1525 - 1625    1660    1760    1798

Elizabethan
Broadside

(1560-1603)

Were Broadside
to identity

Ballad
collection:
Saml Pepys
Thos. d'Urfay
Allan Ramsay

Civil war —
no demand for
literature

Period genuine
journalism,
Balladry,
furtive as a song

Prose
Religious

Bishop
Percy

Period of literary
faking

Bürgers
Needle

German revival /
German folksongs
inspired by Percy

Take?
terrort
under

Samuel Pepys – incidental
collector of Ballads ( most important work was his diary )

Collecting of Ballads in songbooks; such
a collection made by D'Urfey; large
collection called With Mirth or
Pills to Purge Melancholy, "Tom
D'urfeys Pills" English

# THE ATHENÆUM PRESS SERIES

### G. L. KITTREDGE AND C. T. WINCHESTER
#### GENERAL EDITORS

Allan Ramsay (few years after D'Urfey's
collection) Scottish collection "The Ever-
green" also "Tea Table Miscellany"

Scrapbooks of Ballads – manuscript
collections – very valueable
particular collection Sir Humphrey Pitt.

Bishop Thomas Percy interested in
Ballads – worked during time

Romantic awakening – What is a
return to middle ages; Percy had
access to Pitt collection, called Bishop
Percy's Folio Mss. Parts of ballads missing,
burned by cook; Percy filled out stanzas.
First publication of Percy was
Percy's Reliques of Ancient Eng. Poetry.

Bürger – supernatural ballads –
galloping effect in meter
to England in ????? (carried over)
extravagance as great has appearance
in Terror+Wonder School's dacht

Bürger's ballad Leonore – must
popular in England 1790–1800
next in popularity Bürger Wild
Huntsman.

W. Scott – M? Greg Lewis most
affected by Bürger

Athenæum Press Series

# OLD

# ENGLISH BALLADS

SELECTED AND EDITED

BY

## FRANCIS B. GUMMERE

PROFESSOR OF ENGLISH IN HAVERFORD COLLEGE

GINN AND COMPANY

BOSTON · NEW YORK · CHICAGO · LONDON

The Athenæum Press

GINN AND COMPANY · PRO-
PRIETORS · BOSTON · U.S.A.

TO

## PROFESSOR FRANCIS JAMES CHILD.

My dear Mr. Child:

When I ask you to accept the dedication of this book, I am thinking, not of the editor of English and Scottish ballads, the unrivalled master in the investigation of popular poetry, but of the teacher who has taught a host of pupils to welcome honest work in whatever degree of excellence, and of the friend who never failed to help and encourage the humblest of his fellows.

Faithfully yours,

F. B. GUMMERE.

# PREFACE.

THE editor's obligations for help in the making of this book are limited to three sources; but in each case it is hard to render adequate acknowledgment. The authorities of the Harvard College Library have shown the utmost courtesy; Professor Kittredge has helped the editor in revising the proof-sheets of the Introduction, and for the Glossary and Notes has not only given the same generous service, — a service valued best by those who know his command of Middle English, — but has made a number of important suggestions; while Professor Child, in addition to the sympathy and encouragement of which he is so prodigal, has kindly looked through the proof-sheets of the Glossary.

Introduction, Notes and Glossary must speak for themselves; but a word is needed in regard to the Text. The ballads are intended to be representative both in range and in quality. In most instances the editor has selected what seemed to be the best text, although in one or two cases the best had to yield to the suitable. A few omissions were necessary; here and there, but not very often, combinations were made of different texts; and some unimportant substitution of words was allowed as between version and version. The latter freedom, however, was sparingly employed, and was confined mainly to the *Gest.* Absolutely no independent additions were made of any sort; that is to say, no passage, no phrase even, will be found in any of the selections, which is not taken word for word from a recognized text of the ballad in question.

It is perhaps proper to state that the greater part of the Introduction was delivered in the shape of five lectures at the Johns Hopkins University, in the spring of 1893.

F. B. G.

HAVERFORD COLLEGE, 1 March, 1894.


On page 348, note to *Sweet William's Ghost*, 5, 1, and in the Glossary, page 370, *mid-larf* should be explained, after Professor W. P. Ker, as "middle-earth." See the note on cockcrow, page 347.

F. B. G.

19 July, 1914.

# CONTENTS.

# INTRODUCTION.

## I.

IT is a commonplace of criticism that recent literature
has in every way accented the individual ; and we are
wont to charge this difference to the progress made by
civilization from the medieval to the modern point of
view. Ideas and expressions had lain at large in almost
common property ; in verse, translation was as noble
an art as composition ; but when, with the revival of
learning, literature began to take her wares to market,
she sought the critic to serve as watch-dog, and straight-
way wrote down the new crime of plagiarism. Paper
and printer's ink set up a sort of privacy for both the
author and what was once his public ; instead of a
throng of hearers, stood our gentle reader, encouraging
the artist, and luring him more and more to confidences.
It is true that we can find something of this personal
character in the very heart of the middle ages. Added to
such traditions of poetic dignity as the church preserved
from an older literature, came her own teachings in
regard to the value of the individual ; and we certainly
feel a sweep of sentiment, an audacity, one may say, of
individualism, in that typical line of the " Dies Irae " : —

*Quaerens me sedisti lassus !*

Yet this earlier personal element found no echo in popular
poetry of the day. Mainly in a dead tongue, of an
artificial interest, it appealed to a small class of learned

men, and was product as well as property of the schools. The poetry of the masses was objective and impersonal; and even among the learned, despite those conditions which made for a personal attitude, we find poets steadily tending to the objective, and writing generically, merely as representatives of a class. "It seems," says Nyrop, "as if the medieval author held it improper to join his name to a literary composition"; and even Dante, most personal of all poets, names himself but once in the whole Commedia.[1] Our modern period began when the public at large came to be the public of the man of letters, when the poet, full of his own dignity as an artist, went abroad and made friends of all men. With this change, death fell upon that other sort of poetry, so little represented in manuscripts,[2] but so vital and so abundant throughout the middle ages, the poetry which was made for the ear and not for the eye, a poetry full of life, "in which everybody believed and *which everybody could have made*."[3] With the spread of letters among the people, this poetry of the unlettered passed away; the revival of learning, the secularization of art, brought in their train the lapse of impersonal and objective poetry and the rise of the confidential and sentimental poet.

The question of innovations must not delay us. Frenchmen say that Villon brings into their poetry the earliest

[1] Nyrop, *Den oldfranske Heltedigtning*, p. 288. Dante, *Purgat.*, xxx, 55.

[2] For example, compare the praise chanted by monkish chroniclers over King Edgar (Earle, *Two Anglo-Saxon Chronicles*, p. 119) with the dark stories of his cruelty and lust reluctantly told by William of Malmesbury (*Gest. Reg. Ang.*, Bk. II, ed. Stubbs, I, 165) as slurs "which have been cast upon him by ballads,"—*infamias . . . resperserunt cantilenae*. As Müllenhoff says, the middle ages spoke another speech than that of their chronicles.

[3] Gaston Paris, *La Poésie du Moyen Age*, pp. 20, 82 f.

sound of this personal and subjective note,—Villon, with his excellent differences from the pastoral poets of the day, forty feeding like one, his piercingly individual tone, his reckless egotism. When, however, we ask what Englishman first shows the imperious mood of the artist, we are asking a parlous question indeed. We find the thing, with all its pomp, in Shakspere's sonnets, and even in his plays.[1] We find it, with a dramatic mask thinner than usual, in some verses by Tom Nash,[2] where in startling felicity of phrase, —

> *Brightness falls from the air ;*
> *Queens have died young and fair;*
> *Dust hath closed Helen's eye ;*
> *I am sick, I must die,*
>    *Lord have mercy on us !* —

as well as in appeals to the famous dead, we note a parallel to Villon's best-known ballade.[3] But we find it a century earlier in the verses of William Dunbar, who was the first of our poets to see his own work in that mightiest of aids to subjectivity, printer's ink ; and perhaps we shall not err if we assume that Dunbar forms a parallel to Villon in this as in many other respects,[4]

[1] As poetry of the people proper is going out of Europe, the drama comes in ; at first, stiff and impersonal to a fault, it soon follows the new demand for a sentimental note, until in Marlowe and Shakspere we get that intensely personal quality which makes some of their scenes read like a succession of lyrics, and which the late J. A. Symonds has analyzed with such success. It is this "lyric cry" which tells of a new relation between the poet and his public.

[2] In his *Summer's Last Will and Testament ;* a "doleful ditty to the lute." The plague was then raging in London, and the verses have a very personal quality.

[3] For the measureless distance which separates verse of this sort from the *Ubi sunt* strain of medieval poetry, see Sainte-Beuve, *Causeries de Lundi,* XIV, 297 f.

[4] The notes (by Dr. Gregor) in Small's edition of Dunbar, III, 90 ff. point out a likeness in whole and in parts between Dunbar's

and thus takes rank as the first of our sentimental or distinctly lyric poets.

In what poetry, to come closer to our task, must we look for qualities radically different from this artistry and sentiment ? A mere appeal to black-letter will not serve us. What we are wont to call medieval poetry is not the real poetry of the middle ages. We must turn from the printed book ; we must forget even that amiable sinner, the *clerk*, who took his fair hour with a breviary in one hand and Ovid's *Ars Amatoria* in the other ; we must seek poetry which springs from the people, which belongs to no one poet, which appeals to the ear rather than to the eye, and which suggests no confidences.[1] Poetry of this sort lay at the foundation of our early epics ; in modified guise it sought a home in the unlettered and homogeneous communities of the later middle ages ; and with a form yet more changed, it lingered down to our own century in a number of survivals. This seems clear enough, and any one, we say, knows the rural from the lettered muse ; as a matter of fact, however, critics have drawn in vaguest possible outline the boundary between real poetry of the people and certain other forms of verse.

With such confusions we must presently reckon in detail; but it is well to point out a more general blunder. Poetry of the schools and poetry of the people are treated as rival claimants for the throne of excellence. At certain revolutions of taste, men forswear

*Lament for the Makaris* and Villon's two ballades. Mere personality, however, is not the sole test of this new spirit, or we should be obliged to reckon with Dunbar's contemporary, Skelton. *The Garland of Laurell* protests quite superfluously about Skelton poeta.

[1] The *Carmina Burana* have a generical character, but they belong distinctly to the schools. There is a very popular tone in that Latin poem wherein Bishop Golias " confessed his love for good liquor," but it is not poetry of the people.

thin potations in literature, will not hear of Keats or
Shelley, and will have nought but verse dealing with
what Mr. R. L. Stevenson has lately praised as the
better part of existence, — "the eternal life of man
spent under sun and rain, and in rude physical effort."
We take a stanza of " Johnnie Armstrong":

> *Said John, 'Fight on, my merry men all,*
> *I am a little hurt, but I am not slain ;*
> *I will lay me down for to bleed awhile,*
> *And then I'll rise and fight with you again,'*

and we say that here is unaccommodated man, "the thing
itself." We say this rightly, and ought to be content
with such praises ; but we are not content. We go on to
set this rude and bracing verse over against the "Ode to
a Nightingale," or the " Stanzas Written in Dejection near
Naples," and flout the latter heartily, as if, because fresh
air is a good thing, a man ought to open the window and
let a December gale blow upon his back while he reads
before a study-fire. Vilmar, that excellent German,
thought thus to crush Heine with a ballad ; but neither
he nor the more temperate critic has any reason to set
up one standard for two kinds of poetry. An estimate
of poetry of the people based upon the standard of the
schools must lead us into error, as it led Dr. Johnson
into absurdity ; and when enthusiasts for the ballad like
Bürger, or even Jacob Grimm, attempt to judge poetry of
the schools by tests which belong entirely to poetry of
the people, we have confusion even more deplorable.
Outworn poetry of the schools is fain to put on a rural
manner, to catch the trick of simplicity, as when Pru-
dentius, in his "ballad " about a certain martyr, must
bid his hero "give ear to a rustic poet" ; [1] or when, in a

_____

[1] "Audi poetam rusticum." — See Ebert's remarks about this
poem on the martyr Laurentius, which he calls the first example of
a modern ballad. *Geschichte der christl.-latein. Literatur*, I, 252.

famous scene of "Le Misanthrope," the vain, amatorious sonnet is so deftly ridiculed, and the hero recites that pearl of a song about the lover who would fling back King Henry's gift of Paris itself, if it meant the loss of his sweetheart. All this is away from the purpose. One should have nothing to do with the artificiality and badness of the schools, or with the simplicity and goodness of the rural poets. We can delight in "Childe Waters" without bating a jot of our admiration for "Child Roland"; nor do we lay upon lovers of a good ballad the obligation to hate Pope and to writhe in anguish over the "artificial" periods of our literature.

Akin to this confusion of standards, this lack of perspective and tolerance, is the error about which we have already spoken, and into which so many readers and even critics are led by the inadequate nature of their definitions. They make perpetual confusion between poetry of the people and poetry for the people, between a traditional piece of verse and a song written to please the casual crowd of an alley or a concert-hall,[1] — that "popular" poetry here, as well as in Russia, "laboriously produced in the towns, and unblushingly fathered upon soldiers and gypsies." [2] Poetry of the people is the poetry which once came from the people as a whole, from the compact body as yet undivided by lettered or unlettered taste, and represents the sentiment neither of individuals nor of a class. It inclines to the narrative, the concrete and exterior, and it has no mark of the artist and his sentiment. This poetry is supremely difficult to study; for the conditions of any analysis of it are apt to be the conditions of its own decay and disappearance. In general it assumes three forms, — the epos, the song, and the ballad. The question of epic poetry

---

[1] John Ashton, *Modern Street Ballads*, London, 1888.
[2] Ralston, *Songs of the Russian People*, p. 40.

we may not now discuss, except to point out how unstable are the results of critical investigations in its domain ; witness the Homeric problem. The song,[1] spontaneous outburst of emotion, is so often and so clearly a matter of the individual, that it seldom agrees with the conditions of genuine poetry of the people. There remains the ballad, poetry of the people in survival ; and this, in spite of its manifold changes and imperfections, is our best representative of the whole class.

## II.

Error in the comprehension of the ballad goes, then, upon two lines, — there is confusion, more or less deplored, in the name of it ; and there is confusion, for the most part a matter of carelessness, in the treatment of the thing itself. Metes and bounds are seldom clear ;[2] we are confronted not only by the lack of any unequivocal name for this kind of poem, but by a haunting uncertainty in regard to the meaning of the terms used now and then for similar or kindred verse. Thus, when Mr. Saintsbury tells us[3] that "the lack, notorious to this day, of one single original English folk-song of really great beauty, is a rough and general fact," we are at a loss to know how we should understand him. Does he mean by folk-song what a German means by *volkslied*, or does he exclude the narrative ballad? Even if he restricts us to the song pure and simple, like that pearl in the "Misanthrope," what does he understand by a

---

[1] A good example is the well-known Scottish song:—

*O waly, waly up yon bank!*

[2] See, for example, the poems which pass as ballads in S. C. Hall's collection. — In 1860 a collection of well-known modern poems, mainly *vers de société*, was published in New York under the title "Folk Song" !

[3] *Elizabethan Literature*, p. 446.

song of the folk? Chappell, in his invaluable work,[1] shows us that the England of Elizabeth surpassed both Italy and France in the matter of music. High and low, every one loved to sing; every one was expected to take a part, even in difficult songs; and the very barber kept in his shop lute, cittern, or virginal for the amusement of waiting customers. Music was everywhere, and everywhere were songs. How much of all that "masterless" lyric would come under the head of Mr. Saintsbury's folk-song, is a question outside of our present task; enough if we insist upon the indefinite, not to say preposterous, nature of his assertion, and the need of unequivocal terms.[2]

With regard to the name of ballad, we are in no better case.[3] Confusion is rife in the use of the term, and error has even crept into some critical accounts of this confusion. The *ballade* of the schools, to be sure, as it was copied by Chaucer or Gower from the French, need not be reckoned among the immediate causes of trouble;[4] and with it go other poems of different but complicated stanzaic structure.[5] The main source of error lies in the application of the word, however spelled, to almost any short narrative poem, to any short didactic poem, to

---

[1] *Popular Music of the Olden Time*, I, 98. — For an older period of song in England, see ten Brink, *Gesch. d. engl. Lit.*, I, 381 ff. — For the use of "old songs" in a play, see Chappell, I, 72.

[2] In what way would Mr. Saintsbury dispose of the popular Scottish lyric mentioned above?

[3] Wolf, *Lais*, etc., pp. 45, 233.

[4] "This balade," says Chaucer of his "Hyd, Absalon, thy gilte tresses clere," *Legend Goode Women*, 270.

[5] Such is the "balet" printed by Ritson, *Ancient Songs and Ballads*, ed. Hazlitt, p. 149 (in the original ed., p. 86); compare the "balades" named in Lydgate's *Bycorne and Chichevaçhe*. Guest proposed (*Engl. Rhythms*, II, 354) the spelling *ballet* for the related class of poems; but the French *ballade* is surely better.

almost any sort of lyric, and to almost every conceivable form of reviling or grumbling in verse. No better proof of this confusion can be found than in the Register of the Company of Stationers in London.[1] Now and then we meet the traditional ballad of the people: "a ballett of Wakefylde and agrene" (1557–58), is followed by "a ballett of admonyssion to leave swerynge" and "a ballett called *have pytie on the poore*" (1559). John Alde pays his fee for "pryntinge of a balett of Robyn Hod" (1562–63); but compare this batch of seven "ballettes":[2] *Godly Immes used in the churches; who are so mery as thay of y^e low estate; The proverbe is tru yat weddynge ys Destyne; The Robery at Gaddes Hill; holdeth ancer fast; be mery, good Jone; the panges of love.* Moral parodies of a popular song, hymns,[3] satire and personal attack, rimes about a duke's funeral or a campaign in Scotland or any nine days' wonder, — all these, with an occasional ballad of tradition, are entered in the registers under the convenient name.[4] In fact, but for older confusions, we might almost assign the term outright to the realm of trade, the actual making of broadsides,[5] and so give up all attempt to define its literary meaning.

[1] Edited by Arber.

[2] *Ibid.*, I, 96.

[3] The transcriber of the Asloane MS. (see Schipper's account of it, *Poems of Dunbar*, I, 6 ff.) in his table of contents uses "ballat" mainly for religious poems; though *The Devil's Inquest*, a satire by Dunbar, has the same name.

[4] By a sort of synecdoche, any popular line or couplet from one of these broadsides came to be called a ballad. See Murray's *English Dictionary*, s. v. *Ballad*, No. 4.

[5] In the *Athenæum* for April 16th, 1881, Mr. G. Barnett Smith communicates the text of "the oldest English printed ballad in existence," *A Ballade of the Scottyshe Kynge*, by John Skelton, in black-letter, and assigned by authorities of the British Museum to the year 1513. (See also Skelton's Works, ed. Dyce, I, 182 ff., *Skelton Laureate against the Scottes*, especially p. 185 f.) In 1882,

Often, again, the ballad of those days was purely a lyric, whether courtly lay to a mistress' eyebrow, or rough country strains for drink and dance, such as Autolycus laid in for his rural trade. No line was drawn between the song and the ballad. In a well-known dialogue of Walton's "Angler," the milk-woman asks : "What song was it, I pray? Was it *Come, Shepherds, deck your heads*, or *As at noon Dulcina rested*, or *Phillida flouts me*, or *Chevy Chace*, or *Johnny Armstrong*, or *Troy Town?*"[1] We know, too, that Sidney uttered his famous praise of the "*olde song* of Percy and Duglas." A passage in the "Complaynt of Scotland"[2] speaks of certain shepherds who first told pleasant tales, and then sang "sueit sangis," one of which is the lyric "Pastance vitht gude companye," — elsewhere[3] called "The Kyngis Balade," because of its supposed composition by Henry VIII, — and another, the "Hunttis of Chevet," or the older version of Chevy Chace. Finally, the shepherds fell to dancing, and the author, who was looking on, tells us as many of the dances

Mr. John Ashton published this ballad in fac-simile, with a very full introduction (London, Elliot Stock). The poem itself is a taunting affair, quite in Skelton's vein, without narrative, but full of allusions and personal abuse. It has little or nothing to do with our traditional ballads ; it may be compared (*Works*, I, 22) with Skelton's more agreeable "dyvers Balettys and Dyties solacyous," which show French influence on their form, and have a complicated though irregular structure of the stanza. Here narrative occurs ; and in contents, at least, and in the burden (*Hey, lullay, etc.*), one of these poems approaches our traditional ballads, and tells a tale not unlike that of the "Broomfield Hill" (Child, *Ballads*, Part II, p. 390).

[1] Again, in Chapter xiv, "the good old song of the *Hunting in Chevy Chace*, or some other good old ballad." They were all sung. For the tunes, see Chappell, especially I, 260. There is a grouping of lyric as against narrative in the list, but the name is indifferent.

[2] Edited by Murray for the Early English Text Soc., 1872, p. 63 ff.; with commentary on the titles, p. lxxii ff. of the Introduction.

[3] In a Ms. once owned by Ritson, now in the British Museum.

as his "ingyne can put in memorie"; among others, there
were "The Hunt's Up," a lively tune, "Robene hude,"
and "Ihonne Ermistrangis dance." Whether in singing
or even in dancing, little distinction was made between
the narrative song and the pure lyric. Ballads of every
sort were hawked about the land in baskets,[1] or sung by
"blind crowders" as preliminary to a sale. In Beaumont
and Fletcher's "Monsieur Thomas," the fiddler gives a
list of his "best ballads," most of them lyrical; while in
"Rollo"[2] three culprits sing before their execution a
"ballad," with a well-known refrain,[3] in imitation of those
doleful last confessions of criminals, the so-called Good
Nights.

But we may find wider margins for the word. We read
of a translation, made in those days, of "The Canticles
or Balades of Solomon,"[4] a title that would have pleased
Herder. Moreover, alternating with the ballad, comes
another unstable term in the sonnet. The Lamentation
of George Mannington is entered in the books of the
Stationers' Company, 1576, as "a woeful ballad," and is
printed in a collection of poems, 1584, as "a sorrowfull
sonet."[5] The close connection of ballads and the dance
may have been in Udal's mind when he spoke[6] of "wanton
daunsynges or folyshe ballettes wherewith the Gentiles
crie upon theyr devilles"; for tunes were not composed

[1] Country-houses, inns, and the like, were sure to have ballads
upon the walls. (See Addison, *Spectator*, No. 85.) "An honest
alehouse," says Walton's "Angler," "where we shall find a cleanly
room, lavender in the windows, and twenty ballads stuck about the
wall," — cleanly ballads, and old, we feel sure.

[2] End of Act iii.

[3] The tune in Chappell, I, 216. For the "hanging tune" used
for such ballads themselves, see Chappell, I, 162.

[4] Printed in 1549. In the Bishop's Bible it is *The Ballet of Ballets.*

[5] Ritson's *Ancient Songs and Ballads*, Hazlitt, p. 188.

[6] See Richardson's *Dictionary*, s. v.

in that day exclusively for the dance, but any lively ballad
served the turn.

Greater dignity than of the broadsides now and then
invested the ballad, as when Puttenham speaks of the
classical lyric poets writing "songs or ballads of pleasure,"
or calls the *encomia* "ballads of praise," mentioning, too,
the "ballade of birth" — for a prince — and the song at
nuptials "done in ballade wise."[1] This, however, is the
academic use of a term commonly felt to be an affair of
the street or roadside, and distinctly opposed to loftier
efforts of both music and poetry.[2] Among many causes
for this low estate of the ballad must doubtless be reckoned
the scurrilous attacks on people or institutions, which
were printed as broadsides, and often to a popular tune;
here we are not so far, except in a metrical way, from the
*ballade* of Villon and the *ballet* of Dunbar.

> *Thocht I in ballet did with him bourde,*

says the latter in his palinode about James Doig; indeed,
Dunbar's frequently complicated arrangement of the
stanza, and a recurring refrain, suggest models far
removed from the verses of that later rout whom
Shakspere knew, the "scald rhymers" who balladed
out o' tune.[3]

---

[1] Arber's Reprint of Puttenham's *Arte of English Poesie*, pp. 40, 58,
64 ff. Of love-lyrics Puttenham names (p. 60) "odes, songs, elegies,
ballads, sonets, and other ditties." In another place (p. 72) he
mentions "enterlude, song, ballade, carroll, and ditty," as common
names for "our vulgar makings." He himself had made a "brief
*Romance* or historicall ditty in the English tong of the Isle of great
Britaine in short and long meetres, and by breaches or divisions to
be more commodiously song to the harpe . . ." (p. 57).

[2] "Musicians held ballads in contempt, and great poets rarely
wrote in ballad metre." — Chappell, I, 105.

[3] Of course, Dunbar knows the other signification of ballad as an
amorous lyric. See the *Twa Mariit Wemen*, 480; *Targe*, 103
("ballettis in love"); and his complaint of winter as unfavorable to

On the whole, aside from remoter origins, the ballad under Elizabeth, so far as it had any literary meaning, evidently covered on the one hand poems of love or satire which more or less vaguely suggested the French type, and, on the other, poems independent of such influence, pointing back to the traditional ballad, with its refrain, its tune, and its hints of the dance. But any occasional poem, grave or gay, which appeared as a broadside could take the name unchallenged.

In all this coil, two sources of confusion are clear to the critical eye ; and one of them will serve to explain a certain alternation of praise and scorn in contemporary judgment of the Elizabethan ballad. For the less important evil, we have noted a failure to distinguish the lyrical from the narrative. In a merry scene of the Winter's Tale,[1] country-folk "love a ballad in print," for then they are sure it is true, — that is, the narrative ballad, the genuine broadside ; while presently a ballad of the other sort is sung, a part-song, in which the pedler Autolycus joins because it is his "occupation." The second and more serious cause of trouble is the confusion between the ballad of tradition and the verses of men like Elderton, "who did arm himself with ale when he ballated," or Tom Deloney, "the ballading silk-weaver," who could turn into rime a chapter or two from Malory, and so make a ballad of Sir Lancelot.[2] These men often inserted genuine old ballads in collections of their own, and got credit for "Flodden Field" or "The Fair Flower of

the making of "sangis, ballatis, and playis," Works, ed. Small, II, 233. For a "ballad" of praise, in complicated stanza and with constant refrain, see the *Ballade of Lord Bernard Stewart.* A later example of the scurrilous ballad in Scotland is *A Ballat maid upoun Margret Fleming, Satirical Poems of the Reformation,* ed. Cranstoun, Scottish Text Soc., 1891, I, 391 ff., — a woeful affair.

[1] iv, 4.

[2] So think Hales and Furnivall, *Percy Folio,* I, 84.

Northumberland." So the good and the bad fell into
one class. Shakspere loved an old ballad, and speaks
his mind in Orsino's pretty words; but there is sarcasm
in the "ballad-maker" of other passages. Probably
Elizabethans recognized the difference, but they did not
pick terms to tell it. Indeed, much of the balladry con-
demned itself. There was, to be sure, respectable poverty
in the rude chronicles which were beaten into rime, and
Aubrey said that his nurse could repeat in ballads
the history of England from the conquest to the first
Charles;[1] but Mr. Stopford Brooke praises the ballading
gentry too much when he credits them with the educa-
tional value of "a modern weekly review."[2] Much of
their work was mere shreds and tatters of sensation, and
so persistent that "scarce a cat can look out of a gutter
. . . but presently[3] a proper new ballet of a strange sight
is indited."[4] Trash of the sort, "rimes that run in large
in every shop to sell," brought the whole family of ballads
into contempt, and called down the wrath of Puritan
writers even in the days of Elizabeth.[5] These broadsides
were hawked about and sung, like other ballads. Says a
couplet prefixed to one of them :[6]

> *I know no reason but that this harmless riddle*
> *May as well be printed as sung to a fiddle.*

[1] *Percy Folio*, II, 265 ; III, 163.

[2] *Primer of Eng. Lit.*, p. 73.

[3] *I. e.*, 1592. See Chappell, I, 106.

[4] *E. g.*, see Arber *Reg. Stat. Co.*, I, 187, for a ballad on the birth of
a "monsterus pygge."

[5] *Percy Society Publications*, I, p. 49. Ballad-singers were sup-
pressed along with "stage-plays" in 1648.

[6] *Percy Collection of Broadsides*, Vol. III. Under James I,
Deloney and others began to collect their ballads into "little miscel-
lanies," which were called Garlands. More of the sort, with a good
introduction by Chappell, may be found in the Ballad Society's

They had no grace of tradition, these labored verses, whether didactic or scurrilous, and are to be kept carefully sundered from the "bunch of ballets and songs, *all aunctent*,"— that is, ancient in 1575 — owned by Captain Cox,[1] or from such songs as Moros sings by snatches in a comedy[2] of that day, and says he can increase at will :

> *I have twentie mo songs yet;*
> *A fond woman to my mother,*
> *As I was wont in her lappe to sit,*
> *She taught me these and many other.*

Of these two sources of confusion, one is no longer known, while the other, for our sins, abides with us and vexes us daily. Ritson, with good sense of the solidest quality, stated for English usage the distinction which now obtains. "With us," he says,[3] "songs of sentiment,

edition of the *Roxburghe Ballads* (London, 1871 f.); for later times, see the *Bagford Ballads* (Hertford, 1878 f.). John Ashton has published *A Century of Ballads*, 1888.

[1] Furnivall, *Captain Cox*, in Ballad Society Publications, 1871. Laneham wrote his famous letter from Kenilworth in 1575, and is very full of the captain, who hath "great oversight . . . in *matters of storie*," and has at his fingers' ends such "histories" (note the word) as "Robinhood, Clim of the Clough, The King and the Tanner, and The Nutbrown Maid"; while again his "balletts and songs" are such "az Broom broom on hil . . . Bony lass upon a green . . . and a hundred more he hath, fair wrapt up in parchment . . ."

[2] *The Longer Thou Livest the More Foole Thou Art*, often cited : see Ritson, *Anc. Songs and Ball.*, LXXII ff.

[3] "A Historical Essay on the Origin and Progress of National Song," being the introduction to his *Select Collection of English Songs*, 3 vols., 2nd ed., 1813. There is also good material in the introduction to his *Ancient Songs and Ballads*, 1790, and, edited by Hazlitt, 1877 ; see both the "Essay on Minstrels," and his account of old songs and music. In the introduction to his *Ancient Engleish Metrical Romanceës*, he defines ballad as "a lyrical narrative."

expression, or even description, are properly termed
Songs,[1] in contradistinction to mere narrative compositions
which we now denominate Ballads." Germans, too, have
thus cleared the field. "Our mode of speech," says
Scherer,[2] "inclines to call it a song when the singer
speaks of himself, a ballad when he speaks of others." [3]
It is rather the confusion of traditional with artistic or
written ballads,—not so much inferior songs for the
rabble as imitations of the ballad by poets of good rank,
—which still prevails, and allows modern usage to call
by one name "Chevy Chace," "Barbara Frietchie," and
Mr. Gilbert's "Rival Curates." With this word, ballad,
we can do little in the way of reform, save to lament the
equivocation of the fiend who first flung it into our language ; but there is safety in an adjective. Professor
Child takes "popular" for his refuge ; it is, perhaps,
better thus to ignore the distinction of *volkspoesie*
and *volksthümliche poesie*, than to seek a fantastic title.

---

[1] Ritson's taste limped behind his knowledge. He thinks feeble
ballads of Deloney and others better than Chevy Chace ; though
in a note to Captain Car (*Anc. S. and B.*, p. 180 f.) he praises such a
chanted ballad of "the North Countre" at the expense of work by
"a Grub-Street author for the stalls."

[2] *Poetik*, p. 249 ; but see his *Gesch. d. deutsch. Lit.*, p. 257.

[3] We have no space for the detail of German confusions, especially
in the use of Herder's word *volkslied*. The student may consult,
besides the dictionaries, Müllenhoff's introduction to his *Sagen,
Märchen u. Lieder d. Herzogthümer Schleswig-Holstein u. Lauenburg,*
pp. xxx, xxxvi ; Talvj, *Charakteristik u. s. w.*, p. 8 ff. ; Bürger's
*Gedichte*, ed. Tittmann, pp. xliii f., liii f. ; Vilmar, *Handbüchlein f.
Freunde d. deutschen Volksliedes*, p. 138 f. ; Wackernagel, *Poetik*,
p. 96 f. ; Böhme, *Altdeutsches Liederbuch*, pp. xxi f., xxviii f. (who,
while approving Uhland's word *volksballade*, notes that the medieval
term for song or poetry of the people was in Latin *carmen vulgare*,
or *barbarum* or *rusticum*, but never *populare*, and in the vernacular
always Peasants' Song, Mountain Song, what not, until Herder
called the whole genus *volkslied* ) ; and Uhland, *Schriften*, VII, 12
360, and II, 587.

As a mere makeshift, however, one might use the word " communal." A communal ballad is a narrative ballad of tradition which represents a community or folk, not a section or class of that community, and not a single writer.

### III.

Two great authorities, Svend Grundtvig and Ferdinand Wolf, failed to agree in their report about that vexatious matter, the authorship of the ballad ; but on one point they were perfectly united. Alike they insisted that the ballad must be the outcome and the expression of a whole community, and that this community must be homogeneous — must belong to a time when, in a common atmosphere of ignorance, so far as book-lore is concerned, one habit of thought and one standard of action animate every member from prince to ploughboy.[1] Ballads of the primitive type, — of course we do not know them in their original form, — were the product of a people as yet undivided into a lettered and an unlettered class. When learning came among the folk, it drove the ballad first into byways, and then altogether out of living literature. Ballads cannot be made now, at least among civilized races ; nor can a cheap pathos, in slovenly or vulgar

---

[1] Grundtvig wrote an introduction for translations by Rosa Warrens, *Dänische Volkslieder d. Vorzeit*, Hamburg, 1858 ; see especially pp. xvii f., xxii. Wolf did a like office for the same translator in her *Schwedische Volkslieder d. Vorzeit*, 1857. See p. xiv ff. See also Motherwell's attempt (*Minstrelsy*, Amer. ed., I, 16 ff.) to draw " the bounding-line which exists between what is the Oral and what is the Written poetry of a people." This homogeneous character of a ballad-making folk, by the way, is quite enough to explain the high rank of most personages in the ballads, — princes, knights and so on, — without recourse to Wolf's assumption of a direct origin in aristocratic circles (Introd., p. xix). Translator Prior (*Ancient Danish Ballads*, 1860, I, ix) gallantly concludes that for most of the Scandinavian ballads we are indebted to the original composition "of the ladies."

English, even when backed by all the eccentricities of a printing-room, be foisted upon us as poetry of the people.

All writers on the communal ballad are at one in regard to its entire freedom from the subjective element. Nobody has defined so well as Sidney Lanier [1] this triumph of the personal artist in modern letters : —

> *Awful is Art because 'tis free.*
> *The artist trembles o'er his plan*
> *Where men his Self must see.*
> *Who made a song or picture, he*
> *Did it, and not another, God nor man.*

But to this solitary act of the artist in verse, an act which is only heightened by the mirrorings and reactions wrought through transmission on paper, we must oppose, for poetry of the people, a public production and a purely oral and unappropriated transmission. In line with this general necessity, moreover, we may note certain recognized traits of the ballad. Of course, they are characteristic traits of the early community ; " *naïveté*, sympathy, faith," says Weckerlin, [2] not too incisively ; and Wilhelm Grimm is still more hazy in his assertion [3] that what distinguishes a ballad from poems of art is that it "knows no deserts, but thinks of the world as all green and fresh and alive with poetry, with heaven above, and all the hairs counted on every head. Therefore " — like Chaucer's Clerk — " it says nothing but what is needed, what corresponds to reality ; and it despises external splendor." . . . Ferdinand Wolf goes more into particulars, though one must admit that these

[1] *Hymns of the Marshes*, II.

[2] *La Chanson Populaire*, Paris, 1886, p. 21.

[3] He is speaking of the Danish ballads, *Altdänische Heldenlieder*, p. iii. " Like heather on the hill and the birch in the glen " is a similar definition by J. S. Blackie, *Scottish Song*, p. 6 ; another definition, p. 21.

giants of ballad criticism are not too happy in the way of a definition ; the ballad, he says,[1] has "a naïve objectivity, without any reflection, any sentimentalism ; it has lively, erratic narrative, full of leapings and omissions, sudden change from narrative to dialogue, no ornamentation, the art of making with few strokes a vigorous sketch of events and situations." Simplicity of thought and speech, he adds, are in the ballad, and a naturalness that borders on savagery. Another critic[2] insists on the spontaneous character of ballads ; they never give us poetry for poetry's sake, but are born of an occasion, a need ; they have as little subjectivity as speech itself. These are the cardinal virtues of the ballad ;[3] with respect to its conditions, critics unite in regarding oral transmission as its chief available test.[4]

The ballad, then, must give us the sense of tradition, and a flavor of spontaneity ; riches of the emotions and of direct vision, poverty of intellect and reflection. Its poetic diction must be unschooled, close to life, and no dialect, although full of recurring phrases which give occasion for loose talk about the "ballad slang."[5] We

[1] *Romanzenpoesie d. Spanier*, in *Wiener Jahrbücher*, CXVII, 126.

[2] Burdach, in Haupt's *Zeitschrift für deutsches Alterthum*, XXVII, 344.

[3] See also Professor Child in *Johnson's Cyclopædia*, 1893, I, 464, 466.

[4] See Brandl in Paul's *Grundriss d. germ. Philologie*, II, i, 839.

[5] The recurring phrases of the ballad have a well-known parallel in epic, and are a mark of poetry of the people. Thus they are as common in Russian ballads as in English or German : see Bistrom, *Das russische Volksepos* in the *Zeitschr. f. Völkerpsychol., etc.*, V, 188, 193. Motherwell, *Minstrelsy*, Amer. ed., I, 7, calls them "commonplaces . . . an integrant portion of the original mechanism of all our ancient ballads . . . one of their most peculiar and distinctive characteristics." It is evident that such recurring phrases make for the communal character of the ballad. An artist avoids commonplaces, avoids the evident, and seeks to vindicate his own self.

have in the general style of ballads a close parallel to the early stages of so-called figures of speech. The primitive word is a metaphor in an unconscious state; as soon as any distinction can be made between a literal expression and a metaphor, the latter becomes conscious and artistic. But the style of a genuine ballad is not a consciously poetical style; for it is not ballads that form a dialect, it is the schools. From Chaucer to Tennyson,[1] in spite of one reaction after another, the drift of poetry has been to increase and isolate the dialect of the schools; not as a theory, but as a matter of fact, we note in the history of English verse a steady widening of the chasm between the speech of daily life and the language of poetry.[2] A study of German lyric poetry in the twelfth or thirteenth century shows us the same process from a simple popular diction, a style in which there was no thought of expressing individuality, to a complicated and artistic diction, offspring of the schools.

The metre of a ballad,[3] while not obstreperously rough, should be simple; not labored, hardly melodious in our

---

[1] When Tennyson speaks of "the chalice of the grapes of God," or gives the time of day as —

> *Before the crimson-circled star*
> *Had fallen into her father's grave,*

he is reviving the obscure scaldic "kenning" and the mythological puzzle of the most artificial phase in all Germanic poetry.

[2] See the famous remarks of Wordsworth, in his preface to the *Lyrical Ballads*, on these "arbitrary and capricious habits of expression," and the faults of "poetic diction."

[3] For particulars, see appendix on metre. Undoubtedly the prevailing measure is the medieval *septenarius*, domesticated in English verse; but this raises a difficult problem. If popular poetry, like Langland's, held so tenaciously to the old Germanic form — still vigorous a century and a half later in Dunbar's well-known verses — why should the ballads, which we assume to represent tradition in its most positive form, turn from the old, and take up the new and

sense of the word, never saccharine, it should show a clear and certain sense of general harmony. Assonance must often do the work of rime; and sometimes the most heroic "slurring" fails to bring order out of the chaos; in such moments, however, we must think of grammatical changes, of local forms, and of the chances of print.

The antithesis of schools and people would cause us to expect little from ballads in the way of trope or figure; and this we find to be the case.[1] Figures are few and recurrent, always unforced, and for the most part unconscious. Steenstrup, in his excellent study of Scandinavian ballads, says that they "talk like a mother to her child" and have "scarcely a kenning";[2] while Wilhelm Grimm long ago noted the absence of figures in the Nibelungen Lay as compared with the poems of Wolfram.[3]

---

"intellectualized" measure? Where, moreover, were the Anglo-Saxon ballads? Chappell rejects with some sharpness (II, 796) the notion that English popular music was taken or imitated, in the first instance, from the music of the church; but ballad measure and even rime — though this is not at all sure — are now generally referred to such a source.

[1] Here again we have a contrast with Anglo-Saxon poetry, and apparent breach with tradition. Instead of the riot of tropes, the constant "variation," ballads give us naked and literal language. But this is not so hard to explain. We have no simple, popular verse from Anglo-Saxon times; monk and minstrel had made a school.

[2] *Vore Folkeviser*, pp. 196, 204.

[3] *Heldensage*,[2] p. 287. — The absence of similes from old German poetry is so marked that Müllenhoff and Scherer considered the assumption of them sufficient to condemn a certain interpretation,— *Denkmäler*,[2] II, 131. It is the good pastor's zeal, rather than his accuracy, which leads Neocorus (*Chronik*, ed. Dahlmann, I, 176) to remark of the ballads of the Cimbrian peninsula, "dat fast nicht ein Tropus edder Figura in der edlen Redekunst, so nicht in einen edder mehr Gesengen konde gewist werden." Müllenhoff (*Sagen, u.s.w.*, p. xxxiv) notices that the ballads of this same country have really "few figures and comparisons."

The language of primitive or simple passion is iteration, not figure; and the ballads, poor in figures, are full of iteration. In fact, the chief mark of ballad style, as it is found in such survivals as are given in the present collection, is a sort of progressive iteration. The question is repeated with the answer; each increment in a series of related facts has a stanza for itself, identical, save for the new fact, with the other stanzas;[1] and in every way a note of iteration dominates the style of our ballads.

From any list of ballads which agree with these conditions, and spring from the community, it would seem that we ought to exclude the ballad of satire and abuse. It appears at first sight to be hedged about with a singular and personal depravity. We even find evidence of a laureate in this art; for Kluge suggests that our old English word for poet is really the same thing as "scoffer."[2] Every Icelander was expected to hold his own in these encounters, and Gunnlaug Snake-Tongue got the nickname by dexterity in the composition of satiric verses; often such a stanza of sarcasm was cut on a prominent rock, like our modern advertisements. All this, it is true, smacks of the artist; but we find more general satire. We think of those songs which Goethe's Gretchen dreaded, or Shakspere's Helena invited if she should attempt to cure the king and fail. We think of the legions making a ballad about Cæsar, or of Roland and his dread lest he and his men should be held up to ridicule in song.[3] The church had much trouble with these

---

[1] Out of a host of examples we may instance the ballad of "Kemp Owyne."

[2] *Scop.* See Kluge in *Englische Studien,* VIII, 480 ff.; and Müllenhoff on the gloss *scofleod,* in Haupt's *Zst.,* IX, 128. We cannot here discuss the "flyting."

[3] *Chanson de Roland,* 1008 ff. To serve the king, says Roland, one must endure heat and cold, perils of every kind, "so that no

communal songs of satire, and put them down only with
great difficulty; for they seem to have been a legacy
from heathen Europe. They touched politics as well as
religion. Satiric ballads often arose from the hatred of
folk for folk, nation for nation, like the songs made after
Bannockburn, and sung with a refrain "in daunces, in
the carols of the maidens and minstrels of Scotland, to
the reproofe and disdaine of Englishmen."[1] Of more
interest, however, for our present task is the evidence
that a ballad of satire could have a distinctly communal
origin, that its actual creation could be in the community
and — if the expression will pass — by the community.
Moreover, this satiric ballad was sung in the same place,
by the same people, and for the same purpose, as the
heroic ballad of tradition. In Pastor Lyngbye's valuable
book,[2] we read of such a satiric ballad made by the Färöe
Islanders. It is in derision of some unfortunate fisherman, who comes to the public dance, is seized by a couple
of stalwart comrades, and pushed out before the throng
— that is, before the whole community. Then the ballad
which mocks some misadventure of his, known to all the
folk, is sung by the dancing crowd, — a few at first, then
all; with facts so given, spontaneous production is easy
enough; and so, verse upon verse, they make the man

bad songs shall be sung about us," *male cançun ja cantée n'en seit!*
Nyrop quotes *Iliad*, vi, 358, as a parallel case. Moreover, who of
us does not know the remorseless rimes, largely spontaneous, which
a band of children can rain in chorus upon the head of some un-
popular urchin?

[1] Fabyan's *Chronicle*, from which this is taken, was written long
after the event, and is not too trustworthy.

[2] *Færøiske Quæder om Sigurd*, etc., Randers, 1822. P. E. Müller
writes the preface, and quotes from Lyngbye's journal. Our quotation is found at p. 14. A few additional details in V. U. Hammershaimb, *Færøsk Anthologi*, I, Copenhagen, 1891, p. xli ff.

dance to his own shame.[1]  More than this, if the ballad
wins general applause it remains from year to year a
permanent source of pleasure and diversion.  A more
striking antithesis to our ordinary notions could hardly
be found ; the poet or artist vanishes ; the singer, reciter,
publisher, takes the background ; and in the fore-
ground stands the object — not subject merely — of
the song.  Instead of the poet's mood, the poet's
sensations and manner, we have the mood, sensations
and manner of the object which called out the ballad.
What reversal of attitude, compared with Keats and his
nightingale !

This gregarious song of satire, as opposed to the
personal attack, brings us, as the opposition of traditional
and made ballads brought us, to our knottiest problem.
If the chief characteristics of a ballad are those which
belong to the product of a community rather than to the
work of an artist, and so force us to abandon certain
ideas inseparable from recent poetry, how far are we to
go in this surrender of the modern standard, and in what
degree shall we hold the community responsible for the
actual making of a ballad ?  Where, if at all, are we to
admit an individual poet in the process ?

[1] The editor is indebted to Professor G. L. Kittredge for a
reminder of the "communal spontaneity" in that vivid scene of
Bjørnson's *Fiskerjenten* (Chap. V), where the mob sings an insulting
song before poor Petra's door ; and, further, for a reference to
O'Curry, *Manners and Customs of the Ancient Irish*, II, 70, where
we are told that Laidcenn, in revenge for the slaughter of his son,
poured forth for a year his poetic satire upon the men of Leinster,
"so that neither corn, grass, nor foliage could grow for them during
the whole year."  (See II, 216 ff.)  The connection of satiric poetry
with older magic, with runes, charms, and the like, is too wide a
subject for further comment here.

## IV.

The answers to this important question of origins may
be divided into two groups.  One party, formerly strong,
but now in evident minority, declares that the people as
a whole and a unit, make what the phrase says they
make, poetry of the people.  Another party, now in
the majority, asserts that poetry of the people is made
as any other poetry is made, except that it is subject to
purely oral transmission,[1] and therefore to infinite variation and the chances of popular control.

Before we approach this problem by the long path
of a century of criticism, and before we attempt the slow
sifting of other material, it seems in order to get a clear
idea of what the more aggressive party meant by its
claim of communal authorship.  Among the last words
which came from the pen of ten Brink, in a fragment[2]
dealing with theories about poetry of the people, that
accomplished scholar refers explicitly to an article by
Steinthal, in the Journal of Race-Psychology,[3] which
seems to be a confession of faith on the part of those
who, like Jacob Grimm, believe in communal authorship
of the ballad.  In effect, ten Brink signs this declaration,
modifying it here and there, but adhering to the spirit of
it.  Again, in that introduction, already quoted, which
Grundtvig wrote for the translations of Rosa Warrens,[4]
we find words which go far to rank their distinguished

[1] Brandl, in Paul's *Grundriss*, II, i, 839.

[2] See ten Brink in Paul's *Grundr.*, II, i, 515; and also the
former's *Beowulf*, p. 7.

[3] One fairly flounders in the attempt to English this *Zeitschrift
für Völkerpsychologie und Sprachwissenschaft.*

[4] See the passage (p. xxiii) beginning: "Darum ist das Volks-
Individuum als solches, nicht das einfache Menschen-Individuum,
als Dichter der Volkspoesie zu betrachten . . ."

author in the same list of believers with Grimm and
Steinthal.  Despite the coldness or open derision of
other modern critics in regard to this matter of communal authorship, despite the distinct denial of F.
Wolf,[1] we cannot laugh out of court a case defended by
two such advocates as Grundtvig and ten Brink ; and, at
least, we must give it a hearing.

In an opening editorial article, something hazy withal,
Steinthal and Lazarus tell readers of their new journal [2]
what they mean by this race, this "folk."  The spirit
of the race, presently to be set up as poet of our ballad,
would seem to be a "monad" which at once penetrates
and binds together the individuals, yet is really created
and sustained by them.[3]  Not common descent, not common language, make a "folk" ; it is the sense of unity
in all the individuals.  This unity, this spirit of the race,
manifests itself first in speech, then in myth, then in
religious rites, then in poetry, then in art, then in custom ; after long tradition, custom gives birth to law.[4]  In
other words, poetry of the people is made by any given
race through the same mysterious process which forms
speech, cult, myth, custom, or law.

Eight years later,[5] Steinthal grappled directly with the
problem of authorship, and tried to set forth the doctrine
that a whole race can make poems.  The individual, he
maintained, is the outcome of culture and long ages
of development, while primitive races show simply an
aggregate of men.  Sensation, impulse, and sentiment

[1] Wolf is as emphatic on the other side.  Introduction to
*Schwed. Volksl.* (Rosa Warrens), p. xv ; not "von einem nebu-
losen Dichteraggregat, Volk genannt," but "von einem dichtenden
Subject," come our traditional ballads.

[2] 1860.

[3] *Ztst. f. Völkerpsy. u. Sprachw.*, I, 29.

[4] *Ibid.*, 39, 44, 47 ff.

[5] *Ibid.*, V, 1 ff.

must be quite uniform in the uncivilized community, —
what one feels, all feel. A common creative sentiment
throws out the word, and makes language, — throws out
the song, and makes poetry. No one owns a word,[1] a
law, a story, a custom. No one owns a song. "Singing,"
says Steinthal, is what we ought to say, not "song"; for
all is in flux. Dip from the brook a pailful of water, and
one has captured no brook ; write down a version of some
folksong, and it is no folksong more. There is no sta-
bility about it; among Russians or Servians, a song of
eight or ten lines has endless variations. An Italian girl
sang a song several times, but each time sang it with a
difference ; when asked the reason, she said she could
not help it, as the thing came to her so, — *mi viene così.*

With these and other arguments,[2] Steinthal sought to
put on the basis of psychology and common sense a
theory of the ballad already held by many to be vague,
contradictory, and mistaken. Ten Brink plainly tells us,
however, that from this article he has "learned the
most" in regard to the nature and origin of poetry
of the people ; and we shall presently see how he tries
to supply what Steinthal left undone. The weak place
of the essay is its failure to answer the question of
ways and means. How got the apples in ? How does
a song cross the gulf between this spirit of the race, this
latent community of sentiment, and the concrete fact of
melody and words ? If, indeed, we could only assume
the primitive community to have been like the folk
whom Alice met in Wonderland, all "thinking in chorus,"
it would be a plain matter. But it is not a plain matter ;

[1] Scherer's *Poetik* defends the primitive artist even as a maker of
words, and throughout pleads for the unity of poetry against
any hard and fast division into poetry of the people and poetry
of the schools.

[2] Dealing with that outcome of a certain class of ballads, the Epos.

and our prosaic time, to judge by a show of hands, is inclined to side with the late Professor Scherer.[1] He insisted upon oral or written transmission as the only test of poetry of the people and poetry of the schools. " Poetry," he declared, " is one and the same at all times ; it is the times which change."

Clearly we are not to pronounce an off-hand opinion. However tedious the task, we must review the course of criticism in this field, and then try to come to some conclusion for ourselves. We cannot avoid this question of origins, for it involves the essence and the criteria of all ballads of tradition.

## V.

We are now to pass in review a century of criticism, and we must naturally begin with the pioneer, — dithyrambic, impetuous Herder, whose almost truculent enthusiasm first secured a hearing for the claims of popular poetry. Herder, not Percy ; for while the bishop nobly heads the list of collectors and editors, he founded no school of criticism. Moreover, England needed no such trumpetings and onslaught ; she had never allowed a certain homebred fondness for this sort of verse to be crushed by foreign standards. At any time when literary interests seemed utterly hostile to the ballad, some one — Sidney, Addison,[2] Goldsmith, — was sure to say a good word for it. Garrulous Pepys made his collection of broadsides, and

---

[1] See his *Poetik*, Berlin, 1888 ; and his *Jacob Grimm*, 2nd ed., 1885, p. 146.

[2] See especially *Spectator*, 70, 74 ; we note that Ben Jonson, who poured contempt enough on the ballading gentry, would rather have been the author of Chevy Chace " than of all his works." Sidney's praise is well known : see Cook's edition of the *Defense*, p. 29. Dryden had a good opinion of ballads, and so had " the witty Lord Dorset." See *Spectator*, 85, and Percy, preface to the *Reliques*.

Rowe, taking a plot from the ballads, lauded them distinctly in the preface to his " Jane Shore " ; while men of such opposite tastes as Gray and Garrick were interested in songs of the people.

Very different was the state of affairs on the continent. Ballads and songs were looked upon as little better than intellectual outcasts. " Seventy years ago," says Ferdinand Wolf in 1846, at the opening of his classic essay on Spanish Ballads, " seventy years ago, a university professor would have felt insulted by the mere idea of any academic attention to songs of the people, even of his own people." A school of criticism founded on the traditions of the humanists and refinements of Frenchmen like Boileau, would not give the ballad so much as a hearing. Exceptions go for little. Montaigne had said a good word for ballads ; so had Malherbe ; and we remember Molière in the " Misanthrope." But nobody looked on the poetry of the people as a serious literary fact.

So far as Germany is concerned, signs of change appear about the middle of the eighteenth century ; and this change, as everybody knows, was largely inspired by English example. Words like "genius " and "nature " were bandied about ; and while around the latter term gathered the ideas of Rousseau, the former was more and more associated with Shakspere. [1]

Now came a number of important critical treatises, all making in one direction, all insisting on "nature " and " genius." Of prime importance were Young's " Conjectures on Original Composition," translated at once into German, Robert Wood's remarkable essay

[1] In 1737, Germany's leading critic, writing about English drama, had not mentioned the name of Shakspere. In 1762, Wieland's prose translation of his plays was in all hands. Koberstein, *Gesch. d. d. Lit.*, II, 1342.

"On the Original Genius of Homer," and Lowth's Oxford lectures "On the Sacred Poetry of the Hebrews." The old idols began to totter, as when Joseph Warton appeared with an urbane protest against Pope. Nature and humanity should be the field of the poet, and in naturalness and original genius should lie his power. Poetry, said Blair in his Rhetoric, "is the language of the emotions." To this candle-light of the students came the wildfire of Ossian,[1] and at last, in 1765, the sunrise of the Reliques.

Meanwhile, Germany had nearer promptings. About this time were published, in whatever faulty shape, the Nibelungen Lay, the Songs of the Minnesingers, and many of the old Scandinavian poems. Gleim revived the ballad, seriously, and not simply in burlesque, as a form for modern imitation ; and even Lessing, who thought but little of the Nibelungen, had a good word for ballads of the better sort.[2] Then came an oracle ; the famous Magician of the North spoke certain mighty, but nigh unintelligible, words about the nature of poetry.[3] All literary production, contended Hamann, is successful only when it concentrates the entire mental and moral force of the writer upon his work. Divided power is wasted power. The emotions and intellect must work together, and nowhere is this so true as in poetry.

---

[1] Grotesque but well-meant imitations of the ballad were made by Percy's friend Shenstone (*Jemmy Dawson*, about 1745), and later by Mickle (*Hengist and Mey*, a ballad, 1772 ; and the song, *There's nae luck about the House*). Actual forgery of the ballad had already begun ; Lady Wardlaw's *Hardyknut* appeared in 1719.

[2] See No. 33 of the *Briefe die neueste Literatur betreffend*, 19 April, 1759.

[3] See Goethe's admiring account of Hamann, *Wahrheit u. Dichtung*, Hempel ed., III, 63 ff. Devil's advocate, however, is Gervinus (*Gesch. d. d. Lit.*, IV, 436 ff., ed. 1843), who thinks Hamann more than half imbecile.

"Poetry," said he, in memorable phrase, "is the mother-tongue of man"; the less this large utterance is hampered by learned restrictions, the better for poetry and for mankind. Poetry must be spontaneous, immediate, no work of reflection. Now, all these things, and many more, tending to glorify primitive and popular poetry, fell with oracular force upon the ears of Herder.

To study Herder, that eupeptic Carlyle, is to study poetry of the people.[1] His criticism follows a straight path. He is fain to establish the canons and tests of poetry as lying chiefly in its immediate dependence upon nature, upon genius, free from rule or model. He would bring all poetry into connection with its environment of race and country. Following lines which led him through the philosophy of language to the philosophy of history, he treats the human race as a whole, and insists that its childhood was the golden age of poetry, as well in language as in sentiment. "What," he asks, in his essay on the Origin of Language, "what was earliest speech but a collection of the elements of poetry? . . . A dictionary of the soul — what else is poetry?"[2] In his "Letters about Ossian and the Songs of Ancient Races," he tells[3] an imaginary correspondent that "wild," when applied to a primitive race and its poetry, means "livelier, freer, more sensuous, of greater lyric power and range." The further a race is removed from learned habits of thought, the better its "lyrical, living, and dance-like songs." He translates our own ballad "Edward" as a specimen of such natural poetry. Such,

[1] Quotations are from Suphan's admirable edition of Herder's complete works.

[2] *Works*, V, 56.

[3] *Ibid.*, V, 164; written in 1773. See, also, preface to the second part of the *Volkslieder*, *Works*, XXV, 314.

too, was the epos of Homer, such the poems of Ossian ; and these, like all early poetry, were *impromptus.* Elsewhere he couples Homer and Moses as two of the greatest "singers of the people." "Read Homer as if he were singing in the streets !"

After the great period of primitive verse we meet the minstrels, who walked a like spontaneous path of poetry, but with weaker and weaker steps, until, says Herder, "art came along, and extinguished nature." Poetry lost its strength, its inevitableness, and became a tottering thing, like the "corrected exercises of a schoolboy." This is all in the familiar eighteenth century hysterics ; bnt we get a hint of cause and effect, of sober origins, in a prize-essay "On the Causes of Decadence and Corruption in Taste."[1] Homer, says our author, was great because of his contact with an age when "writing and prose were not invented," and when heroic traditions still living in the mouths of the people "*of themselves took on poetic form.*" Here is one of those oracular and nebulous phrases which the age presently hugged so to its heart ; but with Herder it is no theory of origins. It is simply a remark incidental to his purpose of heaping scorn upon the puny schools of his day, and of lauding the poetry of nature and of spontaneity.[2] For he is convinced that the chief shock came to poetry with the invention of printing, with learned verse, and the consequent separation of it from the common people.

[1] *Works*, V, 593 ff. See also 601 f., 613 f., 616 ff. On p. 617 one seems to be reading Taine.

[2] See the essay on Effect of Poetry upon Popular Morals, etc., *Works*, VIII, 334 ff. In another place, however, (XXV, 332 f.) he tells us that if the spirit of a ballad be good, actual contents are of little moment ; for the bad will of itself fall away with time, and the stanzas will right themselves into harmony. But we cannot hold Herder to any theory of origins, because of such figurative talk.

" Aforetime," runs his Jeremiad, " these songs rang out
in a living circle, sung to the harp and animated by the
voice, the vigor and the courage of the singer or poet ;
now " — that is, with printing, — "they stood fixed in
black and white, prettily printed on —— rags ! " The
poet now wrote "for a paper eternity," where once he
had sung to the living heart and to the listening ear.
And this audience of old time was no class, no fragment,
but the race itself. " Folk," cries Herder, " that does
not mean the rabble of the streets." [1]

Thus his doctrine, his sermon. But there is something
to be learned from his selections and translations,[2] which
did so much to beget a taste for ballads. Like Percy,
Herder included in his collection much that could not be
brought under the head of ballads ; bits of the Edda,
soliloquies from Shakspere, even sheer *vers de société*, were
mixed with ballads like " Edward," in order to rescue his
chances with the public.[3] Yet Herder would evidently
include the plays of Shakspere in his poetry of the
people. He cared little or nothing for origins. If a
poem seemed to express thought or emotion of a national
character, if it smacked of outdoor life and not of the
study, it fell under his category of *volkslied*. He did not
ask whether it came from a community or race as a
representative creation, as their own making, but whether,
whatever its origin, it would express any race or community, and correspond to their taste, their sentiment, their

[1] *Works*, XXV, 323.

[2] The first edition was printed in two parts, and bore the title
*Volkslieder* (1777 and 1778 ) ; whereas the second edition was called
*Stimmen der Völker*. But there was a still earlier collection than
these, now first made public by Suphan, which Herder and his wife
sent to the press in 1775 ; for some reason it was withdrawn from
publication.

[3] Later editors of ballad-collections have followed the example
of Percy and Herder, but without their excuse.

collective character.[1]  The traditional element is to a
certain extent his test for a ballad, but he is always
reverting to this note of nationality.[2]  He is glad to
welcome even half barbarous races, provided always their
songs have the stamp of race.  In fact, the wilder the
song the better ; for " nature made man free, joyous,
singing : art and institutions (*zunft*) make him self-
contained, distrustful, dumb ! "  The aim of his collection,
as the second title shows, is to give a sort of human
symphony made up by voices of the nations ; for poetry,
he declares, " is the flower of the idiosyncrasy of a
race, of its speech, land, affairs, prejudices, passions,
presumptions, music, soul."

Herder saw clearly the virtues of natural and spontaneous verse ; but he failed to see what Grundtvig has since
put so strongly, — that the making of the ballad, of poetry
of the people in general, is a closed account.  He thought
to revive such poetry in his own land, ignorant that
while Germany might again array herself as a folk in
arms, she could never again present the spectacle of a
folk in verse.  What he did bring about, besides a new
taste for ballads and the poetry of genius, was a revival
— largely through his influence upon Goethe — of the
national lyric.  Indeed, if one will but consider Herder's
generous enthusiasm, his sweeping claims, his ardor
for nature, genius, inspiration, and all the other war-
cries of the new school in criticism, one readily sees
that his *volkslied* is anything but conterminous with our
ballad.  He is preaching the gospel of universal poetry.

---

[1] Herder's translations are superlatively good.  His remarks about
the task (*Works*, XXV, 333 f.) may be called the very gospel of
translation.  Oddly enough, J. Grimm, Herder's greatest scholar,
denies (*Klein. Schr.*, IV, 399, 423) altogether the possibility of
adequate translations of this sort.

[2] See two essays, *Works*, XXV, 65 ff., 81 ff.

Much the same is to be said of Goethe's influence
upon the study of ballads. Spurred on by Herder at
Strassburg, he collected a few Alsatian songs, and presently began to show their influence upon his own lyric.
On various occasions, mainly in later life, he made
critical comments on ballads as a class, or on poetry of
the people as Herder meant the phrase.[1] In 1823 he
remarks on the fashion in which people "use this word
*volkslieder* so much, and do not know just what is meant
by it." Such poems should really be made, if not among
savages, "at least among uncultivated masses. . . ."
Surely, we shall now have a definition? All he does,
however, is to change *volkslieder* into *lieder des volks*,
and so emphasize the note of nationality. One famous
saying of his may, nevertheless, be quoted as evidence
that he did not favor the nebular hypothesis for the
making of ballads. He is speaking of some Lithu-
anian ballads, which must be regarded, he says, as
coming directly from the people, who stand much nearer
to nature, and thus to poetry, than the educated world,
— surely the voice is the voice of Herder ; but presently
he adds his own clear-cut dictum : "When I think of it
in quiet, it seems wonderful enough that people make so
much of folksongs and rate them so high. There is only
one poetry, the real and the true ; all else is approxima-
tion and show. Poetic talent is given to the peasant
as well as to the knight ; it depends whether each one
lays hold upon his own condition and treats it as it
deserves, in which case the simplest relations will be the
most advantageous."

In many respects, a good pendant to Goethe is

[1] Thus to Eckermann (3 May, 1827) : It was not the authors of
Greek tragedies that really composed them, but, rather, "the time
and the nation." And he goes on to speak in the same way of
Burns.

Wordsworth. Both of them recognized the claims of natural poetry; both essayed to catch its secret; and both fell into a profoundly classical habit, as witness, in Wordsworth's case, the Laodamia and certain parts of the Excursion, — noble utterance, but through and through poetry of the schools. Like Goethe, Wordsworth turned to ballads mainly to teach himself and to help his own work as an artist in verse. Like Goethe, he echoes Herder's doctrine of spontaneity. All good poetry, he tells us,[1] is "the spontaneous overflow of powerful feelings"; but presently comes the definition of poetry as "the breath and finer spirit of all knowledge," . . . "the impassioned expression which is in the countenance of all science," — and we are with the schools again.

Wordsworth can do for our purpose no more than Goethe did; and it is hardly otherwise with a German poet of whom Wordsworth speaks in terms of respect and admiration, the unfortunate Bürger. Bürger, however, at least continued Herder's work in getting a public for the ballad, and was single-hearted in his devotion to poetry of the people; he hit its tone better in his own verse, and gave a better critical account of it, than did his happier brothers of the laurel. "Lenore" had more vogue than any one ballad of Goethe's, and its author made the supreme effort among all modern poets to catch the delight and the secret of a lapsing form. Moreover, in certain essays and prefaces on the nature of poetry, whereby he came into sharp conflict with Schiller, he laid down his confession of faith. Poetry, he contended, belongs not to learning, but to the people. He did not care so much for Herder's notion of nationality, of a folk in verse, as he did for the idea of tradition and unlettered poetry. What he calls "the epos of nature" must be the standard for every

---

[1] Preface to the *Lyrical Ballads.*

poet ; and whoever has mastered this secret can gain all hearts, high or low. Where, one asks, is this "epos of nature" to be found? In our old songs of the people, answers Bürger ; often, we are told in a pretty passage, often he has listened at twilight under the village lindens, or by the spinning-wheel, to ballads and wayside songs ; and that is the best school for any poet, lyric or epic. All poetry — and this is the claim he makes so boldly — even the higher lyric, must be tried by the popular standard. The sole muse of poetry, ran his perilous creed, is the muse of the traditional ballad. Now this sweeping assertion not only went far beyond anything Herder had said, but involved Bürger in contradictions. Herder, indeed, after his vigorous campaign for poetry of the people, had turned from the matter, much as Goethe did, with an audible *majora canamus ;* there is a time, he said,[1] to talk about songs of the people, and a time to talk of them no more ; for him that latter hour had struck, — and so to fresh pastures. He tosses the whole task of collecting, defending and defining these songs, with a sort of scornful good-will, to the Romantic School. But Bürger has no such divided allegiance ; for him there are no *majora ;* and the song of the people is all in all. In the preface to his collected poems,[2] he affirms this article of faith, " in which I firmly believe, the axis on which turns my whole theory of poetry : all representative and plastic art (*bildnerei*) can be and must be of the people, for that is the seal of its perfection."

Of course, Bürger's crux is his definition of folk or people. Having asserted a principle valid for any epoch, he must define " folk " in terms of the present time. He

[1] *Works*, XXV, 545. Herder did not wish to substitute the actual folksong for poetry of higher art : he admits that would be sheer folly. *Works*, XXV, 308.

[2] It is 1778, the year of Herder's first part of the *Volkslieder.*

cannot appeal to the fact of a once homogeneous race or community, and to the expression of that race and time in genuine songs of the people ; he has to fight a desperate battle *pro domo* as well as for his favorites of the past. All he can do is to "hit the average," to take as standard the general taste of the better classes in any given country, and to bid the poet write for this level just as shoemakers make a shoe for general sale, — on the average measure. But in what confusion, in what contradictions, such a theory must involve us ! Poetry of the people is thus inextricably tangled with poetry for the people ; and we flounder hopelessly in this bog which has caught so many students of the ballad.[1]

To put the matter briefly, the criticism which we have so far examined was no real criticism at all. Oracle, eloquence, theory, rhetoric have been with us ; but nothing of the careful and sundering criticism which we need. Discussions about what poetry ought to be, and ought to have been, are interesting ; but in our day they are yielding — as witness Scherer's fragmentary, flippant, unequal, but revolutionary and always stimulating "Poetik" — to the question of what poetry was, and where it began. Nobody dreams of rapid solution, perhaps even of ultimate solution ; but to come as close to the matter as we can is the task of modern poetics. We turn, therefore, to the founder of Germanic philology, confident that we shall get something better than declamation, something more stable than even the righteous eloquence of Herder.

---

[1] This confusion is sharply criticised by Hoffmann von Fallersleben in his book *Unsere volksthümlichen Lieder*, 3d ed., Leipzig, 1869. He gives some amusing specimens of the made ballad, "songs of labor" and what not.

## VI.

In these days of the philological agnostic, it must seem a bit of folly to set up Jacob Grimm, the thrice battered, as a god in poetical criticism. Three distinct theories which he held have been sharply, and in a measure successfully, attacked, — the theory of a native and original Germanic beast-epos ; the theory that our popular tales had their source in ancient Germanic and Aryan myth ; and the theory that poetry of the people "makes itself." Of these, nobody holds any longer to the first. The second is badly damaged, as any one must admit who reads the clear arraignment of it by Cosquin.[1] The third is our present subject for consideration, and we must begin by giving an account of it in Grimm's own words.

Herder,[2] we remember, had spoken in a general way about Homer as a "singer of the people," as the poet of a time when heroic traditions "of themselves took on poetic form." Out of this phrase, Jacob and Wilhelm Grimm made a definite critical proposition, and laid down a doctrine of ballad origins. They maintained that poetry of the people "sings itself," has no indi-

---

[1] *Contes Populaires de Lorraine*, with *un essai sur l'origine et la propagation des contes populaires européens*, 2 vols., Paris, 1886. On p. xii is given the solution of the problem, as against the "vague vaporeux et poétique" of the Grimms, or the fatuity of a later writer, Hahn. Importation from the East, or elsewhere, doubtless explains most of the tales ; but there is some sense in the objection, by anticipation, of Steinthal (on *Mythos, Sage, Märchen u. s. w.*, in his *Zeitschrift*, XVII, 113 ff.), that it is going too far when one assumes, "because Europe imported so much, she must have been herself sterile and unproductive" (p. 123).

[2] Lack of space compels us to leave out of account minor, but deserving critics of the ballad like Görres and Arnim, as well as details about other ballad-collectors, the *Wunderhorn*, and all the rest.

vidual poet behind it, and is a product of the whole
folk. This was a hard saying even to some men of the
Romantic School ; and phrases were bandied about in
regard to such a "spontaneous generation" of the ballad.
To others it seemed as natural an assumption that a
whole nation could create songs, could sing itself into
verse, as that a whole nation could govern itself. But
we must hear Grimm's own words. In one of his earliest
papers,[1] he insists that it is useless to seek after the
author of the Nibelungen Lay, "as, indeed, must be the
case with all national poems, because they belong to
the folk as a whole, and thus everything subjective is
kept in the background." Again, in the same year,[2] "it
is inconsistent," he says, "to think of composing an
epos, for every epos must compose itself, must make
itself, and can be written by no poet." In another article, somewhat later, he notes the great interest felt for
songs of the people, sunders epic from dramatic composition,—the former as poetry of nature, the latter as
poetry of art, — asserts the identity of oldest history and
oldest poetry as the true expression of the nation which
so records itself, and declares that "in epic poetry, deeds
give forth, as it were, a sound of themselves, which
must make its way throughout all the race." When
formal history begins, when learning and culture arrive,
poetry takes flight to the unlettered people, and there
lives on, narrowed in scope, and influenced here and
there by culture, but still a pure ancestral song, the
inherited poetry of the race. Here, of course, belongs
the ballad ; for the ballad is an epos in little. Five years
later,[3] we have the same note in Grimm's "Thoughts
on Myth, Epos and History." In the epos, he contends,

---

[1] 1807. See his *Kleinere Schriften*, IV, 4.

[2] *Ibid.*, IV, 10, note.

[3] *Ibid.*, IV, 74.

there is no poetizing, but poetry pure and simple ; and then, wishing to make himself clearer, he adds the phrase " objective inspiration." [1]

This was the young man ; but what have his maturer years to say about the problem ? In 1845, writing about the great Finnish epos, and in 1859 in his beautiful Discourse on Schiller,[2] he reverts to this theme of early poetry in more cautious and measured terms, we must admit, but substantially in the old spirit. " Epic poetry," he declares in the former essay, " can no more be made than history can be made." It is the "folk" which pours its own flood of poetry over far-off events, and so brings about the epos. In the Discourse on Schiller[3] one hears much the same ; events sing themselves in current of resistless poetry, " behind which the poet utterly disappears." More significant yet is a passage in the Discourse on Lachmann, where Grimm clings as firmly as ever to his theory of poetry of the people and by the people, but allows a certain flexibility and range of interpretation in regard to the manner of this gregarious authorship. " Epic poetry," he says,[4] "is not produced by particular and recognized poets, but rather springs up and spreads a long time among the people themselves, in the mouth of the people, — *however one may choose to understand this in a nearer application.*" [5]

Here, of course, is the weak joint of the armor, the fragile link in the chain of argument. Transmission from the communal mind, from the vague spirit of poetry felt by a homogeneous mass of men, into definite words

[1] " Keine Erdichtung, sondern wahrhafte Dichtung." — " Objective Begeisterung."

[2] *Kl. Schr.*, II, 75 ff. and I, 374 ff.

[3] See p. 380.

[4] *Kleinere Schriften*, I, 155.

[5] " Wie man das nun näher fasse."

and a concrete body of song, yet without any mediation of the artist or maker : this was doubtless as difficult in Grimm's eyes, as it seems impossible in our own. He hardly tried to solve the problem. Poetry for him lay close to religion,— it was religion ; and in his simple reverence for the secret of creation and all human life, he was content to leave the matter as belonging, if not to the sphere of miracle, at least to the sphere of mystery. A passage from his earliest complete book [1] throws some light on this attitude. Heroic legend, he is remarking, is natural poetry ; the joy and sense of ownership felt by a race towards its great men and kings must have "sung itself" ; and yet, just how this was done, he admits, lies beneath the veil. " *One must have faith.*" Faith is the last weapon with which modern criticism is wont to arm itself ; but even the shrewdest investigators are forced to put up with a deal of mystery, and mystery is what Grimm assumed for the process in question.[2] Take the origin of language, a problem always with us. How does a race make its language ? In mass, or by deputy ? Precisely such a problem for Grimm, in whom the lover of words always kept close to the lover of songs, was the communal authorship of poetry ; he believed in it, but could not demonstrate every step of the process. He insisted [3]

---

[1] *Ueber den altdeutschen Meistergesang*, 1811. See especially p. 5 ff.

[2] Save the mark, one is fain to cry, after a course of erudition from the popgun battalion who have been bickering about Grimm's heels and firing so valiantly at his boots, — save the mark ! Shall we be talking forever of the primitive savage, his blank amazement if he could see his descendants and the work of their hands, his utter inability to comprehend our ways, and shall we allow the fellow no poor little trick of deed or word which is not all clear and explicable in our eyes ?

[3] *Ursprung der Sprache*, in *Kl. Schr.*, I, 297. See also the preface to *Deutsche Sagen*, p. ix f.

that problems in one field are pretty sure to be problems in the other. " In the whole range of poetry, nothing stands, in regard to its parts and its development, so near to language and so analogous to it, as the epos." In his admirable essay on the Poetry of Law we meet the same doctrine with a new comparison. " This song belongs to no poet ; he who sang it, simply knew best how to sing it. Even so the law is not made by the judge, who dares not originate it. The singer controls his store of song; the judge puts forth his law." [1]

We have now heard enough from Jacob Grimm to understand what he thought of ballads, and what he had most in mind when he penned his pretty definition of poetry in general as "life itself, taken in its purity and held in the magic of speech." [2] Nor need we delay over the utterances of the more cautious Wilhelm, who was really the first to apply his brother's doctrine of epos and legend directly to actual ballad. [3] We are ready for a voice from the opposition. The Grimms had published a periodical, [4] in which they printed, along with other contributions, their own researches in Germanic philology. The first of these volumes was reviewed [5] by A. W. Schlegel;

[1] Grimm was not content with surmises about the past, but welcomed modern instances and declared them to be supporters of his theory. See *Kl. Schr.*, II, 76 f. ; also IV, 200, where he reviews a collection of modern Servian Ballads. No one claims the making of these, he says ; there are reciters and singers, but no authors.

[2] *Meistergesang*, p. 5.

[3] *Entstehung der altdeutschen Poesie*, 1808, *Kl. Schr.*, I, 92 ff. See also his *Altdänische Heldenlieder*, p. 541 ff. It must be added that Wilhelm is more cautious than Jacob in his application of the famous phrase, as may be seen in another part of his essay. In his *Helden-sage* (2nd ed., p. 345 ff.) he gives another description of primitive poetry, which is marked by little of Jacob's boldness.

[4] *Altdeutsche Wälder*, 3 vols., 1813–1817.

[5] *Heidelberger Jahrbücher*, 1815. A good *résumé* by Scherer in his *Jacob Grimm*, 2nd ed., p. 141 ff.

and some of his severest censure fell upon Jacob Grimm's theory of primitive song. A poem, affirmed the brilliant critic, implies always a poet; a work of art, as every poem must be, whether good or bad, implies an artist; and for poems of any reach or grace, we must assume an artist of the highest class. Legend and epos and song might well belong to the people as their property; but the making of this verse was never a communal process. A stately tower, argued Schlegel, or any building of beauty, means, it is true, that a host of workmen have carried stones from the quarry and reared the walls; but behind them is the shaping thought of the architect. All poetry rests upon a union of nature and art; even the earliest poetry has a purpose and a plan, and therefore belongs to an artist. Nor was it all a world of truth and beauty, mirrored, as Grimm had fabled, in the clear waters of song; there stood the minstrel, ready for hire and salary to sing his master's deeds, to tickle his vanity, and, like a picture-dealer of our day, to furnish a whole row of valiant and deified ancestors. Thus, and with more of the same caustic argument, the self-made song is waved away.[1]

Grimm and Schlegel, the pioneer and the critic, spoke each after his kind and from frankly opposite points of view. Whether we approve or blame either one of them, we have no reason to complain of an indistinct utterance.

[1] There is no doubt that Lachmann shared in a way this opinion about the nebulous and distant character of Grimm's teaching. In 1816 he quotes Schlegel's criticism with approval (see Lachmann, *Kl. Schr.*, I, 2, 65). In his review of von der Hagen's *Nibelungen* (1820) he is more favorable to Grimm: the "poet" of the lay, he says is "the People." His most explicit statement on this subject, however, so far as the present writer can speak, is in his paper on the Hildebrand-Lay, *Kl. Schr.*, I, 407 ff., where he insists that invention and presentation of a folk-song are always separate processes, and further assumes (p. 443) that the folk-singer stands to his material of legend as a poet to the language in which he writes.

It is quite another matter with Uhland, a gentle soul, whose treatise on poetry of the people,[1] left incomplete, and published after his death, is perhaps the most important work of the kind. It has a single purpose, and employs all its writer's store of investigation to one end; while Grimm's utterances on the subject are mainly *obiter dicta*. Yet it suffers, so far as the matter of origin is concerned, from indecision; and we find it hard to say whether Uhland's attitude towards Grimm must be called guarded opposition or modified approval.

Uhland accepts, of course, the doctrine of a homogeneous people as a condition of this sort of poetry, and its dependence upon oral tradition. "Growth or decay of communal poetry," he says,[2] "always depends absolutely upon the part played in it by the race as a compact whole. If the nobler souls draw back, and turn to written literature, communal poetry sinks into poverty and the commonplace." Legend and oral tradition are opposed inevitably to literature and the community of letters. The race must be poetic as a race, as a unit. In the idea of popular poetry, he goes on to say, and in the phrase itself, rests a demand that not only shall the song be popular, but also that the common culture and the popular mode of thought shall be poetic. This is the case with a people in whom the whole intellect is still under control of those mental powers which make for poetry, — powers of imagination, of emotion, — and where the popular intellectual life is saturated with such an influence, and expresses it in speech, in proverbs, in laws, in legends, in songs. Oral tradition, added to

[1] See *Abhandlung über die deutschen Volkslieder*, Vol. III, and *Anmerkungen zu den Volksliedern*, Vol. IV, of Uhland's collected works. There is also material in his *Sagengeschichte d. germ. u. röm. Völker*, VII, 3 ff.

[2] *Schr.*, VII, 7.

all this, rounds the poetry to a common standard, and excludes — at any rate, in our sense of the phrase, — all individual poets. So far in general terms ; but as for the mystery, the actual authorship of poetry of the people, Uhland takes that position of strategy defined by Hosea Biglow as " frontin' south by north." Although, he tells us, " a creation of the mind can never spring immediately from a multitude, although such a creation needs the act and the capacity of individuals, still, as opposed to that importance which rests in formal literature upon the personality, the peculiarities, or the mood of the poet, in poetry of the people there is decided preponderance of the mass over the individual. . . . That impulse, known to the individual man, to create a spiritual image of his life is active in whole races as such, as well as in individuals ; and it is no mere figure of speech that a race can be a poet.[1] Precisely in such common production lies the idea of poetry of the people. True, this poetry can get utterance only through individuals ; but these have little personality, and are lost in the totality of the race." [2] There follow some excellent remarks upon the nature of oral transmission and its workings upon the form and style of a ballad ; but we get no unequivocal words in regard to authorship. We hoped, from this man of sanity and balance, some stay for our feet, some happy compromise between the too ideal Grimm and the too literal Schlegel ; but what does Uhland really teach us ? Certainly no distinct notion about the making of a ballad. He rests too much in a phrase. He avoids the mystery in which Grimm took refuge ; but instead, he flies to images and allegory. He concedes the individual act in authorship, and then denies its significance. What, for example, in explaining the origin of popular song, are we to make of a community

---

[1] " Völker dichten."    [2] VII, 4.

"watered in every part by the gushing springs of poetry"? Where is, where was such a community, how are we to find it ; and when we find it, what will it do for us? We pass from phrase to phrase, all true and beautiful and good, but of scant help for the solution of our problem. It is not only the German who thus disappoints us. We get this same sort of diet from a man not unlike Uhland, save in length of days, a man of taste, of fine tact in collecting ballads, and a poet of merit in his own right, the Scottish Motherwell. Speaking of the communal nature of ballads, he calls them [1] "that body of poetry which has inwoven itself with the feelings and passions of the people, and which shadows forth, as it were, an actual embodiment of their Universal mind, and of its intellectual and moral tendencies." What we wish above all things to know, is the way in which this Universal mind goes about its work ; but neither Uhland nor Motherwell undertakes to tell us.

What shall we conclude? There is a simple remedy for our trouble. The cooler heads of the present, and for some decades past, have been content with an answer that involves no mystery, needs no "community watered by the gushing springs of poetry," and fares very tolerably without a Universal Mind. Modern criticism of ballads began in the mists and shadows of the romantic school ; its work is now going on in the dry light invoked by a band of sleek-headed men who work by day, sleep soundly o' nights, and are troubled by no dreams and mysteries. They hold, with Schlegel, to a very simple solution of our problem. The whole matter is one of oral tradition on one hand, and of scribe's or printer's ink on the other ; and that is all. "Sirs," they tell us, — in the language of one of their predecessors, — as for this ballad, "he hath never fed of the dainties

[1] Introduction to the *Minstrelsy*.

that. are bred in a' book ; he hath not eat paper, as it
were ; he hath not drunk ink ; his intellect is not
replenished . . ." That, surely, is no mystery.

Let us collect a few signatures to this simple statement
of belief.  No man has done more for certain phases of
poetry of the people than Ferdinand Wolf ;[1] and he
definitely rejects "the nebulous poet-aggregate called
folk."  Talvj,[2] too, has no love for Wilhelm Grimm's assertion that ballads make themselves ; and she tells us how
they are made in reality.  Singers, minstrels, compose
them, — blind old men, as in Servia ; or, it may be, in
some idyllic neighborhood, youth and maiden go about
their daily tasks in a spirit of improvisation, and make
little ballads while they herd or spin.  Coming over to
England, we have Bishop Percy's theory of minstrel
authorship, and the scoffs of that very irritable, but
startlingly well-informed person, Joseph Ritson.  Ritson
refers the origin of our English ballads to the reign of
Queen Elizabeth ; and while we can find no mention
of the mystery, we know pretty well what he would have
thought about it.[3]  Of no different opinion, so far as the

---

[1] *Ueber die Lais, Sequenzen, etc.,* 1841 — see pp. 48, 74, 125 ;
*Wiener Jahrbücher,* CXVII, pp. 84 f., 121 f., 127 ; *Proben portug. u.
catalan. Volksromanzen,* Sitzungsberichte d. Wien. Akad., Phil.-Hist.
Cl., XX, 17 ff. (March 12, 1856) ; and especially Introduction, Rosa
Warrens, *Schwedische Volkslieder,* 1857, p. xv.

[2] Mrs. Robinson, born v. Jacob.  See her *Versuch einer Charakteristik d. Volkslieder germanischer Nationen,* pp. 10, 338 f., 403 ff.

[3] See *Historical Essay* in his *Select Collection of English Songs,*
2nd ed., 1813, p. lxviii ; also, in his *Ancient Songs and Ballads,* the
*Observations on the Minstrels,* where he contemptuously concedes
a few songs to the minstrels, but all "merely narrative" (ed. Hazlitt,
p. xxi f.) ; and *Dissertation on Romance and Minstrelsy,* in his
*Ancient Engleish Metrical Romanceës.*  In this dissertation (original
ed. (1802) I, v ff.), Ritson thinks the Gest of Robin Hood may well
have been "composed by a priest in his closet !"

mystery is concerned, was Sir Walter Scott; in his eyes,
the minstrel was quite sufficient to account for minstrelsy, whether of the border or elsewhere. Ballads,
he remarks, often abridged from the romances, may be
originally the work of minstrels "professing the joint
arts of poetry and music," or they may be "the occasional effusions of some self-taught bard." [1] Motherwell,[2]
whom we have already quoted, tells of a custom which
favors the artist in ballad-making. Scottish singers by
profession, he says, preface, supplement, or interlard
their ballads with prose, supplying omissions, or telling
what became of the characters. Some pieces mix poetry
and prose, like a Scandinavian saga; and it is interesting
to note that Scherer deems this to have been the primitive form of all epic.[3] Crossing the channel again, and
coming nearer to our own time, we find so great an
authority as Müllenhoff, while agreeing with Grundtvig
about the necessary conditions of popular poetry, taking
definite stand — if his words are read aright — for individual authorship.[4] Müllenhoff's illustrious scholar and
colleague, Scherer, devotes pages of his brilliant sketch
of Jacob Grimm, and yet more of his *Poetik*, to the
support of Schlegel and the theory of artistry as the
prime factor in early song as well as in early speech.
Again, Professor Paul, who is no lover of Scherer's theories, is one with him in the rejection of this famous
mystery; in times of oral tradition, explains Paul, poets
composed a ballad, or what not, and sang it about the

---

[1] *Minstrelsy* (1802), II, 102; I, c. — He notes (I, xcii) the
account of Irish bards given by Spenser, and thinks an analogy
could be found in "our ancient border poets."

[2] *Minstrelsy*, Amer. ed., I, 19.

[3] *Poetik*, 14 f.

[4] Introduction to the *Sagen, Lieder u. s. w.*, pp. xxvi and xxviii.

land for bread.[1] Nyrop tells us[2] that by 1883 all Scandinavian — or Danish?[3] — scholars had totally given up the
theory that such poetry is the work of a whole people.
He is very emphatic for the artist in all ballads. "Originally there existed no popular singer who did not make
some pretensions as poet,"[4] — and this even before the
real epos had been developed. The Danish trumpet, we
note, gives no uncertain sound ; and, indeed, the energetic
writer might have calmed his fears for Germany by reading
quite as rational and quite as decided a view of the matter
in the pages of Böhme.[5] "It is not true," says Böhme,
"that a whole people ever made songs"; and he goes on
to give us, not a theory, but an actual example of the way
in which poetry of the people was really made. He pro-
duces from the *Limburg Chronicle* a certain leprous monk
of the fourteenth century, who lived by the Rhine and
made the best songs and dance-tunes in the world ; what
he sang, runs the record, all the people loved to sing and
whistle, and gleemen took up his songs and tunes, scatter-
ing them about the land. "There," says Böhme, "we
have the secret about the origins of popular poetry ; the
oft admired and nebulous composition by a poetic multitude is mistake and nonsense. First of all, one man

---

[1] Paul, *Grundriss d. germanischen Philologie*, I, 231 ; see, also,
I, 73.

[2] *Den oldfranske Heltedigtning*, p. 35, note. He is declaring that
a single poet must have composed an epos like the *Chanson de
Roland*. See, also, p. 287 f., where he insists on an author for the
ballad, but allows that oral tradition, singing, destroys the trace of
individuality.

[3] He says : "Den, hos os i det mindste fuldstendig opgivne, tågede
Teori" . . . He fears that in Germany they are coming back to the
heresy. As strong condemnation, too, is in the little book of P.
Friis : *Udsigt over de danske Kæmpeviser, etc.*, Copenhagen, 1875,
p. 7.

[4] Work quoted, p. 291.

[5] *Altdeutsches Liederbuch*, p. xxii.

sings a song, and then others sing it after him, changing
what they do not like." That is all.[1] It cannot be denied
that this view of the matter agrees admirably with our
modern habit of thought, and Böhme finds approval, implied or expressed, from many a minor critic of the ballad,
— for example, to enlarge our borders, from a Dutch
writer, who explicitly commends such a position.[2] Implied approval, distinct enough on the main question,
comes also from the scholars who just now have been
handling these matters in Paul's Germanic Philology.
Professor Brandl[3] recognizes oral tradition as the only
available test of the English ballad, so far as matter is
concerned, and insists further upon a set metrical form.
Lundell, speaking for Scandinavia,[4] thinks that theories
about the origin and development of ballads are still one
and all hypothetical ; but he has no love for the mystery.
Meier,[5] for the Germans, defines a song of the people as
one where " the author or authors " have no intention
of a literary character, no design upon the world of
letters,[6] — a view amiable but vague.

So runs the uniform comment of these certainly able
critics ; and what they assert really amounts to an identi-

[1] Unfortunately for his cause, Böhme does not stop here, but goes
on to define the difference between poetry of the people and that of
the schools, whereby he brings under the second class precisely those
songs of the leprous monk which he has just set up as models of the
first class. Why, he asks, in contradiction of himself, why inquire
for the author of a folk-song when it was never really composed
(*verfasst*) at all ? " It is a masterless and nameless affair " — and he
falls to quoting . . . Jacob Grimm ! See p. xxiii ff.

[2] G. Kalff, *Het Lied in de Middeleeuwen*, Leiden, 1884, p. 38.

[3] *Grundriss d. german. Philol.*, II, i, 839 f.

[4] *Ibid.*, II, i, 724 f.

[5] *Ibid.*, II, i, 741.

[6] We might go on with examples : R. M. Meyer in Haupt's *Zts.,*
XXIX, 121 f. ; Burdach in same journal, XXVII, 344, and so on :
but all would be to one purpose.

fication of the origins of the ballad with the origins of poetry as a thing of literature, barring the facts of environment at the outset and oral tradition in reaching a later public. In both cases the artist is a final cause. Yet all able critics of our day are not on this side. Leaving out of sight for the moment the question of gregarious or communal authorship for itself, we find that a few of our best scholars are unwilling to concede so much to the artist. They wish to keep the ballad, not only in its fate and accidents, but in its origins and its essence, apart from the poem of literature. They may not support Grimm's theory as laid bare by criticism ; but they take up ground not far removed from it. These men are in the first instance Grundtvig and ten Brink. Grundtvig we have already quoted,[1] and ten Brink is presently to be considered. Professor Child, the best living authority on our subject, has devoted his main energies thus far to the editing and comparing of actual ballads, with such result that it is impossible to praise too highly his great collection, now nearly completed ; he has had little to say on the subject of origins.[2] Professor Steenstrup, whose clear and admirable study of Danish ballads [3]

[1] See above, p. xxxv. Pp. xxi–xxiv of the Introduction quoted are surely unequivocal enough ; and we know of no passage in other works where Grundtvig has changed his opinion. His *Udsigt over den Nordiske Oldtids Heroiske Digtning* (1867) protests, it is true, against the German tendency to myth, and against the Scandinavian tendency to find history in everything ; but that is quite apart from our question. Moreover, he is talking of the Eddas and the Sagas.

[2] In Johnson's *Cyclopædia*, 1893, "Ballad Poetry," he names absence of subjectivity and of self-consciousness as prime trait of the ballad, and adds : "Though they do not 'write themselves' as William Grimm has said, though a man and not a people has composed them, still the author counts for nothing, and it is not by mere accident, but with the best reason, that they have come down to us anonymous."

[3] *Vore Folkeviser fra Middelalderen*, Copenhagen, 1891.

is mainly devoted to the demonstration of a total lack of connection between these and the old Scandinavian poems,[1] does not take positive ground on the matter of authorship; some of his investigations,[2] notably a fine chapter on the "I" in ballads, bear that way, and he is emphatic against all poetic individuality, and all lyrical elements; but he nowhere approaches approval of Grimm's mystery.[3] However, be the vote of these two eminent scholars for or against the artist in the ballad, we feel that the outspoken opposition of Grundtvig, master in ballads, and of ten Brink, whose tact and judgment in general literature no one can call

[1] See especially p. 322.

[2] See pp. 32, 37 ff., 204.

[3] We are concerned with Germanic criticism, but allow ourselves a glance at two men of note in Romance territory who seem to be separated from the camp of the *Aufklärer*. Nigra in his admirable study, *La Poesia Popolare Italiana*, prefixed to his *Canti Popolari del Piemonte*, reverts to the analogy in the making of ballads and of language. " Ma la poesia popolare *al pari della lingua è una creazione spontanea essenzialmente etnica*" (p. xviii); and again, (p. xxvii): "La canzone storica popolare . . . è anonima. Non è improvvisata da un poeta popolare [Böhme's leper!] più o meno noto. . . . " For such songs we assume "*un periodo più o meno lungo d'incubazione,* al quale succede una continua elaborazione che si va perpetuando con fasi diverse, finchè la canzone cada a poco a poco nell' oblio, o sia fissata dalla scrittura." Again, it would seem that Gaston Paris is not with the majority. *Hist. Poétique de Charlemagne,* p. 2 : early popular poetry is " improvisée et contemporaine des faits "; *Romania,* XIII, 617 : the songs are " composés non seulement sous l'impression immédiate des faits, mais *par ceux et pour ceux* qui y avaient pris part "; and in the same journal, p. 603, he doubts the existence of any professional minstrels among the primitive Germans, going on to say how "indications prove that later, and even among Anglo-Saxons, skill in composing and singing narrative songs was common with the majority of men, like skill in fighting or in settling matters of law (*dire le droit*)." It was the warriors of early time (*Hist. Poët. de Charl.,* p. 11) " lesquels chantaient eux-mêmes les chants qu'ils avaient composés."

in question, gives us pause when we are asked to set down the problem of the origin of the ballad as a matter definitely adjusted by modern criticism.

It seems to us, and not at all in the way of Uhland's compromise, that the modern school make a very perilous leap when they conclude from the safe assertion of nebulosity and lack of meaning in any notion of the ballad as singing itself, that therefore the primitive ballad, which we do not see and never have seen, was made as any other poem is made, and is differenced simply by oral transmission. Let us frankly give up this phrase, that the ballad "makes itself." Let us go further, and give up for any ballads in our control the assumption that they were made by a whole race or community as such. But let us not surrender so hastily the autonomy of the ballad, the dualism of poetry of the people and poetry of the schools ; let us maintain opposition between the throng and the artist, between the chorus and the lyric. At least, let us not give up all this until we have completed our critical task, until we have rendered better account of the essential elements of the ballad as it must have been at its best.

## VII.

It is impossible to watch a ballad in its making ; that merry art is dead. Even if one could uncover the origins of any English ballad, it is not likely that one would see a folk in verse behind it. It might be traced, like "Thomas Rymer," to some romance, or, like "St. Stephen," to a legend of the church, or, like "King Orfeo," to a distorted tale from the classics. "Mary Hamilton" seems as Scottish and as local as may be ; but for all its versions, the source of it is probably to be found in the court of Peter the Great. "Bewick and Grahame" is surely no loan from abroad ; but it belongs, at the earliest, to the end of the sixteenth century, and by what delusion can we think of Shakspere's countrymen running together some fine day to chant this simple story as a sort of off-hand oratorio ?   Apart, too, from problems of origin and transmission, we must reckon with the changes wrought by migration, which hold good for the ballad as they do for the popular tale.   True, when cynicism or flippancy leads us from the ballad to its source in a *fabliau*, as is the case with "The Boy and the Mantle," we lay these faults to the charge of minstrels, and make due reservations ; but popular tales of humbler and more traditional character will account for many a true ballad,[1] and thus establish its origin in the simple desire for entertainment.   Ballads were quick enough to take up a moving story of any sort ; witness, with its hint of real history, the tale told in "Sir Aldingar," and followed by Grundtvig through so many chances ; or witness the supernatural motive of "Clerk Colven."[2]   The ballad, moreover, is always close to popular legend, and, like the legend, holds peculiar relations with history, borrowing a trait, a fact, a name, or combining widely sundered events, as in "Mary Hamilton."   Legend, again, may combine with legend, and ballad with ballad, as in "The Baron of Brackley," where we are at least tempted to assume two Barons, and a confusion of two traditional songs.   Often this may have been accidental, and often the minstrel's

---

[1] For example, *The Twa Magicians*. See Child's remarks, *Ballads*, I, 401 (Part II) ; and Crane, Introduction to *Chansons Populaires de la France*, New York, 1891, p. xxvi f.

[2] *Danmarks Gamle Folkeviser*, I, 177 ff., and Child, *Ballads*, I (Part II), 374 ff. — In *Mélusine*, I, 1 ff., *De l'étude de la poésie populaire en France*, Gaston Paris is inclined to limit this factor of borrowing as a source of ballads.   Admitting that it has its place, he insists on the analogy of poetry and language, and on "un certain fonds ou patrimoine commun à toute la race aryenne."

flattery or cunning must bear the blame.[1]  Again, the same story may have been told in different settings or about different people ; a striking incident in one ballad may have been transferred to another ballad ; and finally the temper of the singer and the character of his audience may so change with time as to alter the nature of the events, the dignity of the characters, and even the outcome of the story.  In English ballads one can often follow this degeneration, with its lapse in vivid character, and its effacing or rationalizing of the supernatural.[2]  Akin, moreover, to the fates of transmission from age to age, are the chances of migration from race to race.  True, it is to be conceded that the simpler tragic or dramatic motives need no theory of borrowing ; human fate and human emotion — *partout les passions, partout l'inexorable destin*[3] — are enough to account for such epics of the countryside.  But there are other motives and other stories which force us to assume either a common origin, or a passage from land to land ; the distribution and relations of the ballad are as undoubted in the way of fact as they are difficult in the way of explanation, and it is clear that they play no small part in the ballads of this collection.[4]

[1] See Wilhelm Grimm's admirable study, " Ursprung und Fortbildung," in his *Heldensage,*[2] p. 345 ff.  For minstrel's interpolation, and the character of Volker in the Nibelungen, see p. 363.

[2] Not to fall back on " Buchan's parrots," witness the degradation, especially due to broadside influence, shown by comparing two versions (A and B) of " Sir Andrew Barton," or, for a less flagrant case, the substitution of a man for a bird in " Johnie Cock " (A, 21).

[3] Epilogue to *Les Bohémiens,* Mérimée's translation from Pushkin.

[4] For Germanic ballads, Grundtvig and Child have done noble work in this field of comparison.  On the general question of distribution, see Uhland, *Schriften zur Gesch. d. Dichtung u. Sage,* III, 9 f. ;  Motherwell, *Minstrelsy,* Amer. Ed., I, 50 ;  and R. M. Meyer in Haupt's *Zeitschr.,* XXIX, 176, with references in the foot-note. —

All of the English and Scottish ballads, by the very conditions of their preservation, lie this side of the purely communal stage. The "Gest" is an epos in the making, with local traditions and local characters ; its central figure is no immortalized hero, but rather an idealized type of the woodland outlaw, — certainly not a tottering relic of pagan divinity, whether Woden or even Brandl's field-and-forest demigod.[1] This admirable poem shows no defect in sharpness of outline, although transmission and the fusion of several independent ballads have destroyed identity of person and legend ; like any good epic, it bears the double grace of a popular origin and an incipient artistic control. Only madness could regard such an altogether charming piece as mere gregarious makings, like the Färöe ballad of the frustrated fisher, jostled into unity by the chances of time. "Otterburn " and " The Hunting of the Cheviot " are in the same class : traditional verse of the people at its best, handed down by shifty singers. So it is with "Johnie Cock" and "Johnie Armstrong"; each has overwhelmingly popular character, yet a form and a cohesion which suggest the beginning, however feeble, of literary tact. " Kinmont Willie " should be compared with the other two ; whatever Scott's share in it, its literary suggestion is far more prominent. " Sir Andrew Barton " is a good story, well told in parts, but far gone into the way of broadsides. Of the shorter ballads, " Spens," " Brackley," " Mary Hamilton," and others, reveal the charm of tradition and that pathos

Nigra points out (*Canti Popolari del Piemonte*, p. xviii) that the materials of the song go anywhere, while metre, rime, and form in general are borrowed only from "popoli omoglotti." It is evident that border folk could transmit ballads, as they transmitted many things less desirable.

[1] Paul's *Grundriss*, II, i, 844.

which springs from the feeling of a community and not from the sentiment of a poet ; while ballads like " Bonnie George Campbell " and " Three Ravens " show a note of the lyric[1] slowly detaching itself from pure narrative, just as " Lord Randal" and " Edward " lean to the dramatic. " Babylon," " The Twa Sisters," " Child Maurice," lead us back to a simpler tone of tragedy ; " Sweet William's Ghost " and " The Wife of Usher's Well " touch the supernatural world ; the tragedy of love or family relations, in the group which follows, is as direct as possible, yet not without the same suggestion of a fit reporter ; and at last we have the romantic ballad, of which " Young Beichan " is the homeliest and " Childe Waters " the most admirable specimen. Wherever we turn, we find in these ballads something impersonal and communal which we recognize as their differentiating element ; and we also find the agency of a singer, a skilful recording secretary, one might say, who stands between us and the community, running withal the chances of oral transmission.[2]

Such are the sober facts in regard to the ballads of this collection ; but in admitting the agency of reporter

[1] Steenstrup, *Vore Folkeviser*, p. 32, shows that in primitive ballads this lyric note was unknown.

[2] From a count, for which the editor is indebted to Mr. B. Cadbury, late graduate student in Haverford College, of the ballads in the first seven parts of Professor Child's collection, it would seem that of 225 ballads, 113 are Scottish, 80 English, 2 from Shetland, and 30 with both English and Scottish versions ; that 148 are derived from popular tradition, 46 from historical tradition (actual, though distorted events), 9 from traditional history (fable accepted as history), 17 from romances and tales, and 5 from the Bible or sacred legends. Of ballads derived from popular tradition, 38 belong to the Robin Hood cycle ; and of those from historical tradition, 28 refer to warfare and raids of the Scottish border. There are 77 ballads which have counterparts in other languages or show incidents common to continental ballads.

and singer one does not necessarily solve the question of ultimate origins. One knows, for example, that the literary form of certain delightful German stories[1] is chiefly due to Wilhelm Grimm ; but no one dreams that such a concession has anything to do with fixing the origin of popular tales. As little is done for ballads by the frantic appeal to common sense,[2] or by talk of "author and public," and of "prices" and "competition" in the primitive German literary market. This is mere journalism. It is the critic's business to detach from the ballad, which is a compromise between tradition and art, all those elements in which art and the individual can have had no share, and to inquire whether the balance for communal forces can be explained on the simple basis of oral transmission. In other words, to borrow a phrase from M. Cosquin, after the student of ballads has determined the *marque de fabrique*[3] of a given specimen, it is in order for the student of the ballad itself to attack the more general but no less interesting problem, and determine the *marque de fabrique* of the popular elements in all ballads.

In avoiding mysteries we may ignore facts. We have no right to study the exotic of a greenhouse, and assume

---

[1] *Kinder- und Hausmärchen gesammelt durch die Brüder Grimm.*

[2] M. Anatole Loquin in *Mélusine*, IV, 529 ff., reviewing Tiersot's *Chanson Populaire en France*, is very bold. "Find the author!" he commands. Many popular songs ("chants populaires"), he insists, are by known authors (p. 535). Even when Tiersot modestly remarks that these songs are "of the people," the reviewer cries, "Ah, qu'en savez-vous ? *Vous trouveriez-vous donc là, quand ces chants ont été composés ?*"—This is certainly no argument.

[3] *L'Origine des Contes Populaires Européens, mémoire présenté au Congrès des Traditions Populaires de 1889;* mainly a criticism of theories held by Mr. Andrew Lang. See p. 6. Luckily, the task of determining the origin of popular elements in the ballad is not the unstable psychological process for which M. Cosquin has such horror (p. 19) ; it is largely a question of facts.

for it the same conditions of growth and propagation in a soil where it is the hardy product of nature. It is one thing to grant the agency of a singer in gathering and reporting poetry of the people ; it is quite another thing to say that such poetry, as it shades back into scraps of early traditional verse, and then, sheer combination and inference, escapes us in the darkness of prehistoric times, was always of this character, was always something dependent upon the artist. It is one thing to grant the possibility of personal authorship, somewhat in our modern sense, for a ballad like " Bewick and Grahame " ; it is another thing to say that the impersonal character of the ballad itself, a pervading quality which even the " I " of the singer is powerless to affect, rests upon the mere fact of oral transmission. Granted that this impersonal character differences all ballads, what is behind it ? If the ultimate reason for this quality lies in certain conditions of authorship by one man, then the axe is laid to the root of that distinction, still so carefully maintained by good critics, between *volksthümliche poesie* and *volkspoesie.* If M. Loquin is right, we need nothing more than a lively tune and words that take popular fancy, in order to make a ballad now ; and there is no reason why balladry of the best kind should be a closed account. But even modern criticism declares that it is a closed account. What, then, if this impersonal element in the ballad were simply the last active state of a distinct fashion of poetry, once common enough, but vanishing under the triumph of the schools ? What if this impersonal character of the later ballad were due to the purely communal elements of the primitive ballad ? Unfortunately, one cannot make proper connection between the two ; for in English and Scottish ballads one is dealing not with a sequence but with a survival. We have a series of ballads made from the beginning of the

fourteenth century down to the beginning of our own ;
but the Anglo-Saxon ballads are matter of inference.
That Angles and Saxons had ballads, says Brandl,[1] in a
pithy phrase, "is not to be denied if we consider human
nature, and not to be affirmed if we consider our present
sources of information." Certainly, so far as form is
concerned, the ballads are quite opposed to that poetry
handed down to us by the monks who controlled our
literature before the conquest ; though we find ample
evidence that poems in character and contents analogous
to the later ballad were sung in Saxon England. This
cataclysm and breach in traditions was not peculiar to
Great Britain. Steenstrup concludes that there is no
connection between the Scandinavian ballads, which are
like ours in form as well as matter, and the heroic poems
of the Edda. We can hardly doubt that English ballads
could be traced back in an unbroken chain to the
primitive Germanic song ; but we have lost important
links of the chain.[2] What we must do, when we find it

[1] Paul's *Grundriss*, II, i, 840. Merbot (*Aesthetische Studien zur
Ags. Poesie*, Breslau, 1883, p. 19 ff., and especially p. 31) gives a
list of words used by the Anglo-Saxons for different kinds of poetry,
admits the difficulty of drawing conclusions from a language which
rioted in synonyms, and yet concedes that a mass of occasional
poetry (*bismerléoð, brýdléoð, etc.*) may be inferred, of which we have
no actual remains.

[2] Sievers, as is well known, has explained Anglo-Saxon metre as
a recited verse, as *sprechvortrag*, compared with the far older
Germanic verse, which was sung, and naturally had stanzaic form.
This epic verse of the Anglo-Saxon poets was the only form which
the monks preserved as literature, but it is probable that the people
sang their songs in the old fashion. Luick (Paul's *Grundriss*, II, i,
998) assumes that the beginnings of the English riming couplet may
be regarded as the Old-Germanic verse for singing (*altgermanischen
taktierenden Gesangvers*) revived for literary purposes. It is no easy
question ; but one may at least fancy some such explanation for the
underground river of balladry.

impossible to follow the actual ballad, is to follow its elements, and so determine what a rational inference ought to conclude about their origin. Jacob Grimm set up a primitive mystery; Scherer sets up a primitive "entertainer," a singer of songs, teller of tales, lecturer on "the cause of thunder,"[1] in short, an æsthetic purveyor to the Probably Arboreal nobility and gentry. One process is quite as reasonable, and quite as acrobatic, as the other.

What are these elements of the ballad which make for communal origin? Aside from the story, which may be tradition, popular tale, or a loan from abroad, one must reckon with the melody, or the singing of ballads, with the dance, with the refrain or chorus, and with the important element of spontaneity. As a negative but essential element, one must include absolute ignorance of solitary composition and of the ideas attached to literary ownership as we know it.

## VIII.

No one denies the singing of ballads, and for early times no one will deny the prevailingly social character of singing. We know of many ballad-tunes, some of them still current;[2] and evidence is overwhelming that an unsung ballad may go for a contradiction in terms. With later ballads, instrumental accompaniment had its place;[3] but singing is always the chief consideration.

---

[1] See Scherer, *Poetik*, p. 116, on the origin of myths.

[2] See Chappell, Böhme, and other collections. Motherwell, in the Appendix to his *Minstrelsy*, gives thirty-three such tunes taken down from the singing. See also F. Wolf, *Proben portugiesischer . . . Volksromanzen*, above, p. 45.

[3] For the instruments, see Chappell, I, 247 f., and Ritson, *Anc. Songs and Ballads*, p. xlix ff., together with Drayton's *Polyolbion*, Song iv.

Thomas Rymer, in the romance of that name,[1] has choice of two supernatural gifts, surpassing ability either to "harpe" or else to "carpe";[2] and he replies:

> . . . *harpynge kepe I none,*[3]
> *For tonge es chefe of mynstralcye.*

It is true that some of the ballads came to be recited, on account of their great length; and often a monotonous chant or recitative took the place of melody.[4]  But even

[1] See *Thomas of Erceldoune*, ed. Brandl, vv. 313 ff., 687 ff.

[2] That is, to sing and narrate, to narrate in singing.

[3] That is, 'I care not at all for harping.'

[4] Standard passages which discuss this matter are W. Grimm, *Heldensage*,[2] p. 381; Lachmann, *Kl. Schr.*, I, 461 f., and especially 463; Wolf, *Lais*, p. 48 ff.; Müllenhoff, *Sagen u. s. w.*, p. ix.  It is not always clear what antithesis we should understand by the phrase "sing and say."  In *Widsíð*, v. 54, it seems almost a hendiadys, — "to tell in singing"; but *singan oððe secgan* is common elsewhere in Anglo-Saxon, and Puttenham, (*Arte of English Poesie*, ed. Arber, p. 26) remarks that even savages "do sing *and also* say their highest and holiest matter in certain riming versicles."  Chaucer must refer to recitation in his couplet (*Book Duch.*, v. 471 f.) :

> *He sayed a lay, a maner song,*
> *Withoute noote, withoute song ;*

and in the famous line of *Troilus*, v, 257, he uses the antithesis :

> *And red wherso thou be, or elles songe.*

Even in the singing a difference was made between long ballads and the livelier or shorter kind.  Chappell (II, 790 f.) speaks of his third class of "characteristic airs of England," that is, "the historical and very long ballads," as "invariably of simple construction, usually plaintive. . . .  One peculiar feature of these airs is the long interval between each phrase [*sic*], so well calculated for recitation and recovering the breath. . . .  They were rarely if ever used for dancing."  Böhme (*Geschichte des Tanzes*, p. 239) thinks the old narrative songs were given in the recitative of a single person, like modern Russian and Servian ballads ; the bystanders now and then joined in a sort of chorus.  Wissmann (*King Horn, Quellen u. Forschungen*, XLV, p. xxii), conjectures that while the narrative parts

the longer English ballads were often sung, as Chappell distinctly affirms ; and the ordinary ballad, probably all primitive ballads whatsoever, were inseparable from song. Ballads were made for singing, and to some extent were made in singing. The melody was by no means the device of a minstrel to entertain the throng,

of *King Horn* were recited, the dialogue — always in stricter stanzaic form — was sung ; and this would somewhat resemble the mixed song and story (in prose) mentioned by Motherwell in his account of certain Scottish ballads (*Minstrelsy*, Amer. ed., I, 19 ff.) and exemplified by Pitcairn's version of "The Lass of Roch Royal," note to Child, *Ballads*, II, 225 (Part III) Version C, or by Version H in "The Maid Freed from the Gallows," II, 354, — here, however, in a vanishing ratio of recitation or comment. It should be remembered that not only does Scherer (see p. lix, above) regard this mingling of prose and verse as the primitive form of epic, but Joseph Jacobs (note to "Childe Rowland," in *English Fairy-Tales*, p. 240), discussing the *cante-fable*, remarks : "It is indeed unlikely that the ballad itself began as continuous verse, and the *cante-fable* is probably the protoplasm out of which both ballad and folk-tale have been differentiated." That "unlikely," however, very prettily begs the whole question ; and Jamieson's account (*Illustrations of Northern Antiquities*, p. 408) of the romance under discussion, as it was told to him by a country tailor, "an ignorant and dull good sort of man," who "recited in a sort of formal, drowsy, measured, monotonous recitative," will most admirably fit the "say" of our formula, the artist's half of it, but not the "sing," which belongs to ballads of the crowd. Indeed, this seems the best solution of the whole question. "Sing and say" is the antithesis of throng and artist, a dancing multitude and a reciting "entertainer." — It is hardly necessary, so far as ballads are concerned, to take sides in the controversy between Sievers (*Entstehung d. deutschen Reimverses*, Paul-Braune, *Beiträge*, XIII, 135 f.) and Möller, (*Zur althochdeutschen Alliterationspoesie*, 146 ff.). Whether early Germanic verse had no ordered sense of melody and time, — Vigfússon indeed, speaks of "emphatic prose" (*Corpus Poeticum Boreale*, I, 434), — as Sievers asserts, or whether Möller is right in his claims for *takt*, it may be safely assumed that actual ballad verse was always stanzaic and always sung. It was quite distinct from the continuous epic verse.

but the concerted work of a throng to entertain itself ; and this assertion, on the face of it not far from a *petitio principii,* derives its best support from the connection of ballads with the dance.

The dance, in early days, was inseparable from song ; out of its steps and windings came perhaps the fact and certainly the terms of metre.[1] There is no doubt that one must look upon the dance as centre and, in a way, origin of all songs of the people.[2] "*No dance without singing,*" says Böhme, "*and no song without a dance ;* songs for the dance were the earliest of all songs, and melodies for the dance the oldest music of every race.*"[3]

---

[1] Scherer, *Geschichte d. deutschen Sprache,*[2] p. 624. In many tongues, dance and song are convertible terms. Icelandic *danz,* though a foreign word, is used very early in the sense of our "ballad," a song to which people dance : see Cleasby-Vigfússon, *Dictionary,* p. 96, with the classic passage. Our own words, like "ballad" itself, "carol," and others, help the etymological argument. — Religious and social questions cannot be considered here : see Livy, i, 20, on the Salian priests, or Müllenhoff (*Festgabe f. G. Homeyer : über den Schwerttanz,* especially p. 117) on the instrumental accompaniment of the Germanic sword-dance. One is inclined, though Möller explicitly opposes it, to assume a ballad of battle sung to this cadence of step and flashing sword. The Grimms (*Deutsche Sagen,* I, 210) promised a description of the later Hessian sword-dance " with the song of the dancers." See references (for later German literature) in Paul's *Grundriss,* II, i, 835. Scott (see Lockhart's *Life,* ed. 1837, III, 162 : Amer. ed., II, 130) refers to an account of the Shetland sword-dance, and speaks of "the lines, the rhymes, and the form of the dance."

[2] " Mittelpunkt alles Volksgesanges " : Müllenhoff, *Sagen, u. s. w.,* p. xxv. Böhme (*Tanz,* p. 13) thinks all lyric poetry, even, began in the dance. Jeanroy, *Les Origines de la Poésie Lyrique en France,* p. 357 ff., gives ample material from Romance poetry in support of these views ; and he adds : " Dans ces fêtes [dancing and singing] non seulement on chantait les chansons, mais on en composait " (p. 390).

[3] *Altdeutsches Liederbuch,* p. xxxv ; *Geschichte d. Tanzes,* p. 4.

Besides this wider association of song and dance, it is of importance to note the close connection between dancing and the narrative ballad. As early as the seventeenth century, Färöe islanders were known to use their traditional songs as music for the dance ; and later the invaluable work of Lyngbye mentions as favorite not only the satiric ballad, but even the distinctly heroic ballad. Dancing, says Lyngbye,[1] is the islanders' chief amusement. At a given dance, one or more persons begin to sing, then all folk present join in the ballad, or, at the very least, in the refrain. "The purpose of the song is not, like dance-music, simply to order the steps, but at the same time by its meaning and contents to waken certain feelings. One can notice by the demeanor of the dancers that they are not indifferent to the tendency and spirit of the song ;[2] for by their gestures and expressions they take pains, while they dance, to show the various contents of it." Thus, amid conditions which come nearer to the primitive state than any of which we have such accurate knowledge, is found a genuine song of the people, in which dancing is the main fact, singing a necessity, heroic deeds a favorite subject, and spontaneous composition by a part or the whole of the throng a not infrequent factor. We note the present and immediate influence of those doings which the song chances to describe ; no one person is needed to interpret between the fact and the metrical form. In Iceland, to take a different phase of the matter, *rímur*, with metre

---

[1] *Færøiske Quæder*, p. viii. This account is confirmed by later observers. See Maurer in Westermann's *Illustr. Monatsheften*, May, 1863, quoted by Böhme, *Geschichte d. Tanzes*, p. 13 ; and Hammershaimb, *Færøsk Anthologi*, p. xli ff.

[2] "They follow the story with breathless interest," says Hammershaimb ; and he describes the dramatic fervor with which they make real again the ballad of a victorious battle.

like that of our own ballads, have long been used for
the dance, and are often variations of the old sagas.[1]
Something of the same sort, too, is told of dwellers on
the Cimbrian peninsula. Writing in 1652, Giesebrecht
remarks [2] that this folk still loved to dance to songs of
battle and conquest ; while earlier yet, we have the well
known account of Neocorus,[3] much to the same effect.
This chronicler, a priest who writes at the beginning of
the seventeenth century, is full of wonder at the way in
which unschooled peasants answer every poetic demand,
be it grave or merry. One gathers that their favorite
ballads for the dance were of the traditional and heroic
kind. As the Färöe islanders still sang of Sigurd, so the
Cimbrian peasants loved a story of their own victory
in warfare against overwhelming odds. [4] From the
neighboring Frisians, too, we have a ballad, said to be the
only real song of antiquity which the race has preserved ; [5]
and to this solitary song they were wont, two centuries
ago, to tread their only national dance. The dramatic

---

[1] The *rímur* were narrative, the *mansöngr*, to be noted below, were
lyric. From the fourteenth century, these *rímur* were almost the
only poetry known in Iceland, until our own century, — excluding,
of course, clerical religious verse. See Th. Möbius in *Ergänzungsband* of Zacher's *Zeitschrift für deutsche Philologie*, 1874, p. 60.

[2] Quoted by Müllenhoff, *Sagen, u. s. w.*, p. xxii f.

[3] *Chronik*, ed. Dahlmann, I, 176 f ; II, 559 ff.

[4] See also Müllenhoff, *Sagen*, pp. xxv, xxx, xxxv, as well as the
ballads on the battle of Hemmingstede (1500), at p. 59 ff., which
were avowedly used for the national dance. In regard to lighter
ballads of this folk (see Böhme, *Altd. Liederb.*, p. 375 ff.), one may
question the inference of Vogt (Paul's *Grundriss*, II, i, 372) that
the presence of mother, daughter and knight in the "springtanz,"
proves this ballad to be direct copying of Neidhart's well known
peasant-dances, and not a result of the same impulse which found
expression in these dances. The mania for "sources" knows no
limit.

[5] See, for words and music, Böhme, *Altd. Liederb.*, p. 378 f.

action of the dancers was considerable, and the song itself as communal as possible in its character ; dialogue abounds,[1] repetition is constant, variations are progressive, and the events are of the simplest kind. This song was of a cheerful cast ; but such ballads, it may be remarked, were not always of a bright and lively nature. One did not dance simply because one was merry, because one was born under Beatrice's star ; but the slow and stately measure of a tragic ballad could time more solemn steps.[2] The main point, however, is this prevailingly narrative character of the oldest ballads, and their inevitable connection with the dance. Even later narrative ballads, like those of Robin Hood, were more or less used by the dancers. True, because a dance bears the name of a ballad, we cannot conclude that the precise ballad which we now know by that name was always sung as accompaniment of the dance in question ; but when the author of the "Complaynt of Scotland" says that his shepherds danced "Robene hude, thom of lyn,[3] . . . ihonne ermistrangis dance," we see no reason why they

---

[1] On dialogue in the Romance ballads, and its connection with the dance, see Jeanroy, *Origines de la Poésie Lyrique en France*, p. 393.

[2] Dance and song were common at medieval funerals (see Böhme, *Tanz*, p. 10) ; and a pretty little song called the "Dans der Maechdekens," known in Flanders as late as 1840 and sung, on the occasion of a young girl's funeral, by the maidens of her parish, seems to be a distinct survival of the earliest choral dances at a funeral, — those pagan affairs against which the church made war. See Kalff, *Het Lied in de Middeleeuwen*, p. 522 ff. — For the Dance of Death, and all its extravagances, see Böhme, *Tanz*, p. 45 ff.

[3] Not, however, our "Tam Lin." — As to Robin Hood, why should this ballad be shunted off as a "Chanson de Robin," a "merrie and extemporall song"? See Furnivall's *Captain Cox*, quoted in *Complaynt of Scotland*, ed. Murray, p. lxxxviii. Some further references for the connection of ballads and dance are Wolf, *Lais*, 233 ; Steenstrup, *Vore Folkeviser*, 8 f., 23 ff. ; and Schultz, *Das höfische Leben z. Zeit d. Minnesinger*,[2] I, 544 ff.

did not sing ballads of the character indicated by the
titles. England, in those days, had a supreme love of
song ; it had a great reputation as the home of dancing ; [1]
and it had the best of ballads.

For an Elizabethan merry-making one must think of
ballads and their story as ancillary to the dance itself ; [2]
but as one goes further back, events and the ballad
which sings them take a more important place. It was
under escort of song and dance, one may say, that great
national or communal events forced themselves into verse
and found room in popular memory ; such was the case
with that ballad, made in the seventh century to the
honor of St. Faro, and sung by the women " as they
danced and clapped their hands." [3] Unfortunately, one
finds but scant material of this sort ; but in later days,
survivals of the narrative ballad at a dance are plentiful
enough. Such seems to be the *Khorovod,* "blended
dance and song" of the Russians, an immemorial
possession, prominent in all Slavonic poetry of the
people.[4]

The song of satire and mockery has been already
mentioned as favorite for the dance. Historic accounts
of the diversion reach far back into the past, and survivals

[1] Chappell, II, 625 f.

[2] So, too, on an indifferent occasion. "Clap us into *Light o' Love*,"
says Margaret in *Much Ado*, iii, 4 ; "that goes without a burden :
do you sing it, and I'll dance it."

[3] The record is instructive. " Ex qua victoria carmen publicum
juxta rusticitatem per omnium pene volitabat ora ita canentium,
feminaeque choros inde plaudendo componebant." Mabillon, *Acta
Sanctorum ordinis S. Benedicti*, Venetis, 1733, II, 590. So "the
maidens and minstrels of Scotland" (see p. xxxiii, above) danced
and sang those taunting songs about Bannockburn and the English.

[4] Narrative, too, are most of the dance-songs in a modern Russian
cottage, with interesting arrangement of stanza, and the true ballad-
trait of repetition. Ralston, *Songs of the Russian People*, pp. 2 f., 34.

of it linger down to our own day.   Naturally, a lazy race
of aristocrats came to be mere spectators, and watched
some hireling — *jongleur*, minstrel, or what not — harp,
sing and mimic their foe in rude dance and gestures.   In
such case were the Norman revellers whom Hereward
surprised ; [1] but earlier and sounder folk danced to their
own fun, and not by deputy.   Medieval dancers found
good sport of this kind in mocking certain weaknesses of
the clergy ; [2] and in the *schnaderhüpfel*, to which South-
German peasants dance, there is ample satire of the
frankly personal sort.   Occasionally one finds a sort of
erotic satire, easily passing the bounds of decency, in
such guise as the Icelandic *mansöngr*, against which the
bishops had to fight so hard ; men and women in the
dance exchanged satiric stanzas, mostly spontaneous, and
sometimes stretching out to poems.[3]   Among the more
innocent kinds of song which served the same turn

[1] " Joculator psallendo, exprobrans genti Anglorum, et in medio
domus incompositos quasi angligenas fingens saltus."   *Gest. Herew.*,
ed. Michel, *Chron. Angl.-Norm.*, II, 41.

[2] A survival of these adult dances is clearly seen in the Flemish
*Van't Paterken* (Willems, *Oude Vlaemsche Liederen*, No. 125) which
makes mock of monk and nun.   Coussemaker (*Chants Pop. des
Flamands*, p. 328 f.) gives it as a game for children, though evidently
of adult origin ; but this is the right course.   " A children's game,
the last stage of many old ballads " (Child, Ballads, II, 346), shows
us also the last stage of many an old dance.   See Child, I, 354
(Part II), version F of " The Maid Freed from the Gallows."
Müllenhoff asserts that these games give us the best notion to be
had of the old choral hymns in our pagan worship, and collects
some rimes of the sort :   *Sagen*, pp. ix, xxiv, 484 ff.   There is also
good material in Newell, *Games and Songs of American Children*,
New York, 1883, and Jeanroy, *Origines de la Poésie Lyrique en
France*, 1889, p. 394 f.

[3] Möbius in Zacher's *Zeitschrift, Ergänzungsband*, 1874, p. 54.
These duels belong in development to a later stage than the
communal satire against one person, like the Färöe fisherman.

were riddle-ballads,[1] a series of wishes for things quite impossible to attain, monstrous and emulative falsehoods, strife between winter and summer,[2] the dialogue of two lovers, one without and one within the house, and actual hymns.  In short, any doing of man, — *quidquid agunt homines,* — so it went to metre, was welcome for the dance.  Dramatic action was common enough, for the story was made present and belonged to every singer ; and graceful gestures, survival of the older mimicry, were still in vogue for the vanishing Sir Roger de Coverley within memory of living men.  Indeed, a temerarious but catholic taste seems to have led folk to play ball along with their dancing, — as if your modern base-runner should " come home in a coranto " ; and one hears of a gay dame leading some medieval dance, who in the midst of her singing and her winding steps was most regret-tably hit on the head and killed by a bat (*baculus*) which slipped from some man's hand.[3]  The German Neidhart, who has so much to say about peasants' dancing, mentions a gay-colored ball, seemingly as part of the outfit ; while there is distinct tripping of metre, if not of steps, in those dactyls of Walther von der Vogelweide :

[1] See Child, *Ballads*, I, 1 ff.

[2] Uhland, *Volkslieder*, I, 23. — Böhme, *Altdeutsches Liederbuch*, gives a number of the more or less erotic dances.

[3] Probably dancers and ball-players were crowded together.  This " awful example " is from a medieval sermon (often quoted : Schultz, *Das höfische Leben zur Zeit d. Minnesinger*,[2] I, 541, who gives ample material for medieval ball-playing ;  and Uhland, *Schriften*, III, 477, note) against such follies as dancing, and may incidentally explain Edward III's action in forbidding hand-ball, foot-ball, and club-ball to English youth (Strutt, *Sports and Pastimes*, Introduction, section xxxvii).  In the ballads, Sir Hugh seems to have been playing foot-ball, a formidable punter for his tender years ;  the Earl of Murray played at ba' not specified ;  and the four and twenty ladies in " Childe Waters," and in " Tam Lin," were probably tossing and catching.

> *Winter has left us no pleasance at all,*
> *Leafage and heather have fled with the fall,*
> *Bare is the forest and dumb as a thrall:*
> *If the girls by the roadside were tossing the ball,*
> *I could prick up my ears for the singing-birds' call !* [1]

The dancing-song has died out with the good old way of dancing, known now by none but children. Neocorus asserts that before 1559 dancing by pairs or couples was unknown among his happy breed of men; it was the throng, the community, a ring of merry folk going hand in hand, winding and changing, with all voices raised to make the only music. Many considerations already urged, joined with such a statement as that quoted from Böhme in regard to the origin of our oldest narrative folksongs in the dance itself, show how carefully one should regard this singing, dancing, improvising multitude, before one says a last word on the origin of the ballad. To be sure, there is much talk about a leader,[2] one who begins song as well as step; but the more primitive the dance, the less he had to do.[3] Only in later times was conduct of the dance or singing of new verses assigned to one man. Still another advance from primitive ways was the separation of the dance from the song; the former became an affair of couples and instrumental music, the latter, entertainment by a singer with more or

---

[1] Böhme, *Tanz*, p. 4, is inclined to give "ball" equal rights in the facts and etymology of "ballad." He says that "in the dance our oldest epic poems, — narrative folksongs, — were sung, and the dance was the cause of their making; *the dance, and the game of ball that went with it, gave to these poems the name of ballad.*"

[2] "Der des voresingens phlac, Daz was Friderîch," says Neidhart in description of a peasants' dance: *Deutsche Liederdichter,*[3] Bartsch-Golther, xxv, vv. 405 f.

[3] One must carefully distinguish this leader of a communal dance from the artists in dancing, the gleemen, tumblers, jugglers and glee-maidens who are so frequent in pictures in the old MSS.

less in the way of refrain, chorus or burden by the crowd,
until, finally, even this poor communal remnant was lost,
and the ballad turned into a recited story in verse.
The sometime leader is now a minstrel who composes
stanzas, has a latent sense of literary responsibility and
literary property, only to lose his occupation with the
spread of printed books. Reverse the process, and this
leader becomes a hazy impersonality, then vanishes in
the throng. The individual withers as we retrace our
steps in balladry, and the throng, with its refrain, is more
and more.[1]

This refrain is the third and most important element
for the question in hand. According to Ferdinand Wolf,[2]
the refrain is as old as any poetry of the people and
occurs chiefly therein, arising from direct participation
of the folk in songs at worship, feast, dance, game, or
whatever other primitive ceremonies. Classical writers
imitated the popular refrain;[3] and one is sure to find it
wherever one touches the beginnings of vernacular poetry
in Europe. From this purely popular source it passed
not only into poetry of the schools, fairly rioting in such
artificial forms as triolet or ballade, but also into the new
ritual of the church.[4] If, then, as conservative writers

---

[1] Take the process in little. Speaking of St. William of Orange,
the chronicler (*Acta Sanctorum*, May 6, 811) exclaims : " *Qui chori
juvenum, qui conventus populorum* . . . dulce non resonant et
modulatis vocibus decantant, qualis et quantus fuerit . . . ? " Later,
Ordericus Vitalis says of the same hero : " *Vulgo canitur a jocula-
toribus* de illo cantilena." (The quotations are taken from Nyrop,
*Den oldfranske Heltedigtning*, p. 15.) — Is not this the history of
folksong ?

[2] *Lais*, 18 ff. Refrain carried from popular poetry into learned
Latin poetry, pp. 23, 27.

[3] Catullus, lxi, lxii ; or the famous *Pervigilium Veneris*.

[4] Church hymns are now a fine refuge for critics who wish to
explain anything in older vernacular literature. But the early

admit,[1] the so-called narrative lyric, or ballad in stricter sense, was the universal primitive form of poetry of the people, and if, in spite of some faint opposition,[2] our best critics conclude that the refrain was a necessary part of the original ballad,[3] it is clear that a study of the refrain must throw some light on the origins of poetry of the people in general. It is of interest, moreover, to find the refrain best represented in those English and Scottish ballads which spring from pure tradition and are of the most distinctly popular type.[4]

The precise nature of the refrain in any ballad is not always easy to define.[5] Fortunately, in a description of

middle ages took so much into the church from popular and heathen sources, that a subsequent "taking from the church" was often mere recovery of stolen goods.

[1] Steenstrup, *Vore Folkeviser*, p. 53.

[2] Geijer : see Steenstrup, p. 88.

[3] *Ibid.*, pp. 88, 111 : "en folkevise altid har omkvæd." Steenstrup says that out of 502 ballads which he examined, "only about a score" lacked the refrain.

[4] That is, in the first volume of Professor Child's collection, where the two-line stanza and the more popular or traditional ballads occur.

[5] One must distinguish chorus, refrain and burden. Burden is sometimes used in its stricter sense, as defined by Chappell, I, 222 : "The burden of a song, in the old acceptation of the word, was the base, foot, or under-song. It was sung throughout, and not merely at the end of the verse." Thus, in the quotation given above from *Much Ado*, Margaret proposes a song "that goes without a burden" because there was no man on the stage to sing this base or foot ; so that *Light o' Love*, remarks Chappell, was "strictly a ballett, to be sung and danced." Murray's *Dictionary* refers, for this use of the word, to Shakspere's *Lucrece*, 1133 :

> *For burden-wise I'll hum on Tarquin still,*
> *While thou* [*sc.* the nightingale] *on Tereus descant'st better skill.*

But often, again, the burden is confused with the refrain ; see Murray, *Dictionary*, s. v. "Burden," 10 : "the refrain or chorus of a song ; a set of words recurring at the end of each verse." Guest, *English Rhythms*, II, 290, defines "Burthen" as "the return of the

the popular dance in his own day, Neocorus speaks definitely of the parts played by the leader and the throng, so far as the ballad was concerned. The leader of the song, who usually holds a drinking-cup in his hand, and sometimes sings alone, sometimes calls in a colleague, begins the ballad. "And when he has sung a verse, he sings no further, but the whole throng, who either know the ballad, or else have paid close attention to him, repeat and echo the same verse. And when they have brought it to the point where the leader stopped, he begins again, and sings another verse." This is again repeated. Presently, with the singing thus under way, a leader of the dance comes forward, hat in

same words at the close of each stave." The refrain is the repetition of a certain passage at regular intervals, and is thus of service in marking off a stanza : see, for oldest English, *Déor's Song*, or for later rimeless and unsung verse, Tennyson's *Tears, Idle Tears*, or Lamb's *Old Familiar Faces*. In ballads, however, the refrain is undoubtedly the recurring verse or verses sung by the throng in contradistinction to the main body of the ballad, which for later times, was the business of the leader or minstrel. It is no easy matter to adjust the relations of the burden and the refrain. The latter may have been originally more like the burden in its strict meaning, and would thus imply constant, not intermittent, singing of the throng : see Jeanroy, *Poésie Lyrique en France*, p. 104, for a hint in this direction, and Professor Child's note, *Ballads*, I, 7. The question is very complicated : see Valentin, *Studien über die schwedischen Volksmelodien*, p. 9 f. It is, for example, a temptation to infer from the greater proportion of refrains preserved with two-line stanzas, that the four-line stanza was developed out of this two-line stanza with double refrain ; but many facts lie in the way of such an assumption. Rosenberg's plea for the theory is rejected by Steenstrup, *V. F.*, p. 120. It will be best, therefore, for present purposes, to use "refrain" simply as the recurrent passage or passages which seem to have been sung by the crowd, and to leave unsettled the actual manner of singing. The chorus was a whole stanza sung after each new stanza of the ballad, — as in *The Twa Magicians*, Child, *Ballads*, I, 403.

hand, dances about the room, and invites the whole
assembly to join.[1]  Evidently, this is a very elaborate
affair, and for more primitive relations we may certainly
suppose the entire crowd singing to their own steps.[2]
Again, as in Icelandic ballads,[3] we may think of the
leader singing an initial stanza, which the crowd con-
tinue to sing as burden or accompaniment to the new
verses of the leader ; a long burden, overlapping the
stanza, would be partly heard as a refrain.

However all this may have been, the refrain was sung
by the throng, and means more and more as we approach
primitive relations.  In later ballads the refrain bears a
lyrical character, and seems to express the tone or motive
of the whole piece, or even forms a part of the story.[4]
Often it merely states the time of year, reminding one
distantly of the beautiful stanzas which open such a
ballad as "Robin Hood and the Monk"; or else a
double refrain could combine the season of the year with
the mood and feeling of the narrative.  There is also a
merely interjectional refrain, not found in Danish ballads,
but common in German, the *Ha!* or *Eja!* which was
once, in all probability, an outcry of some sort at the
dance.[5]  It is instructive to note more developed forms
of this outcry, — what a French writer has called the
*refrains par onomatopées*, — as well as the half-intelligible,
half-interjectional "refrain without a song."

Whatever the nature of the refrain, it was sung by the
crowd.  Talvj admits this ;[6] but at the same time wrongly

[1] Neocorus, *Chronik*, ed. Dahlmann, I, 177.

[2] Böhme, *Tanz*, p. 229.

[3] See *The Elfin Knight*, and Professor Child's note, *Ballads*, I, 7.

[4] Steenstrup, as quoted above.  Lundell, in Paul's *Grundriss*,
II, i, 728.

[5] Steenstrup, p. 78 ;  Uhland, *Schr.*, III, 392 f.;  Tiersot, *Chanson
Populaire*, p. 124 f.

[6] *Characteristik*, p. 335 f.

attributes the origin of the refrain to an arbitrary and often spontaneous invention of the minstrel. In a practical way, the refrain undoubtedly served to give the leader breathing-space, literal and figurative ; the crowd took up the song, while he either recalled or improvised another stanza.[1] But this accidental advantage is no ultimate reason for the refrain, and dwindles before the significance of the fact that refrains increase in importance as one approaches the beginnings of vernacular poetry, receding, so to speak, from the leader or the minstrel, slipping from his control, and at last dominating the ballad itself. Setting aside the vanity of dogmatizing, one feels inclined to assert that the original ballad must have been sung by all, as it was danced by all ; the division of labor implied in the leader's song and the crowd's refrain surely indicates a later adjustment.

Dr. Meyer[2] attacks the question of origins by a study of the unintelligible refrain. This, he says, was simply the inarticulate cry of primitive man, the sudden sense of fear, delight, wonder, grief, or love, expressed in a melodious sound or series of sounds, — the earliest form of poetry. This sound or series of sounds is preserved by the piety of a later age in its original and now meaningless form, imbedded among the articulate words of a developed song. Take, for example, the threnody. In earliest verse of the sort, says Meyer,[3] one may fancy "a monotonous repetition of emotional sounds." Indeed, we

[1] R. M. Meyer, *Zeitschrift f. vergleichende Literatur*, I, 35, suggests that early poetry may well have had but slight sense of proportion and succession, just as early painting knew no perspective ; and thus the refrain served to keep the general theme in mind and to preserve harmony of arrangement.

[2] In the article just quoted, *Ueber den Refrain, Ztst. f. vgl. Lit.*, I, 34-47.

[3] *Ibid.*, p. 38.

may add that this impulse, in the guise of iteration, plays a leading part in modern poetry of grief, where, too, a measured and harmonious march of verse often testifies to an older stateliness of choral lamentation. The development of a funeral refrain out of these inarticulate sounds of woe is not a hard matter. Emotional utterances, cries of grief, of rage or delight,[1] meaningless at first, soon take on a meaning and form the basis of choral hymns which afterwards began and ended with these cries. In a way, they are the primitive text of the hymn ; later they are the refrain of it ; in any case, they are absolutely communal in origin.[2]

With regard to the meaning of the refrain, and speaking for English and Scottish ballads, we may note a considerable range. Often it is inarticulate, often a series of meaningless words. In "The Fair Flower of Northumberland,"[3] however, the refrain runs very well with a story of escape and elopement across the border :

> *Follow, my love, come over the strand.*

Probably, too, we import no alien sentiment when we note the touch of pathos and comment in the refrain of a traditional version of "Leesome Brand" :[4]

[1] Peace to the *barditus* (Tacitus, *Germania*, c. 3), and German commentators : that way madness lies. Nor need sailors' chanteys be invoked : see Laura Alexandrine Smith, *Music of the Waters*, London, 1888 ; and John Ashton, *Real Sailor Songs*, London, 1891, a sumptuous folio.

[2] These considerations move Meyer to assume four stages of poetry : Primitive, Natural, The People, The Schools. — Scott's "Eleu Loro" in *Marmion* is an example of the inarticulate refrain revived.

[3] Child, *Ballads*, I, 113 f. This is Version A. In B there is no doubt about the corresponding refrain :

> *A may's love whiles is easy won.*

[4] *Ibid.*, I, 184.

> *There is a feast in your father's house,*
> (*The broom blooms bonnie, and so it is fair*)
> *It becomes you and me to be very douce,*
> (*And we'll never gang up to the broom nae mair*).[1]

However, putting the dreams aside,[2] the memories and hauntings provoked by this stretched metre of an antique

---

[1] Of most of these refrains Motherwell remarks that they have meanings lost to our ears, but significant enough to men of older time. Steenstrup says that the refrain "always strikes the 'note' or mood of the ballad." Of merely interjectional or inarticulate refrains we have many cases; for example, the " O " (or " A " : see Webbe, *Discourse of Engl. Poetrie*, ed. Arber, p. 36, with the allusion to "Robyn hoode") at the end of a line : see Nos. 58, B ; 65, E ; 100, F, and others, in Child's *Ballads*. Such, too, are the "Fal, lal" (No. 164) and the frequent "Hay doune" (81, A) with its variations. Combinations of the inarticulate with the articulate refrain meet us in "Earl Brand":

> *Ay lilly o lilly lally*
> *All i the night sae early,* —

and in "Babylon," where a meaning is evident ; while no meaning attaches to refrains like (1) : .

> *Jennifer gentle and rosemaree*
> *As the dew flies over the mulberry tree.*

Refrain of the season is common (4, and see 10, T) :

> *Aye as the gowans grow gay*
> *The first morning in May.*

A refrain, or genuine burden, longer than the stanza of the ballad, is found in "The Elfin Knight," (2, A) : compare "The Twa Sisters," and "The Three Ravens." The iteration of ballads, which may stand in no distant relation to the refrain, is almost identical with the latter in "Lord Randal," or with shorter form, in "Edward." In version J of "Lord Randal" (Child, I, 163 f.) each verse is repeated, in the form *a a b b* for the stanza ; see F in "Lamkin" (Part IV, p. 328). In four-line stanzas the fourth line is often repeated (*a b c b b*): see 33, B, G ; 52, A ; 70, B ; 75, H, and many others. The third and fourth lines may both be repeated: see 58, D ; 87, B ; and so with the first and second: see 97, B. In *a b c b b*, the repeated line is usually shorter by a measure than the fourth. Scott has imitated this refrain in his song in *Rokeby*, — "A weary lot is thine, fair maid."

[2] " La poésie," says Sainte-Beuve in a sentence that applies as well

song, we are at least justified in claiming the refrain, whether for its origin or for its functions in the ballad, as a distinctly communal matter. It is almost the only rudiment of primitive choral poetry[1] surviving to our day ; and it has come down to us as companion of the ballad and the dance. As the throng must find larger and larger sway in times more and more primitive, so, as we approach those times, the refrain loses its air of service and speaks with more masterful accent, the central fact of the ballad.

Song, dance, and refrain have led us towards the primitive throng and away from the modern artist. There is, however, another element which seems to make for communal origins, — the element of spontaneity and rapid improvisation by members of a throng. Early verse was of a momentary and occasional character. Plan and design come with the artist ; planless, spontaneous poetry, offspring of the instant and of the need for expression, is likely to be the product of a throng. The tracks of thought are sure to diverge ; but the impression of a moment may have one form in many minds, and find vent in one and the same outcry.

To review the facts, one finds improvisation dominant in all poetry of the people. In certain parts of Scandinavia it is still usual for nearly every one of the community to sing at call a quatrain of his own making, or at least a variation of some traditional stanza. These

to ballads as to such a verse as Coleridge's "Upon his shield a burning brand," — " la poésie ne consiste pas à tout dire, mais à tout faire rêver."

[1] Lack of space forbids the evident references to religious ceremonies and primitive worship generally. We know that the refrain rang out as Germanic warriors marched to fight : " Sang uuas gisungan, Uuîg uuas bigunnan," says the *Ludwigslied*, Müllenhoff-Scherer, *Denkmäler*, No. xi, v. 48 f. See also Müllenhoff, *de antiq. German. poesi chorica*, Kiel, 1847.

*stev* are described by Landstad [1] as of two kinds, with improvisation for the common and most prominent feature, and communal drinking and dancing as the proper conditions ; although, he remarks, in modern times one is more likely to remember and vary than to compose outright. The variety of *stev* now most popular is the rapid dialogue, in which the singers propose a set of alternate riddles, or express their feelings about something, or else — by preference — gibe and taunt each other. But this duel in song, this attempt to overwhelm one's opponent by sheer profusion of verses, or by extravagant bragging, is in Landstad's opinion only a degeneration of the *stev*. The older and normal *stev* were in close relation with heroic ballads, were less lyric in character, and sang of deeds rather than of personal emotions. Improvisation, however, was a constant factor ; and to this day in Iceland "there is hardly an adult man who cannot in some fashion put verses together." [2] From Norway to Italy, verse-combats and like improvisations were once universal and are still far from uncommon.[3] Especially interesting is the German *schnaderhüpfel*,[4] a short song, usually of four lines, to a simple air, and mainly a pure improvisation ; it seems often to have been composed in the dances of harvest. Schmeller, who lays stress upon the spontaneous element in its making, brings it into parallel with the *stev* of Norway and the *coplas* of Spain ; unquestionably we are dealing with a custom once common among all the peasants of Europe, and, however

[1] *Norske Folkeviser*, p. 365 ff.

[2] Lundell, in Paul's *Grundriss*, II, i, 730.

[3] Gustav Meyer, *Essays und Studien*, p. 366 f., in the essay on the *Schnaderhüpfel*.

[4] See Schmeller, *Bayerisches Wörterbuch*, 1836, III, 499 ; and G. Meyer, in the essay just quoted, p. 332 ff., where he discusses the literature of the subject.

we may be inclined to regard its later forms, with an
evident survival of what we are fain to call communal
poetry.  Significant is the gathering of harvesters,— once
perhaps a whole tribe, or at least, a community, in united
religious rites ;  significant are the dance and its improvised song.  Even the scurrilous quatrain points the
same way ;  it is the spontaneous conversion of a situation
into a ballad ;  and how well this ancient "chaff" could
rival the very wheat of our modern and labored revilings
— Robert Browning on Fitzgerald, for instance, or Mr.
Swinburne in his severely humorous moments — is matter
of record.  Plenty of evidence is forthcoming to prove
how far a peasant even now surpasses, in this power of
spontaneous verse-making, the man of culture and of
learning.[1]  As regards the main question, moreover, it
is well to note that a recent critic combats the derivation of isolated quatrains from some longer poem,[2]
and maintains that such forms as the *schnaderhüpfel*
are in themselves the original, here and there form-
ing a ballad by the slow accretion of many separate
songs.[3]

There is, then, no doubt in regard to the frequency of
improvisation down to this day, not of the ballad, to be
sure, but of what in better times would have gone to the
making of the ballad.  Even some modern ballads seem
to have this spontaneous if not communal origin.  In
the preface written for a translation of contemporary

---

[1] G. Meyer, p. 352, speaks of Weimar peasants who sit in company
and make couplet after couplet, mostly merry, and often coarse.

[2] *Ibid.*, p. 375 f.  Landstad, in his treatment of the *stev*, leaned to
this theory of fragments.

[3] It is interesting to note in the rimes used for children's games a
tendency to the quatrain, with added refrain or chorus, and also with
the assonance and other peculiarities of an old ballad.  See Newell,
*Games and Songs of American Children*, p. 10 f.

Roumanian ballads,[1] Carmen Sylva says that most of them are improvisations, "sung to a monotonous chant," and "usually begin and end with a refrain." This improvisation is not confined to a few singers ;[2] at the dance, or in the spinning-room, a person who would escape his turn to make a stanza, must follow the example set by Cædmon. Cædmon,[3] of course, reminds us of improvisation in our old literature ; and for another proof of the ease with which Englishmen of that day dropped into poetry, one may take threats of the church against any priest who, — welcome, of course, to make a pious chanson as often as he pleased, — should in an unguarded moment "turn gleeman or ale-bard."[4] But we need go no farther afield in search of evidence about this spontaneous character of early poetry ; the difficulty besets us not here, but in the actual process of primitive "making."

[1] *The Bard of the Dimbovitzka*, London, 1892.

[2] Ralston quotes good authority to the same effect for the powers of improvisation shown by peasants, — particularly women, — in Russia. *Songs of Russian People*, pp. 40 f., 54.

[3] Bede, *Hist Eccl.*, iv, 24 (22).

[4] Schmid, *Gesetze d. Angelsachsen*,[2] p. 366 : *gif préost oferdruncen lufige, oððe gliman oððe eala-scop wurðe.* — There are ample hints of improvisation in our older literature. In *Béowulf*, the "king's thane" not only sings a traditional ballad of Sigmund, but seems to improvise a lay about the deed which has just been done (*Béow.*, v. 867 ff.) ; and perhaps the same is true of the warriors who ride about the hero's tomb, and chant his praises. King Cnut has at least the reputation of an early water-poet ; and Hereward plays his harp and sings his own ballad *cunctis admirantibus* (*De Gestis Herewardi* in Michel, *Chron. Norm.*, II, 19). King Horn (*K. H.*, ed. Wissmann, 1485 ff.), in a well known passage, takes his harp, and sings to Rymenhild a lay of his own making.

## IX.

Early poetry was undoubtedly choral, and mainly in the service of communal religious ceremonies ;[1] leader or *vorsinger* becomes more important as the arts are developed and the individual makes himself felt, very much as in the growth of Greek tragedy the chorus retired in favor of the actor.[2] In one way, we must leave, even amid the most primitive relations, ample verge and room enough for an incipient artist in verse. The lover made a love-song ; but it was for singular and practical purposes. It is true that erotic songs were often choral, with epic and dramatic leanings ; as making of the individual, however, they were like the modern Finnish or Italian love-lays about which collectors tell us, and were meant by the lover for his beloved alone.[3] Private sentiment had no public interest. To publish for money one's affairs of the heart would have struck primitive man, as it strikes the modern peasant girl, as absurd in the extreme ; while the making of love-lays to nobody in particular would have baffled primitive logic.[4]

---

[1] See Paul in his *Grundriss*, I, 225 ; Kögel, *ibid.*, II, i, 166 ; Kluge in the *Englische Studien*, VIII, 481.

[2] Such we take to be Müllenhoff's general meaning when (*Lieder u. s. w.*, p. ix) he says that at the tribal wandering (*Völkerwanderung*) song, which had formerly been sung only by a chorus or crowd, now became "free," and was at the discretion of individual singers.

[3] Even J. Grimm seems to have granted lyric equal date with epos : *Kl. Schr.*, II, 75 ; Müllenhoff–Scherer, *Denkmäler*,[3] II, 154 ; Burdach in Haupt's *Zeitschrift*, XXVII, 347 f. ; Talvj, *Charakteristik*, p. 5 f. Of course, as a matter of literature, epic has precedence of record.

[4] A middle-aged gentleman who pays bills and taxes, disciplines his children, and has the minister to dinner, yet frequently, in the magazines, or in a volume of verses, raves, dies, or is ready to embark upon a career of crime, for the sake of a supposititious young woman, challenges even the modern sense of humor.

It is probably safe to say that public poetry of those times was made in public, and by the public.[1]

Here is the obnoxious phrase once more, but this time it must be squarely met and squarely explained. It was this phrase, or something very like it, which ten Brink undertook to justify, directly in his fragment, and indirectly in his book on the Béowulf.[2] First of all, he bids the critic part company with our modern notion of authorship. Solitary composition would have been as hard for primitive man to understand as communal authorship is hard for us. Poetry was a common possession; there was no production, to quote ten Brink's admirable phrase, but reproduction. There were variations, additions, — spontaneous and free; but no composition, no originality, as we mean the term. In a sense, too, their song had neither beginning nor end; it was taken up and put down, but never definitely bounded; as they knew neither writer nor writing, so they knew nothing of the literary unit, the poem in and for itself. All was in flux; out of a common store of tradition, by a spontaneous and universal movement, song rose and fell according to the needs of the community.[3]

Now when Grimm bids one think of a race composing songs, one keeps in mind the modern way of composition and therefore calls the phrase nebulous or silly. From

---

[1] Lyric in epic, emotion called forth by facts, is Gaston Paris's idea of primitive poetry; see *Romania*, XIII, 617. *Ibid.*, p. 618, he defends the analogy between these lyric-epic songs and English ballads of the border; hence, one infers, he regards the latter as a sort of survival of earliest narrative song.

[2] Paul's *Grundriss*, II, i, 512 ff.; ten Brink, *Beowulf, Quellen u. Forschungen*, LXII.

[3] Schlegel's famous image of the tower as poetry and an architect as the poet, proves nothing and really begs the question. A cairn is easily raised by a crowd; plan and making go together, and are absolutely communal. But this sort of argument is useless.

such a point of view it is nebulous; but while one is inclined under any circumstances to reject it in its bare and dogmatic form, there is a measure of truth in it if one renounces all notion of modern authorship. "Let one fancy," says ten Brink, "an epoch where the same culture, the same sentiment, the same expressions, are property of a whole community . . . an epoch where a poem comes to the ears of the listener in the very moment which gives it form, and, treasured in memory, does not live again until it is again delivered by the voice. *Fancy a poetry oscillating perpetually between reminiscence and improvisation.*" [1] If this is true of an age dominated largely by the minstrel, what shall be said for prehistoric times? The singer is agent at once of preservation and of destruction, for he rescues specimens of a type which his incipient artistry is bound to destroy. Hence the absurdity of trying to discover in any published ballad the absolutely impersonal quality of poetry of the people. Successive triumphs of culture involved a series of steps by which the artist came into prominence and was made welcome by a public; as his note grows more insistent, less and less importance attaches to the communal elements of poetry, — singing, dancing, refrain and improvisation. [2] Reverse this course of development; singing and dancing become obligatory, the scope of the refrain widens more and more, improvisation, varying

---

[1] *Beowulf*, p. 105 f. See also pp. 3, 27, 29, 43, 189, 191, 243. Compared with ten Brink's solidity of argument, Scherer's air of profound hinting and the medley of Darwin, Australians, newspapers, and theatre, — brought forth in his *Poetik* to prove primitive authorship nothing else than our own authorship, — seem almost flippant.

[2] Wídsíð, "the Far-wanderer," a blurred, uncertain, dateless figure, without stay in any time or land, a mere preserver of communal makings, may go for the old type of singer; breezy, confidential Déor, first singer of English lyric, may head the modern list. The two stand like sentries at the gates of English song.

with memory, is a necessity; and we have thus, by steps legitimate in every way, taken our narrative ballad back to a communal origin, and removed it from the conditions of individual authorship. Modern critics would teach us that the ballad, made as any other poem is made, gets its impersonal and differencing quality by oral transmission alone; a glance at the relations which melody, dance, refrain and improvisation bear to the later narrative ballad shows us that its earliest form could never have been that of a poem such as individual authors compose, and it is these four elements, moreover, dwindled and uncertain as they are, which give us our best notion of primitive poetry in its habit as it lived.[1]

The ballad, then, is a survival from this vanished world of poetry. The particular ballads of the present collection cannot be referred directly to communal authorship; but their differencing qualities, the impersonality, the hint of something which we cannot define but as little can deny, are due to this older connection, and are not to be explained by mere oral transmission.[2] Sincere,

---

[1] The relations of ballad and epos, intricate enough in detail, offer no difficulties from this point of view. Germ or aftergrowth of the epos, the ballad has its independent place as a poetical fact. If, however, the reader cherishes a Shandean love of comparisons, let him make what he can of this (from Ferdinand Wolf, in *Wiener Jahrbücher*, CXVII, 87): "The pure and original epos is the evening-dream after sunset, sinking peacefully into vague memories of the past; the lyric-epic ballad (*volkslied*) is the shadow of the forward-hastening star of day." Wolf was one of the first to protest against "nebulous" definitions.

[2] Nigra compares the changes of a ballad with the changes of a dialect; new words or phrases do not destroy the general character of a dialect, and modern phrases or turns of thought make nothing against the traditional ballad. Yet another parallel between the making of ballads and the making of language may be drawn from the reference of Schleicher (*Compendium*,[4] p. 641, note) to that hesitation felt by all Aryan languages to put forth stems for the

strong, rough, these "canticles of love and woe" still speak the speech of a mass, still feel as a community feels, and touch the heart not as a whisper of private sympathy, but as a great cry of delight or grief from the crowd. They are alien to our introspective age. How few of them, too, have come down to us, and how broken and baffled is the story which they tell! Whatever the critical view of its origin, all lovers of the ballad will join in the quaint laments of Neocorus [1] for the vanished lays of old, and mourn the *quae supersunt* which must be written upon even the richest of our collections.

first and second persons of the pronoun, "as indeed in many tongues there is evident shyness to name the *I* and the *thou.*"

[1] "Help Gott, wo manige leffliche schone Gesenge an Wort uund Wisen, ach wo vele, sonderlich der olden Leder, . . . sin undergangen!" *Chronik*, ed. Dahlmann, I, 176.

Characteristics of Robin Hood

yeoman
proud
courteous
pious
chivalrous to woman
kind to the poor
companionable
hostile to landed clergy
"   " representatives of the law
devoted to person of king
bold + skilled in combat
roughly humorous

# BALLADS.

—◆—

## A GEST OF ROBYN HODE.

1.  Lythe and listin, gentilmen,
      That be of frebore blode;
    I shall you tel of a gode yeman,
      His name was Robyn Hode.

2.  Robyn was a prude outlaw,
      Whyles he walked on grounde;
    So curteyse an outlaw as he was one
      Was never non yfounde.

3.  Robyn stode in Bernesdale,
      And lenyd hym to a tre;
    And bi him stode Litell Johnn,
      A gode yeman was he.

4.  And alsoo dyd gode Scarlok,
      And Much, the miller's son;
    There was none ynch of his bodi
      But it was worth a grome.

5.  Than bespake Lytell Johnn
      All untoo Robyn Hode:
    Maister, and ye wolde dyne betyme
      It wolde doo you moche gode.

6.   Than bespake hym gode Robyn :
     To dyne have I noo lust,
  Till that I have som bolde baron,
     Or som unkouth gest.

7.   .    .    .    .    .    .
     That may pay for the best,
  Or some knyght or som squyer
     That dwelleth here bi west.

8.   A gode maner than had Robyn ;
     In londe where that he were,
  Every day or he wold dyne
     Thre messis wolde he here.

9.   The one in the worship of the Fader,
     And another of the Holy Gost,
  The thirde was of Our dere Lady
     That he loved allther moste.

10.   Robyn loved Oure dere Lady ;
     For dout of dydly synne,
  Wolde he never do compani harme
     That any woman was in.

11.   ' Maistar,' than sayde Lytil Johnn,
     ' And we our borde shal sprede,
  Tell us wheder that we shall go
     And what life that we shall lede.

12.   ' Where we shall take, where we shall leve,
     Where we shall abide behynde ;
  Where we shall robbe, where we shall reve,
     Where we shall bete and bynde.'

13. 'Thereof no force,' than sayde Robyn ;
    'We shall do well inowe ;
But loke ye do no husbonde harme
    That tilleth with his ploughe.

14. 'No more ye shall no gode yeman
    That walketh by grene-wode shawe ;
Ne no knyght ne no squyer
    That wol be a gode felawe.

15. 'These bisshoppes and these archebishoppes,
    Ye shall them bete and bynde ;
The hye sherif of Notyngham,
    Hym holde ye in your mynde.'

16. 'This worde shalbe holde,' sayde Lytell Johnn,
    'And this lesson we shall lere ;
It is fer dayes ; God sende us a gest,
    That we were at our dynere.'

17. 'Take thy gode bowe in thy honde,' sayde Robyn ;
    'Late Much wende with the ;
And so shal Willyam Scarlok,
    And no man abyde with me.

18. 'And walke up to the Saylis
    And so to Watlinge Strete,
And wayte after some unkuth gest,
    Up chaunce ye may them mete.

19. 'Be he erle, or ani baron,
    Abbot, or ani knyght,
Bringhe hym to lodge to me ;
    His dyner shall be dight.'

20. They wente up to the Saylis,
    These yemen all three ;
    They loked est, they loked weest,
    They myght no man see.

21. But as they loked in to Bernysdale,
    Bi a dernë strete,
    Than came a knyght ridinghe ;
    Full sone they gan hym mete.

22. All dreri was his semblaunce,
    And lytell was his pryde ;
    His one fote in the styrop stode,
    That othere wavyd beside.

23. His hode hanged in his iyn two ;
    He rode in symple aray ;
    A soriar man than he was one
    Rode never in somer day.

24. Litell Johnn was full curteyes,
    And sette hym on his kne :
    'Welcom be ye, gentyll knyght,
    Welcom ar ye to me.

25. 'Welcom be thou to grenë wode,
    Hendë knyght and fre ;
    My maister hath abiden you fastinge,
    Syr, al these oures thre.'

26. 'Who is thy maister?' sayde the knyght ;
    Johnn sayde, 'Robyn Hode';
    'He is a gode yoman,' sayde the knyght,
    'Of hym I have herde moche gode.

27.   'I graunte,' he sayde, ' with you to wende,
          My bretherne, all in fere ;
      My purpos was to have dyned to day
          At Blith or Dancastere.'

28.   Furth than went this gentyl knight,
          With a carefull chere ;
      The teris oute of his iyen ran,
          And fell downe by his lere.

29.   They brought him to the lodgë-dore ;
          Whan Robyn gan hym see,
      Full curtesly dyd of his hode
          And sette hym on his knee.

30.   'Welcome, sir knight,' than sayde Robyn,
          ' Welcome art thou to me ;
      I have abyden you fastinge, sir,
          All these ouris thre.'

31.   Than answered the gentyll knight,
          With wordes fayre and fre :
      'God the save, goode Robyn,
          And all thy fayre meynë.'

32.   They wasshed togeder and wyped bothe,
          And sette to theyr dynere ;
      Brede and wyne they had right ynoughe,
          And noumbles of the dere.

33.   Swannes and fessauntes they had full gode,
          And foules of the ryvere ;
      There fayled none so litell a birde
          That ever was bred on bryre.

34.  'Do gladly, sir knight,' sayde Robyn;
        'Gramarcy, sir,' sayde he;
     'Suche a dinere had I nat
        Of all these wekys thre.

35.  'If I come ageyne, Robyn,
        Here by thys contrë,
     As gode a dyner I shall the make
        As thou haest made to me.'

36.  'Gramarcy, knyght,' sayde Robyn;
        'My dyner whan I have,
     I was never so gredy, by dere worthi God,
        My dyner for to crave.

37.  'But pay or ye wende,' sayde Robyn;
        'Me thynketh it is gode ryght;
     It was never the maner, by dere worthi God,
        A yoman to pay for a knyght.'

38.  'I have nought in my coffers,' saide the knyght,
        'That I may profer for shame':
     'Litell John, go loke,' sayde Robyn,
        'Ne lat not for no blame.

39.  'Tel me truth,' than saide Robyn,
        'So God have parte of the':
     'I have no more but ten shelynges,' sayde the
           knyght,
        'So God have parte of me.'

40.  'If thou have no more,' sayde Robyn,
        'I woll nat one peny;
     And yf thou have nede of any more,
        More shall I lend the.

41.    'Go nowe furth, Litell Johnn,
           The truth tell thou me ;
        If there be no more but ten shelinges,
           No peny that I se.'


42.    Lyttell Johnn sprede downe hys mantell
           Full fayre upon the grounde,
        And there he fonde in the knyghtes cofer
           But even halfe a pounde.


43.    Littell Johnn let it lye full styll,
           And went to hys maysteer full lowe ;
        'What tydynges, Johnn ?' sayde Robyn ;
           'Sir, the knyght is true inowe.'


44.    'Fyll of the best wine,' sayde Robyn,
           'The knyght shall begynne ;
        Moche wonder thinketh me
           Thy clothynge is so thinne.


45.    'Tell me one worde,' sayde Robyn,
           'And counsel shal it be ;
        I trowe thou wert made a knyght of force,
           Or ellys of yemanry.


46.    'Or ellys thou hast been a sori husbande,
           And lyved in stroke and strife ;
        An okerer, or ellis a lechoure,' sayde Robyn,
           'Wyth wronge hast led thy lyfe.'


47.    'I am none of those,' sayde the knyght,
           'By God that madë me ;
        An hundred wynter here before
           Myn auncetres knyghtes have be.

48.   'But oft it hath befal, Robyn,
          A man hath be disgrate;
      But God that sitteth in heven above
          May amende his state.

49.   'Withyn this two yere, Robyne,' he sayde,
          'My neghbours well it knowe,
      Foure hundred pounde of gode money
          Ful well than myght I spende.

50.   'Nowe have I no gode,' saide the knyght,
          'God hath shapen such an ende,
      But my chyldren and my wyfe,
          Tyll God yt may amende.'

51.   'In what maner,' than sayde Robyn,
          'Hast thou lorne thy rychesse?'
      'For my greate foly,' he sayde,
          'And for my kyndenesse.

52.   'I hade a sone, forsoth, Robyn,
          That shulde have ben myn ayre,
      Whanne he was twenty wynter olde,
          In felde wolde just full fayre.

53.   'He slewe a knyght of Lancashire,
          And a squyer bolde;
      For to save him in his ryght
          My godes beth sette and solde.

54.   'My londes beth sette to wedde, Robyn,
          Untyll a certayn day,
      To a ryche abbot here besyde
          Of Seynt Mari Abbey.'

55. 'What is the som?' sayde Robyn;
    'Trouth than tell thou me';
'Sir,' he sayde, 'foure hundred pounde;
    The abbot told it to me.'

56. 'Nowe and thou lese thy lond,' sayde Robyn,
    'What shall fall of the?'
'Hastely I wol me buske [sayd the knyght]
    Over the saltë see,

57. 'And se where Criste was quyke and dede,
    On the mount of Calverë;
Fare wel, frende, and have gode day;
    It may not better be.'

58. Teris fell out of hys eyen two;
    He wolde have gone hys way;
'Farewel, frendes, and have gode day,
    I have no more to pay.'

59. 'Where be thy frendes?' sayde Robyn:
    'Syr, never one wol me knowe;
While I was ryche ynowe at home
    Great boste than wolde they blowe.

60. 'And nowe they renne away fro me,
    As bestis on a rowe;
They take no more hede of me
    Thanne they me never sawe.'

61. For ruthe thanne wept Litell Johnn,
    Scarlok and Much in fere;
'Fyl of the best wyne,' sayde Robyn,
    'For here is a symple chere.

62.    'Hast thou any frends,' sayde Robyn,
            'Thy borowes that wyll be?'
       'I have none,' than sayde the knyght,
            'But God that dyed on tree.'


63.    'Do away thy japis,' sayde Robyn,
            'Thereof wol I right none;
       Wenest thou I wolde have God to borowe,
            Peter, Poule, or Johnn?


64.    'Nay, by hym that made me,
            And shope both sonne and mone,
       Fynde me a better borowe,' sayde Robyn,
            'Or money getest thou none.'


65.    'I have none other,' sayde the knyght,
            'The sothe for to say,
       But yf yt be Our dere Lady;
            She fayled me never or thys day.'


66.    'By dere worthy God,' sayde Robyn,
            'To seche all Englonde thorowe,
       Yet fonde I never to my pay
            A moche better borowe.


67.    'Come nowe furth, Litell Johnn,
            And go to my tresourë,
       And bringe me foure hundered pound,
            And loke well tolde it be.'


68.    Furth than went Litell Johnn,
            And Scarlok went before;
       He tolde oute four hundred pounde
            By eight and twenty score.

69.  'Is thys well tolde?' sayde litell Much;
        Johnn sayde: 'What greveth the?
     It is almus to helpe a gentyll knyght
        That is fal in povertë.

70.  'Master,' than sayde Lityll John,
        'His clothinge is full thynne;
     Ye must gyve the knight a lyveray,
        To lappe his body therein.

71.  'For ye have scarlet and grene, mayster,
        And many a riche aray;
     Ther is no marchaunt in mery Englond
        So ryche, I dare well say.'

72.  'Take hym thre yerdes of every colour,
        And loke well mete that it be';
     Lytell Johnn toke none other mesure
        But his bowë-tree.

73.  And at every handfull that he met
        He lept over fotes three;
     'What devylles drapar,' sayd litell Much,
        'Thynkest thou for to be?'

74.  Scarlok stode full stil and loughe,
        And sayd, 'By God Almyght,
     Johnn may gyve hym gode mesure,
        For it costeth hym but lyght.'

75.  'Mayster,' than said Litell Johnn
        All unto Robyn Hode,
     'Ye must give the knight a hors
        To lede home al this gode.'

76.  'Take him a gray coursar,' sayde Robyn,
        'And a saydle newe;
     He is Oure Ladye's messangere;
        God graunt that he be true.'


77.  'And a gode palfray,' sayde lytell Much,
        'To mayntene hym in his right';
     'And a peyre of botes,' sayde Scarlok,
        'For he is a gentyll knight.'


78.  'What shalt thou gyve hym, Litell John?' [said
            Robyn;]
        'Sir, a peyre of gilt sporis clene,
     To pray for all this company;
        God bringe hym oute of tene.'


79.  'Whan shal mi day be,' said the knight,
        'Sir, and your wyll be?'
     'This day twelve moneth,' saide Robyn,
        'Under this grene-wode tre.


80.  'It were greate shame,' sayde Robyn,
        'A knight alone to ryde,
     Withoutë squyre, yoman, or page,
        To walkë by his syde.


81.  'I shal the lende Litell Johnn, my man,
        For he shalbe thy knave;
     In a yeman's stede he may the stande,
        If thou greate nedë have.

## THE SECONDE FYTTE.

82.  Now is the knight gone on his way;
        This game hym thought full gode;
      Whanne he loked on Bernesdale
        He blessyd Robyn Hode.

83.  And whanne he thought on Bernysdale,
        On Scarlok, Much and Johnn,
      He blessyd them for the best company
        That ever he in come.

84.  Then spake that gentyll knyght,
        To Lytel Johan gan he saye,
      'To-morrowe I must to Yorke toune
        To Saynt Mary abbay.

85.  'And to the abbot of that place
        Foure hundred pounde I must pay;
      And but I be there upon this nyght
        My londe is lost for ay.'

86.  The abbot sayd to his covent,
        There he stode on grounde,
      'This day twelfe moneth came a knyght
        And borowed foure hondred pounde.

87.  ['He borowed four hondred pounde]
        Upon his londe and fee;
      But he come this ylkë day
        Disherited shall he be.'

88.  'It is full erely,' sayd the pryoure,
        The day is not yet ferre gone;
      I had lever to pay an hondred pounde,
        And lay it downe anone.

89.　'The knyght is ferre beyonde the see,
　　　　In Englonde is his ryght,
　　And suffreth honger and colde
　　　　And many a sory nyght.


90.　'It were grete pytë,' said the pryoure,
　　　　'So to have his londe;
　　And ye be so lyght of your consyence,
　　　　Ye do to hym moch wronge.'


91.　'Thou arte ever in my berde,' sayd the abbot,
　　　　'By God and Saynt Rycharde';
　　With that cam in a fat-heded monke,
　　　　The heygh selerer.


92.　'He is dede or hanged,' sayd the monke,
　　　　'By God that bought me dere,
　　And we shall have to spende in this place
　　　　Foure hondred pounde by yere.'


93.　The abbot and the hy selerer
　　　　Sertë forthe full bolde,
　　The highe justyce of Englonde
　　　　The abbot there dyde holde.


94.　The hye justyce and many mo
　　　　Had taken into theyr honde
　　Holy all the knyghtes det,
　　　　To put that knyght to wronge.


95.　They demed the knyght wonder sore,
　　　　The abbot and his meynë:
　　'But he come this ylkë day
　　　　Disherited shall he be.'

96.  'He wyll not come yet,' sayd the justyce,
        'I dare well undertake';
     But in sorowe tymë for them all
        The knyght came to the gate.

97.  Than bespake that gentyll knyght
        Untyll his meynë:
     'Now put on your symple wedes
        That ye brought fro the see.'

98.  [They put on their symple wedes,]
        They came to the gates anone;
     The porter was redy hymselfe
        And welcomed them everychone.

99.  'Welcome, syr knyght,' sayd the porter,
        'My lorde to mete is he,
     And so is many a gentyll man,
        For the love of the.'

100. The porter swore a full grete othe:
        'By God that madë me,
     Here be the best coresed hors
        That ever yet sawe I me.

101. 'Lede them in to the stable,' he sayd,
        'That eased myght they be';
     'They shall not come therin,' sayd the knyght,
        'By God that dyed on a tre.'

102. Lordës were to mete isette
        In that abbotes hall;
     The knyght went forth and kneled downe,
        And salued them grete and small.

103.   'Do gladly, syr abbot,' sayd the knyght,
         'I am come to holde my day':
       The fyrst word that the abbot spake,
         'Hast thou brought my pay?'

104.   'Not one peny,' sayd the knyght,
         'By God that maked me';
       'Thou art a shrewed dettour,' sayd the abbot;
         'Syr justyce, drynke to me.

105.   'What doost thou here,' sayd the abbot,
         'But thou haddest brought thy pay?'
       'For God,' than sayed the knyght,
         'To pray of a lenger daye.'

106.   'Thy daye is broke,' sayd the justyce,
         'Londe gettest thou none':
       'Now, good syr justyce, be my frende
         And fende me of my fone!'

107.   'I am holde with the abbot,' sayd the justyce,
         'Both with cloth and fee':
       'Now, good syr sheryf, be my frende!'
         'Nay, for God,' sayd he.

108.   'Now, good syr abbot, be my frende,
         For thy curteysë,
       And holde my londës in thy honde
         Tyll I have made the gree!

109.   'And I wyll be thy true servaunte,
         And trewely serve the,
       Tyll ye have foure hondred pounde
         Of money good and free.'

110. The abbot sware a full grete othe,
'By God that dyed on a tree,
Get thy londe where thou may,
For thou getest none of me.'

111. 'By dere worthy God,' then sayd the knyght,
'That all this worldë wrought,
But I have my londe agayne,
Full dere it shall be bought.

112. 'God, that was of a mayden borne,
Leve us well to spede !
For it is good to assay a frende
Or that a man have nede.'

113. The abbot lothely on hym gan loke,
And vylaynesly hym gan call ;
'Out,' he sayd, 'thou false knyght,
Spede the out of my hall ! '

114. 'Thou lyest,' then sayd the gentyll knyght,
'Abbot, in thy hal ;
False knyght was I never,
By God that made us all.'

115. Up then stode that gentyll knyght,
To the abbot sayd he,
'To suffre a knyght to knele so longe,
Thou canst no curteysye.

116. 'In joustes and in tournaments
Full ferre than have I be,
And put myself as ferre in prees
As ony that ever I see.'

117. 'What wyll ye gyve more,' sayd the justyce,
    ' And the knyght shall make a releyse?
And elles dare I safly swere
    Ye holde never your londe in pees.'

118. 'An hondred pounde,' sayd the abbot;
    The justice sayd, 'Gyve hym two';
'Nay, be God,' sayd the knyght,
    ' Ye get not my land so.

119. 'Though ye wolde gyve a thousand more,
    Yet were ye never the nere;
Shal there never be myn heyre
    Abbot, justice ne frere.'

120. He stert hym to a borde anone,
    Tyll a table rounde,
And there he shoke oute of a bagge
    Even four hundred pound.

121. 'Have here thi golde, sir abbot,' saide the knight,
    ' Which that thou lentest me;
Had thou ben curtes at my comynge,
    I would have rewarded thee.'

122. The abbot sat styll, and ete no more,
    For all his ryall fare;
He cast his hede on his shulder,
    And fast began to stare.

123. 'Take me my golde agayne,' saide the abbot,
    ' Sir justice, that I toke the';
Not a peni,' said the justice,
    ' Bi God, that dyed on tree.'

124.    'Sir abbot, and ye men of lawe,
            Now have I holde my daye;
        Now shall I have my londe agayne,
            For ought that you can saye.'


125.    The knyght stert out of the dore,
            Awaye was all his care,
        And on he put his good clothynge
            The other he lefte there.


126.    He wente hym forth full mery syngynge,
        ·   As men have told in tale;
        His lady met hym at the gate,
            At home in Verysdale.


127.    'Welcome, my lorde,' sayd his lady;
            'Syr, lost is all your good?'
        'Be mery, dame,' sayd the knyght,
            'And pray for Robyn Hode,


128.    'That ever his soule be in blysse:
            He holpe me out of tene;
        Ne had be his kyndёnesse,
            Beggers had we bene.


129.    'The abbot and I accorded ben,
            He is served of his pay;
        The god yoman lent it me
            As I cam by the way.'


130.    This knight than dwelled fayre at home,
            The sothe for to saye,
        Tyll he had got four hundred pound,
            Al redy for to pay.

131.    He purveyed him an hundred bowes,
            The strynges well ydyght,
        An hundred shefe of arowes gode,
            The hedys burneshed full bryght;

132.    And every arowe an ellë longe,
            With pecok well idyght,
        Inocked all with whyte silver;
            It was a semely syght.

133.    He purveyed him an hondreth men,
            Well harnessed in that stede,
        And hym selfe in that same suite,
            And clothed in whyte and rede.

134.    He bare a launsgay in his honde,
            And a man ledde his male,
        And reden with a lyght songe
            Unto Bernysdale.

135.    [But at Wentbrydge] there was a wrastelyng,
            And there taryed was he,
        And there was all the best yemen
            Of all the west countree.

136.    A full fayre game there was up set,
            A whyte bulle up i-pyght,
        A grete courser, with sadle and brydil,
            With golde burnyssht full bryght.

137.    A payre of gloves, a rede golde rynge,
            A pype of wyne, in fay;
        What man that bereth hym best i-wys
            The pryce shall bere away.

138.   There was a yoman in that place,
         And best worthy was he,
       And for he was ferre and frembde bested,
         Slayne he shulde have be.


139.   The knight had ruthe of this yoman,
         In place where that he stode ;
       He sayde that yoman shulde have no harme,
         For love of Robyn Hode.


140.   The knyght pressed in to the place,
         An hundreth folowed hym free,
       With bowes bent and arowes sharpe,
         For to shende that companye.


141.   They shulderd all and made hym rome,
         To wete what he wolde say ;
       He toke the yeman bi the hande,
         And gave hym al the play.


142.   He gave hym five marke for his wyne,
         There it lay on the molde,
       And bad it shulde be set a broche,
         Drynkë who so wolde.


143.   Thus longe taried this gentyll knyght,
         Tyll that play was done ;
       So longe abode Robyn fastinge
         Thre houres after the none.

Little John lost in translation

## THE THIRDE FYTTE.

144. Lyth and lystyn, gentilmen,
    All that nowe be here;
Of Litell Johnn, that was the knightes man,
    Goode myrth ye shall here.

145. It was upon a mery day
    That yonge men wolde go shete;
Lytell Johnn fet his bowe anone,
    And sayde he wolde them mete.

146. Thre tymes Litell Johnn shet aboute,
    And alway cleft the wande;
The proude sherif of Notingham
    By the markes gan stande.

147. The sherif swore a full greate othe:
    'By hym that dyede on a tre,
This man is the best arschere
    That ever I dyd see.

148. 'Say me nowe, wight yonge man,
    What is nowe thy name?
In what countre were thou borne,
    And where is thy wonynge wane?'

149. 'In Holdernes, sir, I was borne,
    I-wys al of my dame;
Men cal me Reynolde Grenelef
    Whan I am at home.'

150. 'Sey me, Reynolde Grenelefe,
    Wolde thou dwell with me?
And every yere I woll the gyve
    Twenty marke to thy fee.'

151. 'I have a maister,' sayde Litell Johnn,
    'A curteys knight is he ;
May ye levë gete of hym,
    The better may it be.'

152. The sherif gate Litell John
    Twelve moneths of the knight ;
Therefore he gave him right anone
    A gode hors and a wight.

153. Nowe is Litell John the sherifes man,
    God lende us well to spede !
But alwey thought Lytell John
    To quyte hym wele his mede.

154. 'Nowe so God me helpe,' sayde Litell John,
    'And by my true leutye,
I shall be the worst servaunt to hym
    That ever yet had he.'

155. It fell upon a Wednesday
    The sherif on huntynge was gone,
And Litel John lay in his bed,
    And was foriete at home.

156. Therfore he was fastinge
    Til it was past the none ;
'Gode sir stuarde, I pray to the,
    Gyve me my dynere,' saide Litell John.

157. 'It is to longe for Grenelefe
    Fastinge thus for to be ;
Therfor I pray the, sir stuarde,
    Mi dyner gif thou me.'

158.   'Shalt thou never ete ne drynke,' saide the stuarde,
           'Tyll my lorde be come to towne :'
       'I make myn avowe to God,' saide Litell John,
           'I had lever to crake thy crowne.'


159.   The boteler was full uncurteys,
           There he stode on flore ;
       He start to the botery
           And shet fast the dore.


160.   Lytell Johnn gave the boteler suche a tap
           His backe went nere in two ;
       Though he liveth an hundred wynter,
           The wors he still shall goe.


161.   He sporned the dore with his fote ;
           It went open wel and fyne ;
       And there he made large lyveray,
           Bothe of ale and of wyne.


162.   'Sith ye wol nat dyne,' sayde Litell John,
           'I shall gyve you to drinke ;
       And though ye lyve an hundred wynter,
           On Lytel Johnn ye shall thinke.'


163.   Litell John ete, and Litel John drank,
           The whilë that he wolde ;
       The sherife had in his kechyn a coke,
           A stoute man and a bolde.


164.   'I make myn avowe to God,' saide the coke,
           'Thou arte a shrewde hyne
       In ani householde for to dwel,
           For to aske thus to dyne.'

165.   And there he lent Litell John
            Godë strokis thre ;
        'I make myn avowe,' sayde Lytell John,
            ' These strokis lyked well me.

166.   ' Thou arte a bolde man and a hardy,
            And so thinketh me ;
        And or I pas fro this place
            Assayed better shalt thou be,'

167.   Lytell Johnn drew a ful gode sworde,
            The coke toke another in hande ;
        They thought no thynge for to fle,
            But stifly for to stande.

168.   There they faught sore togedere
            Two mylë way and more ;
        Myght neyther other harme done,
            The mountnaunce of an owre.

169.   ' I make myn avowe to God,' sayde Litell Johnn,
            ' And by my true lewtë ;
        Thou art one of the best sworde-men
            That ever yit sawe I me.

170.   ' Cowdest thou shote as well in a bowe,
            To grene wode thou shuldest with me,
        And two times in the yere thy clothinge
            Chaunged shuldë be ;

171.   ' And every yere of Robyn Hode
            Twenty merke to thy fe : '
        ' Put up thy swerde,' saide the coke,
            ' And felowes woll we be.'

172.    Thanne he fet to Lytell Johnn
            The nowmbles of a do,
        Gode brede and full gode wyne;
            They ete and drank theretoo.


173.    And when they had dronkyn well,
            Theyre trouthes togeder they plight
        That they wolde be with Robyn
            That ylkë samë nyght.


174.    They dyd them to the tresoure-hows,
            As fast as they myght gone;
        The lokkes, that were of full gode stele,
            They brake them everichone.


175.    They toke away the silver vessell,
            And all that thei might get;
        Pecis, masars, ne sponis,
            Wolde thei not forget.


176.    Also they toke the gode pens,
            Thre hundred pounde and more,
        And did them streyte to Robyn Hode,
            Under the grene wode hore.


177.    'God the save, my dere mayster,
            And Criste the save and se!'
        And thanne sayde Robyn to Litell Johnn,
            'Welcome myght thou be.


178.    'Also be that fayre yeman
            Thou bryngest there with the;
        What tydynges fro Notyngham?
            Lytill Johnn, tell thou me.'

179.  '.Well the gretith the proude sheryf,
          And sendeth the here by me
      His coke and his silver vessell,
          And thre hundred pounde and thre.'


180.  'I make myne avowe to God,' sayde Robyn,
          'And to the Trenytë,
      It was never by his gode wyll
          This gode is come to me.'


181.  Lytyll Johnn there hym bethought
          On a shrewde wyle;
      Fyve myle in the forest he ran,
          Hym happed all his wyll.


182.  Than he met the proude sheref,
          Huntynge with houndes and horne;
      Lytell Johnn coude of curtesye,
          And knelyd hym beforne.


183.  'God the save, my dere mayster,
          And Criste the save and se!'
      'Reynolde Grenelefe,' sayde the shyref,
          'Where hast thou nowe be?'


184.  'I have be in this forest;
          A fayre syght can I se;
      It was one of the fayrest syghtes
          That ever yet sawe I me.


185.  'Yonder I sawe a ryght fayre harte,
          His coloure is of grene;
      Seven score of dere upon a herde
          Be with hym all bydene.

186.    ' Their tyndes are so sharp, maister,
        Of sexty, and well mo,
    That I durst not shote for drede,
        Lest they wolde me slo.'

187.    ' I make myn avowe to God,' sayde the shyref,
        ' That syght wolde I fayne se :'
    ' Buske you thyderwarde, mi dere mayster,
        Anone, and wende with me.'

188.    The sherif rode, and Litell Johnn
        Of fote he was full smerte,
    And whane they came before Robyn,
        ' Lo, here is the mayster-herte.'

189.    Still stode the proude sherief,
        A sory man was he ;
    ' Wo the worthe, Raynolde Grenelefe,
        Thou hast betrayed me.'

190.    ' I make myn avowe to God,' sayde Litell Johnn,
        ' Mayster, ye be to blame ;
    I was mysserved of my dynere
        When I was with you at home.'

191.    Sone he was to souper sette,
        And served with silver white,
    And when the sherif sawe his vessell,
        For sorowe he myght nat ete.

192.    ' Make glad chere,' sayde Robyn Hode,
        ' Sherif, for charitë,
    And for the love of Litill Johnn
        Thy lyfe I graunt to the.'

193.  Whan they had souped well,
          The day was al gone ;
      Robyn commaunded Litell Johnn
          To drawe of his hose and shone ;

194.  His kirtell, and his cote a pye,
          That was fured well and fine,
      And toke hym a grene mantel,
          To lap his body therein.

195.  Robyn commaundyd his wight yonge men,
          Under the grene wode tree,
      They shulde lye in that same sute
          That the sherif myght them see.

196.  All nyght lay the proude sherif
          In his breche and in his schert ;
      No wonder it was, in grene wode,
          Though his sydes gan to smerte.

197.  ' Make glad chere,' sayde Robyn Hode,
          ' Sheref, for charitë ;
      For this is our ordre i-wys
          Under the grene-wode tree.'

198.  ' This is harder order,' sayde the sherief,
          ' Than any ankir or frere ;
      For all the golde in mery Englonde
          I wolde nat longe dwell her.'

199.  'All this twelve monthes,' sayde Robin,
          ' Thou shalt dwell with me ;
      I shall the teche, proude sherif,
          An outlawe for to be.'

200.   ' Or I here another nyght lye,' sayde the sherif,
           ' Robyn, nowe pray I the,
       Smyte of mijn hede rather to-morowe,
           And I forgyve it the.


201.   ' Lat me go,' than sayde the sherif,
           ' For saynte charite,
       And I woll be the best frende
           That ever yet had ye.'


202.   ' Thou shalt swere me an othe,' sayde Robyn,
           ' On my bright bronde ;
       Shalt thou never awayte me scathe
           By water ne by lande.


203.   ' And if thou fynde any of my men,
           By nyght or by day,
       Upon thyn othe thou shalt swere
           To helpe them that thou may.'


204.   Nowe hathe the sherif sworne his othe,
           And home he began to gone ;
       He was as full of grene wode
           As ever was hepe of stone.

## The Fourth Fytte.

205.   The sherif dwelled in Notingham;
       He was fayne he was agone;
   And Robyn and his mery men
       Went to wode anone.

206.   'Go we to dyner,' sayde Littell Johnn;
       Robyn Hode sayde, 'Nay;
   For I drede Our Lady be wroth with me,
       For she sent me nat my pay.'

207.   'Have no doute, maister,' sayde Litell Johnn;
       'Yet is not the sonne at rest;
   For I dare say, and savely swere,
       The knight is true and truste.'

208.   'Take thy bowe in thy hande,' sayde Robyn,
       'Late Much wende with the,
   And so shal Wyllyam Scarlok,
       And no man abyde with me.

209.   'And walke up under the Sayles,
       And to Watlynge-strete,
   And wayte after some unketh gest;
       Up-chaunce ye may them mete.

210.   'Whether he be messengere,
       Or a man that myrthës can,
   Of my good he shall have some,
       Yf he be a pore man.'

211.   Forth then stert Lytel Johan,
       Half in tray and tene,
   And gyrde hym with a full good swerde,
       Under a mantel of grene.

212.   They went up to the Sayles,
           These yemen all thre ;
       They loked est, they loked west,
           They myght no man se.


213.   But as they loked in Bernysdale,
           By the hyë waye,
       Than were they ware of two blacke monkes,
           Eche on a good palferay.


214.   Then bespake Lytell Johan,
           To Much he gan say,
       ' I dare lay my lyfe to wedde,
           These monkes have brought our pay.


215.   ' Make glad chere,' sayd Lytell Johan,
           ' And frese our bowes of ewe,
       And loke your hertes be seker and sad.
           Your strynges trusty and trewe.


216.   ' The monke hath two and fifty men,
           And seven somers full stronge ;
       There rydeth no bysshop in this londe
           So ryally, I understond.


217.   ' Brethern,' sayd Lytell Johan,
           ' Here are no more but we thre ;
       But we brynge them to dyner,
           Our mayster dare we not se.


218.   ' Bende your bowes,' sayd Lytell Johan,
           ' Make all yon prese to stonde ;
       The formost monke, his lyfe and his deth
           Is closed in my honde.

219. 'Abyde, chorle monke,' sayd Lytell Johan,
 ' No ferther that thou gone ;
Yf thou doost, by dere worthy God,
 Thy deth is in my honde.

220. ' And evyll thryfte on thy hede,' sayd Lytell Johan,
 ' Ryght under thy hattes bonde,
For thou hast made our mayster wroth,
 He is fastynge so longe.'

221. 'Who is your mayster?' sayd the monke;
 Lytell Johan sayd, Robyn Hode;
' He is a stronge thefe,' sayd the monke,
 ' Of hym herd I never good.'

222. ' Thou lyest,' than sayd Lytell Johan,
 ' And that shall rewë the;
He is a yeman of the forest,
 To dyne he hath bodë the.'

223. Much was redy with a bolte,
 Redly and anone,
He set the monke to-fore the brest,
 To the grounde that he can gone.

224. Of two and fyfty wyght yonge yemen
 There abode not one,
Saf a lytell page and a grome,
 To lede the somers with Lytel Johan.

225. They brought the monke to the lodge-dore,
 Whether he were loth or lefe,
For to speke with Robyn Hode,
 Maugre in theyr tethe.

226.    Robyn dyde a downe his hode,
            The monke whan that he se ;
        The monke was not so curteyse,
            His hode then let he be.


227.    'He is a chorle, mayster, by dere worthy God,'
            Than sayd Lytell Johan :
        'Thereof no force,' sayd Robyn,
            'For curteysy can he none.


228.    'How many men,' sayd Robyn,
            'Had this monke, Johan ?'
        'Fyfty and two whan that we met,
            But many of them be gone.'


229.    'Let blowe a horne,' sayd Robyn,
            'That felaushyp may us knowe ;'
        Seven score of wyght yemen,
            Came pryckynge on a rowe.


230.    And everych of them a good mantell
            Of scarlet and of raye ;
        All they came to good Robyn,
            To wyte what he wolde say.


231.    They made the monke to wasshe and wype,
            And syt at his denere,
        Robyn Hode and Lytell Johan
            They served him both in-fere.


232.    'Do gladly, monke,' sayd Robyn.
            'Gramercy, syr,' sayd he.
        'Where is your abbay, whan ye are at home,
            And who is your avowë ?'

233.  'Saynt Mary abbay,' sayd the monke,
        'Though I be symple here.'
      'In what offyce?' said Robyn:
        'Syr, the hye selerer.'

234.  'Ye be the more welcome,' sayd Robyn,
        'So ever mote I the:
      Fyll of the best wyne,' sayd Robyn,
        'This monke shall drynke to me.

235.  'But I have grete mervayle,' sayd Robyn,
        Of all this longë day;
      I drede Our Lady be wroth with me,
        She sent me not my pay.'

236.  'Have no doute, mayster,' sayd Lytell Johan,
        'Ye have no nede, I saye;
      This monke hath brought it, I dare well swere,
        For he is of her abbay.'

237.  'And she was a borowe,' sayd Robyn,
        'Betwene a knyght and me,
      Of a lytell money that I hym lent,
        Under the grene-wode tree.

238.  'And yf thou hast that sylver ibrought,
        I pray the let me se;
      And I shall helpë the eftsones,
        Yf thou have nede to me.'

239.  The monke swore a full grete othe,
        With a sory chere,
      'Of the borowehode thou spekest to me,
        Herde I never ere.'

240.   'I make myn avowe to God,' sayd Robyn,
           'Monke, thou art to blame ;
       For God is holde a ryghtwys man,
           And so is his dame.


241.   'Thou toldest with thyn owne tonge,
           Thou may not say nay,
       How thou arte her servaunt,
           And servest her every day.


242.   'And thou art made her messengere,
           My money for to pay ;
       Therefore I cun the morë thanke
           Thou arte come at thy day.


243.   'What is in your cofers?' sayd Robyn,
           'Trewe than tell thou me :'
       'Syr,' he sayd, 'twenty marke,
           Al so mote I the.'


244.   'Yf there be no more,' sayd Robyn,
           'I wyll not one peny ;
       Yf thou hast myster of ony more,
           Syr, more I shall lende to the.


245.   'And yf I fynde more,' sayd Robyn,
           'I-wys thou shalte it for gone ;
       For of thy spendynge-sylver, monke,
           Thereof wyll I ryght none.


246.   'Go nowe forthe, Lytell Johan,
           And the trouth tell thou me ;
       If there be no more but twenty marke,
           No peny that I se.'

247.   Lytell Johan spred his mantell downe,
      As he had done before,
  And he tolde out of the monkes male
      Eyght hondred pounde and more.

248.   Lytell Johan let it lye full styll,
      And went to his mayster in hast;
  'Syr,' he sayd, 'the monke is trewe ynowe,
      Our Lady hath doubled your cast.'

249.   'I make myn avowe to God,' sayd Robyn —
      'Monke, what tolde I the? —
  Our Lady is the trewest woman
      That ever yet founde I me.

250.   'By dere worthy God,' sayd Robyn,
      'To seche all Englond thorowe,
  Yet founde I never to my pay
      A moche better borowe.

251.   'Fyll of the best wyne, and do hym drynke,' sayd
      Robyn,
      'And grete well thy lady hende,
  And yf she have nede to Robyn Hode,
      A frende she shall hym fynde.

252.   'And yf she nedeth ony more sylver,
      Come thou agayne to me,
  And, by this token she hath me sent,
      She shall have such thre.'

253.   The monke was goynge to London ward,
      There to hold grete mote,
  The knyght that rode so hye on hors,
      To brynge hym under fote.

254.    'Whether be ye away?' sayd Robyn :
            'Syr, to maners in this londe,
        Too reken with our reves,
            That have done moch wronge.'


255.    'Come now forth, Lytell Johan,
            And harken to my tale ;
        A better yemen I knowe none,
            To seke a monkës male.'


256.    'How moch is in yonder other corser?' sayd
                Robyn,
            'The soth must we see :'
        By Our Lady,' than sayd the monke,
            'That were no curteysye,


257.    'To bydde a man to dyner,
            And syth hym bete and bynde.'
        'It is our olde maner,' sayd Robyn,
            'To leve but lytell behynde.'


258.    The monke toke the hors with spore,
            No lenger wolde he abyde :
        'Aske to drynke,' than sayd Robyn,
            'Or that ye forther ryde.'


259.    'Nay, for God,' than sayd the monke,
            'Me reweth I cam so nere ;
        For better chepe I myght have dyned
            In Blythe or in Dankestere.'


260.    'Grete well your abbot,' sayd Robyn,
            'And your pryour, I you pray,
        And byd hym send me such a monke
            To dyner every day.'

261. Now lete we that monke be styll,
     And speke we of that knyght:
Yet he came to holde his day,
     Whyle that it was lyght.

262. He dyde him streyt to Bernysdale,
     Under the grene-wode tre,
And he founde there Robyn Hode,
     And all his mery meynë.

263. The knyght lyght doune of his good palfray;
     Robyn whan he gan see,
So curteysly he dyde adoune his hode,
     And set hym on his knee.

264. 'God the save, Robyn Hode,
     And all this company:'
'Welcome be thou, gentyll knyght,
     And ryght welcome to me.'

265. Than bespake hym Robyn Hode,
     To that knyght so fre:
What nede dryveth the to grene-wode?
     I praye the, syr knyght, tell me.

266. 'And welcome be thou, gentyll knyght,
     Why hast thou be so longe?'
'For the abbot and the hye iustyce
     Wolde have had my londe.'

267. 'Hast thou thy londe agayne?' sayd Robyn;
     'Treuth than tell thou me:'
'Ye, for God,' sayd the knyght,
     'And that thanke I God and the.

268. 'But take no grefe, that I have be so longe ;
  I came by a wrastelynge,
 And there I holpe a pore yeman,
  With wronge was put behynde.'

269. 'Nay, for God,' sayd Robyn,
  'Syr knyght, that thanke I the ;
 What man that helpeth a good yeman,
  His frende than wyll I be.'

270. 'Have here foure hondred pounde,' sayd the
  knyght,
  'The whiche ye lent to me ;
 And here is also twenty marke
  For your curteysy.'

271. 'Nay, for God,' sayd Robyn,
  'Thou broke it well for ay ;
 For Our Lady, by her hye selerer,
  Hath sent to me my pay.

272. 'And yf I toke it i-twyse,
  A shame it were to me ;
 But trewely, gentyll knyght,
  Welcome arte thou to me.'

273. Whan Robyn had tolde his tale,
  He leugh and made good chere :
 'By my trouthe,' then sayd the knyght,
  'Your money is redy here.'

274. 'Broke it well,' said Robyn,
  'Thou gentyll knyght so fre ;
 And welcome be thou, gentyll knyght,
  Under my trystell-tre.

275.　'But what shall these bowes do?' sayd Robyn,
　　　　'And these arowes ifedred fre?'
　　　'By God,' than sayd the knyght,
　　　　'A pore present to the.'


276.　'Come now forth, Lytell Johan,
　　　　And go to my treasurë,
　　　And brynge me there foure hondred pounde;
　　　　The monke over-tolde it me.


277.　'Have here foure hondred pounde,
　　　　Thou gentyll knyght and trewe,
　　　And bye thee hors and harnes good,
　　　　And gylte thy spores all newe.


278.　'And yf thou fayle ony spendynge,
　　　　Com to Robyn Hode,
　　　And by my trouth thou shalt none fayle,
　　　　The whyles I have any good.


279.　'And broke well thy foure hondred pound,
　　　　Whiche I lent to the,
　　　And make thy selfe no more so bare,
　　　　By the counsell of me.'


280.　Thus than holpe hym good Robyn,
　　　　The knyght all of his care:
　　　God, that syt in heven hye,
　　　　Graunte us well to fare!

## The Fyfth Fytte.

281.    Now hath the knyght his leve i-take,
        And wente hym on his way;
    Robyn Hode and his mery men
        Dwelled styll full many a day.

282.    Lyth and lysten, gentil men,
        And herken what I shall say,
    How the proud sheryfe of Notyngham
        Dyde crye a full fayre play;

283.    That all the best archers of the north
        Sholde come upon a day,
    And he that shoteth allther best
        The game shall bere away.

284.    He that shoteth allther best,
        Furthest fayre and lowe,
    At a payre of fynly buttes,
        Under the grene wode shawe,

285.    A ryght good arowe he shall have,
        The shaft of sylver whyte,
    The hede and feders of ryche rede golde,
        In Englond is none lyke.

286.    This than herde good Robyn,
        Under his trystell-tre:
    'Make you redy, ye wyght yonge men;
        That shotynge wyll I se.

287.    'Buske you, my mery yonge men;
        Ye shall go with me;
    And I wyll wete the shryvës fayth,
        Trewe and yf he be.'

288.  Whan they had theyr bowes i-bent,
      Theyr takles fedred fre,
    Seven score of wyght yonge men
      Stode by Robyns kne.


289.  Whan they cam to Notyngham,
      The buttes were fayre and longe;
    Many was the bolde archere
      That shot with bowës stronge.


290.  ' There shall but syx shote with me;
      The other shal kepe my he[ve]de,
    And stande with good bowes bent,
      That I be not desceyved.'


291  The fourth outlawe his bowe gan bende,
      And that was Robyn Hode,
    And that behelde the proud sheryfe,
      All by the but he stode.


292.  Thryës Robyn shot about,
      And alway he slist the wand,
    And so dyde good Gylberte
      With the whytë hande.


293.  Lytell Johan and good Scatheloke
      Were archers good and fre ;
    Lytell Much and good Reynolde,
      The worste wolde they not be.


294.  Whan they had shot aboute,
      These archours fayre and good,
    Evermore was the best,
      For soth, Robyn Hode.

295.  Hym was delyvered the good arowe,
          For best worthy was he;
      He toke the yeft so curteysly,
          To grene-wode wolde he.

296.  They cryed out on Robyn Hode,
          And grete hornes gan they blowe:
      'Wo worth the, treason!' sayd Robyn,
          'Full evyl thou art to knowe.

297.  'And wo be thou! thou proude sheryf,
          Thus gladdynge thy gest;
      Other wyse thou behote me
          In yonder wylde forest.

298.  'But had I the in grene-wode,
          Under my trystell-tre,
      Thou sholdest leve me a better wedde
          Than thy trewe lewtë.'

299.  Full many a bowë there was bent,
          And arowes let they glyde;
      Many a kyrtell there was rent,
          And hurt many a syde.

300.  The outlawes shot was so stronge
          That no man myght them dryve,
      And the proud sheryfes men,
          They fled away full blyve.

301.  Robyn sawe the busshement to-broke,
          In grene wode he wolde have be;
      Many an arowe there was shot
          Amonge that company.

302.    Lytell Johan was hurte full sore,
            With an arowe in his kne,
        That he myght neyther go nor ryde;
            It was full grete pytë.

303.    'Mayster,' then sayd Lytell Johan,
            'If ever thou lovedst me,
        And for that ylkë lordës love
            That dyed upon a tre,

304.    'And for the medes of my servyce,
            That I have served the,
        Lete never the proude sheryf
            Alyve now fyndë me.

305.    'But take out thy browne swerde,
            And smyte all of my hede,
        And gyve me woundës depe and wyde;
            No lyfe on me be lefte.'

306.    'I wolde not that,' sayd Robyn,
            'Johan, that thou were slawe,
        For all the golde in mery Englonde,
            Though it lay now on a rawe.'

307.    'God forbede,' sayd Lytell Much,
            'That dyed on a tre,
        That thou sholdest, Lytell Johan,
            Parte our company.'

308.    Up he toke hym on his backe,
            And bare hym well a myle;
        Many a tyme he layd him downe,
            And shot another whyle.

309.    Then was there a fayre castell,
            A lytell within the wode ;
        Double-dyched it was about,
            And walled, by the rode.


310.    And there dwelled that gentyll knyght,
            Syr Rychard at the Lee,
        That Robyn had lent his good,
            Under the grene-wode tree.


311.    In he toke good Robyn,
            And all his company :
        'Welcome be thou, Robyn Hode,
            Welcome arte thou to me ;


312.    'And moche I thanke the of thy comfort,
            And of thy curteysye,
        And of thy grete kyndenesse,
            Under the grene-wode tre.


313.    'I love no man in all this worlde
            So much as I do the ;
        For all the proud sheryf of Notyngham,
            Ryght here shalt thou be.


314.    'Shutte the gates, and drawe the brydge,
            And let no man come in,
        And arme you well, and make you redy,
            And to the walles ye wynne.


315.    'For one thynge, Robyn, I the behote ;
            I swere by Saynt Quyntyne,
        These forty dayes thou wonnest with me,
            To soupe, ete, and dyne.'

316.  Bordes were layde, and clothes were spredde,
          Redely and anone ;
      Robyn Hode and his mery men
          To metë can they gone.

--•◦•--

### The Sixth Fytte.

317.  Lythe and lysten, gentylmen,
          And herkyn to your songe ;
      Howe the proude shyref of Notyngham,
          And men of armys stronge,

318.  Full fast cam to the hye shyref,
          The contrë up to route,
      And they besette the knyghtes castell,
          The wallës all aboute.

319.  The proude shyref loude gan crye,
          And sayde, 'Thou traytour knight,
      Thou kepest here the kynges enemys,
          Agaynst the lawe and right.'

320.  'Syr, I wyll avowe that I have done,
          The dedys that here be dyght,
      Upon all the landës that I have,
          As I am a trewe knyght.

321.  'Wende furth, sirs, on your way,
          And do no more to me
      Tyll ye wyt oure kyngës wille,
          What he wyll say to the.'

322.   The shyref thus had his answere,
      Without any lesynge;
    Forth he yede to London towne,
      All for to tel our kinge.

323.   Ther he telde him of that knight,
      And eke of Robyn Hode,
    And also of the bolde archars,
      That were soo noble and gode.

324.   'He wyll avowe that he hath done,
      To mayntene the outlawes stronge;
    He wyll be lorde, and set you at nought,
      In all the northe londe.'

325.   'I wil be at Notyngham,' saide our kynge,
      'Within this fourteenyght,
    And take I wyll Robyn Hode
      And so I wyll that knight.

326.   'Go nowe home, shyref,' sayde our kynge,
      'And do as I byd the;
    And ordeyn gode archers ynowe,
      Of all the wyde contrë.'

327.   The shyref had his leve i-take,
      And went hym on his way,
    And Robyn Hode to grene wode,
      Upon a certen day.

328.   And Lytel John was hole of the arowe
      That shot was in his kne,
    And dyd hym streyght to Robyn Hode,
      Under the grene wode tree.

329.   Robyn Hode walked in the forest,
           Under the levys grene ;
       The proude shyref of Notyngham
           Thereof he had grete tene.


330.   The shyref there fayled of Robyn Hode,
           He myght not have his pray ;
       Than he awayted this gentyll knyght,
           Bothe by nyght and day.


331.   Ever he wayted the gentyll knyght,
           Syr Richarde at the Lee,
       As he went on haukynge by the ryver-syde,
           And lete his haukës flee.


332.   Toke he there this gentyll knight,
           With men of armys stronge,
       And led hym to Notynghamwarde,
           Bounde bothe fote and hande.


333.   The sheref sware a full grete othe,
           Bi him that dyed on rode,
       He had lever than an hundred pound
           That he had Robyn Hode.


334.   This harde the knyghtës wyfe,
           A fayr lady and a free ;
       She set hir on a gode palfrey,
           To grene wode anone rode she.


335.   Whanne she cam in the forest,
           Under the grene wode tree,
       Fonde she there Robyn Hode,
           And al his fayre menë.

336.　'God the save, gode Robyn,
　　　　　And all thy company ;
　　　For Our dere Ladyes sake,
　　　　　A bone graunte thou me.


337.　'Late never my wedded lorde
　　　　　Shamefully slayne be ;
　　　He is fast bound to Notinghamwarde,
　　　　　For the love of the.'


338.　Anone than saide goode Robyn
　　　　　To that lady so fre,
　　　'What man hath your lorde ytake?'
　　　　　'The proude shirife,' than sayd she.


339.　·　·　·　·　·　·
　　　　　'For soth as I the say ;
　　　He is nat yet thre mylës
　　　　　Passed on his way.'


340.　Up than sterte gode Robyn,
　　　　　As man that had ben wode :
　　　'Buske you, my mery men,
　　　　　For hym that dyed on rode.


341.　'And he that this sorowe forsaketh,
　　　　　By hym that dyed on tre,
　　　Shall he never in grene wode
　　　　　No lenger dwel with me.'


342.　Sone there were gode bowës bent,
　　　　　Mo than seven score ;
　　　Hedge ne dyche spared they none
　　　　　That was them before.

343. 'I make myn avowe to God,' sayde Robyn,
    'The sherif wolde I fayne see ;
And if I may him take,
    I-quyt then shall he be.'


344. And when they came to Notingham,
    They walked in the strete ;
And with the proude sherif i-wys
    Sonë can they mete.


345. 'Abyde, thou proude sherif,' he sayde,
    'Abyde, and speke with me ;
Of some tidinges of oure kinge
    I wolde fayne here of the.


346. 'This seven yere, by dere worthy God,
    Ne yede I this fast on fote ;
I make myn avowe to God, thou proude sherif,
    It is not for thy gode.'


347. Robyn bent a full goode bowe,
    An arrowe he drowe at wyll ;
He hit so the proude sherife
    Upon the grounde he lay full still.


348. And or he myght up aryse,
    On his fete to stonde,
He smote of the sherifs hede
    With his bright bronde.


349. 'Lye thou there, thou proude sherife ;
    Evyll mote thou thryve :
There myght no man to the truste
    The whyles thou were a lyve.'

350. His men drewe out theyr bryght swerdes,
  That were so sharpe and kene,
 And layde on the sheryves men,
  And dryved them downe bydene.


351. Robyn stert to that knyght,
  And cut a two his bonde,
 And toke hym in his hand a bowe,
  And bad hym by hym stonde.


352. 'Leve thy hors the behynde,
  And lerne for to renne ;
 Thou shalt with me to grene wode,
  Through myre, mosse, and fenne.


353. 'Thou shalt with me to grene wode,
  Without ony leasynge,
 Tyll that I have gete us grace
  Of Edwarde, our comly kynge.'


THE SEVENTH FYTTE.

354. The kynge came to Notynghame,
  With knyghtes in grete araye,
 For to take that gentyll knyght
  And Robyn Hode, and yf he may.


355. He asked men of that countrë,
  After Robyn Hode,
 And after that gentyll knyght,
  That was so bolde and stout.

356.   Whan they had tolde hym the case
      Our kynge understode ther tale,
  And seased in his honde
      The knyghtës londës all.


357.   All the passe of Lancasshyre
      He went both ferre and nere,
  Tyll he came to Plomton Parke ;
      He faylyd many of his dere.


358.   There our kynge was wont to se
      Herdës many one,
  He coud unneth fynde one dere,
      That bare ony good horne.


359.   The kynge was wonder wroth with all,
      And swore by the Trynytë,
  'I wolde I had Robyn Hode,
      With eyen I myght hym se.


360.   'And he that wolde smyte of the knyghtës hede,
      And brynge it to me,
  He shall have the knyghtës londes,
      Syr Rycharde at the Le.


361.   'I gyve it hym with my charter,
      And sele it with my honde,
  To have and holde for ever more,
      In all mery Englonde.'


362.   Than bespake a fayre olde knyght,
      That was treue in his fay :
  'A, my leegë lorde the kynge,
      One worde I shall you say.

363.    'There is no man in this countrë
            May have the knyghtës londes,
        Whyle Robyn Hode may ryde or gone,
            And bere a bowe in his hondes,

364.    'That he ne shall lese his hede,
            That is the best ball in his hode :
        Give it no man, my lorde the kynge,
            That ye wyll any good.'

365.    Half a yere dwelled our comly kynge
            In Notyngham, and well more ;
        Coude he not here of Robyn Hode,
            In what countrë that he were.

366.    But alway went good Robyn
            By halke and eke by hyll,
        And alway slewe the kyngës dere,
            And welt them at his wyll.

367.    Than bespake a proude fostere,
            That stode by our kyngës kne :
        'Yf ye wyll see good Robyn,
            Ye must do after me.

368.    'Take fyve of the best knyghtes
            That be in your lede,
        And walke downe by yon abbay,
            And gete you monkës wede.

369.    And I wyll be your ledes-man,
            And lede you the way,
        And or ye come to Notyngham,
            Myn hede then dare I lay,

370.    That ye shall mete with good Robyn,
            On lyve yf that he be ;
        Or ye come to Notyngham,
            With eyen ye shall hym se.


371.    Full hastely our kynge was dyght,
            So were his knyghtës fyve,
        Everych of them in monkës wede,
            And hasted them thyder blyve.


372.    Our kynge was grete above his cole,
            A brode hat on his crowne,
        Ryght as he were abbot-lyke,
            They rode up into the towne.


373.    Styf botes our kynge had on,
            Forsoth as I you say ;
        He rode syngynge to grene wode,
            The covent was clothed in graye.


374.    His male-hors and his grete somers
            Folowed our kynge behynde,
        Tyll they came to grene wode,
            A myle under the lynde.


375.    There they met with good Robyn,
            Stondynge on the waye,
        And so dyde many a bolde archere,
            For soth as I you say.


376.    Robyn toke the kyngës hors,
            Hastely in that stede,
        And sayd, Syr abbot, by your leve,
            A whyle ye must abyde.

377. 'We be yemen of this foreste,
    Under the grene-wode tre;
We lyve by our kyngës dere,
    Other shift have not wee.

378. 'And ye have chyrches and rentës both,
    And gold full grete plentë;
Gyve us some of your spendynge,
    For saynt charytë.'

379. Than bespake our cumly kynge,
    Anone than sayd he;
'I brought no more to grene-wode
    But forty pounde with me.

380. 'I have layne at Notyngham,
    This fourtynyght with our kynge,
And spent I have full moche good
    On many a grete lordynge.

381. 'And I have but forty pounde,
    No more than have I me:
But if I had an hondred pounde,
    I would give it to thee.'

382. Robyn toke the forty pounde,
    And departed it in two partye;
Halfendell he gave his mery men,
    And bad them mery to be.

383. Full curteysly Robyn gan say;
    'Syr, have this for your spendyng;
We shall mete another day';
    'Gramercy,' than sayd our kynge.

384.  'But well the greteth Edwarde, our kynge,
          And sent to the his seale,
      And byddeth the com to Notyngham,
          Both to mete and mele.'


385.  He toke out the brode targe,
          And sone he lete hym se ;
      Robyn coud his courteysy,
          And set hym on his kne.


386.  'I love no man in all the worlde
          So well as I do my kynge ;
      Welcome is my lordës seale ;
          And, monke, for thy tydynge,


387.  'Syr abbot, for thy tydynges,
          To day thou shalt dyne with me,
      For the love of my kynge,
          Under my trystell-tre.'


388.  Forth he lad our comly kynge,
          Full fayre by the honde ;
      Many a dere there was slayne,
          And full fast dyghtande.


389.  Robyn toke a full grete horne,
          And loude he gan blowe ;
      Seven score of wyght yonge men
          Came redy on a rowe.


390.  All they kneled on theyr kne,
          Full fayre before Robyn :
      The kynge sayd hym selfe untyll,
          And swore by Saynt Austyn,

391.    'Here is a wonder semely sight;
            Me thynketh, by Goddës pyne,
        His men are more at his byddynge
            Then my men be at myn.'


392.    Full hastely was theyr dyner idyght,
            And therto gan they gone;
        They served our kynge with all theyr myght,
            Both Robyn and Lytell Johan.


393.    Anone before our kynge was set
            The fattë venyson,
        The good whyte brede, the good rede wyne,
            And therto the fyne ale and browne.


394.    'Make good chere,' said Robyn,
            'Abbot, for charytë;
        And for this ylkë tydynge,
            Blyssed mote thou be.


395.    'Now shalte thou se what lyfe we lede,
            Or thou hens wende;
        Than thou may enfourme our kynge,
            Whan ye togyder lende.'


396.    Up they sterte all in hast,
            Theyr bowes were smartly bent;
        Our kynge was never so sore agast,
            He wende to have be shente.


397.    Two yerdes there were up set,
            Thereto gan they gange;
        By fyfty pase, our kynge sayd,
            The merkës were to longe.

398.   On every syde a rose-garlonde,
       They shot under the lyne :
   'Who so fayleth of the rose-garlonde,' sayd Robyn,
       'His takyll he shall tyne,

399.   'And yelde it to his mayster,
       Be it never so fyne ;
   For no man wyll I spare,
       So drynke I ale or wyne ;

400.   'And bere a buffet on his hede,
       I-wys ryght all bare : '
   And all that fell in Robyns lote,
       He smote them wonder sare.

401.   Twyse Robyn shot aboute,
       And ever he cleved the wande,
   And so dyde good Gylberte
       With the whytë hande.

402.   Lytell Johan and good Scathelocke,
       For nothynge wolde they spare ;
   When they fayled of the garlonde,
       Robyn smote them full sore.

403.   At the last shot that Robyn shot,
       For all his frendës fare,
   Yet he fayled of the garlonde
       Thre fyngers and mare.

404.   Than bespake good Gylberte,
       And thus he gan say ;
   'Mayster,' he sayd, 'your takyll is lost,
       Stande forth and take your pay.'

405. 'If it be so,' sayd Robyn,
      'That may no better be,
     Syr abbot, I delyver the myn arowe,
      I pray the, syr, serve thou me.'

406. 'It falleth not for myn ordre,' sayd our kynge,
      'Robyn, by thy leve,
     For to smyte no good yeman,
      For doute I sholde hym greve.'

407. 'Smyte on boldely,' sayd Robyn,
      'I give the largë leve:'
     Anone our kynge, with that worde,
      He folde up his sleve,

408. And sych a buffet he gave Robyn,
      To grounde he yede full nere:
     'I make myn avowe to God,' sayd Robyn,
      'Thou arte a stalworthe frere.

409. 'There is pith in thyn arme,' sayd Robyn,
      'I trowe thou canst well shete;'
     Thus our kynge and Robyn Hode
      Togeder gan they mete.

410. Robyn behelde our comly kynge
      Wystly in the face,
     So dyde Syr Rycharde at the Le,
      And kneled downe in that place.

411. And so dyde all the wylde outlawes,
      Whan they se them knele:
     'My lorde the kynge of Englonde,
      Now I knowe you well.'

412.     ' Mercy then, Robyn,' sayd our kynge,
      ' Under your trystyll-tre,
   Of thy goodnesse and thy grace,
      For my men and me ! '

413.     ' Yes, for God,' sayd Robyn,
      ' And also God me save,
   I aske mercy, my lorde the kynge,
      And for my men I crave.'

414.     ' Yes, for God,' than sayd our kynge,
      ' And therto sent I me,
   With that thou leve the grene-wode,
      And all thy company ;

415.     ' And come home, syr, to my courte,
      And there dwell with me.'
   ' I make myn avowe to God,' sayd Robyn,
      ' And ryght so shall it be.

416.     ' I wyll come to your courte,
      Your servyse for to se,
   And brynge with me of my men
      Seven score and thre.

417.     ' But me lyke well your servyse,
      I wyll come agayne full soone,
   And shote at the donnë dere,
      As I am wonte to done.'

## The Eighth Fytte.

418. 'Haste thou ony grene cloth,' sayd our kynge,
'That thou wylte sell nowe to me?'
'Ye, for God,' sayd Robyn,
'Thyrty yerdes and thre.'

419. 'Robyn,' sayd our kynge,
'Now pray I the,
Sell me some of that cloth,
To me and my meynë.'

420. 'Yes, for God,' then sayd Robyn,
'Or elles I were a fole;
Another day ye wyll me clothe,
I trowe, ayenst the Yole.'

421. The kynge kest of his cole then,
A grene garment he dyde on,
And every knyght also, iwys,
Another had full sone.

422. Whan they were clothed in Lyncolne grene,
They keste away theyr graye;
'Now we shall to Notyngham,'
All thus our kynge gan say.

423. They bente theyr bowes and forth they went,
Shotynge all in-fere,
Towarde the towne of Notyngham,
Outlawes as they were.

424. Our kynge and Robyn rode togyder,
For soth as I you say,
And they shote plucke-buffet,
As they went by the way.

425.   And many a buffet our kynge wan
       Of Robyn Hode that day,
    And nothynge spared good Robyn
       Our kynge when he did pay.

426.   'So God me helpë,' sayd our kynge,
       'Thy game is nought to lere;
    I sholde not get a shote of the,
       Though I shote all this yere.'

427.   All the people of Notyngham
       They stode and behelde;
    They sawe nothynge but mantels of grene
       That covered all the felde.

428.   Than every man to other gan say,
       'I drede our kynge be slone;
    Come Robyn Hode to the towne, i-wys
       On lyve he lefte never one.'

429.   Full hastely they began to fle,
       Both yemen and knaves,
    And olde wyves that myght evyll goo,
       They hypped on theyr staves.

430.   The kynge loughe full fast,
       And commaunded theym agayne;
    When they se our comly kynge,
       I-wys they were full fayne.

431.   They ete and dranke, and made them glad,
       And sange with notës hye;
    Than bespake our comly kynge
       To Syr Richarde at the Lee.

432.    He gave hym there his londe agayne,
            A good man he bad hym be;
        Robyn thanked our comly kynge,
            And set hym on his kne.


433.    Had Robyn dwelled in the kynges courte
            But twelve monethes and thre,
        That he had spent an hondred pounde,
            And all his mennes fe.


434.    In every place where Robyn came
            Ever more he layde downe,
        Both for knyghtës and for squyres,
            To gete hym grete renowne.


435.    By than the yere was all agone
            He had no man but twayne,
        Lytell Johan and good Scathelocke,
            With hym all for to gone.


436.    Robyn sawe yonge men shote
            Full faire upon a day;
        'Alas!' than sayd good Robyn,
            'My welthe is went away.


437.    'Somtyme I was an archere good,
            A styffe and eke a stronge;
        I was compted the best archere
            That was in mery Englonde.


438.    'Alas!' then sayd good Robyn,
            'Alas and well a woo!
        Yf I dwele lenger with the kynge,
            Sorowe wyll me sloo.'

439.    Forth than went Robyn Hode
      Tyll he came to our kynge :
  'My lorde the kynge of Englonde,
      Graunte me myn askynge.

440.   'I made a chapell in Bernysdale,
      That semely is to se,
  It is of Mary Magdaleyne,
      And thereto wolde I be.

441.   'I myght never in this seven nyght
      No tyme to slepe ne wynke,
  Nother all these seven dayes
      Nother ete ne drynke.

442.   'Me longeth sore to Bernysdale,
      I may not be therfro ;
  Barefote and wolwarde I have hyght
      Thyder for to go.'

443.   'Yf it be so,' than sayd our kynge,
      'It may no better be ;
  Seven nyght I gyve the leve,
      No lengre, to dwell fro me.'

444.   'Gramercy, lorde,' then sayd Robyn,
      And set hym on his kne ;
  He toke his leve full courteysly,
      To grene wode then went he.

445.   Whan he came to grene wode,
      In a mery mornynge,
  There he herde the notës small
      Of byrdës mery syngynge.

446.    'It is ferre gone,' sayd Robyn,
             'That I was last here ;
        Me lyste a lytell for to shote
             At the donnë dere.'


447.    Robyn slewe a full grete harte ;
             His horne than gan he blow,
        That all the outlawes of that forest
             That horne coud they knowe,


448.    And gadred them togyder,
             In a lytell throwe.
        Seven score of wyght yonge men
             Came redy on a rowe,


449.    And fayre dyde of theyr hodes,
             And set them on theyr kne :
        'Welcome,' they sayd, 'our mayster,
             Under this grene-wode tre.'


450.    Robyn dwelled in grene wode
             Twenty yere and two ;
        For all drede of Edwarde our kynge,
             Agayne wolde he not goo.


451.    Yet he was begyled, i-wys,
             Through a wycked woman,
        The pryoresse of Kyrkësly,
             That nye was of hys kynne :


452.    For the love of a knyght,
             Syr Roger of Donkesly,
        That was her ownë speciall ;
             Full evyll mote they the !

453.    They toke togyder theyr counsell
      Robyn Hode for to sle,
   And how they myght best do that dede,
      His banis for to be.


454.    Than bespake good Robyn,
      In place where as he stode,
   'To morow I muste to Kyrke[s]ly,
      Craftely to be leten blode.'


455.    Syr Roger of Donkestere,
      By the pryoresse he lay,
   And there they betrayed good Robyn Hode,
      Through theyr falsë playe.


456.    Cryst have mercy on his soule,
      That dyed on the rode !
   For he was a good outlawe,
      And dyde pore men moch god.

## ROBIN HOOD AND GUY OF GISBORNE.

1.    When shawes beene sheene, and shradds full fayre,
          And leeves both large and longe,
       Itt is merry, walking in the fayre fforrest,
          To heare the small birds songe.

2.    The woodweele sang, and wold not cease,
          Amongst the leaves a lyne ;
       And it is by two wight yeomen,
          By deare God, that I meane.

          .    .    .    .    .    .    .    .

3.    'Me thought they did mee beate and binde,
          And tooke my bow mee froe ;
       If I bee Robin a-live in this lande,
          I 'le be wrocken on both them towe.'

4.    'Sweavens are swift, master,' quoth John,
          'As the wind that blowes ore a hill ;
       Ffor if itt be never soe lowde this night,
          To-morrow it may be still.'

5.    'Buske yee, bowne yee, my merry men all,
          Ffor John shall goe with mee ;
       For I 'le goe seeke yond wight yeomen
          In greenwood where thé bee.'

6.    Thé cast on their gowne of greene,
          A shooting gone are they,
       Until they came to the merry greenwood,
          Where they had gladdest bee ;
       There were thé ware of a wight yeoman,
          His body leaned to a tree.

7.    A sword and a dagger he wore by his side,
         Had beene many a man's bane,
      And he was cladd in his capull-hyde,
         Topp, and tayle, and mayne.


8.    'Stand you still, master,' quoth Litle John,
         'Under this trusty tree,
      And I will goe to yond wight yeoman,
         To know his meaning trulye.'


9.    'A, John, by me thou setts noe store,
         And that's a ffarley thinge ;
      How offt send I my men beffore,
         And tarry my-selfe behinde ?


10.   'It is noe cunning a knave to ken,
         And a man but heare him speake ;
      And itt were not for bursting of my bowe,
         John, I wold thy head breake.'


11.   But often words they breeden bale,
         That parted Robin and John ;
      John is gone to Barnesdale,
         The gates he knowes eche one.


12.   And when hee came to Barnesdale,
         Great heavinesse there hee hadd ;
      He ffound two of his fellowes
         Were slaine both in a slade,


13.   And Scarlett a ffoote flyinge was,
         Over stockes and stone,
      For the sheriffe with seven score men
         Fast after him is gone.

14. 'Yett one shoote I'le shoote,' sayes Litle John,
    'With Crist his might and mayne ;
    I'le make yond fellow that flyes soe fast
        To be both glad and ffaine.'

15. John bent up a good veiwe bow,
        And ffetteled him to shoote ;
    The bow was made of a tender boughe,
        And fell downe to his foote.

16. 'Woe worth thee, wicked wood,' sayd Litle John,
        'That ere thou grew on a tree !
    Ffor this day thou art my bale,
        My boote when thou shold bee !'

17. This shoote it was but looselye shott,
        The arrowe flew in vaine,
    And it mett one of the sheriffe's men ;
        Good William a Trent was slaine.

18. It had beene better for William a Trent
        To hange upon a gallowe
    Then for to lye in the greenwoode,
        There slaine with an arrowe.

19. And it is sayd, when men be mett,
        Six can doe more than three :
    And they have tane Litle John,
        And bound him ffast to a tree.

20. 'Thou shalt be drawen by dale and downe,'
            quoth the sheriffe,
        'And hanged hye on a hill :'
    'But thou may ffayle,' quoth Litle John,
        'If itt be Christ's owne will.'

21.   Let us leave talking of Litle John,
          For hee is bound fast to a tree,
      And talke of Guy and Robin Hood
          In the green woode where they bee.

22.   How these two yeomen together they mett,
          Under the leaves of lyne,
      To see what marchandise they made
          Even at that same time.

23.   'Good morrow, good fellow,' quoth Sir Guy;
          'Good morrow, good ffellow,' quoth hee;
      'Methinkes by this bow thou beares in thy hand,
          A good archer thou seems to bee.

24.   'I am wilfull of my way,' quoth Sir Guye,
          'And of my morning tyde :'
      'I'le lead thee through the wood,' quoth Robin,
          'Good ffellow, I'le be thy guide.'

25.   'I seeke an outlaw,' quoth Sir Guye,
          'Men call him Robin Hood;
      I had rather meet with him upon a day
          Then forty pound of golde.'

26.   'If you tow mett, itt wold be seene whether were
              better
          Afore yee did part awaye;
      Let us some other pastime find,
          Good ffellow, I thee pray.

27.   'Let us some other masteryes make,
          And wee will walke in the woods even;
      Wee may chance meet with Robin Hoode
          Att some unsett steven.'

28.  They cutt them downe the summer shroggs
         Which grew both under a bryar,
     And sett them three score rood in twinn,
         To shoote the prickes full neare.


29.  'Leade on, good ffellow,' sayd Sir Guye,
         'Lead on, I doe bidd thee :'
     'Nay, by my faith,' quoth Robin Hood,
         'The leader thou shalt bee.'


30.  The first good shoot that Robin ledd,
         Did not shoote an inch the pricke ffroe ;
     Guy was an archer good enoughe,
         But he cold neere shoote soe.


31.  The second shoote Sir Guy shott,
         He shott within the garlande ;
     But Robin Hoode shott it better than hee,
         For he clove the good pricke-wande.


32.  'God's blessing on thy heart !' sayes Guye,
         'Goode ffellow, thy shooting is goode ;
     For an thy hart be as good as thy hands,
         Thou were better than Robin Hood.


33.  'Tell me thy name, good ffellow,' quoth Guy,
         'Under the leaves of lyne :'
     'Nay, by my faith,' quoth good Robin,
         'Till thou have told me thine.'


34.  'I dwell by dale and downe,' quoth Guye,
         'And I have done many a curst turne ;
     And he that calles me by my right name,
         Calles me Guye of good Gysborne.'

35. 'My dwelling is in the wood,' sayes Robin ;
     'By thee I set right nought ;
    My name is Robin Hood of Barnesdale,
     A ffellow thou has long sought.'


36. He that had neither beene a kithe nor kin
     Might have seene a full fayre sight,
    To see how together these yeomen went,
     With blades both browne and bright.


37. To have seene how these yeomen together fought
     Two howers of a summer's day ;
    Itt was neither Guy nor Robin Hood
     That ffettled them to flye away.


38. Robin was reacheles on a roote,
     And stumbled at that tyde,
    And Guy was quicke and nimble with-all,
     And hitt him ore the left side.


39. 'Ah, deere Lady !' sayd Robin Hoode,
     'Thou art both mother and may !
    I thinke it was never man's destinye
     To dye before his day.'


40. Robin thought on Our Lady deere,
     And soone leapt up againe,
    And thus he came with an awkwarde stroke ;
     Good Sir Guy hee has slayne.


41. He tooke Sir Guy's head by the hayre,
     And sticked itt on his bowe's end :
    'Thou hast beene traytor all thy liffe,
     Which thing must have an ende.'

42.   Robin pulled forth an Irish kniffe,
         And nicked Sir Guy in the fface,
      That hee was never on a woman borne
         Cold tell who Sir Guye was.


43.   Saies, Lye there, lye there, good Sir Guye,
         And with me be not wrothe ;
      If thou have had the worse stroakes at my hand,
         Thou shalt have the better cloathe.


44.   Robin did off his gowne of greene,
         Sir Guye hee did it throwe ;
      And hee put on that capull-hyde
         That cladd him topp to toe.


45.   ' The bowe, the arrowes, and litle horne,
         And with me now I 'le beare ;
      Ffor now I will goe to Barnesdale,
         To see how my men doe ffare.'


46.   Robin sett Guye's horne to his mouth,
         A lowd blast in it he did blow ;
      That beheard the sheriffe of Nottingham,
         As he leaned under a lowe.


47.   ' Hearken ! hearken !' sayd the sheriffe,
         ' I heard noe tydings but good ;
      For yonder I heare Sir Guye's horne blowe,
         For he hath slaine Robin Hoode.


48.   ' For yonder I heare Sir Guye's horne blow,
         Itt blowes soe well in tyde,
      For yonder comes that wighty yeoman,
         Cladd in his capull-hyde.

49. 'Come hither, thou good Sir Guy,
  Aske of mee what thou wilt have : '
 'I 'le none of thy gold,' sayes Robin Hood,
  'Nor I 'le none of itt have.


50. 'But now I have slaine the master,' he sayd,
  'Let me goe strike the knave ;
 This is all the reward I aske,
  Nor noe other will I have.'


51. 'Thou art a madman,' said the shiriffe,
  'Thou sholdest have had a knight's ffee ;
 Seeing thy asking hath beene soe badd,
  Well granted it shall be.'


52. But Litle John heard his master speake,
  Well he knew that was his steven ;
 'Now shall I be loset,' quoth Litle John,
  'With Christ's might in heaven.'


53. But Robin hee hyed him towards Litle **John,**
  Hee thought hee wold loose him belive ;
 The sheriffe and all his companye
  Fast after him did drive.


54. 'Stand abacke ! stand abacke !' sayd Robin ;
  'Why draw you mee soe neere ?
 Itt was never the use in our countrye
  One's shrift another shold heere.'


55. But Robin pulled forth an Irysh kniffe,
  And losed John hand and ffoote,
 And gave him Sir Guye's bow in his hand.
  And bade it be his boote.

56.   But John tooke Guye's bow in his hand
    (His arrowes were rawstye by the roote);
The sherriffe saw Litle John draw a bow
    And ffettle him to shoote.


57.   Towards his house in Nottingham
    He ffled full fast away,
And soe did all his companye,
    Not one behind did stay.


58.   But he cold neither soe fast goe,
    Nor away soe fast runn,
But Litle John, with an arrow broade,
    Did cleave his heart in twinn.

## ROBIN HOOD AND THE MONK.

1. In somer, when the shawes be sheyne,
   And leves be large and long,
   Hit is full mery in feyre foreste
   To here the foulys song:

2. To se the dere draw to the dale,
   And leve the hilles hee,
   And shadow hem in the levës grene,
   Under the grene-wode tre.

3. Hit befel on Whitsontide,
   Erly in a May mornyng,
   The son up feyre can shyne,
   And the briddis mery can syng.

4. 'This is a mery mornyng,' seid Litull John,
   'Be hym that dyed on tre;
   A more mery man then I am one
   Lyves not in Christiantë.

5. 'Pluk up thi hert, my dere mayster,'
   Litull John can sey,
   And thynk hit is a full fayre tyme
   In a mornyng of May.'

6. 'Ye, on thyng greves me,' seid Robyn,
   'And does my hert mych woo;
   That I may not no solem day
   To mas nor matyns goo.

7.  'Hit is a fourtnet and more,' seid he,
        'Syn I my savyour see;
    To day wil I to Notyngham,
        With the myght of mylde Marye.'

8.  Than spake Moche, the mylner sun,
        Ever more wel hym betyde!
    'Take twelve of thi wyght yemen,
        Well weppynd, be thi side.
    Such on wolde thi selfe slon,
        That twelve dar not abyde.'

9.  'Of all my mery men,' seid Robyn,
        'Be my feith I wil non have,
    But Litull John shall beyre my bow,
        Til that me list to drawe.'

10. 'Thou shall beyre thin own,' seid Litull Jon,
        'Maister, and I wyl beyre myne,
    And we well shete a peny,' seid Litull Jon,
        'Under the grene-wode lyne.'

11. 'I wil not shete a peny,' seyd Robyn Hode,
        'In feith, Litull John, with the,
    But ever for on as thou shetis,' seide Robyn,
        'In feith I holde the thre.'

12. Thus shet thei forth, these yemen too,
        Bothe at buske and brome,
    Til Litull John wan of his maister
        Five shillings to hose and shone.

13. A ferly strife fel them betwene,
        As they went bi the wey;
    Litull John seid he had won five shillings,
        And Robyn Hode seid schortly nay.

14.  With that Robyn Hode lyed Litul Jon,
         And smote hym with his hande;
     Litul Jon waxed wroth therwith,
         And pulled out his bright bronde.


15.  'Were thou not my maister,' seid Litull John,
         'Thou shuldis by hit ful sore;
     Get the a man wher thou wilt,
         For thou getis me no more.'


16.  Then Robyn goes to Notyngham,
         Hym selfe mornyng allone,
     And Litull John to mery Scherwode,
         The pathes he knew ilkone.


17.  Whan Robyn came to Notyngham,
         Sertenly withouten layn,
     He prayed to God and myld Mary
         To bryng hym out save agayn.


18.  He gos in to Seynt Mary chirch,
         And kneled down before the rode;
     Alle that ever were the church within
         Beheld wel Robyn Hode.


19.  Beside hym stod a gret-hedid munke,
         I pray to God woo he be!
     Fful sone he knew gode Robyn,
         As sone as he hym se.


20.  Out at the durre he ran,
         Fful sone and anon;
     Alle the gatis of Notyngham
         He made to be sparred everychon.

21.   'Rise up,' he seid, 'thou prowde schereff,
          Buske the and make the bowne ;
      I have spyed the kynggis felon,
          Ffor sothe he is in this town.


22.   'I have spyed the false felon,
          As he stondis at his masse ;
      Hit is long of the,' seide the munke,
          'And ever he fro us passe.


23.   'This traytur name is Robyn Hode,
          Under the grene-wode lynde ;
      He robbyt me onys of a hundred pound,
          Hit shalle never out of my mynde.'


24.   Up then rose this prowde shereff,
          And radly made hym yare ;
      Many was the moder son
          To the kyrk with hym can fare.


25.   In at the durres thei throly thrast,
          With staves ful gode wone ;
      'Alas, alas !' seid Robyn Hode,
          'Now mysse I Litull John.'


26.   But Robyn toke out a too-hond sworde,
          That hangit down be his kne ;
      Ther as the schereff and his men stode thyckust,
          Thedurwarde wolde he.


27.   Thryes thorowout them he ran then
          For sothe as I yow sey,
      And woundyt mony a moder son,
          And twelve he slew that day.

28.   His sworde upon the schireff hed
          Sertanly he brake in too ;
      'The smyth that the made,' seid Robyn,
          'I pray God wyrke hym woo.


29.   'Ffor now am I weppynlesse,' seid Robyn,
          ' Alasse ! agayn my wylle ;
      But if I may fle these traytors fro,
          I wot thei wil me kyll.'


30.   Robyn in to the churchë ran,
          Throout hem everilkon,


      *    *    *    *    *    *    *    *


31.   Sum fel in swonyng as thei were dede,
          And lay stil as any stone ;
      Non of theym were in her mynde
          But only Litull Jon.


32.   'Let be your rule,' seid Litull Jon,
          'Ffor his luf that dyed on tre,
      Ye that shulde be dughty men ;
          Het is gret shame to se.


33.   'Oure maister has bene hard bystode
          And yet scapyd away ;
      Pluk up your hertis, and leve this mone,
          And harkyn what I shal say.


34.   'He has servyd Oure Lady many a day,
          And yet wil, securly ;
      Therfor I trust in hir specialy
          No wyckud deth shal he dye.

35.    ' Therfor be glad,' seid Litul John,
           ' And let this mournyng be ;
       And I shal be the munkis gyde,
           With the myght of mylde Mary.


36.    .    .    .    .    .    .      .
           ' We will go but we too ;
       And I mete hym,' seid Litul John,

           .    .    .    .    .    .


37.    ' Loke that ye kepe wel owre tristil-tre,
           Under the levys smale,
       And spare non of this venyson,
           That gose in thys vale.'


38.    Fforthe then went these yemen too,
           Litul John and Moche on fere,
       And lokid on Moch emys hows,
           The hye way lay full nere.


39.    Litul John stode at a wyndow in the mornyng,
           And lokid forth at a stage ;
       He was war wher the munke came ridyng,
           And with hym a litul page.


40.    ' Be my feith,' seid Litul John to Moch,
           ' I can the tel tithyngus gode ;
       I se wher the munke cumys rydyng,
           I know hym be his wyde hode.'


41.    They went in to the way, these yemen bothe,
           As curtes men and hende ;
       Thei spyrred tithyngus at the munke,
           As they hade bene his frende.

42. 'Ffro whens come ye?' seid Litull Jon,
    'Tel us tithyngus, I yow pray,
Off a false owtlay, callid Robyn Hode,
    Was takyn yisterday.

43. 'He robbyt me and my felowes bothe
    Of twenti marke in serten;
If that false owtlay be takyn,
    Ffor sothe we wolde be fayn.'

44. 'So did he me,' seid the munke,
    'Of a hundred pound and more;
I layde furst hande hym apon,
    Ye may thonke me therfore.'

45. 'I pray God thanke you,' seid Litull John,
    'And we wil when we may;
We wil go with you, with your leve,
    And bryng yow on your way.

46. 'Ffor Robyn Hode hase many a wilde felow,
    I tell you in certen;
If thei wist ye rode this way,
    In feith ye shulde be slayn.'

47. As thei went talking be the way,
    The munke and Litull John,
John toke the munkis horse be the hede,
    Fful sone and anon.

48. Johne toke the munkis horse be the hed,
    Ffor sothe as I yow say;
So did Much the litull page,
    Ffor he shulde not scape away.

49.    Be the golett of the hode
            John pulled the munke down;
       John was nothyng of hym agast,
            He lete hym falle on his crown.


50.    Litull John was sore agrevyd,
            And drew owt his swerde in hye;
       This munke saw he shulde be ded,
            Lowd mercy can he crye.


51.    'He was my maister,' seid Litull John,
            'That thou hase browght in bale;
       Shalle thou never cum at our kyng,
            Ffor to telle hym tale.'


52.    John smote of the munkis hed,
            No longer wolde he dwell;
       So did Moch the litull page,
            Ffor ferd lest he wolde tell.


53.    Ther thei beryed hem bothe,
            In nouther mosse nor lyng,
       And Litull John and Much infere
            Bare the letturs to oure kyng.


54.    .      .      .      .      .      .      .
            He knelid down upon his kne:
       'God yow save, my lege lorde,
            Jhesus yow save and se!


55.    'God yow save, my lege kyng!'
            To speke John was full bolde;
       He gaf hym the letturs in his hond,
            The kyng did hit unfold.

56.   The kyng red the letturs anon,
         And seid, 'So mot I the,
     Ther was never yoman in mery Inglond
         I longut so sore to se.

57.   'Wher is the munke that these shuld have
             brought?'
         Oure kyng can say:
     'Be my trouth,' seid Litull John,
         'He dyed after the way.'

58.   The kyng gaf Moch and Litul Jon
         Twenti pound in sertan,
     And made theim yemen of the crown,
         And bade theim go agayn.

59.   He gaf John the seel in hand,
         The sheref for to bere,
     To bryng Robyn hym to,
         And no man do hym dere.

60.   John toke his leve at oure kyng,
         The sothe as I yow say;
     The next way to Notyngham
         To take, he yede the way.

61.   Whan John came to Notyngham
         The gatis were sparred ychon;
     John callid up the porter,
         He answerid sone anon.

62.   'What is the cause,' seid Litul Jon,
         'Thou sparris the gates so fast?'
     'Because of Robyn Hode,' seid the porter,
         'In depe prison is cast.

63. 'John and Moch and Wyll Scathlok,
        Ffor sothe as I yow say,
    Thei slew oure men upon our wallis,
        And sawten us every day.'


64. Litull John spyrred after the schereff,
        And sone he hym fonde ;
    He oppyned the kyngus prive seell,
        And gaf hym in his honde.


65. Whan the scheref saw the kyngus seell,
        He did of his hode anon :
    'Wher is the munke that bare the letturs?'
        He seid to Litull John.


66. 'He is so fayn of hym,' seid Litul John,
        'Ffor sothe as I yow say,
    He has made hym abot of Westmynster,
        A lorde of that abbay.'


67. The scheref made John gode chere,
        And gaf hym wyne of the best;
    At nyght thei went to her bedde,
        And every man to his rest.


68. When the scheref was on slepe,
        Dronken of wyne and ale,
    Litul John and Moch for sothe
        Toke the way unto the jale.


69. Litul John callid up the jayler,
        And bade hym rise anon ;
    He seyd Robyn Hode had brokyn prison,
        And out of hit was gon.

70.　The porter rose anon sertan,
　　　As sone as he herd John calle;
　　Litul John was redy with a swerd,
　　　And bare hym to the walle.

71.　'Now wil I be porter,' seid Litul John,
　　　'And take the keyes in honde':
　　He toke the way to Robyn Hode,
　　　And sone he hym unbonde.

72.　He gaf hym a gode swerd in his hond,
　　　His hed therwith for to kepe,
　　And ther as the walle was lowyst
　　　Anon down can thei lepe.

73.　Be that the cok began to crow,
　　　The day began to spryng;
　　The scheref fond the jaylier ded,
　　　The comyn bell made he ryng.

74.　He made a crye thoroout al the town,
　　　Wheder he be yoman or knave,
　　That cowthe bryng hym Robyn Hode,
　　　His warison he shuld have.

75.　'Ffor I dar never,' said the scheref,
　　　'Cum before oure kyng;
　　Ffor if I do, I wot serten
　　　Ffor sothe he wil me heng.'

76.　The scheref made to seke Notyngham,
　　　Bothe be strete and stye,
　　And Robyn was in mery Scherwode,
　　　As light as lef on lynde.

77.   Then bespake gode Litull John,
          To Robyn Hode can he say,
      'I have done the a gode turn for an evyll,
          Quyte the whan thou may.

78.   'I have done the a gode turne,' seid Litull John,
          'Ffor sothe as I yow say ;
      I have brought the under grene-wode lyne ;
          Ffare wel, and have gode day.'

79.   'Nay, be my trouth,' seid Robyn Hode,
          'So shall hit never be ;
      I make the maister,' seid Robyn Hode,
          'Off alle my men and me.'

80.   'Nay, be my trouth,' seid Litull John,
          'So shalle hit never be ;
      But lat me be a felow,' seid Litull John,
          'No noder kepe I be.'

81.   Thus John gate Robyn Hod out of prison,
          Sertan withoutyn layn ;
      Whan his men saw hym hol and sounde,
          Ffor sothe they were full fayne.

82.   They filled in wyne, and made hem glad,
          Under the levys smale,
      And gete pastes of venyson,
          That gode was with ale.

83.   Than worde came to oure kyng
          How Robyn Hode was gon,
      And how the scheref of Notyngham
          Durst never loke hym upon.

84.    Then bespake oure cumly kyng,
         In an angur hye:
    'Litull John hase begyled the schereff,
         In faith so hase he me.


85.    'Litul John has begyled us bothe,
         And that full wel I se;
    Or ellis the schereff of Notyngham
         Hye hongut shulde he be.


86.    'I made hem yemen of the crowne,
         And gaf hem fee with my hond;
    I gaf hem grith,' seid oure kyng,
         'Thorowout all mery Inglond.


87.    'I gaf theym grith,' then seid oure kyng;
         'I say, so mot I the,
    Ffor sothe soch a yeman as he is on
         In all Inglond ar not thre.


88.    'He is trew to his maister,' seid our kyng;
         'I sey, be swete Seynt John,
    He lovys better Robyn Hode
         Then he dose us ychon.


89.    'Robyn Hode is ever bond to hym,
         Bothe in strete and stalle;
    Speke no more of this mater,' seid oure kyng,
         'But John has begyled us alle.'


90.    Thus endys the talkyng of the munke
         And Robyn Hode i-wysse;
    God, that is ever a crowned kyng,
         Bryng us all to his blisse!

## ROBIN HOOD'S DEATH.

1.  'I WILL never eate nor drinke,' Robin Hood said,
        ' Nor meate will doo me noe good,
    Till I have beene att merry Churchlees,
        My vaines for to let blood.'

2.  'That I reade not,' said Will Scarllett,
        ' Master, by the assente of me,
    Without halfe a hundred of your best bowmen
        You take to goe with yee.

3.  ' For there a good yeoman doth abide
        Will be sure to quarrell with thee,
    And if thou have need of us, master,
        In faith we will not flee.'

4.  ' And thou be feard, thou William Scarlett,
        Att home I read thee bee ':
    ' And you be wrothe, my deare master,
        You shall never heare more of mee.'

5.  ' For there shall noe man with mee goe,
        Nor man with mee ryde,
    And Litle John shall be my man,
        And beare my benbow by my side.'

6.  ' You'st beare your bowe, master, your selfe,
        And shoote for a peny with mee ':
    ' To that I doe assent,' Robin Hood sayd,
        ' And soe, John, lett it bee.'

7.  They two bolde children shotten together,
        All day theire selfe in ranke,
    Untill they came to blacke water,
        And over it laid a planke.

8.  Upon it there kneeled an old woman,
        Was banning Robin Hoode;
    'Why dost thou bann Robin Hood?' said Robin,

        .   .   .   .   .   .   .   .   .

        *   *   *   *   *   *   *   *

9.  .   .   .   .   .   .   .   .   .
        'To give to Robin Hoode;
    Wee weepen for his deare body,
        That this day must be lett bloode.'

10. 'The dame prior is my aunt's daughter,
        And nie unto my kinne;
    I know shee wold me noe harme this day,
        For all the world to winne.'

11. Forth then shotten these children two,
        And they did never lin,
    Untill they came to merry Churchlees,
        To merry Churchlees with-in.

12. And when they came to merry Churchlees,
        They knoced upon a pin;
    Upp then rose dame prioresse,
        And lett good Robin in.

13. Then Robin gave to dame prioresse
        Twenty pound in gold,
    And bad her spend while that wold last,
        And shee shold have more when shee wold.

14.   And downe then came dame prioresse,
          Downe she came in that ilke,
      With a pair off blood-irons in her hands,
          Were wrapped all in silke.

15.   ' Sett a chaffing-dish to the fyer,' said dame
              prioresse,
          ' And stripp thou up thy sleeve ':
      I hold him but an unwise man
        · That will noe warning leeve.

16.   Shee laid the blood-irons to Robin Hood's vaine,
          Alacke, the more pitye !
      And pearct the vaine, and let out the bloode,
          That full red was to see.

17.   And first it bled, the thicke, thicke bloode,
          And afterwards the thinne,
      And well then wist good Robin Hoode
          Treason there was within.

18.   ' What cheere my master ? ' said Litle John ;
          ' In faith, John, litle goode ';

      .       .       .       .       .       .       .

          .       .       .       .       .       .

      *     *     *     *     *     *     *     *

19.   ' I have upon a gowne of greene,
          Is cut short by my knee,
      And in my hand a bright browne brand
          That will well bite of the.'

20.   But forth then of a shot-windowe
          Good Robin Hood he could glide ;
      Red Roger, with a grounden glave,
          Thrust him through the milk-white side.

21.  But Robin was light and nimble of foote,
      And thought to abate his pride,
  Ffor betwixt his head and his shoulders
      He made a wound full wide.

22.  Says, ' Ly there, ly there, Red Roger,
      The doggs they must thee eate ;
  For I may have my houzle,' he said,
      ' For I may both goe and speake.

23.  ' Now give me mood,' Robin said to Litle John,
      ' Give me mood with thy hand ;
  I trust to God in heaven soe hye
      My houzle will me bestand.'

24.  ' Now give me leave, give me leave, master,' he
      said,
      ' For Christ's love give leave to me,
  To set a fier within this hall,
      And to burn up all Churchlee.'

25.  ' That I reade not,' said Robin Hoode then,
      ' Litle John, for it may not be ;
  If I shold doe any widow hurt, at my latter end,
      God,' he said ' wold blame me ;

26.  ' But take me upon thy backe, Litle John,
      And beare me to yonder streete,
  And there make me a full fayre grave,
      Of gravell and of greete.

27.  ' And sett my bright sword at my head,
      Mine arrowes at my feete,
  And lay my vew-bow by my side,
      My met-yard wi . . . .

*1. Difference in subj. matter*

*2. (more) national interest*

*3. Interest in names of characters —*

*4. formulaic epithets*

*5. More intimate knowledge of characters*

*6. scenes definitely located*

## THE BATTLE OF OTTERBURN.

1. Yt felle abowght the Lamasse tyde,
   Whan husbondes wynnes ther haye,
   The dowghtye Dowglasse bowynd hym to ryde,
   In Ynglond to take a praye.

*7. These are minstrel ballads*

2. The yerlle of Fyffe, wythowghten stryffe,
   He bowynd hym over Sulway;
   The grete wolde ever to-gether ryde;
   That raysse they may rewe for aye.

3. Over Hoppertope hyll they cam in,
   And so down by Rodclyffe crage;
   Upon Grene Lynton they lyghted dowyn,
   Styrande many a stage.

4. And boldely brente Northomberlond,
   And haryed many a towyn;
   They dyd owr Ynglyssh men grete wrange,
   To battell that were not bowyn.

5. Than spake a berne upon the bent,
   Of comforte that was not colde,
   And sayd, 'We have brente Northomberlond,
   We have all welth in holde.

6. 'Now we have haryed all Bamborowe schyre,
   All the welth in the world have wee;
   I rede we ryde to Newe Castell,
   So styll and stalworthlye.'

*Differences between these and all other ballads*

7. Upon the morowe, when it was day,
   The standerds schone fulle bryght;
   To the Newe Castell the toke the waye,
   And thether they cam fulle ryght.

8. Syr Henry Perssy laye at the New Castell,
   I tell yow wythowtten drede;
   He had byn a march-man all hys dayes,
   And kepte Barwyke upon Twede.

9. To the Newe Castell when they cam,
   The Skottes they cryde on hyght,
   'Syr Hary Perssy, and thow byste within,
   Com to the fylde, and fyght.

10. 'For we have brente Northomberlonde,
    Thy erytage good and ryght,
    And syne my logeyng I have take,
    Wyth my brande dubbyd many a knyght.'

*satirical*

11. Syr Harry Perssy cam to the walles,
    The Skottyssch oste for to se,
    And sayd, 'And thow hast brente Northomberlond,
    Full sore it rewyth me.

12. 'Yf thou hast haryed all Bamborowe schyre,
    Thow hast done me grete envye;
    For the trespasse thow hast me done,
    The tone of us schall dye.'

13. 'Where schall I byde the?' sayd the Dowglas,
    'Or where wylte thow com to me?'
    'At Otterborne, in the hygh way,
    Ther mast thow well logeed be.

14.   'The roo full rekeles ther sche rinnes,
          To make the game and glee;
      The fawken and the fesaunt both,
          Amonge the holtes on hye.


15.   'Ther mast thow have thy welth at wyll,
          Well looged ther mast be;
      Yt schall not be long or I com the tyll,'
          Sayd Syr Harry Perssye.


16.   'Ther schall I byde the,' sayd the Dowglas,
          'By the fayth of my bodye':
      'Thether schall I com,' sayd Syr Harry Perssy
          'My trowth I plyght to the.'


17.   A pype of wyne he gave them over the walles,
          For soth as I yow saye;
      Ther he mayd the Dowglasse drynke,
          And all hys ost that daye.


18.   The Dowglas turnyd hym homewarde agayne,
          For soth withowghten naye;
      He toke his logeyng at Oterborne,
          Upon a Wedynsday.


19.   And ther he pyght hys standerd dowyn,
          Hys gettyng more and lesse,
      And syne he warned hys men to goo
          To chose ther geldynges gresse.


20.   A Skottysshe knyght hoved upon the bent,
          A wache I dare well saye;
      So was he ware on the noble Perssy
          In the dawnyng of the daye.

21. He prycked to hys pavyleon dore,
    As faste as he myght ronne ;
    'Awaken, Dowglas,' cryed the knyght,
    'For hys love that syttes in trone.

22. 'Awaken, Dowglas,' cryed the knyght,
    'For thow maste waken wyth wynne ;
    Yender have I spyed the prowde Perssye,
    And seven stondardes wyth hym.'

23. 'Nay by my trowth,' the Dowglas sayed,
    'It ys but a fayned taylle ;
    He durst not loke on my brede banner
    For all Ynglonde so haylle.

24. 'Was I not yesterdaye at the Newe Castell,
    That stondes so fayre on Tyne ?
    For all the men the Perssy had,
    He coude not garre me ones to dyne.'

25. He stepped owt at his pavelyon dore,
    To loke and it were lesse :
    'Araye yow, lordynges, one and all,
    For here bygynnes no peysse.

26. 'The yerle of Mentaye, thow arte my eme, *uncle*
    The fowarde I gyve to the :
    The yerlle of Huntlay, cawte *wary* and kene,
    He schall be wyth the.

27. 'The lorde of Bowghan, in armure bryght,
    On the other hand he schall be ;
    Lord Jhonstoune and Lorde Maxwell,
    They to schall be with me.

Epithet – Homeric

28.  'Swynton, fayre fylde upon your pryde!
     To batell make yow bowen
   Syr Davy Skotte, Syr Water Stewarde,
     Syr Jhon of Agurstone!'

29.  The Perssy cam byfore hys oste,
     Wych was ever a gentyll knyght;
   Upon the Dowglas lowde can he crye,
     'I wyll holde that I have hyght. *promised*

30.  'For thou haste brente Nórthomberlonde,
     And done me grete envye;
   For thys trespasse thou hast me done,
     The tone of us schall dye.'

31.  The Dowglas answerde hym agayne,
     Wyth grett wurdes upon hye,
   And sayd, 'I have twenty agaynst thy one,
     Byholde, and thou maste see.'

32.  Wyth that the Perssy was grevyd sore,
     For soth as I yow saye;
   He lyghted dowyn upon his foote,
     And schoote hys horsse clene awaye.

33.  Every man sawe that he dyd soo,
     That ryall was ever in rowght;
   Every man schoote hys horsse hym froo,
     And lyght hym rowynde abowght.

34.  Thus Syr Hary Perssye toke the fylde,
     For soth as I yow saye;
   Jhesu Cryste in hevyn on hyght
     Dyd helpe hym well that daye.

Epithet doesnt distinguish – associated over and over – doughty Douglas

35. But nyne thowzand, ther was no moo,
  The cronykle wyll not layne ;
  Forty thowsande of Skottes and fowre
   That day fowght them agayne.


36. But when the batell byganne to joyne,
  In hast ther cam a knyght ;
  The letters fayre furth hath he tayne,
   And thus he sayd full ryght :


37. ' My lorde your father he gretes yow well,
  Wyth many a noble knyght ;
  He desyres yow to byde
   That he may see thys fyght.


38. ' The Baron of Grastoke ys com out of the west,
  With hym a noble companye ;
  All they loge at your fathers thys nyght,
   And the batell fayne wolde they see.'


39. ' For Jhesus love,' sayd Syr Harye Perssy,
  ' That dyed for yow and me,
  Wende to my lorde my father agayne,
   And saye thow sawe me not with yee.


40. ' My trowth ys plyght to yonne Skottysh knyght,
  It nedes me not to layne,
  That I schulde byde hym upon thys bent,
   And I have hys trowth agayne.


41. ' And if that I weynde of thys growende,
  For soth, onfowghten awaye,
  He wolde me call but a kowarde knyght
   In hys londe another daye.

*played*

42.　' Yet had I lever to be rynde and rente,
　　　　By Mary, that mykkel maye,
　　　Then ever my manhood schulde be reprovyd
　　　　Wyth a Skotte another daye.


43.　' Wherefore schote, archars, for my sake,
　　　　And let scharpe arowes flee ;
　　　Mynstrells, playe up for your waryson,
　　　　And well quyt it schall bee.


44.　' Every man thynke on hys trewe-love,
　　　　And marke hym to the Trenite ;
　　　For to God I make myne avowe
　　　　Thys day wyll I not flee.'


45.　The blodye harte in the Dowglas armes,
　　　　Hys standerde stood on hye,
　　　That every man myght full well knowe ;
　　　　By syde stode starrës thre.


46.　The whyte lyon on the Ynglyssh perte,
　　　　For soth as I yow sayne,
　　　The lucettes and the cressawntes both;
　　　　The Skottes faught them agayne.


47.　Upon Sent Androwe lowde can they crye,
　　　　And thrysse they schowte on hyght,
　　　And syne merked them one owr Ynglysshe men,
　　　　As I have tolde yow ryght.


48.　Sent George the bryght, owr ladyes knyght,
　　　　To name they were full fayne ;
　　　Owr Ynglyssh men they cryde on hyght,
　　　　And thrysse the schowtte agayne.

49. Wyth that scharpe arowes bygan to flee,
     I tell yow in sertayne ;
    Men of armes byganne to joyne,
     Many a dowghty man was ther slayne.

50. The Perssy and the Dowglas mette,
     That ether of other was fayne ;
    They swapped together whyll that the swette,
     Wyth swordes of fyne collayne :

*Single combat organized according to rules of chivalry*

51. Tyll the bloode from ther bassonnettes ranne,
     As the roke doth in the rayne ;
    'Yelde the to me,' sayd the Dowglas,
     'Or elles thow schalt be slayne.

52. 'For I see by thy bryght bassonet,
     Thow arte sum man of myght ;
    And so I do by thy burnysshed brande ;
     Thow arte an yerle, or elles a knyght.'

53. 'By my good faythe,' sayd the noble Perssye,
     'Now haste thou rede full ryght ;
    Yet wyll I never yelde me to the,
     Whyll I may stonde and fyght.'

54. They swapped together whyll that they swette,
     Wyth swordës scharpe and long ;
    Ych on other so faste thee beette,
     Tyll ther helmes cam in peyses dowyn.

55. The Perssy was a man of strenghth,
     I tell yow in thys stounde ;
    He smote the Dowglas at the swordes length
     That he fell to the growynde.

56.   The sworde was scharpe, and sore can byte,
          I tell yow in sertayne ;
      To the harte he cowde hym smyte,
          Thus was the Dowglas slayne.


57.   The stonderdes stode styll on eke a syde,
          Wyth many a grevous grone ;
      Ther the fowght the day, and all the nyght,
          And many a dowghty man was slayne.


58.   Ther was no freke that ther wolde flye,
          But styffely in stowre can stond,
      Ychone hewyng on other whyll they myght drye,
          Wyth many a bayllefull bronde.


59.   Ther was slayne upon the Skottës syde,
          For soth and sertenly,
      Syr James a Dowglas ther was slayne,
          That day that he cowde dye.


60.   The yerlle of Mentaye he was slayne,
          Grysely groned upon the growynd ;
      Syr Davy Skotte, Syr Water Stewarde,
          Syr Jhon of Agurstoune.


61.   Syr Charllës Morrey in that place,
          That never a fote wold flee ;
      Syr Hewe Maxwell, a lord he was,
          Wyth the Dowglas dyd he dye.


62.   Ther was slayne upon the Skottës syde,
          For soth as I yow saye,
      Of fowre and forty thowsande Scottes
          Went but eyghtene awaye.

63.   Ther was slayne upon the Ynglysshe syde,
         For soth and sertenlye,
      A gentell knyght, Syr Jhon Fechewe,
         Yt was the more pety.


64.   Syr James Hardbotell ther was slayne,
         For hym ther hartes were sore;
      The gentyll Lovell ther was slayne,
         That the Perssys standerd bore.


65.   Ther was slayne upon the Ynglyssh perte,
         For soth as I yow saye,
      Of nyne thowsand Ynglyssh men
         Fyve hondert cam awaye.


66.   The other were slayne in the fylde;
         Cryste kepe ther sowlles from wo!
      Seyng ther was so fewe fryndes
         Agaynst so many a foo.


67.   Then on the morne they mayde them beerys
         Of byrch and haysell graye;
      Many a wydowe, wyth wepyng teyres,
         Ther makes they fette awaye.


68.   Thys fraye bygan at Otterborne,
         Bytwene the nyght and the day;
      Ther the Dowglas lost hys lyffe,
         And the Perssy was lede awaye.


69.   Then was ther a Scottysh prisoner tayne,
         Syr Hewe Mongomery was hys name;
      For soth as I yow saye,
         He borowed the Perssy home agayne.

70.   Now let us all for the Perssy praye
      To Jhesu most of myght,
      To bryng hys sowlle to the blysse of heven,
      For he was a gentyll knyght.

Last two verses of benediction
are an indication of the
minstrel ballads —

Rhyme tag — meaningless
phrase for sake of rhyme

similes an indication of
minstrel ballad

expression of feeling a
minstrel in tribulation  ——

## THE HUNTING OF THE CHEVIOT.

1.  The Persë owt off Northombarlonde,
       and avowe to God mayd he
    That he wold hunte in the mowntayns
       off Chyviat within days thre,
    In the magger of doughtë Dogles,
       and all that ever with him be.


2.  The fattiste hartes in all Cheviat
       he sayd he wold kyll, and cary them away :
    ' Be my feth,' sayd the dougheti Doglas agayn,
       ' I wyll let that hontyng yf that I may.'


3.  Then the Persë owt off Banborowe cam,
       with him a myghtee meany,
    With fifteen hondrith archares bold off blood and
       bone ;
       the wear chosen owt of shyars thre.


4.  This begane on a Monday at morn,
       in Cheviat the hillys so he ;
    The chylde may rue that ys unborn,
       it wos the more pittë.


5.  The dryvars thorowe the woodës went,
       for to reas the dear ;
    Bomen byckarte upponè the bent
       with ther browd aros cleare.

6.   Then the wyld thorowe the woodës went,
       on every sydë shear ;
     Greahondës thorowe the grevis glent,
       for to kyll thear dear.


7.   This begane in Chyviat the hyls abone,
       yerly on a Monnyn-day ;
     Be that it drewe to the oware off none,
       a hondrith fat hartës ded ther lay.


8.   The blewe a mort uppone the bent,
       the semblyde on sydis shear ;
     To the quyrry then the Persë went,
       to se the bryttlynge off the deare.


9.   He sayd, 'It was the Duglas promys
       this day to met me hear ;
     But I wyste he wolde faylle, verament ;'
       a great oth the Persë swear.


10.  At the laste a squyar off Northomberlonde
       lokyde at his hand full ny ;
     He was war a the doughetie Doglas commynge,
       with him a myghttë meany.


11.  Both with spear, bylle, and brande,
       yt was a myghtti sight to se ;
     Hardyar men, both off hart nor hande,
       wear not in Cristiantë.


12.  The wear twenti hondrith spear-men good,
       withoute any feale ; *fail*
     The wear borne along be the watter a Twyde,
       yth bowndës of Tividale.

13. 'Leave of the brytlyng of the dear,' he sayd,
    'and to your boÿs lock ye tayk good hede;
For never sithe ye wear on your mothars borne
    had ye never so mickle nede.'

14. The dougheti Dogglas on a stede,
    he rode alle his men beforne;
His armor glytteryde as dyd a glede;
    a boldar barne was never born.

15. 'Tell me whos men ye ar,' he says,
    'or whos men that ye be:
Who gave youe leave to hunte in this Chyviat
    chays,
    in the spyt of myn and of me.'

16. The first mane that ever him an answear mayd,
    yt was the good lord Persë:
'We wyll not tell the whoys men we ar,' he says,
    'nor whos men that we be;
But we wyll hounte hear in this chays,
    in the spyt of thyne and of the.'

17. 'The fattiste hartës in all Chyviat
    we have kyld, and cast to carry them away:
'Be my troth,' sayd the doughetë Dogglas agayn,
    'therfor the ton of us shall de this day.'

18. Then sayd the doughtë Doglas
    unto the lord Persë:
'To kyll alle thes giltles men,
    alas, it wear great pittë!

19. 'But, Persë, thowe art a lord of lande,
    I am a yerle callyd within my contrë;
Let all our men uppone a parti stande,
    and do the battell off the and of me.'

20.  ' Nowe Cristes cors on his crowne,' sayd the lord
          Persë,
              ' who-so-ever ther-to says nay;
     Be my troth, doughttë Doglas,' he says,
          ' thow shalt never se that day.


21.  ' Nethar in Ynglonde, Skottlonde, nar France,
          nor for no man of a woman born,
     But, and fortune be my chance,
          I dar met him, on man for on.'


22.  Then bespayke a squyar off Northombarlonde,
          Richard Wytharyngton was his nam :
     ' It shall never be told in Sothe-Ynglonde,' he
          says,
          ' to Kyng Herry the Fourth for sham.


23.  ' I wat youe byn great lordës twaw,
          I am a poor squyar of lande :
     I wylle never se my captayne fyght on a fylde,
          and stande my selffe and loocke on,
     But whylle I may my weppone welde,
          I wylle not fayle both hart and hande.'


24.  That day, that day, that dredfull day !
          the first fit here I fynde ;
     And youe wyll here any mor a the hountyng a the
          Chyviat,
          yet ys ther mor behynde.



25.  The Yngglyshe men hade ther bowys yebent,
          ther hartes wer good yenoughe ;
     The first off arros that the shote off,
          seven skore spear-men the sloughe.

26. Yet byddys the yerle Doglas uppon the bent,
    a captayne good yenoughe,
And that was sene verament,
    for he wrought hom both woo and wouche.


27. The Dogglas partyd his ost in thre,
    lyk a cheffe cheften off pryde;
With suar spears off myghttë tre,
    the cum in on every syde:


28. Thrughe our Yngglyshe archery
    gave many a wounde fulle wyde;
Many a doughetë the garde to dy,
    which ganyde them no pryde.


29. The Ynglyshe men let ther boÿs be,
    and pulde owt brandes that wer brighte;
It was a hevy syght to se
    bryght swordes on basnites lyght.


30. Thorowe ryche male and myneyeple,
    many sterne the strocke done streght;
Many a freyke that was fulle fre,
    ther undar foot dyd lyght.


31. At last the Duglas and the Persë met,
    lyk to captayns of myght and of mayne;
The swapte togethar tylle the both swat,
    with swordes that wear of fyn myllan.


32. Thes worthë freckys for to fyght,
    ther-to the wear fulle fayne,
Tylle the bloode owte off thear basnetes sprente,
    as ever dyd heal or rayn.

33. 'Yelde the, Persë,' sayde the Doglas,
   'and i feth I shalle the brynge
   Wher thowe shalte have a yerls wagis
   of Jamy our Skottish kynge.

34. 'Thou shalte have thy ransom fre,
   I hight the hear this thinge;
   For the manfullyste man yet art thowe
   that ever I conqueryd in filde fighttynge.'

35. 'Nay,' sayd the lord Persë,
   'I tolde it the beforne,
   That I wolde never yeldyde be
   to no man of a woman born.'

36. With that ther cam an arrowe hastely,
   forthe off a myghttë wane;
   Hit hathe strekene the yerle Duglas
   in at the brest-bane.

37. Thorowe lyvar and longës bathe
   the sharpe arrowe ys gane,
   That never after in all his lyffe-days
   he spayke mo wordës but ane:
   That was,'Fyghte ye, my myrry men, whyllys ye may,
   for my lyff-days ben gan.'

38. The Persë leanyde on his brande,
   and sawe the Duglas de;
   He tooke the dede mane by the hande,
   and sayd, 'Wo ys me for the !

39. 'To have savyde thy lyffe, I wolde have partyde with
   my landes for years thre,
   For a better man, of hart nare of hande,
   was nat in all the north contrë.'

40.  Off all that se a Skottishe knyght,
        was callyd Ser Hewe the Monggombyrry;
     He sawe the Duglas to the deth was dyght,
        he spendyd a spear, a trusti tre.


41.  He rod uppone a corsiare
        throughe a hondrith archery :
     He never stynttyde, nar never blane,
        tylle he cam to the good lord Persë.


42.  He set uppone the lorde Persë
        a dynte that was full soare ;
     With a suar spear of a myghttë tre
        clean thorow the body he the Persë ber,


43.  A the tothar syde that a man myght se
        a large cloth-yard and mare :
     Towe bettar captayns wear nat in Cristiantë
        then that day slan wear ther.


44.  An archar off Northomberlonde
        say slean was the lord Persë ;
     He bar a bende bowe in his hand,
        was made off trusti tre.


45.  An arow, that a cloth-yarde was lang,
        to the harde stele halyde he ;
     A dynt that was both sad and soar
        he sat on Ser Hewe the Monggombyrry.


46.  The dynt yt was both sad and sar,
        that he of Monggomberry sete ;
     The swane-fethars that his arrowe bar
        with his hart-blood the wear wete.

47.    Ther was never a freake wone foot wolde fle,
      but still in stour dyd stand,
   Heawyng on yche othar, whylle the myghte dre
      with many a balfull brande.

48.    This battell begane in Chyviat
      an owar befor the none,
   And when even-songe bell was rang,
      the battell was nat half done.

49.    The tocke . . . on ethar hande
      be the lyght off the mone ;
   Many hade no strenght for to stande,
      in Chyviat the hillys abon.

50.    Of fifteen hondrith archars of Ynglonde
      went away but seventi and thre ;
   Of twenti hondrith spear-men of Skotlonde,
      but even five and fifti.

51.    But all wear slayne Cheviat within ;
      the hade no strengthe to stand on hy ;
   The chylde may rue that ys unborne,
      it was the mor pittë.

52.    Thear was slayne, withe the lord Persë,
      Sir Johan of Agerstone,
   Ser Rogar, the hinde Hartly,
      Ser Wyllyam, the bolde Hearone.

53.    Ser Jorg, the worthë Loumle,
      a knyghte of great renowen,
   Ser Raff, the ryche Rugbe,
      with dyntes wear beaten dowene.

54. For Wetharryngton my harte was wo,
      that ever he slayne shulde be;
   For when both his leggis wear hewyne in to,
      yet he knyled and fought on hys kny.


55. Ther was slayne, with the dougheti Duglas,
      Ser Hewe the Monggombyrry,
   Ser Davy Lwdale, that worthë was,
      his sistar's son was he.


56. Ser Charls a Murrë in that place,
      that never a foot wolde fle;
   Ser Hewe Maxwelle, a lorde he was,
      with the Doglas dyd he dey.


57. So on the morrowe the mayde them byears
      off birch and hasell so gray;
   Many wedous, with wepyng tears,
      cam to fache ther makys away.


58. Tivydale may carpe off care,
      Northombarlond may mayk great mon,
   For towe such captayns as slayne wear thear,
      on the March-parti shall never be non.


59. Word ys commen to Eddenburrowe,
      to Jamy the Skottische kynge,
   That dougheti Duglas, lyff-tenant of the Marches,
      he lay slean Chyviot within.


60. His handdës dyd he weal and wryng,
      he sayd, 'Alas, and woe ys me!
   Such an othar captayn Skotland within,'
      he sayd, 'ye-feth shuld never be.'

61.    Worde ys commyn to lovly Londone,
           till the fourth Harry our kynge,
       That lord Persë, leyff-tenante of the Marchis,
           he lay slayne Chyviat within.

62.    'God have merci on his solle,' sayde Kyng Harry,
           'good lord, yf thy will it be !
       I have a hondrith captayns in Ynglonde,' he sayd,
           'as good as ever was he :
       But, Persë, and I brook my lyffe,
           thy deth well quyte shall be.'

63.    As our noble kynge mayd his avowe,
           lyke a noble prince of renowen,
       For the deth of the lord Persë
           he dyde the battell of Hombyll-down ;

64.    Wher syx and thrittë Skottishe knyghtes
           on a day wear beaten down :
       Glendale glytteryde on ther armor bryght,
           over castille, towar, and town.

65.    This was the hontynge off the Cheviat,
           that tear begane this spurn ;
       Old men that knowen the grownde well yenoughe
           call it the battell of Otterburn.

66.    At Otterburn begane this spurne
           uppone a Monnynday ;
       Ther was the doughtë Doglas slean,
           the Persë never went away.

67.    Ther was never a tym on the Marche-partës
           sen the Doglas and the Persë met,
       But yt ys mervele and the rede blude ronne not,
           as the reane doys in the stret.

68.  Jhesue Crist our balys bete,
        and to the blys us brynge !
    Thus was the hountynge of the Chivyat :
        God send us alle good endyng !

## KINMONT WILLIE.

1.  O have ye na heard o the fause Sakelde?
     O have ye na heard o the keen Lord Scroop?
  How they hae taen bauld Kinmont Willie,
     On Hairibee to hang him up?

2.  Had Willie had but twenty men,
     But twenty men as stout as he,
  Fause Sakelde had never the Kinmont taen,
     Wi eight score in his companie.

3.  They band his legs beneath the steed,
     They tied his hands behind his back;
  They guarded him, fivesome on each side,
     And they brought him ower the Liddel-rack.

4.  They led him thro the Liddel-rack,
     And also thro the Carlisle sands;
  They brought him to Carlisle castell,
     To be at my Lord Scroope's commands.

5.  'My hands are tied, but my tongue is free,
     And whae will dare this deed avow?
  Or answer by the Border law?
     Or answer to the bauld Buccleuch!'

6.  'Now haud thy tongue, thou rank reiver!
     There's never a Scot shall set ye free;
  Before ye cross my castle-yate,
     I trow ye shall take farewell o me.'

7. 'Fear na ye that, my lord,' quo Willie ;
    ' By the faith o my body, Lord Scroope,' he said,
    ' I never yet lodged in a hostelrie,
       But I paid my lawing before I gaed.'

8. Now word is gane to the bauld Keeper, *of the Marches*
       In Branksome Ha where that he lay,
    That Lord Scroope has taen the Kinmont Willie,
       Between the hours of night and day.

9. He has taen the table wi his hand,
       He garrd the red wine spring on hie ;
    ' Now Christ's curse on my head,' he said,
       ' But avenged of Lord Scroope I 'll be !

10. 'O is my basnet a widow's curch,
       Or my lance a wand of the willow-tree,
    Or my arm a ladye's lilye hand,
       That an English lord should lightly me ?

11. 'And have they taen him, Kinmont Willie,
       Against the truce of Border tide,
    And forgotten that the bauld Buccleuch
       Is keeper here on the Scottish side ?

12. 'And have they een taen him, Kinmont Willie,
       Withouten either dread or fear,
    And forgotten that the bauld Buccleuch
       Can back a steed, or shake a spear ?

13. 'O were there war between the lands,
       As well I wot that there is none,
    I would slight Carlisle castell high,
       Tho it were builded of marble stone.

14.   'I would set that castell in a low,
          And sloken it with English blood;
      There's nevir a man in Cumberland
          Should ken where Carlisle castell stood.


15.   'But since nae war's between the lands,
          And there is peace, and peace should be,
      I'll neither harm English lad or lass,
          And yet the Kinmont freed shall be!'


16.   He has calld him forty marchmen bauld,
          I trow they were of his ain name,
      Except Sir Gilbert Elliott, calld
          The Laird of Stobs, I mean the same.


17.   He has calld him forty marchmen bauld,
          Were kinsmen to the bauld Buccleuch,
      With spur on heel, and splent on spauld,
          And gleuves of green, and feathers blue.


18.   There were five and five before them a',
          Wi hunting-horns and bugles bright;
      And five and five came wi Buccleuch,
          Like Warden's men, arrayed for fight.


19.   And five and five like a mason-gang,
          That carried the ladders lang and hie;
      And five and five like broken men;
          And so they reached the Woodhouselee.


20.   And as we crossd the Bateable Land,
          When to the English side we held,
      The first o men that we met wi,
          Whae sould it be but fause Sakelde!

21.  'Where be ye gaun, ye hunters keen?'
        Quo fause Sakelde ; 'come tell to me';
    'We go to hunt an English stag,
        Has trespassd on the Scots countrie.'

22.  'Where be ye gaun, ye marshal-men?'
        Quo fause Sakelde ; 'come tell me true';
    'We go to catch a rank reiver,
        Has broken faith wi the bauld Buccleuch.'

23.  'Where are ye gaun, ye mason-lads,
        Wi a' your ladders lang and hie?'
    'We gang to herry a corbie's nest,
        That wons not far frae Woodhouselee.'

24.  'Where be ye gaun, ye broken men?'
        Quo fause Sakelde ; 'come tell to me';
    Now Dickie of Dryhope led that band,
        And the nevir a word o lear had he.

25.  'Why trespass ye on the English side?
        Row-footed outlaws, stand!' quo he;
    The neer a word had Dickie to say,
        Sae he thrust the lance thro his fause bodie.

26.  Then on we held for Carlisle toun,
        And at Staneshaw-bank the Eden we crossd;
    The water was great, and meikle of spait,
        But the nevir a horse nor man we lost.

27.  And when we reachd the Staneshaw-bank,
        The wind was rising loud and hie;
    And there the laird garrd leave our steeds,
        For fear that they should stamp and nie.

28. And when we left the Staneshaw-bank,
   The wind began full loud to blaw;
  But 't was wind and weet, and fire and sleet,
   When we came beneath the castel-wa.


29. We crept on knees, and held our breath,
   Till we placed the ladders against the wa;
  And sae ready was Buccleuch himsell
   To mount the first before us a'.


30. He has taen the watchman by the throat,
   He flung him down upon the lead:
  ' Had there not been peace between our lands,
   Upon the other side thou hadst gaed.


31. ' Now sound out, trumpets!' quo Buccleuch;
   ' Let 's waken Lord Scroope right merrilie!'
  Then loud the Warden's trumpets blew
   ' O whae dare meddle wi me?'


32. Then speedilie to wark we gaed,
   And raised the slogan ane and a',
  And cut a hole thro a sheet of lead,
   And so we wan to the castel-ha.


33. They thought King James and a' his men
   Had won the house wi bow and spear;
  It was but twenty Scots and ten,
   That put a thousand in sic a stear!


34. Wi coulters and wi forehammers,
   We garrd the bars bang merrilie,
  Untill we came to the inner prison,
   Where Willie o Kinmont he did lie.

35.   And when we cam to the lower prison,
          Where Willie o Kinmont he did lie,
      'O sleep ye, wake ye, Kinmont Willie,
          Upon the morn that thou 's to die?'

36.   'O I sleep saft, and I wake aft,
          It 's lang since sleeping was fleyd frae me;
      Gie my service back to my wyfe and bairns,
          And a' gude fellows that speer for me.'

37.   Then Red Rowan has hente him up,
          The starkest man in Teviotdale:
      'Abide, abide now, Red Rowan,
          Till of my Lord Scroope I take farewell.

38.   'Farewell, farewell, my gude Lord Scroope!
          My gude Lord Scroope, farewell!' he cried;
      'I 'll pay you for my lodging-maill
          When first we meet on the border-side.'

39.   Then shoulder high, with shout and cry,
          We bore him down the ladder lang;
      At every stride Red Rowan made,
          I wot the Kinmont's airns playd clang.

40.   'O mony a time,' quo Kinmont Willie,
          'I have ridden horse baith wild and wood;
      But a rougher beast than Red Rowan
          I ween my legs have neer bestrode.

41.   'And mony a time,' quo Kinmont Willie,
          'I 've pricked a horse out oure the furs;
      But since the day I backed a steed,
          I nevir wore sic cumbrous spurs.'

42.   We scarce had won the Staneshaw-bank,
      When a' the Carlisle bells were rung,
  And a thousand men, in horse and foot,
      Cam wi the keen Lord Scroope along.

43.   Buccleuch has turned to Eden Water,
      Even where it flowd frae bank to brim,
  And he has plunged in wi a' his band,
      And safely swam them thro the stream.

44.   He turned him on the other side,
      And at Lord Scroope his glove flung he
  'If ye like na my visit in merry England,
      In fair Scotland come visit me!'

45.   All sore astonished stood Lord Scroope,
      He stood as still as rock of stane;
  He scarcely dared to trew his eyes,
      When thro the water they had gane.

46.   'He is either himsell a devil frae hell,
      Or else his mother a witch maun be;
  I wad na have ridden that wan water
      For a' the gowd in Christentie.'

*element of humor had no place in the first ballads —*

*Nature background probably introduced by Scott.*

*Not a border ballad; &c its way to bring an outlaw ballad*

*might be written*

# JOHNIE COCK.

1. Up Johnie raise in a May morning,
     Calld for water to wash his hands,
   And he has calld for his gude gray hunds
     That lay bund in iron bands, bands,
     That lay bund in iron bands.

2. 'Ye 'll busk, ye 'll busk my noble dogs,
     Ye 'll busk and mak them boun,
   For I 'm going to the Braidscaur hill
     To ding the dun deer doun.'

3. Johnie's mother has gotten word o that,
     And care-bed she has taen :
   'O Johnie, for my benison,
     I beg you 'l stay at hame ;
   For the wine so red, and the well-baken bread,
     My Johnie shall want nane.

4. 'There are seven forsters at Pickeram Side,
     At Pickeram where they dwell,
   And for a drop of thy heart's bluid
     They wad ride the fords of hell.'

5. But Johnie has cast aff the black velvet,
     And put on the Lincoln twine,
   And he is on to gude greenwud
     As fast as he could gang.

6. Johnie lookit east, and Johnie lookit west,
     And he lookit aneath the sun,
   And there he spied the dun deer sleeping
     Aneath a buss o whun.

7.   Johnie shot, and the dun deer lap,
       And she lap wondrous wide,
     Until they came to the wan water,
       And he stemd her of her pride.


8.   He 'as taen out the little pen-knife,
       'Twas full three quarters long,
     And he has taen out of that dun deer
       The liver bot and the tongue.


9.   They eat of the flesh, and they drank of the blood,
       And the blood it was so sweet,
     Which caused Johnie and his bloody hounds
       To fall in a deep sleep.


10.  By then came an old palmer,
       And an ill death may he die!
     For he 's away to Pickram Side
       As fast as he can drie.


11.  'What news, what news?' says the Seven Forsters,
       'What news have ye brought to me?'
     'I have noe news,' the palmer said,
       'But what I saw with my eye.


12.  'As I cam in by Braidisbanks,
       And down among the whuns,
     The bonniest youngster eer I saw
       Lay sleepin amang his hunds.


13.  'The shirt that was upon his back
       Was o the holland fine;
     The doublet which was over that
       Was o the Lincoln twine.'

14.  Up bespake the Seven Forsters,
         Up bespake they ane and a':
     'O that is Johnie o Cockleys Well,
         And near him we will draw.'

15.  O the first stroke that they gae him,
         They struck him off by the knee;
     Then up bespake his sister's son:
         'O the next 'll gar him die!'

16.  'O some they count ye well-wight men,
         But I do count ye nane;
     For you might well ha wakend me,
         And askd gin I wad be taen.

17.  'The wildest wolf in aw this wood
         Wad not ha done so by me;
     She'd ha wet her foot ith wan water,
         And sprinkled it oer my brae,
     And if that wad not ha wakend me,
         She wad ha gone and let me be.

18.  'O bows of yew, if ye be true,
         In London, where ye were bought,
     Fingers five, get up belive,
         Manhuid shall fail me nought.'

19.  He has killd the Seven Forsters,
         He has killd them all but ane,
     And that wan scarce to Pickeram Side,
         To carry the bode-words hame.

20.  'Is there never a [bird] in a' this wood
         That will tell what I can say;
     That will go to Cockleys Well,
         Tell my mither to fetch me away?'

21. There was a [bird] into that wood,
    That carried the tidings away,
And many ae was the well-wight man
    At the fetching o Johnie away.

## JOHNIE ARMSTRONG.

1.  There dwelt a man in faire Westmerland,
      Jonnë Armestrong men did him call,
    He had nither lands nor rents coming in,
      Yet he kept eight score men in his hall.

2.  He had horse and harness for them all,
      Goodly steeds were all milke-white;
    O the golden bands an about their necks,
      And their weapons, they were all alike.

3.  Newes then was brought unto the king
      That there was sicke a won as hee,
    That livëd lyke a bold out-law,
      And robbëd all the north country.

4.  The king he writt an a letter then,
      A letter which was large and long;
    He signëd it with his owne hand,
      And he promised to doe him no wrong.

5.  When this letter came Jonnë untill,
      His heart was as blyth as birds on the tree:
    'Never was I sent for before any king,
      My father, my grandfather, nor none but mee.

6.  'And if wee goe the king before,
      I would we went most orderly;
    Every man of you shall have his scarlet cloak,
      Laced with silver laces three.

7.    ' Every won of you shall have his velvett coat,
          Laced with silver lace so white ;
      O the golden bands an about your necks,
          Black hatts, white feathers, all alyke.'

8.    By the morrow morninge at ten of the clock,
          Towards Edenburough gon was hee,
      And with him all his eight score men ;
          Good lord, it was a goodly sight for to see !

9.    When Jonnë came befower the king,
          He fell downe on his knee ;
      ' O pardon, my soveraine leige,' he said,
          ' O pardon my eight score men and mee.'

10.   ' Thou shalt have no pardon, thou traytor strong,
          For thy eight score men nor thee ;
      For to-morrow morning by ten of the clock,
          Both thou and them shall hang on the gallow-
              tree.'

11.   But Jonnë looked over his left shoulder,
          Good Lord, what a grevious look looked hee !
      Saying, ' Asking grace of a graceles face —
          Why there is none for you nor me.'

12.   But Jonnë had a bright sword by his side,
          And it was made of the mettle so free,
      That had not the king stept his foot aside,
          He had smitten his head from his faire boddë.

13.   Saying, ' Fight on, my merry men all,
          And see that none of you be taine ;
      For rather than men shall say we were hangd,
          Let them report how we were slaine.'

14. Then, God wott, faire Eddenburrough rose,
    And so besett poore Jonnë rounde,
    That fower score and tenn of Jonnës best **men**
    Lay gasping all upon the ground.

15. Then like a mad man Jonnë laide about,
    And like a mad man then fought hee,
    Untill a falce Scot came Jonnë behinde,
    And runn him through the faire boddee.

16. Saying, ' Fight on, my merry men all,
    I am a little hurt, but I am not slain ;
    I will lay me down for to bleed a while,
    Then I 'le rise and fight with you again.'

17. Newes then was brought to young Jonnë Arme-
        strong,
    As he stood by his nurses knee,
    Who vowed if ere he lived for to be a man,
    O the treacherous Scots revengd hee 'd be.

## SIR ANDREW BARTON.

1.   As itt beffell in midsumer-time,
        When burds singe sweetlye on every tree,
     Our noble king, King Henery the Eighth,
        Over the river of Thames past hee.

2.   Hee was no sooner over the river,
        Downe in a fforrest to take the ayre,
     But eighty merchants of London cittye
        Came kneeling before King Henery there.

3.   'O yee are welcome, rich merchants,
        [Good saylers, welcome unto me !']
     They swore by the rood the were saylers good,
        But rich merchants they cold not bee.

4.   'To Ffrance nor Fflanders dare we nott passe,
        Nor Burdeaux voyage wee dare not ffare,
     And all ffor a ffalse robber that lyes on the seas,
        And robbs us of our merchants-ware.'

5.   King Henery was stout, and he turned him about,
        And swore by the Lord that was mickle of might,
     'I thought he had not beene in the world through-
           out,
        That durst have wrought England such unright.'

6.   But ever they sighed, and said, alas !
        Unto King Harry this answere againe :
     'He is a proud Scott that will rob us all
        If wee were twenty shipps and hee but one.'

7. The king looket over his left shoulder,
      Amongst his lords and barrons soe ffree :
   'Have I never lord in all my realme
      Will ffeitch yond traitor unto mee ? '

8. 'Yes, that dare I ! ' sayes my Lord Chareles Howard,
      Neere to the king wheras hee did stand ;
   'If that Your Grace will give me leave,
      My selfe wilbe the only man.'

9. 'Thou shalt have six hundred men,' saith our king,
      'And chuse them out of my realme soe ffree :
   Besids marriners and boyes,
      To guide the great shipp on the sea.'

10. 'I 'le goe speake with Sir Andrew,' sais Charles, my
         Lord Haward,
      'Upon the sea, if hee be there ;
   I will bring him and his shipp to shore,
      Or before my prince I will never come neere.'

11. The ffirst of all my lord did call,
      A noble gunner he was one ;
   This man was three score yeeres and ten,
      And Peeter Simon was his name.

12. 'Peeter,' sais hee, 'I must sayle to the sea,
      To seeke out an enemye ; God be my speed !
   Before all others I have chosen thee ;
      Of a hundred guners thoust be my head.'

13. 'My lord,' sais hee, 'if you have chosen mee
      Of a hundred gunners to be the head,
   Hange me at your maine-mast tree
      If I misse my marke past three pence bread.'

*ornamental repetition*

14. The next of all my lord he did call,
    A noble bowman hee was one;
In Yorekeshire was this gentleman borne,
    And William Horsley was his name.

15. 'Horsley,' says hee, 'I must sayle to the sea,
    To seeke out an enemye; God be my speede!
Before all others I have chosen thee;
    Of a hundred bowemen thoust be my head.'

16. 'My lord,' sais hee, 'if you have chosen mee
    Of a hundred bowemen to be the head,
Hang me att your mainemast tree
    If I misse my marke past twelve pence bread.'

17. With pikes, and gunnes, and bowemen bold,
    This noble Howard is gone to the sea
On the day before midsummer-even,
    And out att Thames mouth sayled they.

18. They had not sayled dayes three
    Upon their journey they tooke in hand,
But there they mett with a noble shipp,
    And stoutely made itt both stay and stand.

19. 'Thou must tell me thy name,' sais Charles, my
        lord Haward,
    'Or who thou art, or ffrom whence thou came,
Yea, and where thy dwelling is,
    To whom and where thy shipp does belong.'

20. 'My name,' sayes hee, 'is Henery Hunt,
    With a pure hart and a penitent mind;
I and my shipp they doe belong
    Unto the New-castle that stands upon Tine.'

21.  'Now thou must tell me, Harry Hunt,
         As thou hast sayled by day and by night,
     Hast thou not heard of a stout robber?
         Men calls him Sir Andrew Bartton, Knight.'


22.  But ever he sighed, and sayd, 'Alas!
         Ffull well, my lord, I know that wight!
     He robd me of my merchants ware,
         And I was his prisoner but yesternight.


23.  'As I was sayling uppon the sea,
         And Burdeaux voyage as I did ffare,
     He clasped me to his hachborde,
         And robd me of all my merchants-ware.


24.  'And I am a man both poore and bare,
         And every man will have his owne of me,
     And I am bound towards London to ffare,
         To complaine to my prince Henerye.'


25.  'That shall not need,' sais my Lord Haward;
         'If thou canst lett me this robber see,
     Ffor every peny he hath taken thee ffroe,
         Thou shalt be rewarded a shilling,' quoth hee.


26.  'Now God fforefend,' saies Henery Hunt,
         'My lord, you shold worke soe ffar amisse!
     God keepe you out of that traitors hands!
         For you wott ffull litle what a man hee is.


27.  'Hee is brasse within, and steele without,
         And beames hee beares in his topcastle stronge;
     His shipp hath ordinance cleane round about;
         Besids, my lord, hee is verry well mand.

28.   'He hath a pinnace, is deerlye dight,
          Saint Andrews crosse, that is his guide ;
      His pinnace beares nine score men and more,
          Besids fifteen cannons on every side.

29.   'If you were twenty shippes, and he but one,
          Either in hachbord or in hall,
      He wold overcome you everyone,
          And if his beames they doe downe ffall.'

30.   'This is cold comfort,' sais my Lord Haward,
          'To wellcome a stranger thus to the sea ;
      I 'le bring him and his shipp to shore,
          Or else into Scottland hee shall carrye mee.'

31.   'Then you must gett a noble gunner, my lord,
          That can sett well with his eye,
      And sinke his pinnace into the sea,
          And soone then overcome will hee bee.

32.   'And when that you have done this,
          If you chance Sir Andrew for to bord,
      Lett no man to his topcastle goe ;
          And I will give you a glasse, my lord,

33.   'And then you need to ffeare no Scott,
          Whether you sayle by day or by night ;
      And to-morrow, by seven of the clocke,
          You shall meete with Sir Andrew Bartton, Knight.

34.   'I was his prisoner but yester night,
          And he hath taken mee sworne,' quoth hee ;
      'I trust my Lord God will me fforgive
          And if that oath then broken bee.

35.   'You must lend me sixe peeces, my lord,' quoth hee,
    'Into my shipp, to sayle the sea,
And to-morrow, by nine of the clocke,
    Your Honour againe then will I see.'

\*    \*    \*    \*    \*    \*    \*

36.   And the hache-bord where Sir Andrew lay
    Is hached with gold deerlye dight:
'Now by my ffaith,' sais Charles, my lord Haward,
    'Then yonder Scott is a worthye wight!

37.   'Take in your ancyents and your standards,
    Yea that no man shall them see,
And put me forth a white willow wand,
    As merchants use to sayle the sea.'

38.   But they stirred neither top nor mast,
    But Sir Andrew they passed by:
'Whatt English are yonder,' said Sir Andrew,
    'That can so litle curtesye?

39.   'I have beene admirall over the sea
    More then these yeeres three;
There is never an English dog, nor Portingall,
    Can passe this way without leave of mee.

40.   'But now yonder pedlers, they are past,
    Which is no litle greffe to me:
Ffeich them backe,' sayes Sir Andrew Bartton,
    'They shall all hang att my maine-mast tree.'

41.   With that the pinnace itt shott of,
    That my Lord Haward might itt well ken;
Itt stroke downe my lords fforemast,
    And killed fourteen of my lord his men.

42.   'Come hither, Simon!' sayes my lord Haward,
          'Looke that thy words be true thou sayd;
      I 'le hang thee att my maine-mast tree
          If thou misse thy marke past twelve pence bread.'


43.   Simon was old, but his hart itt was bold;
          Hee tooke downe a peece, and layd itt ffull lowe;
      He put in chaine yeards nine,
          Besids other great shott lesse and more.


44.   With that hee lett his gun-shott goe;
          Soe well hee settled itt with his eye,
      The ffirst sight that Sir Andrew sawe,
          Hee see his pinnace sunke in the sea.


45.   When hee saw his pinace sunke,
          Lord! in his hart hee was not well:
      'Cutt my ropes! itt is time to be gon!
          I 'le goe ffeitch yond pedlers backe my selfe!'


46.   When my Lord Haward saw Sir Andrew loose,
          Lord! in his hart that hee was ffaine:
      'Strike on your drummes, spread out your ancyents!
          Sound out your trumpetts! sound out amaine!'


47.   'Ffight on, my men!' sais Sir Andrew Bartton;
          'Weate, howsoever this geere will sway;
      Itt is my Lord Admirall of England
          Is come to seeke mee on the sea.'


48.   Simon had a sonne; with shott of a gunn —
          Well Sir Andrew might itt ken —
      He shott itt in att a privye place,
          And killed sixty more of Sir Andrews men.

49.  Harry Hunt came in att the other syde,
        And att Sir Andrew hee shott then;
     He drove downe his fformast-tree,
        And killed eighty more of Sir Andriwes men.


50.  'I have done a good turne,' sayes Harry Hunt;
        'Sir Andrew is not our kings ffreind;
     He hoped to have undone me yesternight,
        But I hope I have quitt him well in the end.'


51.  'Ever alas!' sayd Sir Andrew Barton,
        'What shold a man either thinke or say?
     Yonder ffalse theeffe is my strongest enemye,
        Who was my prisoner but yesterday.


52.  'Come hither to me, thou Gourden good,
        And be thou readye att my call,
     And I will give thee three hundred pound
        If thou wilt lett my beames downe ffall.'


53.  With that hee swarved the maine-mast tree,
        Soe did he itt with might and maine;
     Horseley, with a bearing arrow,
        Stroke the Gourden through the braine.


54.  And he ffell into the haches againe,
        And sore of this wound that he did bleed;
     Then word went throug Sir Andrews men,
        That the Gourden hee was dead.


55.  'Come hither to me, James Hambliton,
        Thou art my sisters sonne, I have no more;
     I will give thee six hundred pound
        If thou will lett my beames downe ffall.'

56. With that he swarved the maine-mast tree,
    Soe did hee itt with might and maine :
    Horseley, with another broad arrow,
    Strake the yeaman through the braine.

57. That hee ffell downe to the haches againe ;
    Sore of his wound that hee did bleed ;
    Covetousness getts no gaine,
    Itt is verry true, as the Welchman sayd.

58. But when hee saw his sisters sonne slaine,
    Lord ! in his heart hee was not well :
    'Goe ffeitch me down my armour of prove,
    Ffor I will to the topcastle my-selfe.

59. 'Goe ffeitch me downe my armour of prooffe,
    For itt is guilded with gold soe cleere ;
    God be with my brother, John of Bartton !
    Amongst the Portingalls hee did itt weare.'

60. But when hee had his armour of prooffe,
    And on his body hee had itt on,
    Every man that looked att him
    Sayd, Gunn nor arrow hee neede feare none !

61. 'Come hither, Horsley !' sayes my lord Haward,
    'And looke your shaft that itt goe right ;
    Shoot a good shoote in the time of need,
    And ffor thy shooting thoust be made a knight.'

62. 'I 'le doe my best,' sayes Horsley then,
    'Your Honor shall see beffore I goe ;
    If I shold be hanged att your mainemast,
    I have in my shipp but arrowes tow.'

63.  But att Sir Andrew hee shott then ;
        Hee made sure to hitt his marke ;
     Under the spole of his right arme
        He smote Sir Andrew quite throw the hart.

64.  Yett ffrom the tree hee wold not start,
        But hee clinged to itt with might and maine ;
     Under the coller then of his jacke,
        He stroke Sir Andrew thorrow the braine.

65.  ' Ffight on, my men,' sayes Sir Andrew Bartton,
        ' I am hurt, but I am not slaine ;
     I 'le lay mee downe and bleed a-while,
        And then I 'le rise and ffight againe.

66.  ' Ffight on, my men,' sayes Sir Andrew Bartton,
        ' These English doggs they bite soe lowe ;
     Ffight on ffor Scottland and Saint Andrew
        Till you heare my whistle blowe ! '

67.  But when the cold not heare his whistle blow,
        Sayes Harry Hunt, ' I 'le lay my head
     You may bord yonder noble shipp, my lord,
        For I know Sir Andrew hee is dead.'

68.  With that they borded this noble shipp,
        Soe did they itt with might and maine ;
     The ffound eighteen score Scotts alive,
        Besids the rest were maimed and slaine.

69.  My lord Haward tooke a sword in his hand,
        And smote of Sir Andrews head ;
     The Scotts stood by did weepe and mourne,
        But never a word durst speake or say.

70.   He caused his body to be taken downe,
          And over the hatch-bord cast into the sea,
      And about his middle three hundred crownes :
          'Wheresoever thou lands, itt will bury thee.'

71.   With his head they sayled into England againe,
          With right good will, and fforce and main,
      And the day beffore Newyeeres even
          Into Thames mouth they came againe.

72.   My lord Haward wrote to King Heneryes grace,
          With all the newes hee cold him bring :
      'Such a Newyeeres gifft I have brought to your
              Grace,
          As never did subject to any king.

73.   'Ffor merchandyes and manhood,
          The like is nott to be ffound ;
      The sight of these wold doe you good,
          Ffor you have not the like in your English ground.'

74.   But when hee heard tell that they were come,
          Full royally hee welcomed them home ;
      Sir Andrews shipp was the kings Newyeeres guifft ;
          A braver shipp you never saw none.

75.   Now hath our king Sir Andrews shipp,
          Besett with pearles and precyous stones ;
      Now hath England two shipps of warr,
          Two shipps of warr, before but one.

76.   'Who holpe to this ? ' sayes King Henerye,
          'That I may reward him ffor his paine : '
      'Harry Hunt, and Peeter Simon,
          William Horseleay, and I the same.'

77.   'Harry Hunt shall have his whistle and chaine,
          And all his jewells, whatsoever they bee,
      And other rich giffts that I will not name,
          For his good service he hath done mee.

78.   'Horslay, right thoust be a knight,
          Lands and livings thou shalt have store;
      Howard shalbe erle of Nottingham,
          And soe was never Haward before.

79.   'Now, Peeter Simon, thou art old;
          I will maintaine thee and thy sonne;
      Thou shalt have five hundred pound all in gold
          Ffor the good service that thou hast done.'

80.   Then King Henerye shiffted his roome;
          In came the Queene and ladyes bright;
      Other arrands they had none
          But to see Sir Andrew Bartton, Knight.

81.   But when they see his deadly fface,
          His eyes were hollow in his head;
      'I wold give a hundred pound,' sais King Henerye,
          'The man were alive as hee is dead!

82.   'Yett ffor the manfull part that hee hath playd,
          Both heere and beyond the sea,
      His men shall have halfe a crowne a day
          To bring them to my brother, King Jamye.'

## BROWN ROBYN'S CONFESSION.

1.   It fell upon a Wodensday
        Brown Robyn's men went to sea,
     But they saw neither moon nor sun
        Nor starlight wi their ee.

2.   'We'll cast kevels us amang,
        See wha the unhappy man may be;'
     The kevel fell on Brown Robyn,
        The master-man was he.

3.   'It is nae wonder,' said Brown Robyn,
        'Altho I dinna thrive,
     For    .    .    .    .    .    .

        .    .    .    .    .    .    .

4.   'But tie me to a plank o wude
        And throw me in the sea;
     And if I sink, ye may bid me sink,
        But if I swim, just lat me be.'

5.   They've tyed him to a plank o wude,
        And thrown him in the sea;
     He didna sink, tho they bade him sink;
        He swimd, and they lat him bee.

6.   He hadna been into the sea
        An hour but barely three,
     Till by it came Our Blessed Lady,
        Her dear young son her wi.

7. 'Will ye gang to your men again,
    Or will ye gang wi me?
   Will ye gang to the high heavens,
    Wi my dear son and me?'


8. 'I winna gang to my men again,
    For they would be feared at mee;
   But I woud gang to the high heavens,
    Wi thy dear son and thee.'


9. 'It's for nae honour ye did to me, Brown Robyn,
    It's for nae guid ye did to mee;
   But a' is for your fair confession
    You've made upon the sea.'

## SIR PATRICK SPENS.

1. The king sits in Dumferling toune,
    Drinking the blude-reid wine :
   ' O whar will I get guid sailor,
    To sail this schip of mine?'

2. Up and spak an eldern knicht,
    Sat at the kings richt kne :
   ' Sir Patrick Spence is the best sailor,
    That sails upon the se.'

3. The king has written a braid letter,
    And signd it wi his hand,
   And sent it to Sir Patrick Spence,
    Was walking on the sand.

4. The first line that Sir Patrick red,
    A loud lauch lauched he ;
   The next line that Sir Patrick red,
    The teir blinded his ee.

5. ' O wha is this has don this deid,
    This ill deid don to me,
   To send me out this time o' the yeir,
    To sail upon the se !

6. ' Mak hast, mak haste, my mirry men all,
    Our guid schip sails the morne :'
   ' O say na sae, my master deir,
    For I feir a deadlie storme.

7. 'Late late yestreen I saw the new moone,
    Wi the auld moone in hir arme,
And I feir, I feir, my deir master,
    That we will cum to harme.'

8. O our Scots nobles wer richt laith
    To weet their cork-heild schoone;
Bot lang owre a' the play wer playd,
    Thair hats they swam aboone.

9. O lang, lang may their ladies sit,
    Wi thair fans into their hand,
Or eir they se Sir Patrick Spence
    Cum sailing to the land.

10. O lang, lang may the ladies stand,
    Wi thair gold kems in their hair,
Waiting for thair ain deir lords,
    For they'll se thame na mair.

11. Haf owre, haf owre to Aberdour,
    It's fiftie fadom deip,
And thair lies guid Sir Patrick Spence,
    Wi the Scots lords at his feit.

## CAPTAIN CAR OR EDOM O GORDON.

1.   It befell at Martynmas,
         When wether waxed colde,
     Captaine Care said to his men,
         We must go take a holde.


         Syck, sike, and to-towe sike,
             And sike and like to die ;
         The sikest nighte that ever I abode,
             God lord have mercy on me !


2.   ' Haille, master, and wether you will,
         And wether ye like it best ; '
     ' To the castle of Crecrynbroghe,
         And there we will take our reste.'


3.   ' I knowe wher is a gay castle,
         Is builded of lyme and stone ;
     Within their is a gay ladie,
         Her lord is riden and gone.'


4.   The ladie she lend on her castle-walle,
         She loked upp and downe ;
     There was she ware of an host of men,
         Come riding to the towne.


5.   ' Se yow, my meri men all,
         And se yow what I see ?
     Yonder I see an host of men,
         I muse who they shold bee.'

6.  She thought he had ben her wed lord,
        As he comd riding home ;
    Then was it traitur Captaine Care
        The lord of Ester-towne.

7.  They wer no soner at supper sett,
        Then after said the grace,
    Or Captaine Care and all his men
        Wer lighte aboute the place.

8.  'Gyve over thi howsse, thou lady gay,
        And I will make the a bande ;
    To-nighte thou shall ly within my armes,
        To-morrowe thou shall ere my lande.'

9.  Then bespacke the eldest sonne,
        That was both whitt and redde :
    'O mother dere, geve over your howsse,
        Or elles we shalbe deade.'

10. 'I will not geve over my hous,' she saithe,
        'Not for feare of my lyffe ;
    It shalbe talked throughout the land,
        The slaughter of a wyffe.

11. 'Fetch me my pestilett,
        And charge me my gonne,
    That I may shott at this bloddy butcher,
        The lord of Easter-towne.'

12. Styfly upon her wall she stode,
        And lett the pellettes flee ;
    But then she myst the blody bucher,
        And she slew other three.

13. 'I will not geve over my hous,' she saithe,
      'Netheir for lord nor lowne ;
    Nor yet for traitour Captaine Care,
      The lord of Easter-towne.

14. 'I desire of Captine Care,
      And all his bloddye band,
    That he would save my eldest sonne,
      The eare of all my lande.'

15. 'Lap him in a shete,' he sayth,
      'And let him downe to me,
    And I shall take him in my armes,
      His waran shall I be.'

16. The captayne sayd unto him selfe ;
      Wyth sped, before the rest,
    He cut his tonge out of his head,
      His hart out of his brest.

17. He lapt them in a handkerchef,
      And knet it of knotes three,
    And cast them over the castell-wall,
      At that gay ladye.

18. 'Fye upon the, Captayne Care,
      And all thy bloddy band !
    For thou hast slayne my eldest sonne,
      The ayre of all my land.'

19. Then bespake the yongest sonne,
      That sat on the nurse's knee,
    Sayth, 'Mother gay, geve over your house ;
      For the smoake it smoothers me.'

20. Out then spake the Lady Margaret,
   As she stood on the stair ;
  The fire was at her goud garters,
   The lowe was at her hair.


21. ‘ I wold geve my gold,’ she saith,
   ‘ And so I wolde my ffee,
  For a blaste of the westryn wind,
   To dryve the smoke from thee.


22. ‘ Fy upon the, John Hamleton,
   That ever I paid the hyre !
  For thou hast broken my castle-wall,
   And kyndled in the ffyre.’


23. The lady gate to her close parler,
   The fire fell aboute her head ;
  She toke up her children two,
   Seth, ‘ Babes, we are all dead.’


24. Then bespake the hye steward,
   That is of hye degree ;
  Saith, ‘ Ladie gay, you are in close,
   Wether ye fighte or flee.’


25. Lord Hamleton dremd in his dream,
   In Carvall where he laye,
  His halle were all of fyre,
   His ladie slayne or daye.


26. ‘ Busk and bowne, my mery men all,
   Even and go ye with me ;
  For I dremd that my hall was on fyre,
   My lady slayne or day.’

27. He buskt him and bownd hym,
    And like a worthi knighte;
    And when he saw his hall burning,
    His harte was no dele lighte.

28. He sett a trumpett till his mouth,
    He blew as it plesd his grace;
    Twenty score of Hamlentons
    Was light aboute the place.

29. 'Had I knowne as much yesternighte
    As I do to-daye,
    Captaine Care and all his men
    Should not have gone so quite.

30. 'Fye upon the, Captaine Care,
    And all thy blody bande!
    Thou haste slayne my lady gay,
    More wurth then all thy lande.

31. 'If thou had ought eny ill will,' he saith,
    'Thou shoulde have taken my lyffe,
    And have saved my children thre,
    All and my lovesome wyffe.'

## THE BARON OF BRACKLEY.

1. Inverey cam doun Deeside, whistlin and playin,
   He was at brave Braikley's yett ere it was dawin.

2. He rappit fu loudly an wi a great roar,
   Cried, 'Cum doun, cum doun, Braikley, and open
   the door.

3. 'Are ye sleepin, Baronne, or are ye wakin?
   Ther's sharpe swords at your yett, will gar your
   blood spin.

4. 'Open the yett, Braikley, and lat us within,
   Till we on the green turf gar your bluid rin.'

5. Up spak his ladie, at his bak where she lay,
   'Get up, get up, Braikley, an be not afraid;
   The'r but young hir'd widifus wi belted plaids.'

6. 'Cum kiss me, mi Peggy, I'le nae langer stay,
   For I will go out and meet Inverey.

7. 'But haud your tongue, Peggy, and mak nae sic din,
   For yon same hir'd widifus will prove themselves
   men.'

8. She called on her marys, they cam to her hand;
   Cries, 'Bring me your rocks, lassies, we will them
   command.

9. 'Get up, get up, Braikley, and turn bak your ky,
   Or me an mi women will them defy.

10. 'Cum forth then, mi maidens, and show them some
　　　　play ;　.
　　We'll ficht them, and shortly the cowards will fly.

11. 'Gin I had a husband, whereas I hae nane,
　　He woud nae ly i his bed and see his ky taen.

12. 'Ther's four-and-twenty milk-whit calves, twal o
　　　　them ky,
　　In the woods o Glentanner, it's ther thei a' ly.

13. 'Ther's goat i the Etnach, and sheep o the brae,
　　An a' will be plundered by young Inverey.'

14. 'Now haud your tongue, Peggy, and gie me a gun,
　　Ye'll see me gae furth, but I'll never cum in.

15. 'Call mi brother William, mi unkl also,
　　Mi cousin James Gordon ; we'll mount and we'll go.'

16. When Braikley was ready and stood i the closs,
　　He was the bravest baronne that eer mounted horse.

17. Whan all wer assembled o the castell green,
　　No man like brave Braikley was ther to be seen.

18. 　.　　.　　.　　.　　.　　.　　.　　.　　.
　　'Turn bak, brother William, ye are a bridegroom ;

19. 'Wi bonnie Jean Gordon, the maid o the mill ;
　　O sichin and sobbin she'll soon get her fill.'

20. 'I'm no coward, brother, 'tis kend I'm a man ;
　　I'll ficht i your quarral as lang's I can stand.

21. 'I'll ficht, my dear brother, wi heart and gudewill,
And so will young Harry that lives at the mill.

22. 'But turn, mi dear brother, and nae langer stay :
What'll cum o your ladie, gin Braikley thei slay?

23. 'What'll cum o your ladie and bonnie young son?
O what'll cum o them when Braikley is gone?'

24. 'I never will turn : do you think I will fly?
But here I will ficht, and here I will die.'

25. 'Strik dogs,' crys Inverey, 'and ficht till ye're slayn,
For we are four hundred, ye are but four men.

26. 'Strik, strik, ye proud boaster, your honour is gone,
Your lands we will plunder, your castell we'll burn.'

27. At the head o the Etnach the battel began,
At Little Auchoilzie thei killd the first man.

28. First thei killd ane, and soon they killd twa,
Thei killd gallant Braikley, the flour o them a',

29. Thei killd William Gordon, and James o the Knox,
And brave Alexander, the flour o Glenmuick.

30. What sichin and moaning was heard i the glen,
For the Baronne o Braikley, who basely was slayn!

31. 'Cam ye bi the castell, and was ye in there?
Saw ye pretty Peggy tearing her hair?'

32. 'Yes, I cam by Braikley, and I gaed in there,
And there saw his ladie braiding her hair.

33. 'She was rantin, and dancin, and singin for joy,
    And vowin that nicht she woud feest Inverey.

34. 'She eat wi him, drank wi him, welcomd him in,
    Was kind to the man that had slain her baronne.'

35. Up spake the son on the nourice's knee,
    'Gin I live to be a man, revenged I'll be.'

36. Ther's dool i the kitchin, and mirth i the ha,
    The Baronne o Braikley is dead and awa.

# THE BONNY EARL OF MURRAY.

1. Ye Highlands, and ye Lawlands,
   Oh where have you been?
   They have slain the Earl of Murray,
   And they layd him on the green.

2. 'Now wae be to thee, Huntly!
   And wherefore did you sae?
   I bade you bring him wi you,
   But forbade you him to slay.'

3. He was a braw gallant,
   And he rid at the ring;
   And the bonny Earl of Murray,
   Oh he might have been a king!

4. He was a braw gallant,
   And he playd at the ba;
   And the bonny Earl of Murray
   Was the flower amang them a

5. He was a braw gallant,
   And he playd at the glove;
   And the bonny Earl of Murray,
   Oh he was the Queen's love!

6. Oh lang will his lady
   Look o'er the Castle Down,
   Eer she see the Earl of Murray
   Come sounding thro the town!

## YOUNG WATERS.

1. About Yule, when the wind blew cule,
   And the round tables began,
   A there is cum to our king's court
   Mony a well-favourd man.

2. The queen luikt owre the castle-wa,
   Beheld baith dale and down,
   And then she saw Young Waters
   Cum riding to the town.

3. His footmen they did rin before,
   His horsemen rade behind;
   Ane mantel of the burning gowd
   Did keip him frae the wind.

4. Gowden-graithd his horse before,
   And siller-shod behind;
   The horse Young Waters rade upon
   Was fleeter than the wind.

5. Out then spake a wylie lord,
   Unto the queen said he:
   O tell me wha 's the fairest face
   Rides in the company?'

6. 'I 've sene lord, and I 've sene laird,
   And knights of high degree,
   But a fairer face than Young Waters
   Mine eyne did never see.'

7.  Out then spack the jealous king,
        And an angry man was he :
    'O if he had been twice as fair,
        You micht have excepted me.'

8.  'You 're neither laird nor lord,' she says,
        'Bot the king that wears the crown ;
    There is not a knight in fair Scotland
        Bot to thee maun bow down.'

9.  For a' that she could do or say,
        Appeasd he wad nae bee,
    Bot for the words which she had said,
        Young Waters he maun dee.

10. They hae taen Young Waters,
        And put fetters to his feet ;
    They hae taen Young Waters,
        And thrown him in dungeon deep.

11. 'Aft have I ridden thro Stirling town,
        In the wind bot and the weit ;
    Bot I neir rade thro Stirling town
        Wi fetters at my feet.

12. 'Aft have I ridden thro Stirling town,
        In the wind bot and the rain ;
    Bot I neir rade thro Stirling town
        Neir to return again.'

13. They hae taen to the heiding-hill
        His young son in his craddle,
    And they hae taen to the heiding-hill
        His horse bot and his saddle.

14.    They hae taen to the heiding-hill
          His lady fair to see,
       And for the words the queen had spoke
          Young Waters he did dee.

Are the last two scenes any more than a formal lament? If so—should the last two scenes be regarded as separate scenes or as narrative?

Last five stanzas merely descriptive elaboration—

## MARY HAMILTON.

1. Word's gane to the kitchen,
    And word's gane to the ha,
   That Marie Hamilton has born a bairn
    To the hichest Stewart of a'.

2. She's tyed it in her apron
    And she's thrown it in the sea ;
   Says, 'Sink ye, swim ye, bonny wee babe,
    You'll ne'er get mair o me.'

3. Down then cam the auld Queen,
    Goud tassels tying her hair :
   'O Marie, where's the bonny wee babe
    That I heard greet sae sair?'

4. 'There was never a babe intill my room,
    As little designs to be ;
   It was but a touch o my sair side,
    Came o'er my fair bodie.'

5. 'O Marie, put on your robes o black,
    Or else your robes o brown,
   For ye maun gang wi me the night,
    To see fair Edinbro town.'

6. 'I winna put on my robes o black,
    Nor yet my robes o brown ;
   But I 'll put on my robes o white,
    To shine through Edinbro town.'

7. When she gaed up the Cannogate,
    She laughd loud laughters three;
But when she cam down the Cannogate
    The tear blinded her ee.

8. When she gaed up the Parliament stair,
    The heel cam aff her shee;
And lang or she cam down again
    She was condemnd to dee.

9. When she cam down the Cannogate,
    The Cannogate sae free,
Many a ladie lookd o'er her window,
    Weeping for this ladie.

10. 'Make never meen for me,' she says,
    'Make never meen for me;
Seek never grace frae a graceless face,
    For that ye'll never see.

11. 'Bring me a bottle of wine,' she says,
    'The best that eer ye hae,
That I may drink to my weil-wishers,
    And they may drink to me.

12. 'And here's to the jolly sailor lad
    That sails upon the faem;
And let not my father nor mother get wit
    But that I shall come again.

13. 'And here's to the jolly sailor lad
    That sails upon the sea;
But let not my father nor mother get wit
    O the death that I maun dee.

*Interpret M.H. by the public that composed her.*

14. 'Oh little did my mother think,
      The day she cradled me,
   What lands I was to travel through,
      What death I was to dee.

*People of that time had little love for nobility*

15. 'Oh little did my father think,
      The day he held up me,
   What lands I was to travel through,
      What death I was to dee.

16. 'Last night I washd the Queen's feet,
      And gently laid her down;
   And a' the thanks I've gotten the nicht
      To be hangd in Edinbro town!

17. 'Last nicht there was four Maries,
      The nicht there 'll be but three;
   There was Marie Seton, and Marie Beton.
      And Marie Carmichael, and me.'

*Character of Mary Hamilton chief note in his ballad; her cool indifference to death*

# BONNIE GEORGE CAMPBELL.

1. High upon Highlands,
    and low upon Tay,
Bonnie George Campbell
    rade out on a day.

2. Saddled and bridled
    and gallant rade he;
Hame cam his guid horse,
    but never cam he.

3. Out cam his auld mither
    greeting fu' sair,
And out cam his bonnie bride
    riving her hair.

4. Saddled and bridled
    and booted rade he;
Toom hame cam the saddle,
    but never cam he.

5. 'My meadow lies green,
    and my corn is unshorn,
My barn is to build,
    and my babe is unborn.'

6. Saddled and bridled
    and booted rade he;
Toom hame cam the saddle,
    but never cam he.

## BESSIE BELL AND MARY GRAY.

1. O Bessie Bell and Mary Gray,
       They war twa bonnie lasses !
   They bigget a bower on yon burn-brae,
       And theekit it oer wi rashes.

2. They theekit it oer wi rashes green,
       They theekit it oer wi heather ;
   But the pest cam frae the burrows-town,
       And slew them baith thegither.

3. They thought to lie in Methven kirk-yard
       Amang their noble kin ;
   But they maun lye in Stronach haugh,
       To biek forenent the sin.

4. And Bessie Bell and Mary Gray,
       They war twa bonnie lasses ;
   They biggit a bower on yon burn-brae,
       And theekit it oer wi rashes.

# SIR HUGH.

1.    Four and twenty bonny boys
      Were playing at the ba,
   And by it came him sweet Sir Hugh,
      And he playd oer them a'.

2.    He kickd the ba with his right foot,
      And catchd it wi his knee,
   And throuch-and-thro the Jew's window
      He gard the bonny ba flee.

3.    He's doen him to the Jew's castell,
      And walkd it round about;
   And there he saw the Jew's daughter
      At the window looking out.

4.    'Throw down the ba, ye Jew's daughter,
      Throw down the ba to me!'
   'Never a bit,' says the Jew's daughter,
      'Till up to me come ye.'

5.    'How will I come up?   How can I come up?
      How can I come to thee?
   For as ye did to my auld father,
      The same ye 'll do to me.'

6.    She's gane till her father's garden,
      And pu'd an apple, red and green;
   'T was a' to wyle him sweet Sir Hugh,
      And to entice him in.

7. She 's led him in through ae dark door,
    And sae has she thro nine ;
She 's laid him on a dressing-table,
    And stickit him like a swine.

8. And first came out the thick, thick blood,
    And syne came out the thin,
And syne came out the bonny heart's blood ;
    There was nae mair within.

9. She 's rowd him in a cake o lead,
    Bade him lie still and sleep ;
She 's thrown him in Our Lady's draw-well,
    Was fifty fathom deep.

10. When bells were rung, and mass was sung,
    And a' the bairns came hame,
When every lady gat hame her son,
    The Lady Maisry gat nane.

11. She 's taen her mantle her about,
    Her coffer by the hand,
And she 's gane out to seek her son,
    And wanderd oer the land.

12. She 's doen her to the Jew's castell,
    Where a' were fast asleep :
'Gin ye be there, my sweet Sir Hugh,
    I pray you to me speak.'

13. She 's doen her to the Jew's garden,
    Thought he had been gathering fruit :
'Gin ye be there, my sweet Sir Hugh,
    I pray you to me speak.'

14.   She neard Our Lady's deep draw-well,
      Was fifty fathom deep :
   'Whareer ye be, my sweet Sir Hugh,
      I pray you to me speak.'

15.   'Gae hame, gae hame, my mither dear,
      Prepare my winding sheet,
   And at the back o merry Lincoln
      The morn I will you meet.'

16.   Now Lady Maisry is gane hame,
      Made him a winding sheet,
   And at the back o merry Lincoln
      The dead corpse did her meet.

17.   And a' the bells o merry Lincoln
      Without men's hands were rung,
   And a' the books o merry Lincoln
      Were read without man's tongue,
   And neer was such a burial
      Sin Adam's days begun.

## THE THREE RAVENS.

1. There were three ravens sat on a tree,
      Downe a downe, hay down, hay downe,
   There were three ravens sat on a tree,
      With a downe,
   There were three ravens sat on a tree,
   They were as blacke as they might be.
      With a downe derrie, derrie, derrie, downe, downe.

2. The one of them said to his mate,
   'Where shall we our breakfast take?'

3. 'Downe in yonder greene field
   There lies a knight slain under his shield.

4. 'His hounds they lie down at his feete,
   So well they can their master keepe.

5. 'His haukes they flie so eagerly,
   There's no fowle dare him come nie.'

6. Downe there comes a fallow doe,
   As great with young as she might goe.

7. She lift up his bloudy hed,
   And kist his wounds that were so red.

8. She got him up upon her backe,
   And carried him to earthen lake.

9. She buried him before the prime,
   She was dead herselfe ere even-song time.

10. God send every gentleman
    Such haukes, such hounds, and such a leman.

## LORD RANDAL.

1.  'O where hae ye been, Lord Randal, my son?
    O where hae ye been, my handsome young man?'
    'I hae been to the wild wood ; mother, make my bed
        soon,
    For I'm weary wi hunting, and fain wald lie down.'

2.  'Where gat ye your dinner, Lord Randal, my son?
    Where gat ye your dinner, my handsome young
        man?'
    'I din'd wi my true-love ; mother, make my bed soon,
    For I'm weary wi hunting, and fain wald lie down.'

3.  'What gat ye to your dinner, Lord Randal, my son?
    What gat ye to your dinner, my handsome young
        man?'
    'I gat eels boiled in broo ; mother, make my bed
        soon,
    For I'm weary wi hunting, and fain wald lie down.'

4.  'What became of your bloodhounds, Lord Randal,
        my son?
    What became of your bloodhounds, my handsome
        young man?'
    'O they swelld and they died ; mother, make my bed
        soon,
    For I'm weary wi hunting, and fain wald lie down.'

5.  'O I fear ye are poisond, Lord Randal, my son!
    O I fear ye are poisond, my handsome young man!'
    'O yes! I am poisond ; mother, make my bed soon,
    For I'm sick at the heart, and I fain wald lie down.'

# EDWARD.

1. 'Why dois your brand sae drap wi bluid,
        Edward, Edward,
    Why dois your brand sae drap wi bluid,
        And why sae sad gang yee O?'
    'O I hae killed my hauke sae guid,
        Mither, mither,
    O I hae killed my hauke sae guid,
        And I had nae mair bot hee O.'

2. 'Your haukis bluid was nevir sae reid,
        Edward, Edward,
    Your haukis bluid was never sae reid,
        My deir son I tell thee O.'
    'O I hae killed my reid-roan steid,
        Mither, mither,
    O I hae killed my reid-roan steid,
        That erst was sae fair and frie O.'

3. 'Your steid was auld, and ye hae gat mair,
        Edward, Edward,
    Your steid was auld, and ye hae gat mair,
        Sum other dule ye drie O.'
    'O I hae killed my fadir deir,
        Mither, mither,
    O I hae killed my fadir deir,
        Alas, and wae is mee O!'

4. 'And whatten penance wul ye drie, for that,
        Edward, Edward,
    And whatten penance wul ye drie, for that?
        My deir son, now tell me O.'

'Ile set my feit in yonder boat,
   Mither, mither,
Ile set my feit in yonder boat,
  And Ile fare ovir the sea O.'


5. 'And what wul ye doe wi your towirs and your ha,
    Edward, Edward,
 And what wul ye doe wi your towirs and your ha,
  That were sae fair to see O?'
'Ile let thame stand tul they doun fa,
   Mither, mither,
Ile let thame stand tul they doun fa,
  For here nevir mair maun I bee O.'


6. 'And what wul ye leive to your bairns and your wife,
    Edward, Edward,
 And what wul ye leive to your bairns and your wife,
  Whan ye gang ovir the sea O?'
'The warldis room, late them beg thrae life,
   Mither, mither,
The warldis room, late them beg thrae life,
  For thame nevir mair wul I see O.'


7. 'And what wul ye leive to your ain mither dear,
    Edward, Edward,
 And what wul ye leive to your ain mither dear?
  My deir son, now tell me O.'
'The curse of hell frae me sall ye beir,
   Mither, mither,
The curse of hell frae me sall ye beir,
  Sic counseils ye gave to me O.'

## THE TWA SISTERS.

1. There was twa sisters in a bowr,
     Edinburgh, Edinburgh,
   There was twa sisters in a bowr,
     Stirling for ay,
   There was twa sisters in a bowr,
   There came a knight to be their wooer.
   Bonny Saint Johnston stands upon Tay.

2. He courted the eldest wi glove an ring,
   But he lovd the youngest above a' thing.

3. He courted the eldest wi brotch an knife,
   But lovd the youngest as his life.

4. The eldest she was vexed sair,
   An much envi'd her sister fair.

5. Upon a morning fair an clear,
   She cried upon her sister dear:

6. 'O sister, come to yon sea stran,
   An see our father's ships come to lan.'

7. She 's taen her by the milk-white han,
   An led her down to yon sea stran.

8. The youngest stood upon a stane,
   The eldest came and threw her in.

9. She took her by the middle sma,
   An dashd her bonnie back to the jaw.

10. 'O sister, sister, tak my han,
    An Ise mack you heir to a' my lan.

11. 'O sister, sister, tak my middle,
    An yes get my goud and my gouden girdle.

12. 'O sister, sister, save my life,
    An I swear Ise never be nae man's wife.'

13. 'Foul fa the han that I should tacke,
    It twind me an my warldes make.

14. 'Your cherry cheeks an yellow hair
    Gars me gae maiden for evermair.'

15. Sometimes she sank, an sometimes she swam,
    Till she came down yon bonny mill-dam.

16. O out it came the miller's son,
    An saw the fair maid swimmin in.

17. 'O father, father, draw your dam,
    Here's either a mermaid or a swan.'

18. The miller quickly drew the dam,
    And there he found a drownd woman.

19. You coudna see her yellow hair
    For gold and pearle that were so rare.

20. You coudna see her middle sma
    For gouden girdle that was sae braw.

21. You coudna see her fingers white
    For gouden rings that was sae gryte.

22. An by there came a harper fine,
    That harped to the king at dine.

23. When he did look that lady upon,
    He sighd and made a heavy moan.

24. He's taen three locks o her yallow hair,
    An wi them strung his harp sae fair.

25. The first tune he did play and sing,
    Was, ' Farewell to my father the king.'

26. The nextin tune that he playd syne,
    Was, ' Farewell to my mother the queen.'

27. The lasten tune that he playd then,
    Was, ' Wae to my sister, fair Ellen.'

## THE TWA BROTHERS.

1. There were twa brethren in the north,
    They went to the school thegither;
   The one unto the other said,
    'Will you try a warsle afore?'

2. They warsled up, they warsled down,
    Till Sir John fell to the ground,
   And there was a knife in Sir Willie's pouch,
    Gied him a deadlie wound.

3. 'Oh brither dear, take me on your back,
    Carry me to yon burn clear,
   And wash the blood from off my wound,
    And it will bleed nae mair.'

4. He took him up upon his back,
    Carried him to yon burn clear,
   And washd the blood from off his wound,
    But aye it bled the mair.

5. 'Oh brither dear, take me on your back,
    Carry me to yon kirk-yard,
   And dig a grave baith wide and deep,
    And lay my body there.'

6. He's taen him up upon his back,
    Carried him to yon kirk-yard,
   And dug a grave baith deep and wide,
    And laid his body there.

7.   'But what will I say to my father dear,
        Gin he chance to say, Willie, whar 's John?'
     'Oh say that he 's to England gone,
        To buy him a cask of wine.'

8.   'And what will I say to my mother dear,
        Gin she chance to say, Willie, whar's John?'
     'Oh say that he 's to England gone,
        To buy her a new silk gown.'

9.   'And what will I say to my sister dear,
        Gin she chance to say, Willie, whar 's John?'
     'Oh say that he 's to England gone,
        To buy her a wedding ring.'

10.  'But what will I say to her you loe dear,
        Gin she cry, Why tarries my John?'
     'Oh tell her I lie in Kirk-land fair,
        And home again will never come.'

## BEWICK AND GRAHAME.

1. Old Grahame he is to Carlisle gone,
    Where Sir Robert Bewick there met he;
In arms to the wine they are gone,
    And drank till they were both merry.

2. Old Grahame he took up the cup,
    And said, 'Brother Bewick, here's to thee,
And here's to our two sons at home,
    For they live best in our country.'

3. 'Nay, were thy son as good as mine,
    And of some books he could but read,
With sword and buckler by his side,
    To see how he could save his head,

4. 'They might have been calld two bold brethren
    Where ever they did go or ride;
They might have been calld two bold brethren,
    They might have crackd the Border-side.

5. 'Thy son is bad, and is but a lad,
    And bully to my son cannot be;
For my son Bewick can both write and read,
    And sure I am that cannot he.'

6. 'I put him to school, but he would not learn,
    I bought him books, but he would not read;
But my blessing he's never have
    Till I see how his hand can save his head.'

7.   Old Grahame called for an account,
     And he askd what was for to pay;
  There he paid a crown, so it went round,
     Which was all for good wine and hay.

8.   Old Grahame is into the stable gone,
     Where stood thirty good steeds and three;
  He's taken his own steed by the head,
     And home rode he right wantonly.

9.   When he came home, there did he espy
     A loving sight to spy or see,
  There did he espy his own three sons,
     Young Christy Grahame, the foremost was he.

10.   There did he espy his own three sons,
     Young Christy Grahame, the foremost was he:
  'Where have you been all day, father,
     That no counsel you would take by me?'

11.   'Nay, I have been in Carlisle town,
     Where Sir Robert Bewick there met me;
  He said thou was bad, and calld thee a lad,
     And a baffled man by thou I be.

12.   'He said thou was bad, and calld thee a lad,
     And bully to his son cannot be;
  For his son Bewick can both write and read,
     And sure I am that cannot thee.

13.   'I put thee to school, but thou would not learn,
     I bought thee books, but thou would not read;
  But my blessing thou's never have
     Till I see with Bewick thou can save thy head.'

14.    'Oh, pray forbear, my father dear;
           That ever such a thing should be!
       Shall I venture my body in field to fight
           With a man that's faith and troth to me?'


15.    'What's that thou sayst, thou limmer loon?
           Or how dare thou stand to speak to me?
       If thou do not end this quarrel soon,
           Here is my glove thou shalt fight me.'


16.    Christy stoopd low unto the ground,
           Unto the ground, as you'll understand:
       'O father, put on your glove again,
           The wind hath blown it from your hand.'


17.    'What's that thou sayst, thou limmer loon?
           Or how dare thou stand to speak to me?
       If thou do not end this quarrel soon,
           Here is my hand thou shalt fight me.'


18.    Christy Grahame is to his chamber gone,
           And for to study, as well might be,
       Whether to fight with his father dear,
           Or with his bully Bewick he.


19.    'If it be my fortune my bully to kill,
           As you shall boldly understand,
       In every town that I ride through,
           They'll say, There rides a brotherless man!


20.    'Nay, for to kill my bully dear,
           I think it will be a deadly sin;
       And for to kill my father dear,
           The blessing of heaven I ne'er shall win.

21. 'O give me my blessing, father,' he said,
    'And pray well for me for to thrive;
  If it be my fortune my bully to kill,
    I swear I'll neer come home alive.'

22. He put on his back a good plate-jack,
    And on his head a cap of steel,
  With sword and buckler by his side;
    O gin he did not become them weel!

23. 'O fare thee well, my father dear!
    And fare thee well, thou Carlisle town!
  If it be my fortune my bully to kill,
    I swear I'll neer eat bread again.'

24. Now we'll leave talking of Christy Grahame,
    And talk of him again belive;
  But we will talk of bonny Bewick,
    Where he was teaching his scholars five.

25. Now when he had learnd them well to fence,
    To handle their swords without any doubt,
  He's taken his own sword under his arm,
    And walkd his father's close about.

26. He lookd between him and the sun,
    To see what farleys he could see;
  There he spy'd a man with armour on,
    As he came riding over the lee.

27. 'I wonder much what man yon be
    That so boldly this way does come;
  I think it is my nighest friend,
    I think it is my bully Grahame.

28.   'O welcome, O welcome, bully **Grahame** !
          O man, thou art my dear, welcome !
      O man, thou art my dear, welcome !
          For I love thee best in Christendom.'


29.   'Away, away, O bully Bewick,
          And of thy bullyship let me **be** !
      The day is come I never thought on ;
          Bully, I 'm come here to fight with thee.'


30.   'O no ! not so, O bully Grahame !
          That eer such a word should spoken be !
      I was thy master, thou was my scholar :
          So well as I have learned thee.'


31.   'My father he was in Carlisle town,
          Where thy father Bewick there met he ;
      He said I was bad, and he called me a lad,
          And a baffled man by thou I be.'


32.   'Away, away, O bully **Grahame**,
          And of all that talk, man, let us be !
      We 'll take three men of either side
          To see if we can our fathers agree.'


33.   'Away, away, O bully Bewick,
          And of thy bullyship let me **be** !
      But if thou be a man, as I trow thou art,
          Come over this ditch and fight with me.'


34.   'O no, not so, my bully Grahame !
          That eer such a word should spoken be !
      Shall I venture my body in field to fight
          With a man that 's faith and troth to me ?'

35. 'Away, away, O bully Bewick,
     And of all that care, man, let us be !
If thou be a man, as I trow thou art,
     Come over this ditch and fight with me.'


36. 'Now, if it be my fortune thee, Grahame, to kill,
     As God's will, man, it all must be ;
But if it be my fortune thee, Grahame, to kill,
     'Tis home again I 'll never gae.'


37. 'Thou art of my mind, then, bully Bewick,
     And sworn-brethren will we be ;
If thou be a man, as I trow thou art,
     Come over this ditch and fight with me.'


38. He flang his cloak from off his shoulders,
     His psalm-book out of his hand flung he,
He clapd his hand upon the hedge,
     And oer lap he right wantonly.


39. When Grahame did see his bully come,
     The salt tear stood long in his eye :
'Now needs must I say that thou art a man,
     That dare venture thy body to fight with me.


40. 'Now I have a harness on my back ;
     I know that thou hath none on thine ;
But as little as thou hath on thy back,
     Sure as little shall there be on mine.'


41. He flang his jack from off his back,
     His steel cap from his head flang he ;
He's taken his sword into his hand,
     He's tyed his horse unto a tree.

42.  Now they fell to it with two broad swords,
         For two long hours fought Bewick and he;
     Much sweat was to be seen on them both,
         But never a drop of blood to see.


43.  Now Grahame gave Bewick an ackward stroke,
         An ackward stroke surely struck he;
     He struck him now under the left breast,
         Then down to the ground as dead fell he.


44.  'Arise, arise, O bully Bewick,
         Arise, and speak three words to me!
     Whether this be thy deadly wound,
         Or God and good surgeons will mend thee.'


45.  'O horse, O horse, O bully Grahame,
         And pray do get thee far from me!
     Thy sword is sharp, it hath wounded my heart,
         And so no further can I gae.


46.  'O horse, O horse, O bully Grahame,
         And get thee far from me with speed!
     And get thee out of this country quite!
         That none may know who's done the deed.'


47.  'O if this be true, my bully dear,
         The words that thou dost tell to me,
     The vow I made, and the vow I'll keep,
         I swear I'll be the first to die.'


48.  Then he stuck his sword in a moudie-hill,
         Where he lap thirty good foot and three;
     First he bequeathed his soul to God,
         And upon his own sword-point lap he.

49. Now Grahame he was the first that died,
    And then came Robin Bewick to see;
'Arise, arise, O son,' he said,
    'For I see thou's won the victory.

50. 'Arise, arise, O son,' he said,
    'For I see thou's won the victory;'
'Father, could ye not drunk your wine at home,
    And letten me and my brother be?

51. 'Nay, dig a grave both low and wide,
    And in it us two pray bury;
But bury my bully Grahame on the sun-side,
    For I'm sure he's won the victory.'

52. Now we'll leave talking of these two brethren,
    In Carlisle town where they lie slain,
And talk of these two good old men,
    Where they were making a pitiful moan.

53. With that bespoke now Robin Bewick:
    'O man was I not much to blame?
I have lost one of the liveliest lads
    That ever was bred unto my name.'

54. With that bespoke my good lord Grahame:
    'O man, I have lost the better block;
I have lost my comfort and my joy,
    I have lost my key, I have lost my lock.

55. 'Had I gone through all Ladderdale,
    And forty horse had set on me,
Had Christy Grahame been at my back,
    So well as he would guarded me.'

56.   I have no more of my song to sing,
        But two or three words to you I'll name ;
    But 'twill be talked in Carlisle town
        That these two old men were all the blame.

## THE CRUEL BROTHER.

1. There was three ladies playd at the ba,
    With a hey ho and a lillie gay, *refrain*
   There came a knight and played oer them a',
    As the primrose spreads so sweetly. *refrain*

2. One o them was clad in red:
   He asked if she wad be his bride.

3. One o them was clad in green:
   He asked if she wad be his queen.

4. The last o them was clad in white:
   He asked if she wad be his heart's delight.

5. 'Ye may ga ask my father, the king:
   Sae maun ye ask my mither, the queen.

6. 'Sae maun ye ask my sister Anne:
   And dinna forget my brither John.'

7. He has asked her father, the king:
   And sae did he her mither, the queen.

8. And he has asked her sister Anne:
   But he has forgot her brother John.

9. Now, when the wedding day was come,
   The knight would take his bonny bride home.

10.   And many a lord and many a knight
      Came to behold that ladie bright.


11.   And there was nae man that did her see,
      But wishd himself bridegroom to be.


12.   Her father dear led her down the stair,
      And her sisters twain they kissd her there.


13.   Her mother dear led her thro the closs,
      And her brother John set her on her horse.


14.   She leand her oer the saddle-bow,
      To give him a kiss ere she did go.


15.   He has taen a knife, baith lang and sharp,
      And stabbd that bonny bride to the heart.


16.   She hadno ridden half thro the town,
      Until her heart's blude staind her gown.


17.   'Ride up, ride up,' said the foremost man ;
      'I think our bride comes hooly on.'


18.   'Ride up, ride up,' said the second man;
      'I think our bride looks pale and wan.'


19.   'O lead me gently up yon hill,
      And I'll there sit down, and make my will.'


20.   'O what will you leave to your father dear ?'
      'The silver-shod steed that brought me here.'


21.   'What will you leave to your mother dear ?'
      'My velvet pall and my silken gear.'

22.   'What will you leave to your sister Anne?'
      'My silken scarf and my gowden fan.'

23.   'What will you leave to your sister Grace?'
      'My bloody cloaths to wash and dress.'

24.   'What will you leave to your brother John?'
      'The gallows-tree to hang him on.'

25.   'What will you leave to your brother John's wife?'
      'The wilderness to end her life.'

# BABYLON; OR THE BONNIE BANKS O FORDIE.

1. There were three ladies lived in a bower,
     Eh vow bonnie, – *refrain of two lines.*
   And they went out to pull a flower
       On the bonnie banks o Fordie.

2. They hadna pu 'ed a flower but ane,
   When up started to them a banisht man.
       *On the bonnie banks o Fordie*

3. He 's taen the first sister by her hand,
   And he 's turned her round and made her stand.

4. 'It 's whether will ye be a rank robber's wife,
   Or will ye die by my wee pen-knife?'

5. 'It 's I 'll not be a rank robber's wife,
   But I 'll rather die by your wee pen-knife.'

6. He 's killed this may, and he 's laid her by,
   For to bear the red rose company.

7. He 's taken the second ane by the hand,
   And he 's turned her round and made her stand.

8. 'It 's whether will ye be a rank robber's wife,
   Or will ye die by my wee pen-knife?'

9. 'I 'll not be a rank robber's wife,
   But I 'll rather die by your wee pen-knife.'

10. He's killed this may, and he's laid her by,
    For to bear the red rose company.

11. He's taken the youngest ane by the hand,
    And he's turned her round, and made her stand.

12. Says, 'Will ye be a rank robber's wife,
    Or will ye die by my wee pen-knife?'

13. 'I'll not be a rank robber's wife,
    Nor will I die by your wee pen-knife.

14. 'For I hae a brother in this wood,
    And gin ye kill me, it's he'll kill thee.'

15. 'What's thy brother's name? Come tell to me.
    'My brother's name is Baby Lon.'

16. 'O sister, sister, what have I done!
    O have I done this ill to thee!

17. 'O since I've done this evil deed,
    Good sall never be seen o me.'

18. He's taken out his wee pen-knife,
    And he's twyned himsel o his ain sweet life.

## CHILD MAURICE.

1.  Childe Maurice hunted ithe silver wood,
      He hunted it round about,
    And noebodye that he found therin,
      Nor none there was with-out.

2.  He sayes, 'Come hither, thou litle foot-page,
      That runneth lowlye by my knee,
    For thou shalt goe to John Stewards wife
      And pray her speake with mee.

3.  '    .    .    .    .    .    .    .    .    .
         .    .    .    .    .    .    .    .
    I, and greete thou doe that ladye well,
      Ever soe well froe mee.

4.  'And, as it falls, as many times
      As knotts beene knitt on a kell,
    Or marchant men gone to leeve London
      Either to buy ware or sell.

5.  'And, as it falles, as many times
      As any hart can thinke,
    Or schoole-masters are in any schoole-house
      Writing with pen and inke :
    For if I might, as well as shee may,
      This night I wold with her speake.

6.  'And heere I send her a mantle of greene,
      As greene as any grasse,
    And bid her come to the silver wood,
      To hunt with Child Maurice.

7.  'And there I send her a ring of gold,
       A ring of precyous stone,
    And bidd her come to the silver wood,
       Let for no kind of man.'

8.  One while this litle boy he yode,
       Another while he ran,
    Untill he came to John Stewards hall,
       I-wis he never blan.

9.  And of nurture the child had good,
       Hee ran up hall and bower free,
    And when he came to this lady faire,
       Sayes, 'God you save and see!

10. 'I am come from Child Maurice,
       A message unto thee ;
    And Child Maurice, he greetes you well,
       And ever soe well from mee.

11. 'And, as it falls, as oftentimes
       As knotts beene knitt on a kell,
    Or marchant men gone to leeve London
       Either for to buy ware or sell.

12. 'And as oftentimes he greetes you well
       As any hart can thinke,
    Or schoolemasters are in any schoole,
       Wryting with pen and inke.

13. 'And heere he sends a mantle of greene,
       As greene as any grasse,
    And he bids you come to the silver wood,
       To hunt with Child Maurice.

14.  'And heere he sends you a ring of gold,
         A ring of the precyous stone ;
     He prayes you to come to the silver wood,
         Let for no kind of man.'

15.  'Now peace, now peace, thou litle footpage,
         For Christes sake, I pray thee !
     For if my lord heare one of these words,
         Thou must be hanged hye !'

16.  John Steward stood under the castle wall,
         And he wrote the words everye one,

     .   .   .   .   .   .   .   .   .   .

         .   .   .   .   .   .   .   .   .

17.  And he called unto his hors-keeper,
         'Make readye you my steede !'
     I, and soe ne did to his chamberlaine,
         'Make readye thou my weede !'

18.  And he cast a lease upon his backe,
         And he rode to the silver wood,
     And there he sought all about,
         About the silver wood.

19.  And there he found him Child Maurice
         Sitting upon a blocke,
     With a silver combe in his hand,
         Kembing his yellow lockes.

     *   *   *   *   *   *   *   *

20.  But then stood up him Child Maurice,
         And sayd these words trulye :
     'I doe not know your ladye,' he said,
         'If that I doe her see.'

21.   He sayes, 'How now, how now, Child Maurice?
          Alacke, how may this bee?
      For thou hast sent her love-tokens,
          More now then two or three;

22.   'For thou hast sent her a mantle of greene,
          As greene as any grasse,
      And bade her come to the silver woode
          To hunt with Child Maurice.

23.   'And thou hast sent her a ring of gold,
          A ring of precyous stone,
      And bade her come to the silver wood,
          Let for noe kind of man.

24.   'And by my faith, now, Child Maurice,
          The tone of us shall dye!'
      'Now be my troth,' sayd Child Maurice,
          'And that shall not be I.'

25.   But hee pulled forth a bright browne sword,
          And dryed it on the grasse,
      And soe fast he smote at John Steward,
          I-wisse he never did rest.

26.   Then hee pulled forth his bright browne sword,
          And dryed it on his sleeve,
      And the first good stroke John Stewart stroke,
          Child Maurice head he did cleeve.

27.   And he pricked it on his swords poynt,
          Went singing there beside,
      And he rode till he came to that ladye faire,
          Wheras this ladye lyed.

28. And sayes, 'Dost thou know Child Maurice head,
    If that thou dost it see?
And lap it soft, and kisse it oft,
    For thou lovedst him better than mee.'


29. But when shee looked on Child Maurice head,
    She never spake words but three:
'I never beare no childe but one,
    And you have slaine him trulye.'


30. Sayes, 'Wicked be my merrymen all,
    I gave meate, drinke, and clothe!
But cold they not have holden me
    When I was in all that wrath!


31. 'For I have slaine one of the curteousest knights
    That ever bestrode a steed,
Soe have I done one of the fairest ladyes
    That ever ware womans weede!'

# THE WIFE OF USHER'S WELL.

1. There lived a wife at Usher's Well,
   And a wealthy wife was she;
   She had three stout and stalwart sons,
   And sent them oer the sea.

2. They hadna been a week from her,
   A week but barely ane,
   When word came to the carline wife
   That her three sons were gane.

3. They hadna been a week from her,
   A week but barely three,
   When word came to the carlin wife
   That her sons she'd never see.

4. 'I wish the wind may never cease,
   Nor fashes in the flood,
   Till my three sons come hame to me,
   In earthly flesh and blood.'

5. It fell about the Martinmass,
   When nights are lang and mirk,
   The carlin wife's three sons came hame,
   And their hats were o the birk.

6. It neither grew in syke nor ditch,
   Nor yet in ony sheugh;
   But at the gates o Paradise,
   That birk grew fair eneugh.

7. ' Blow up the fire, my maidens !
 Bring water from the well !
For a' my house shall feast this night,
 Since my three sons are well.'

8. And she has made to them a bed,
 She 's made it large and wide,
And she 's ta'en her mantle her about,
 Sat down at the bed-side.

   \*  \*  \*  \*  \*  \*  \*

9. Up then crew the red, red cock,
 And up and crew the gray ;
The eldest to the youngest said,
 ' 'T is time we were away.'

10. The cock he hadna craw'd but once,
 And clappd his wings at a',
When the youngest to the eldest said,
 ' Brother, we must awa.

11. ' The cock doth craw, the day doth daw,
 The channerin worm doth chide ;
Gin we be mist out o our place,
 A sair pain we maun bide.

12. ' Fare ye weel, my mother dear !
 Fareweel to barn and byre !
And fare ye weel, the bonny lass
 That kindles my mother's fire !'

## CLERK COLVEN.

1.  Clark Colven and his gay ladie,
      As they walked to yon garden green,
    A belt about her middle gimp,
      Which cost Clark Colven crowns fifteen:

2.  'O hearken weel now, my good lord,
      O hearken weel to what I say;
    When ye gang to the wall o Stream,
      O gang nae neer the well-fared may.'

3.  'O haud your tongue, my gay ladie,
      Tak nae sic care o me;
    For I nae saw a fair woman
      I like so well as thee.'

4.  He mounted on his berry-brown steed,
      And merry, merry rade he on,
    Till he came to the wall o Stream,
      And there he saw the mermaiden.

5.  'Ye wash, ye wash, ye bonny may,
      And ay 's ye wash your sark o silk:'
    'It 's a' for you, ye gentle knight,
      My skin is whiter than the milk.'

6.  He's taen her by the milk-white hand,
      He's taen her by the sleeve sae green,
    And he's forgotten his gay ladie,
      And away with the fair maiden.

\*    \*    \*    \*    \*    \*    \*

7.  'Ohon, alas!' says Clark Colven,
        'And aye sae sair 's I mean my head!'
    And merrily leugh the mermaiden,
        'O win on till you be dead.

8.  'But out ye tak your little pen-knife,
        And frae my sark ye shear a gare;
    Row that about your lovely head,
        And the pain ye 'll never feel nae mair.'

9.  Out he has taen his little pen-knife,
        And frae her sark he 's shorn a gare,
    Rowed that about his lovely head,
        But the pain increased mair and mair.

10. 'Ohon, alas!' says Clark Colven,
        'An aye sae sair 's I mean my head!'
    And merrily laughd the mermaiden,
        'It will ay be war till ye be dead.'

11. Then out he drew his trusty blade,
        And thought wi it to be her dead,
    But she 's become a fish again,
        And merrily sprang into the fleed.

12. He 's mounted on his berry-brown steed,
        And dowy, dowy, rade he home,
    And heavily, heavily lighted down
        When to his ladie's bower-door he came.

13. 'Oh, mither, mither, mak my bed,
        And, gentle ladie, lay me down;
    Oh, brither, brither, unbend my bow,
        'T will never be bent by me again.'

14.   His mither she has made his bed,
         His gentle ladie laid him down,
         His brither he has unbent his bow,
         'T was never bent by him again.

*Repetition*
*Lament in the conclusion*

## FAIR MARGARET AND SWEET WILLIAM.

1.  As it fell out on a long summer's day,
        Two lovers they sat on a hill;
    They sat together that long summer's day,
        And could not talk their fill.

2.  'I see no harm by you, Margaret,
        Nor you see none by me;
    Before tomorrow eight a clock
        A rich wedding shall you see.'

3.  Fair Margaret sat in her bower-window,
        A combing of her hair,
    And there she spy'd Sweet William and his bride,
        As they were riding near.

4.  Down she layd her ivory comb,
        And up she bound her hair;
    She went her way forth of her bower,
        But never more did come there.

5.  When day was gone, and night was come,
        And all men fast asleep,
    Then came the spirit of Fair Margaret,
        And stood at William's feet.

6.  'God give you joy, you two true lovers,
        In bride-bed fast asleep;
    Loe I am going to my green grass grave,
        And am in my winding-sheet.'

7.  When day was come, and night was gone,
     And all men wak'd from sleep,
Sweet William to his lady said,
    ' My dear, I have cause to weep.

8.  ' I dreamed a dream, my dear lady;
     Such dreams are never good;
I dreamed my bower was full of red swine,
    And my bride-bed full of blood.'

9.  ' Such dreams, such dreams, my honoured lord,
     They never do prove good,
To dream thy bower was full of swine,
    And thy bride-bed full of blood.'

10.  He called up his merry men all,
     By one, by two, and by three,
Saying, ' I'll away to Fair Margaret's bower,
    By the leave of my lady.'

11.  And when he came to Fair Margaret's bower,
     He knocked at the ring;
So ready was her seven brethren
    To let Sweet William in.

12.  He turned up the covering-sheet:
     ' Pray let me see the dead;
Methinks she does look pale and wan,
    She has lost her cherry red.

13.  ' I'll do more for thee, Margaret,
     Than any of thy kin;
For I will kiss thy pale wan lips,
    Tho a smile I cannot win.'

14.  With that bespeak her seven brethren,
        Making most piteous moan :
     'You may go kiss your jolly brown bride,
        And let our sister alone.'

15.  'If I do kiss my jolly brown bride,
        I do but what is right ;
     For I made no vow to your sister dear,
        By day nor yet by night.

16.  'Pray tell me then how much you'll deal
        Of your white bread and your wine ;
     So much as is dealt at her funeral today
        Tomorrow shall be dealt at mine.'

17.  Fair Margaret dy'd today, today,
        Sweet William he dy'd the morrow ;
     Fair Margaret dy'd for pure true love,
        Sweet William he dy'd for sorrow.

18.  Margaret was buried in the lower chancel,
        Sweet William in the higher ;
     Out of her breast there sprung a rose,
        And out of his a brier.

19.  They grew as high as the church-top,
        Till they could grow no higher,
     And then they grew in a true lover's knot,
        Which made all people admire.

## SWEET WILLIAM'S GHOST.

1. Whan bells war rung, an mass was sung,
   A wat a' man to bed were gone,
   Clark Sanders came to Margret's window,
   With mony a sad sigh and groan.

2. 'Are ye sleeping, Margret,' he says,
   'Or are ye waking, presentlie?
   Give me my faith and trouth again,
   A wat, true-love, I gied to thee.'

3. 'Your faith and trouth ye's never get,
   Nor our true love shall never twin,
   Till ye come with me in my bower,
   And kiss me both cheek and chin.'

4. 'My mouth it is full cold, Margret,
   It has the smell now of the ground;
   And if I kiss thy comely mouth,
   Thy life-days will not be long.

5. 'Cocks are crowing a merry mid-larf,
   I wat the wild fule boded day;
   Gie me my faith and trouth again,
   And let me fare me on my way.'

6. 'Thy faith and trouth thou shall na get,
   Nor our true love shall never twin,
   Till ye tell me what comes of women
   Awat that dy's in strong traveling.'

7.   'Their beds are made in the heavens high,
         Down at the foot of our good Lord's knee,
     Well set about wi gilly-flowers,
         A wat sweet company for to see.

8.   'O cocks are crowing a merry mid-larf,
         A wat the wild fule boded day ;
     The salms of Heaven will be sung,
         And ere now I 'll be missed away.'

9.   Up she has taen a bright long wand,
         And she has straked her trouth thereon ;
     She has given it him out at the shot-window,
         Wi mony a sad sigh and heavy groan.

10.  'I thank you, Margret, I thank you, Margret,
         And I thank you heartilie ;
     Gin ever the dead come for the quick,
         Be sure, Margret, I'll come again for thee.'

11.  It's hose and shoon an gound alane
         She clame the wall and followed him,
     Until she came to a green forest,
         On this she lost the sight of him.

12.  'Is there any room at your head, Sanders ?
         Is there any room at your feet ?
     Or any room at your twa sides ?
         Where fain, fain woud I sleep.'

13.  'There is nae room at my head, Margret,
         There is nae room at my feet ;
     There is room at my twa sides,
         For ladys for to sleep.

14.   'Cold meal is my covering owre,
          But an my winding sheet :
      My bed it is full low, I say,
          Among hungry worms I sleep.

15.   'Cold meal is my covering owre,
          But an my winding sheet :
      The dew it falls nae sooner down
          Than ay it is full weet.'

*demands of Margret before she will give it to him — mechanical standing repetition*

## EARL BRAND.

1.   Oh did ye ever hear o brave **Earl Bran**?
       Ay lally, o lilly lally.
     He courted the king's daughter of fair England
       All i the night sae early.

2.   She was scarcely fifteen years of age
     Till sae boldly she came to his bedside.

3.   'O Earl Bran, fain wad I see
     A pack of hounds let loose on the lea.'

4.   'O lady, I have no steeds but one,
     And thou shalt ride, and I will run.'

5.   'O Earl Bran, my father has two,
     And thou shall have the best o them a'.

6.   They have ridden oer moss and moor,
     And they met neither rich nor poor.

7.   Until they met with old Carl Hood ;
     He comes for ill, but never for good.

8.   'Earl Bran, if ye love me,
     Seize this old carl, and gar him die.'

9.   'O lady fair, it wad be sair,
     To slay an old man that has grey hair.

10.  'O lady fair, I'll no do sae,
     I'll gie him a pound and let him gae.'

11. 'O where hae ye ridden this lee lang day?
O where hae ye stolen this lady away?'

12. 'I have not ridden this lee lang day,
Nor yet have I stolen this lady away.

13. 'She is my only, my sick sister,
Whom I have brought from Winchester.'

14. 'If she be sick, and like to dead,
Why wears she the ribbon sae red?

15. 'If she be sick, and like to die,
Then why wears she the gold on high?'

16. When he came to this lady's gate,
Sae rudely as he rapped at it.

17. 'O where's the lady o this ha?'
'She's out with her maids to play at the ba.'

18. 'Ha, ha, ha! ye are a' mistaen:
Gae count your maidens oer again.'

19. The father armed fifteen of his best men,
To bring his daughter back again.

20. Oer her left shoulder the lady looked then:
'O Earl Bran, we both are tane.'

21. 'If they come on me ane by ane,
Ye may stand by and see them slain.

22. 'But if they come on me one and all,
Ye may stand by and see me fall.'

23.  They have come on him ane by ane,
     And he has killed them all but ane.


24.  And that ane came behind his back,
     And he's gien him a deadly whack.


25.  But for a' sae wounded as Earl Bran was,
     He has set his lady on her horse.


26.  They rode till they came to the water o Doune,
     And then he alighted to wash his wounds.


27.  'O Earl Bran, I see your heart's blood!'
     'Tis but the gleat o my scarlet hood.'


28.  They rode till they came to his mother's gate,
     And sae rudely as he rapped at it.


29.  'O my son's slain, my son's put down,
     And a' for the sake of an English loun.'


30.  'O say not sae, my dear mother,
     But marry her to my youngest brother.


     *    *    *    *    *    *    *


31.  'This has not been the death o ane,
     But it's been that o fair seventeen.'

## YOUNG HUNTING.

1. 'O lady, rock never your young son young
      One hour longer for me,
   For I have a sweetheart in Garlick's Wells
      I love thrice better than thee.

2. 'The very soles of my love's feet
      Is whiter than thy face':
   'But nevertheless na, Young Hunting,
      Ye'll stay wi me all night.'

3. She has birld in him Young Hunting
      The good ale and the beer,
   Till he was as fou drunken
      As any wild-wood steer.

4. She has birld in him Young Hunting
      The good ale and the wine,
   Till he was as fou drunken
      As any wild-wood swine.

5. And she has minded her on a little penknife,
      That hangs low down by her gare,
   And she has gien him Young Hunting
      A deep wound and a sare.

6. Out an spake the bonny bird,
      That flew aboon her head:
   'Lady, keep well thy green clothing
      Fra that good lord's blood.'

7.   'O better I'll keep my green clothing
          Fra that good lord's blood
     Nor thou can keep thy flattering tongue,
          That flatters in thy head.

8.   'Light down, light down, my bonny bird,
          Light down upon my hand,
     And ye shall hae a cage o the gowd
          Where ye hae but the wand.

9.   'O siller, O siller shall be thy hyre,
          And goud shall be thy fee,
     And every month into the year
          Thy cage shall changed be.'

10.  'I winna light down, I shanna light down,
          I winna light on thy hand;
     For soon, soon wad ye do to me
          As ye done to Young Hunting"

11.  She has booted and spurd him Young Hunting
          As he had been gan to ride,
     A hunting-horn about his neck,
          And the sharp sword by his side;
     And she has had him to yon wan water,
          For a' man calls it Clyde.

12.  The deepest pot intill it a'
          She has puttin Young Hunting in;
     A green turff upon his breast,
          To hold that good lord down.

13.  It fell once upon a day
          The king was going to ride,
     And he sent for him Young Hunting,
          To ride on his right side.

14.    She has turnd her right and round about,
        She sware now by the corn :
    'I saw na thy son, Young Hunting,
        Sen yesterday at morn.'

15.    She has turnd her right and round about,
        She sware now by the moon :
    'I saw na thy son, Young Hunting,
        Sen yesterday at noon.

16.    'It fears me sair in Clyde Water
        That he is drownd therein':
    O they hae sent for the king's duckers
        To duck for Young Hunting.

17.    They ducked in at the tae water-bank,
        They ducked out at the tither :
    'We'll duck no more for Young Hunting
        Altho he were our brither.'

18.    Out an spake the bonny bird,
        That flew aboon their heads :
    'Dive on, dive on, ye divers all,
        For there he lies indeed.

19.    'O he is na drownd in Clyde Water,
        He is slain and put therein ;
    The lady that lives in yon castle
        Slew him and put him in.

20.    'Leave off your ducking on the day,
        And duck upon the night ;
    Where ever that sakeless knight lyes slain,
        The candles will shine bright.'

21.    They left off their ducking on the day,
           And duckd upon the night,
       And where that sakeless knight lay slain,
           The candles shone full bright.


22.    The deepest pot intill it a'
           They got Young Hunting in;
       A green turff upon his breast,
           To hold that good lord down.


23.    O they hae sent aff men to the wood
           To hew down baith thorn and fern,
       That they might get a great bonefire
           To burn that lady in.
       ' Put na the wyte on me,' she says,
           ' It was her May Catheren.'


24.    When they had taen her May Catheren,
           In the bonefire set her in,
       It wad na take upon her cheeks,
           Nor take upon her chin,
       Nor yet upon her yellow hair,
           To heall the deadly sin.


25.    Out they hae taen her May Catheren,
           And they hae put that lady in;
       O it took upon her cheek, her cheek,
           And it took upon her chin,
       And it took on her fair body,
           She burnt like hoky-gren.

# FAIR JANET.

1. 'Ye maun gang to your father, Janet,
    Ye maun gang to him soon;
  Ye maun gang to your father, Janet,
    In case that his days are dune.'

*Transition*

2. Janet's awa to her father,
    As fast as she could hie:
  'O what's your will wi me, father?
    O what's your will wi me?'

3. 'My will wi you, Fair Janet,' he said,
    'It is both bed and board;
  Some say that ye loe Sweet Willie,
    But ye maun wed a French lord.'

4. 'A French lord maun I wed, father?
    A French lord maun I wed?
  Then, by my sooth,' quo Fair Janet,
    'He's neer enter my bed.'

*Trans.*

5. Janet's awa to her chamber,
    As fast as she could go;
  Wha's the first ane that tapped there,
    But Sweet Willie her jo?           *2 scene*

6. 'O we maun part this love, Willie,
    That has been lang between;
  There's a French lord coming oer the sea,
    To wed me wi a ring;
  There's a French lord coming oer the sea,
    To wed and tak me hame.'

7.  ‘ If we maun part this love, Janet,
        It causeth mickle woe ;
    If we maun part this love, Janet,
        It makes me into mourning go.’

8.  ‘ But ye maun gang to your three sisters,
        Meg, Marion, and Jean ;
    Tell them to come to Fair Janet,
        In case that her days are dune.’

9.  Willie’s awa to his three sisters,
        Meg, Marion, and Jean :
    ‘ O haste, and gang to Fair Janet,
        I fear that her days are dune.’

10. Some drew to them their silken hose,
        Some drew to them their shoon,
    Some drew to them their silk manteils,
        Their coverings to put on,
    And they’re awa to Fair Janet,
        By the hie light o the moon.

*    *    *    *    *    *    *    *

11. ‘ O I have born this babe, Willie,
        Wi mickle toil and pain ;
    Take hame, take hame your babe, Willie,
        For nurse I dare be nane.’

12. He’s tane his young son in his arms,
        And kisst him cheek and chin,
    And he’s awa to his mother’s bower,
        By the hie light o the moon.

13.   'O open, open, mother,' he says,
          'O open, and let me in;
      The rain rains on my yellow hair,
          And the dew drops o'er my chin,
      And I hae my young son in my arms,
          I fear that his days are dune.'

14.   With her fingers lang and sma
          She lifted up the pin,
      And with her arms lang and sma
          Received the baby in.

15.   'Gae back, gae back now, Sweet Willie,
          And comfort your fair lady;
      For where ye had but ae nourice,
          Your young son shall hae three.'

16.   Willie he was scarce awa,
          And the lady put to bed,
      When in and came her father dear:
          'Make haste, and busk the bride.'

17.   'There's a sair pain in my head, father,
          There's a sair pain in my side;
      And ill, O ill, am I, father,
          This day for to be a bride.'

18.   'O ye maun busk this bonny bride,
          And put a gay mantle on;
      For she shall wed this auld French lord,
          Gin she should die the morn.'

19.   Some put on the gay green robes,
          And some put on the brown;
      But Janet put on the scarlet robes,
          To shine foremost through the town.

20.   And some they mounted the black steed,
      And some mounted the brown ;
     But Janet mounted the milk-white steed,
      To ride foremost through the town.

21.   'O wha will guide your horse, Janet?
      O wha will guide him best?'
     'O wha but Willie, my true love?
      He kens I loe him best.'

22.   And when they cam to Marie's kirk,
      To tye the haly ban,
     Fair Janet's cheek looked pale and wan,
      And her colour gaed and cam.

23.   When dinner it was past and done,
      And dancing to begin,
     'O we'll go take the bride's maidens,
      And we'll go fill the ring.'

24.   O ben then cam the auld French lord,
      Saying, 'Bride, will ye dance with me?'
     'Awa, awa, ye auld French Lord,
      Your face I downa see.'

25.   O ben then cam now Sweet Willie,
      He cam with ane advance :
     'O I'll go tak the bride's maidens,
      And we'll go tak a dance.'

26.   'I've seen ither days wi you, Willie,
      And so has mony mae,
     Ye would hae danced wi me mysel,
      Let a' my maidens gae.'

27.  O ben then cam now Sweet Willie,
        Saying, ' Bride, will ye dance wi me?'
     ' Aye, by my sooth, and that I will,
        Gin my back should break in three.'

28.  She hadna turned her through the dance,
        Through the dance but thrice,
     When she fell down at Willie's feet,
        And up did never rise.

29.  Willie 's taen the key of his coffer,
        And gien it to his man :
     ' Gae hame, and tell my mother dear
        My horse he has me slain ;
     Bid her be kind to my young son,
        For father he has nane.'

30.  The tane was buried in Marie's kirk,
        And the tither in Marie's quire ;
     Out of the tane there grew a birk,
        And the tither a bonny brier.

## LADY MAISRY.

1.  The young lords o the north country
        Have all a-wooing gone,
    To win the love of Lady Maisry,
        But o them she woud hae none.

2.  O they hae courted Lady Maisry
        Wi' a' kin kind of things ;
    An they hae sought her Lady Maisry
        Wi' brotches, an wi' rings.

3.  An they ha sought her Lady Maisry
        Frae father and frae mother ;
    An they ha sought her Lady Maisry
        Frae sister and frae brother.

4.  An they ha followd her Lady Maisry
        Thro chamber an thro ha ;
    But a' that they coud say to her,
        Her answer still was Na.

5.  'O had your tongues, young men,' she says,
        'An think nae mair o me ;
    For I 've gien my love to an English lord,
        An think nae mair o me.'

6.  Her father's kitchy-boy heard that,
        An ill death may he die !
    An he is on to her brother,
        As fast as gang coud he.

7.   'O is my father an my mother well,
     But an my brothers three ?
  Gin my sister Lady Maisry be well,
     There 's naething can ail me.'

8.   'Your father an your mother is well,
     But an your brothers three ;
  Your sister Lady Maisry 's well,
     So big wi bairn gangs she.'

9.   'Gin this be true you tell to me,
     My malison light on thee !
  But gin it be a lie you tell,
     You sal be hangit hie.'

10.   He 's done him to his sister's bowr,
     Wi meikle doole an care ;
  An there he saw her Lady Maisry
     Kembing her yallow hair.

11.   'O wha is aught that bairn,' he says,
     'That ye sae big are wi ?
  And gin ye winna own the truth,
     This moment ye sall dee.'

12.   She turnd her right and roun about,
     And the kem fell frae her han ;
  A trembling seizd her fair body,
     An her rosy cheek grew wan.

13.   'O pardon me, my brother dear,
     An the truth I 'll tell to thee ;
  My bairn it is to Lord William,
     An he is betrothd to me.'

14.   'O coudna ye gotten dukes, or lords,
          Intill your ain country,
      That ye draw up wi an English dog,
          To bring this shame on me?


15.   'But ye maun gi up the English lord,
          Whan your young babe is born;
      For, gin you keep by him an hour langer,
          Your life sall be forlorn.'


16.   'I will gi up this English blood,
          Till my young babe be born;
      But the never a day nor hour langer,
          Tho my life should be forlorn.'


17.   'O whare is a' my merry young men,
          Whom I gi meat and fee,
      To pu the thistle and the thorn,
          To burn this wile whore wi?'


18.   'O whare will I get a bonny boy,
          To help me in my need,
      To rin wi hast to Lord William,
          And bid him come wi speed?'


19.   O out it spake a bonny boy,
          Stood by her brother's side:
      'O I would run your errand, lady,
          Oer a' the world wide.


20.   'Aft have I run your errands, lady,
          Whan blawn baith win and weet;
      But now I'll rin your errand, lady,
          Wi sat tears on my cheek.'

21.   O whan he came to broken briggs,
      He bent his bow and swam,
    An whan he came to the green grass growin,
      He slackd his shoon and ran.

22.   O whan he came to Lord William's gates,
      He baed na to chap or ca,
    But set his bent bow till his breast,
      An lightly lap the wa ;
    An, or the porter was at the gate,
      The boy was i the ha.

23.   'O is my biggins broken, boy?
      Or is my towers won?
    Or is my lady lighter yet,
      Of a dear daughter or son?'

24.   'Your biggin is na broken, sir,
      Nor is your towers won ;
    But the fairest lady in a' the lan
      For you this day maun burn.'

25.   'O saddle me the black, the black,
      Or saddle me the brown ;
    O saddle me the swiftest steed
      That ever rade frae a town.'

26.   Or he was near a mile awa,
      She heard his wild horse sneeze :
    'Mend up the fire, my false brother,
      It's na come to my knees.'

27.   O whan he lighted at the gate,
      She heard his bridle ring :
    'Mend up the fire, my false brother,
      It's far yet frae my chin.

28.   ' Mend up the fire to me, brother,
        Mend up the fire to me ;
      For I see him comin hard an fast,
        Will soon men't up to thee.


29.   'O gin my hands had been loose, Willy,
        Sae hard as they are boun,
      I would have turnd me frae the gleed,
        And castin out your young son.'


30.   'O I 'll gar burn for you, Maisry,
        Your father an your mother ;
      And I 'll gar burn for you, Maisry,
        Your sister an your brother.


31.   'An I 'll gar burn for you, Maisry,
        The chief of a' your kin ;
      And the last bonfire that I come to,
        Mysel I will cast in.'

## THE LASS OF ROCH ROYAL.

1.  'O wha will shoe my fu fair foot?
    And wha will glove my hand?
    And wha will lace my middle jimp
      Wi the new made London band?

2.  'And wha will kaim my yellow hair
    Wi the new made silver kaim?
    And wha will father my young son,
      Till Love Gregor come hame?'

3.  'Your father will shoe your fu fair foot,
    Your mother will glove your hand;
    Your sister will lace your middle jimp
      Wi the new made London band.

4.  'Your brother will kaim your yellow hair,
    Wi the new made silver kaim;
    And the King of Heaven will father your bairn,
      Till Love Gregor come hame.'

5.  'But I will get a bonny boat,
    And I will sail the sea,
    For I maun gang to Love Gregor,
      Since he canno come hame to me.'

6.  O she has gotten a bonny boat,
    And sailld the sa't sea fame;
    She langd to see her ain true-love,
      Since he could no come hame.

7.  'O row your boat, my mariners,
     And bring me to the land,
For yonder I see my love's castle,
     Close by the sa't sea strand.'

8.  She has taen her young son in her arms,
     And to the door she's gone,
And lang she's knocked and sair she ca'd,
     But answer got she none.

9.  'O open the door, Love Gregor,' she says,
     'O open and let me in;
For the wind blows thro my yellow hair,
     And the rain draps oer my chin.'

10.  'Awa, awa, ye ill woman,
     You'r nae come here for good;
You'r but some witch or wile warlock,
     Or mermaid of the flood.'

11.  'I am neither a witch nor a wile warlock,
     Nor mermaid of the sea,
I am Fair Annie of Rough Royal;
     O open the door to me.'

12.  'Gin ye be Annie of Rough Royal —
     And I trust ye are not she —
Now tell me some of the love-tokens
     That past between you and me.'

13.  'O dinna ye mind now, Love Gregor,
     When we sat at the wine,
How we changed the rings frae our fingers?
     And I can show thee thine.

14.  'O yours was good, and good enneugh,
      But ay the best was mine;
  For yours was o the good red goud,
      But mine o the diamonds fine.

15.  'But open the door now, Love Gregor,
      O open the door I pray,
  For your young son that's in my arms,
      Will be dead ere it be day.'

16.  'Awa, awa, ye ill woman,
      For here ye shanno win in;
  Gae drown ye in the raging sea,
      Or hang on the gallows-pin.'

17.  When the cock had crawn, and day did dawn,
      And the sun began to peep,
  Then it raise him Love Gregor,
      And sair sair did he weep.

18.  'O I dreamd a dream, my mother dear,
      The thoughts o it gars me greet,
  That Fair Annie of Rough Royal
      Lay cauld dead at my feet.'

19.  'Gin it be for Annie of Rough Royal
      That ye mak a' this din,
  She stood a' last night at this door,
      But I trow she wan no in.'

20.  'O wae betide ye, ill woman,
      An ill dead may ye die!
  That ye woud no open the door to her,
      Nor yet woud waken me.'

21. O he has gone down to yon shore-side,
    As fast as he could fare ;
    He saw Fair Annie in her boat,
        But the wind it tossed her sair.

22. And 'Hey, Annie !' and 'How, Annie !
        O Annie, winna ye bide ? '
    But ay the mair that he cried Annie,
        The braider grew the tide.

23. And 'Hey, Annie !' and 'How, Annie !
        Dear Annie, speak to me ! '
    But ay the louder he cried Annie,
        The louder roared the sea.

24. The wind blew loud, the sea grew rough,
        And dashd the boat on shore ;
    Fair Annie floats on the raging sea,
        But her young son raise no more.

25. Love Gregor tare his yellow hair,
        And made a heavy moan ;
    Fair Annie's corpse lay at his feet,
        But her bonny young son was gone.

26. O cherry, cherry was her cheek,
        And gowden was her hair,
    But clay cold were her rosey lips,
        Nae spark of life was there.

27. And first he's kissed her cherry cheek,
        And neist he's kissed her chin ;
    And saftly pressed her rosey lips,
        But there was nae breath within.

28.  'O wae betide my cruel mother,
      And an ill dead may she die!
   For she turnd my true-love frae my door,
      When she came sae far to me.'

Last scene narrative because there was only one person left; also it is last scene

Repetition marks off this scenes; stanza 20 & 28

*Prowess & adventure
not so sentimental
or long drawn out*

## WILLIE AND LADY MAISRY.

1.  Willie was a widow's son,
        And he wore a milk-white weed, O;
    And weel could Willie read and write,
        Far better ride on steed, O.

2.  Lady Maisry was the first lady
        That drank to him the wine,
    And aye as the healths gade round and round,
        'Laddy, your love is mine.'

3.  Lady Maisry was the first ladye
        That drank to him the beer,
    And aye as the healths gade round and round,
        'Laddy, you're welcome here.

*repetition*

4.  'You must come into my bower
        When the evening bells do ring,
    And you must come into my bower
        When the evening mass doth sing.'

*Introductory scene
developed from intro.*

5.  He's taen four and twenty braid arrows,
        And laced them in a whang,
    And he's awa to Lady Maisry's bower
        As fast as he can gang.

*trans.*

6.  He set ae foot on the wall,
        And the other on a stane,
    And he's killed a' the king's life-guards,
        And he's killed them every man.

*Peace dift*

7. 'Oh open, open, Lady Maisry,
      Open and let me in;
   The weet weets a' my yellow hair,
      And the dew draps on my chin.'

8. With her feet as white as sleet,
      She strode her bower within,
   And with her fingers long and small
      She's looten Sweet Willie in.

9. She's louten down unto her foot
      To loose Sweet Willie's shoon;
   The buckles were sa stiff they wodna lowse,
      The blood had frozen in.

10. 'O Willie, Willie, I fear that thou
      Has bred me dule and sorrow;
    The deed that thou has dune this nicht
      Will kythe upon the morrow.'

11. In then came her father dear,
      And a broad sword by his gare,
    And he's gien Willie, the widow's son,
      A deep wound and a sair.

12. 'Lye yont, lye yont, Willie,' she says,
      'Your sweat weets a' my side;
    Lye yont, lye yont, Willie,' she says,
      'For your sweat I downa bide.'

13. She turned her back unto the wa,
      Her face unto the room,
    And there she saw her auld father,
      Walking up and down.

14.    'Woe be to you, father,' she said,
         'And an ill deed may you die!
       For ye 've killed Willie, the widow's son,
         And he would have married me.'


15.   She turned her back unto the room,
         Her face unto the wa,
       And with a deep and heavy sich
         Her heart it brak in twa.

## LORD THOMAS AND FAIR ANNET.

1.   Lord Thomas and Fair Annet
       Sate a' day on a hill ;
     Whan night was cum, and sun was sett,
       They had not talkt their fill.

2.   Lord Thomas said a word in jest,
       Fair Annet took it ill :
     'A, I will nevir wed a wife
       Against my ain friends' will.'

3.   'Gif ye wull nevir wed a wife,
       A wife wull neir wed yee :'
     Sae he is hame to tell his mither,
       And knelt upon his knee.

4.   'O rede, O rede, mither,' he says,
       'A gude rede gie to mee :
     O sall I tak the nut-browne bride,
       And let Faire Annet bee ?'

5.   'The nut-browne bride haes gowd and gear,
       Fair Annet she has gat nane ;
     And the little beauty Fair Annet haes,
       O it wull soon be gane.'

6.   And he has till his brother gane :
       'Now, brother, rede ye mee ;
     A, sall I marrie the nut-browne bride,
       And let Fair Annet bee ?'

7.　'The nut-browne bride has oxen, brother,
　　　　The nut-browne bride has kye :
　　　I wad hae ye marrie the nut-browne bride,
　　　　And cast Fair Annet bye.'

8.　'Her oxen may dye i the house, billie,
　　　　And her kye into the byre,
　　　And I sall hae nothing to mysell,
　　　　Bot a fat fadge by the fyre.'

9.　And he has till his sister gane :
　　　　'Now sister, rede ye mee;
　　　O sall I marrie the nut-browne bride,
　　　　And set Fair Annet free?'

10.　'I 'se rede ye tak Fair Annet, Thomas,
　　　　And let the browne bride alane;
　　　Lest ye sould sigh, and say, Alace,
　　　　What is this we brought hame !'

11.　'No, I will tak my mither's counsel,
　　　　And marrie me owt o hand;
　　　And I will tak the nut-browne bride;
　　　　Fair Annet may leive the land.'

12.　Up then rose Fair Annet's father,
　　　　Twa hours or it wer day,
　　　And he is gane into the bower
　　　　Wherein Fair Annet lay.

13.　'Rise up, rise up, Fair Annet,' he says,
　　　　'Put on your silken sheene;
　　　Let us gae to St. Marie's kirke,
　　　　And see that rich weddeen.'

14.  'My maides, gae to my dressing-roome,
        And dress to me my hair;
     Whaireir yee laid a plait before,
        See yee lay ten times mair.

15.  'My maides, gae to my dressing-room,
        And dress to me my smock;
     The one half is o the holland fine,
        The other o needle-work.'

16.  The horse Fair Annet rade upon,
        He amblit like the wind;
     Wi siller he was shod before,
        Wi burning gowd behind.

17.  Four and twenty siller bells
        Wer a' tyed till his mane,
     And yae tift o the norland wind,
        They tinkled ane by ane.

18.  Four and twenty gay gude knichts
        Rade by Fair Annet's side,
     And four and twenty fair ladies,
        As gin she had bin a bride.

19.  And whan she cam to Marie's kirk,
        She sat on Marie's stean:
     The cleading that Fair Annet had on
        It skinkled in their een.

20.  And whan she cam into the kirk,
        She shimmered like the sun;
     The belt that was about her waist,
        Was a' wi pearles bedone.

21.   She sat her by the nut-browne bride,
          And her een they wer sae clear,
      Lord Thomas he clean forgat the bride,
          Whan Fair Annet drew near.


22.   He had a rose into his hand,
          He gae it kisses three,
      And reaching by the nut-browne bride,
          Laid it on Fair Annet's knee.


23.   Up than spak the nut-browne bride,
          She spak wi meikle spite:
      'And whair gat ye that rose-water,
          That does mak yee sae white?'


24.   'O I did get the rose-water
          Whair ye wull neir get nane,
      For I did get that very rose-water
          Into my mither's wame.'


25.   The bride she drew a long bodkin
          Frae out her gay head-gear,
      And strake Fair Annet unto the heart,
          That word spak nevir mair.


26.   Lord Thomas he saw Fair Annet wex pale,
          And marvelit what mote bee;
      But whan he saw her dear heart's blude,
          A' wood-wroth wexed hee.


27.   He drew his dagger, that was sae sharp,
          That was sae sharp and meet,
      And drave it into the nut-browne bride,
          That fell deid at his feit.

28.  ' Now stay for me, dear Annet,' he sed,
         ' Now stay, my dear,' he cry'd ;
     Then strake the dagger untill his heart,
         And fell deid by her side.

29.  Lord Thomas was buried without kirk-wa,
         Fair Annet within the quiere ;
     And o the tane thair grew a birk,
         The other a bonny briere.

30.  And ay they grew, and ay they threw,
         As they wad faine be neare ;
     And by this ye may ken right weil
         They were twa luvers deare.

## FAIR MARY OF LIVINGSTON.

1.  ' When we were sisters seven,
        And five of us dyed wi child,
    And there is nane but you and I, Mazery,
        And we 'll go maidens mild.'

2.  But there came knights, and there came squires,
        An knights of high degree ;
    She pleasd hersel in Levieston,
        Thay wear a comly twa.

3.  He has bought her rings for her fingers,
        And garlands for her hair,
    The broochis till her bosome braid ;
        What wad my love ha mair ?
    And he has brought her on to Livingston,
        And made her lady thear.

4.  She had na been in Livingston
        A twelvemonth and a day,
    Till she was as big wi bairn
        As any lady could gae.

5.  ' O whare will I get a bonny boy,
        That will win both hoos and shoon,
    That will win his way to Little Snoddown,
        To my mother, the Queen ? '

6.  Up and stands a bonny boy,
        Goude yellow was his hair ;
    I wish his mother mickle grace at him,
        And his trew-love mickle mare.

7.   'Here am I a bonny boy,
         That will win baith hose an shoon,
     That will win my way to Little Snoddown,
         To thy mother, the Queen.'


8.   'Here is the rings frae my fingers,
         The garlands frae my hair,
     The broches frae my bosom braid;
         Fray me she 'll nere get mare.


9.   'Here it is my weeding-goun,
         It is a' goude but the hem;
     Gi it to my sister Allen,
         For she is left now bird her lane.


10.  'When you come where brigs is broken,
         Ye 'l bent your bow and swim;
     An when ye come whare green grass grows,
         Ye 'l slack your shoon and run.


11.  'But when you come to yon castle,
         Bide neither to chap nor ca,
     But you 'l set your bent bow to your breast,
         And lightly loup the wa,
     And gin the porter be half-gate,
         Ye 'll be ben throw the ha.'


12.  O when he came where brigs was broken,
         He bent his bow and swam;
     And when he came where green grass grows,
         He slackd his shoon an ran.

13.　　And when he came to yon castel,
　　　　　He stayed neither to chap no ca'l,
　　　And bent his bow unto his breast,
　　　　　And lightly lap the wa'l;
　　　And gin the porter was hafe-gate,
　　　　　He was ben throw the ha'l.

14.　　'O peace be to you, ladies a'l!
　　　　　As ye sit at your dine
　　　Ye ha little word of Lady Mazery,
　　　　　For she drees mickel pine.

15.　　'Here is the rings frae her fingers,
　　　　　The garlands frae her hair,
　　　The broches frae her bosome brade;
　　　　　Fray her ye 'l nere get mare.

16.　　'Here it is her weeding-goun,
　　　　　It is a' goude but the hem;
　　　Ye 'll gi it to her sister Allen,
　　　　　For she is left bird her lane.'

17.　　She ca'd the table wi her foot,
　　　　　And coped it wi her tae,
　　　Till siller cups an siller cans
　　　　　Unto the floor did gae.

18.　　'Ye wash, ye wash, ye bonny boy,
　　　　　Ye wash, and come to dine;
　　　It does not fit a bonny boy
　　　　　His errant for to tine.

19.　　'Ge saddle to me the black, the black,
　　　　　Ge saddle to me the brown,
　　　Ge saddle to me the swiftest steed
　　　　　That ever rid frae a town.'

20.    The first steed they saddled to her,
           He was the bonny black;
       He was a good steed, and a very good steed,
           But he tiyrd eer he wan the slack.


21.    The next steed they saddled to her,
           He was the bonny brown;
       He was a good steed, and a very good steed,
           But he tiyird ere he wan the town.


22.    The next steed they saddled to her,
           He was the bonny white;
       Fair fa the mair that fo'd the fole
           That carried her to Mazeree's lear !


23.    As she gaed in at Leivingston,
           Thare was na mickel pride;
       The scobs was in her lovely mouth,
           And the razer in her side.


24.    The knight he knocked his white fingers,
           The goude rings flew in twa :
       'Halls and bowers they shall go wast
           Ere my bonny love gie awa !'


25.    The knight he knocked his white fingers,
           The goude rings flew in foure :
       'Halls and bowers they shall go waste,
           Ere my bonny lady gie it ore !'


26.    'O hold your toung now, Livingston,
           Let all your folly abee;
       I bear the burden in my breast,
           Mun suffer them to dee.'

27.    Out and speaks her Bird Allen,
        For she spake ay through pride :
   ' That man shall near be born,' she says,
      ' Shall ever make me his bride.'


28.    ' O hold your toung now, Bird Allen,
        Let all your folly abee ;
   For you shall marry a man,' she says,
      ' Tho ye shoud live but rathes three.'

## CHILD WATERS.

1. Childe Watters in his stable stoode,
   And stroaket his milke-white steede;
   To him came a ffaire young ladye
   As ere did weare womans weede.

2. Saies, 'Christ you save, good Chyld Waters!'
   Sayes, 'Christ you save and see!
   My girdle of gold which was too longe
   Is now to short ffor mee.

3. 'And all is with one chyld of yours,
   I ffeele sturre att my side:
   My gowne of greene, it is to strayght;
   Before it was to wide.'

4. 'If the child be mine, faire Ellen,' he sayd,
   'Be mine, as you tell mee,
   Take you Cheshire and Lancashire both,
   Take them your owne to bee.

5. 'If the child be mine, ffaire Ellen,' he said,
   'Be mine, as you doe sweare,
   Take you Cheshire and Lancashire both,
   And make that child your heyre.'

6. Shee saies, 'I had rather have one kisse,
   Child Waters, of thy mouth,
   Then I would have Cheshire and Lancashire both,
   That lyes by north and south.

7. 'And I had rather have a twinkling,
       Child Waters, of your eye,
    Then I would have Cheshire and Lancashire both,
       To take them mine oune to bee!'

8. 'To-morrow, Ellen, I must forth ryde
       Soe ffar into the north countrye;
    The ffairest lady that I can ffind,
       Ellen, must goe with mee.'
    'And ever I pray you, Child Watters,
       Your ffootpage let me bee!'

9. 'If you will my ffootpage be, Ellen,
       As you doe tell itt mee,
    Then you must cut your gownne of greene
       An inch above your knee.

10. 'Soe must you doe your yellow lockes
       Another inch above your eye;
    You must tell no man what is my name;
       My ffootpage then you shall bee.'

11. All this long day Child Waters rode,
       Shee ran bare ffoote by his side;
    Yett was he never soe curteous a knight,
       To say, 'Ellen will you ryde?'

12. But all this day Child Waters rode,
       She ran barffoote thorow the broome;
    Yett he was never soe curteous a knight
       As to say, 'Put on your shoone.'

13. 'Ride softlye,' shee said, 'Child Watters:
       Why do you ryde soe ffast?
    The child, which is no mans but yours,
       My bodye itt will burst.'

14.　He sayes, 'Sees thou yonder water, Ellen,
　　　　That fflowes from banke to brim ?'
　　　'I trust to God, Child Waters,' shee sayd,
　　　　'You will never see mee swime.'

15.　But when shee came to the waters side,
　　　　Shee sayled to the chinne :
　　　'Except the lord of heaven be my speed,
　　　　Now must I learne to swime.'

16.　The salt waters bare up Ellens clothes,
　　　　Our Ladye bare upp her chinne,
　　　And Child Waters was a woe man, good Lord,
　　　　To ssee faire Ellen swime.

17.　And when shee over the water was,
　　　　Shee then came to his knee :
　　　He said, 'Come hither, ffaire Ellen,
　　　　Loe yonder what I see !

18.　'Seest thou not yonder hall, Ellen ?
　　　　Of redd gold shine the yates ;
　　　There 's four and twenty ffayre ladyes,
　　　　The ffairest is my wordlye make.

19.　'Seest thou not yonder hall, Ellen ?
　　　　Of redd gold shineth the tower ;
　　　There is four and twenty ffaire ladyes,
　　　　The fairest is my paramoure.'

20.　'I doe see the hall now, Child Waters,
　　　　That of redd gold shineth the yates ;
　　　God give good then of your selfe,
　　　　And of your wordlye make !

21.   'I doe see the hall now, Child Waters,
          That of redd gold shineth the tower;
      God give good then of your selfe,
          And of your paramoure!'

22.   There were four and twenty ladyes,
          Were playing att the ball;
      And Ellen, was the ffairest ladye,
          Must bring his steed to the stall.

23.   There were four and twenty faire ladyes
          Was playing att the chesse;
      And Ellen, shee was the ffairest ladye,
          Must bring his horsse to grasse.

24.   And then bespake Child Waters sister,
          And these were the words said shee:
      'You have the prettyest ffootpage, brother,
          That ever I saw with mine eye;

25.   'But that his belly it is soe bigg,
          His girdle goes wondrous hye;
      And ever I pray you, Child Waters,
          Let him go into the chamber with me.'

26.   'It is more meete for a little ffootpage,
          That has run through mosse and mire,
      To take his supper upon his knee
          And sitt downe by the kitchin fyer,
      Then to go into the chamber with any ladye
          That weares so rich attyre.'

27.   'I pray you now, good Child Waters,
          That I may creepe in att your bedds feete,
      For there is noe place about this house
          Where I may say a sleepe.'

28.  This night and itt drove on affterward
        Till itt was neere the day :
     He sayd, ' Rise up, my litle ffoote page,
        And give my steed corne and hay ;
     And soe doe thou the good blacke oates,
        That he may carry me the better away.'

29.  And up then rose ffaire Ellen,
        And gave his steed corne and hay,
     And soe shee did the good blacke oates,
        That he might carry him the better away.

30.  Shee layned her backe to the manger side,
        And greivouslye did groane ;
     And that beheard his mother deere,
        And heard her make her moane.

31.  Shee said, ' Rise up, thou Child Waters !
        I thinke thou art a cursed man ;
     For yonder is a ghost in thy stable,
        That greivously doth groane,
     Or else some woman laboures of child,
        Shee is soe woe begone !'

32.  But up then rose Child Waters,
        And did on his shirt of silke ;
     Then he put on his other clothes
        On his body as white as milke.

33.  And when he came to the stable dore,
        Full still that hee did stand,
     That hee might heare now faire Ellen,
        How shee made her monand.

34.    Shee said, ' Lullabye, my owne deere child !
       Lullabye, deere child, deere !
   I wold thy father were a king,
       Thy mother layd on a beere ! '


35.    ' Peace now,' he said, ' good faire Ellen !
       And be of good cheere, I thee pray,
   And the bridall and the churching both,
       They shall bee upon one day.'

## FAIR ANNIE.

1.  ' It 's narrow, narrow, make your bed,
        And learn to lie your lane ;
    For I 'm ga'n oer the sea, Fair Annie,
        A braw bride to bring hame.
    Wi her I will get gowd and gear ;
        Wi you I neer got nane.

2.  ' But wha will bake my bridal bread,
        Or brew my bridal ale ?
    And wha will welcome my brisk bride,
        That I bring oer the dale ? '

3.  ' It 's I will bake your bridal bread,
        And brew your bridal ale ;
    And I will welcome your brisk bride,
        That you bring oer the dale.'

4.  ' But she that welcomes my brisk bride
        Maun gang like maiden fair ;
    She maun lace on her robe sae jimp,
        And braid her yellow hair.'

5.  ' But how can I gang maiden-like,
        When maiden I am nane ?
    Have I not born seven sons to thee,
        And am with child again ? '

6.  She 's taen her young son in her arms,
        Another in her hand,
    And she 's up to the highest tower,
        To see him come to land.

7.   'Come up, come up, my eldest son,
        And look oer yon sea-strand,
     And see your father's new-come bride,
        Before she come to land.'

8.   'Come down, come down, my mother dear,
        Come frae the castle wa !
     I fear, if langer ye stand there,
        Ye 'll let yoursell down fa.'

9.   And she gaed down, and farther down,
        Her love's ship for to see,
     And the topmast and the mainmast
        Shone like the silver free.

10.  And she 's gane down, and farther down,
        The bride's ship to behold,
     And the topmast and the mainmast
        They shone just like the gold.

11.  She 's taen her seven sons in her hand,
        I wot she didna fail ;
     She met Lord Thomas and his bride,
        As they came oer the dale.

12.  'You 're welcome to your house, Lord Thomas,
        You 're welcome to your land ;
     You 're welcome with your fair ladye,
        That you lead by the hand.

13.  'You 're welcome to your ha's, ladye,
        You 're welcome to your bowers ;
     You 're welcome to your hame, ladye,
        For a' that 's here is yours.'

14. She hang ae napkin at the door,
    Another in the ha,
  And a' to wipe the trickling tears,
    Sae fast as they did fa.

15. And aye she served the long tables,
    With white bread and with wine;
  And aye she drank the wan water,
    To had her colour fine.

16. And aye she served the lang tables,
    With white bread and with brown;
  And ay she turned her round about,
    Sae fast the tears fell down.

17. And he's taen down the silk napkin,
    Hung on a silver pin,
  And aye he wipes the tear trickling
    A' down her cheek and chin.

18. And aye he turned him round about,
    And smil'd amang his men;
  Says, 'Like ye best the old ladye,
    Or her that's new come hame?'

19. When bells were rung, and mass was sung,
    And a' men bound to bed,
  Lord Thomas and his new-come bride
    To their chamber they were gaed.

20. Annie made her bed a little forbye,
    To hear what they might say;
  'And ever alas,' Fair Annie cried,
    'That I should see this day!

21.    'Gin my seven sons were seven young rats,
            Running on the castle wa,
        And I were a gray cat mysell,
            I soon would worry them a'.


22.    'Gin my seven sons were seven young hares,
            Running oer yon lilly lee,
        And I were a grew hound mysell,
            Soon worried they a' should be.'


23.    And wae and sad Fair Annie sat,
            And drearie was her sang,
        And ever, as she sobbd and grat,
            'Wae to the man that did the wrang!'


24.    'My gown is on,' said the new-come bride,
            'My shoes are on my feet,
        And I will to Fair Annie's chamber,
            And see what gars her greet.


25.    'What ails ye, what ails ye, Fair Annie,
            That ye make sic a moan?
        Has your wine barrels cast the girds,
            Or is your white bread gone?


26.    'O wha was 't was your father, Annie,
            Or wha was 't was your mother?
        And had ye ony sister, Annie,
            Or had ye ony brother?'


27.    'The Earl of Wemyss was my father,
            The Countess of Wemyss my mother;
        And a' the folk about the house
            To me were sister and brother.'

28.  ' If the Earl of Wemyss was your father,
        I wot sae was he mine ;
      And it shall not be for lack o gowd
        That ye your love sall tyne.


29.  ' For I have seven ships o mine ain,
        A' loaded to the brim,
      And I will gie them a' to thee,
        Wi' four to thine eldest son :
      But thanks to a' the powers in heaven
        That I gae maiden hame ! '

## WILLIE'S LADY.

1.  Willie has taen him oer the fame,
    He 's woo'd a wife and brought her hame.

2.  He 's woo'd her for her yellow hair,
    But his mother wrought her mickle care,

3.  And mickle dolour gard her dree,
    For lighter she can never be.

4.  But in her bower she sits wi pain,
    And Willie mourns oer her in vain.

5.  And to his mother he has gone,
    That vile rank witch of vilest kind.

6.  He says : ' My ladie has a cup
    Wi gowd and silver set about.

7.  ' This goodlie gift shall be your ain,
    And let her be lighter o her young bairn.'

8.  ' Of her young bairn she 'll neer be lighter,
    Nor in her bower to shine the brighter.

9.  ' But she shall die and turn to clay,
    And you shall wed another may.'

10. ' Another may I 'll never wed,
    Another may I 'll neer bring hame.'

11. But sighing says that weary wight,
    ' I wish my life were at an end.'

12. 'Ye doe ye unto your mother again,
    That vile rank witch of vilest kind.

13. 'And say your ladie has a steed,
    The like o'm's no in the lands of Leed.

14. 'For he is golden shod before,
    And he is golden shod behind.

15. 'And at ilka tet of that horse's main
    There's a golden chess and a bell ringing.

16. 'This goodlie gift shall be your ain,
    And let me be lighter of my young bairn.'

17. 'O her young bairn she'll neer be lighter,
    Nor in her bower to shine the brighter.

18. 'But she shall die and turn to clay,
    And ye shall wed another may.'

19. 'Another may I'll never wed,
    Another may I'll neer bring hame.'

20. But sighing said that weary wight,
    'I wish my life were at an end.'

21. 'Ye doe ye unto your mother again,
    That vile rank witch of vilest kind.

22. 'And say your ladie has a girdle,
    It's red gowd unto the middle.

23. 'And ay at every silver hem
    Hangs fifty silver bells and ten.

24.   ' That goodlie gift shall be her ain,
      And let me be lighter of my young bairn.'

25.   'O her young bairn she 's neer be lighter,
      Nor in her bower to shine the brighter.

26.   ' But she shall die and turn to clay,
      And you shall wed another may.'

27.   ' Another may I 'll never wed,
      Another may I 'll neer bring hame.'

28.   But sighing says that weary wight,
      ' I wish my life were at an end.'

29.   Then out an spake the Billy Blin,
      He spake aye in good time.

30.   ' Ye doe ye to the market-place,
      And there ye buy a loaf of wax.

31.   ' Ye shape it bairn and bairnly like,
      And in twa glassen een ye pit ;

32.   ' And bid her come to your boy's christening ;
      Then notice weel what she shall do.

33.   ' And do you stand a little forebye,
      And listen weel what she shall say.'

34.   ' O wha has loosed the nine witch knots
      That was amo that ladie's locks ?

35.   ' And wha has taen out the kaims o care
      That hangs amo that ladie's hair ?

36.  'And wha's taen down the bush o woodbine
     That hang atween her bower and mine?

37.  'And wha has killd the master kid
     That ran beneath that ladie's bed?

38.  'And wha has loosed her left-foot shee,
     And lotten that lady lighter be?'

39.  O Willie has loosed the nine witch knots
     That was amo that ladie's locks.

40.  And Willie's taen out the kaims o care
     That hang amo that ladie's hair.

41.  And Willie's taen down the bush o woodbine
     That hang atween her bower and thine.

42.  And Willie has killed the master kid
     That ran beneath that ladie's bed.

43.  And Willie has loosed her left-foot shee,
     And letten his ladie lighter be.

44.  And now he's gotten a bonny young son,
     And mickle grace be him upon.

*Written for amusement of apprenti*

*Good horrible example*

*Immortalized middle class heu*

*apprentices*

## YOUNG BEICHAN.

1.　In London city was Beichan born,
　　　He longd strange countries for to see,
　　But he was taen by a savage Moor,
　　　Who handld him right cruely.

2.　For thro his shoulder he put a bore,
　　　An thro the bore has pitten a tree,
　　An he's gard him draw the carts o wine,
　　　Where horse and oxen had wont to be.

3.　He's casten him in a dungeon deep,
　　　Where he coud neither hear nor see;
　　He's shut him up in a prison strong,
　　　An he's handld him right cruely.

4.　The savage Moor had but ae dochter,
　　　And her name it was Susie Pye,
　　And ilka day as she took the air,
　　　The prison door she passed bye.

5.　But it fell ance upon a day,
　　　As she was walking, she heard him sing;
　　She listend to his tale of woe,
　　　A happy day for young Beichan!

6.　'My hounds they all go masterless,
　　　My hawks they flee frae tree to tree,
　　My youngest brother will heir my lands,
　　　My native land I'll never see.'

7. 'O were I but the prison-keeper,
    As I'm a ladie o hie degree,
I soon wad set this youth at large,
    And send him to his ain countrie.'

8. She went away into her chamber,
    All nicht she never closd her ee;
And when the morning begoud to dawn,
    At the prison door alane was she.

9. 'O hae ye ony lands or rents,
    Or citys in your ain country,
Coud free you out of prison strong,
    An coud mantain a lady free?'

10. 'O London city is my own,
    An other citys twa or three,
Coud loose me out o prison strong,
    An coud mantain a lady free.'

11. O she has bribed her father's men
    Wi meikle goud and white money,
She's gotten the key o the prison doors,
    And she has set young Beichan free.

12. She's gi'n him a loaf o good white bread,
    But an a flask o Spanish wine,
An she bad him mind on the ladie's love
    That sae kindly freed him out o pine.

13. 'Go set your foot on good ship-board,
    An haste you back to your ain country,
An before that seven years has an end,
    Come back again, love, and marry me.'

14.    It was long or seven years had an end
            She longd fu sair her love to see;
       She's set her foot on good ship-board,
            An turnd her back on her ain country.


15.    She's saild up, so has she doun,
            Till she came to the other side;
       She's landed at young Beichan's gates,
            An I hop this day she sal be his bride.


16.    'Is this young Beichan's gates?' says she,
            'Or is that noble prince within?'
       'He's up the stairs wi his bonny bride,
            An monny a lord and lady wi him.'


17.    'O has he taen a bonny bride,
            An has he clean forgotten me!'
       An sighing said that gay lady,
            'I wish I were in my ain country!'


18.    But she's pitten her han in her pocket,
            And gin the porter guineas three;
       Says, 'Take ye that, ye proud porter,
            An bid the bridegroom speak to me.'


19.    O whan the porter came up the stair,
            He's fa'n low down upon his knee;
       'Won up, won up, ye proud porter,
            An what makes a' this courtesy?'


20.    'O I've been porter at your gates
            This mair nor seven years an three,
       But there is a lady at them now
            The like of whom I never did see.

*middle class attempt to perpetual aristocracy*

21.   'For on every finger she has a ring,
          And on the mid-finger she has three,
      An there 's as meikle goud aboon her brow
          As would buy an earldome o lan to me.'


22.   Then up it started young Beichan,
          An sware so loud by our Lady,
      'It can be nane but Susie Pye,
          That has come oer the sea to me.'


23.   O quickly ran he down the stair,
          O fifteen steps he has made but three ;
      He 's tane his bonny love in his arms,
          An a wot he kissd her tenderly.


24.   'O hae you tane a bonny bride ?
          An hae you quite forsaken me ?
      An hae ye quite forgotten her
          That gae you life and liberty ? '


25.   She 's lookit oer her left shoulder
          To hide the tears stood in her ee ;
      'Now fare the well, young Beichan,' she says,
          'I 'll strive to think nae mair on thee.'


26.   'Take back your daughter, madam,' he says,
          'An a double dowry I 'll gi her wi ;
      For I maun marry my first true love,
          That 's done and suffered so much for me.'


27.   He 's take his bonny love by the han,
          And led her to yon fountain stane ;
      He 's changed her name frae Susie Pye,
          An he 's cald her his bonny love, Lady Jane.

## HIND HORN.

1.  In Scotland there was a babie born,
       Lill lal, etc.
     And his name it was called young Hind Horn.
       With a fal lal, etc.

2.  He sent a letter to our king
     That he was in love with his daughter Jean.

3.  The king an angry man was he ;
     He sent young Hind Horn to the sea.

4.  He 's gien to her a silver wand,
     With seven living lavrocks sitting thereon.

5.  She 's gien to him a diamond ring,
     With seven bright diamonds set therein.

6.  ' When this ring grows pale and wan,
     You may know by it my love is gane.'

7.  One day as he looked his ring upon,
     He saw the diamonds pale and wan.

8.  He left the sea and came to land,
     And the first that he met was an old beggar man.

9.  ' What news, what news ? ' said young Hind Horn ;
     ' No news, no news,' said the old beggar man.

10. ' No news,' said the beggar, ' no news at a',
     But there is a wedding in the king's ha.

11. 'But there is a wedding in the king's ha,
    That has halden these forty days and twa.'

12. 'Will ye lend me your begging coat?
    And I'll lend you my scarlet cloak.

13. 'Will you lend me your beggar's rung?
    And I'll gie you my steed to ride upon.

14. 'Will you lend me your wig o hair,
    To cover mine, because it is fair?'

15. The auld beggar man was bound for the mill,
    But young Hind Horn for the king's hall.

16. The auld beggar man was bound for to ride,
    But young Hind Horn was bound for the bride.

17. When he came to the king's gate,
    He sought a drink for Hind Horn's sake.

18. The bride came down with a glass of wine,
    When he drank out the glass, and dropt in the ring.

19. 'O got ye this by sea or land?
    Or got ye it off a dead man's hand?'

20. 'I got not it by sea, I got it by land,
    And I got it, madam, out of your own hand.'

21. 'O I'll cast off my gowns of brown,
    And beg wi you frae town to town.

22. 'O I'll cast off my gowns of red,
    And I'll beg wi you to win my bread.'

23.　'Ye needna cast off your gowns of brown,
　　　For I 'll make you lady o many a town.

24.　'Ye needna cast off your gowns o red,
　　　It 's only a sham, the begging o my bread.'

## KATHARINE JAFFRAY.

1. There livd a lass in yonder dale,
   And doun in yonder glen, O,
   And Kathrine Jaffray was her name,
   Well known by many men, O.

2. Out came the Laird of Lauderdale,
   Out frae the South Countrie,
   All for to court this pretty maid,
   Her bridegroom for to be.

3. He has teld her father and mither baith,
   And a' the rest o her kin,
   And has teld the lass hersell,
   And her consent has win.

4. Then came the Laird of Lochinton,
   Out frae the English border,
   All for to court this pretty maid,
   Well mounted in good order.

5. He 's teld her father and mither baith,
   As I hear sindry say,
   But he has nae teld the lass her sell,
   Till on her wedding day.

6. When day was set, and friends were met,
   And married to be,
   Lord Lauderdale came to the place,
   The bridal for to see.

7.   'O are you come for sport, young man?
      Or are you come for play?
   Or are you come for a sight o our bride,
      Just on her wedding day?'

8.   'I'm nouther come for sport,' he says,
      'Nor am I come for play;
   But if I had one sight o your bride,
      I'll mount and ride away.'

9.   There was a glass of the red wine
      Filld up them atween,
   And ay she drank to Lauderdale,
      Wha her true-love had been.

10.   Then he took her by the milk-white hand,
      And by the grass-green sleeve,
   And he mounted her high behind him there,
      At the bridegroom he askt nae leive.

11.   Then the blude run down by the Cowden Banks,
      And down by Cowden Braes,
   And ay she gard the trumpet sound,
      'O this is foul, foul play!'

12.   Now a' ye that in England are,
      Or are in England born,
   Come nere to Scotland to court a lass,
      Or else ye'l get the scorn.

13.   They haik ye up and settle ye by,
      Till on your wedding day,
   And gie ye frogs instead o fish,
      And play ye foul, foul play.

# THE GAY GOSHAWK.

1.   'O well's me o my gay goss-hawk,
     That he can speak and flee ;
  He'll carry a letter to my love,
     Bring back another to me.'

2.   'O how can I your true-love ken,
     Or how can I her know ?
  Whan frae her mouth I never heard couth,
     Nor wi my eyes her saw.'

3.   'O well sal ye my true-love ken,
     As soon as you her see ;
  For, of a' the flowrs in fair Englan,
     The fairest flowr is she.

4.   'At even at my love's bowr-door
     There grows a bowing birk,
  And sit ye down and sing thereon
     As she gangs to the kirk.

5.   'An four-and-twenty ladies fair
     Will wash and go to kirk,
  But well shall ye my true-love ken,
     For she wears goud on her skirt.

6.   'An four-an-twenty gay ladies
     Will to the mass repair,
  But well sal ye my true-love ken,
     For she wears goud on her hair.'

7.   O even at that lady's bowr door
         There grows a bowing birk,
     And she sat down and sang thereon,
         As she ged to the kirk.


8.   'O eat and drink, my marys a',
         The wine flows you among,
     Till I gang to my shot-window,
         An hear yon bonny bird's song.


9.   'Sing on, sing on, my bonny bird,
         The song ye sang the streen,
     For I ken by your sweet singin,
         You 're frae my true-love sen.'


10.  O first he sang a merry song,
         An then he sang a grave ;
     An then he peck'd his feathers gray,
         To her the letter gave.


11.  'Ha, there 's a letter frae your love,
         He says he sent you three ;
     He canno wait your love langer,
         But for your sake he 'll die.


12.  'He bids you write a letter to him ;
         He says he 's sent you five ;
     He canna wait your love langer,
         Tho you 're the fairest woman alive.'


13.  'Ye bid him bake his bridal bread,
         And brew his bridal ale,
     An I 'll meet him in fair Scotlan
         Lang, lang or it be stale.'

14. She 's doen her to her father dear,
    Fa'n low down on her knee :
'A boon, a boon, my father dear,
    I pray you, grant it me.'

15. 'Ask on, ask on, my daughter,
    And granted it sal be ;
Except ae squire in fair Scotlan,
    An him you sall never see.'

16. 'The only boon, my father dear,
    That I do crave of thee,
Is, gin I die in southin lans,
    In Scotland to bury me.

17. 'An the firstin kirk that ye come till,
    Ye gar the bells be rung,
An the nextin kirk that ye come till,
    Ye gar the mess be sung.

18. 'And the thirdin kirk that ye come till,
    You deal gold for my sake,
An the fourthin kirk that ye come till,
    You tarry there till night.'

19. She is doen her to her bigly bowr,
    As fast as she coud fare,
An she has tane a sleepy draught,
    That she had mixd wi care.

20. She 's laid her down upon her bed,
    An soon she 's fa'n asleep,
And soon o'er every tender limb
    Cauld death began to creep.

21.  Whan night was flown, an day was come,
        Nae ane that did her see
     But thought she was as surely dead
        As ony lady coud be.


22.  Her father an her brothers dear
        Gard make to her a bier ;
     The tae half was o guid red gold,
        The tither o silver clear.


23.  Her mither an her sisters fair
        Gard work for her a sark ;
     The tae half was o cambrick fine,
        The tither o needle wark.


24.  The firstin kirk that they came till,
        They gard the bells be rung,
     And the nextin kirk that they came till,
        They gard the mess be sung.


25.  The thirdin kirk that they came till,
        They dealt gold for her sake,
     An the fourthin kirk that they came till,
        Lo, there they met her make !


26.  ' Lay down, lay down the bigly bier,
        Lat me the dead look on ; '
     Wi cherry cheeks and ruby lips
        She lay an smiled on him.


27.  'O ae sheave o your bread, true-love,
        An ae glass o your wine,
     For I hae fasted for your sake
        These fully days is nine.

28.   ' Gang hame, gang hame, my seven bold
            brothers,
        Gang hame and sound your horn ;
    An ye may boast in southin lans
        Your sister 's play'd you scorn.'

# KING ESTMERE.

1.  Hearken to me, gentlemen,
        Come and you shall heare ;
    Ile tell you of two of the boldest brether
        That ever borne were.


2.  The tone of them was Adler Younge,
        The tother was Kyng Estmere ;
    The were as bolde men in their deeds
        As any were, farr and neare.


3.  As they were drinking ale and wine
        Within his brother's halle,
    'When will ye marry a wyfe, brother,
        A wyfe to glad us all ? '


4.  Then bespake him Kyng Estmere,
        And answered him hartilye :
    'I know not that ladye in any land,
        That is able to marry with mee.'


5.  'Kyng Adland hath a daughter, brother,
        Men call her bright and sheene ;
    If I were kyng here in your stead,
        That ladye shold be my queene.'


6.  Saies, 'Reade me, reade me, deare brother,
        Throughout merry England,
    Where we might find a messenger
        Betwixt us towe to sende.'

7. Saies, 'You shal ryde yourselfe, brother,
  Ile beare you companye ;
 Many a man throughe fals messengers is deceived,
  And I feare lest soe shold wee.'

8. Thus the renisht them to ryde
  Of twoe good renisht steeds,
 And when the came to King Adlands halle,
  Of redd gold shone their weeds.

9. And when the came to Kyng Adlands hall
  Before the goodlye gate,
 There they found good Kyng Adland
  Rearing himselfe theratt.

10. 'Now Christ thee save, good Kyng Adland ;
  Now Christ you save and see ; '
 Sayd, 'You be welcome, King Estmere,
  Right hartilye to mee.'

11. 'You have a daughter,' said Adler Younge,
  ' Men call her bright and sheene,
 My brother wold marrye her to his wiffe,
  Of Englande to be queene.'

12. 'Yesterday was att my deere daughter
  The king his sonne of Spayn,
 And then she nicked him of naye,
  And I doubt sheele do you the same.'

13. 'The Kyng of Spayne is a foule paynim
  And 'leeveth on Mahound,
 And pitye it were that fayre ladye,
  Shold marrye a heathen hound.'

14.   'But grant to me,' sayes Kyng Estmere,
          'For my love I you praye,
      That I may see your daughter deere
          Before I goe hence awaye.'

15.   'Although itt is seven years and more
          Since my daughter was in halle,
      She shall come once downe for your sake,
          To glad my guestës alle.'

16.   Downe then came that mayden fayre,
          With ladyes laced in pall,
      And halfe a hundred of bold knightes,
          To bring her from bowre to hall·
      And as many gentle squiers,
          To tend upon them all.

17.   The talents of golde were on her head sette
          Hanged low downe to her knee,
      And everye ring on her small finger
          Shone of the chrystall free.

18.   Saies, 'God you save, my deere madam,'
          Saies, 'God you save and see;'
      Said, 'You be welcome, Kyng Estmere,
          Right welcome unto mee.

19.   'And, if you love me, as you saye,
          Soe well and hartilee,
      All that ever you are comen about
          Soone sped now itt shal bee.'

20.   Then bespake her father deare :
          'My daughter, I saye naye ;
      Remember well the Kyng of Spayne,
          What he sayd yesterdaye.

21.    ' He wold pull downe my halles and castles,
            And reave me of my lyfe :
        I cannot blame him if he doe,
            If I reave him of his wyfe.'


22.    ' Your castles and your towres, father,
            Are stronglye built aboute,
        And therefore of the king his sonne of Spaine
            We neede not stande in doubt.


23.    ' Plight me your troth, nowe, Kyng Estmere,
            By heaven and your righte hand,
        That you will marrye me to your wyfe,
            And make me queene of your land.'


24.    Then Kyng Estmere he plight his troth,
            By heaven and his righte hand,
        That he wolde marrye her to his wyfe,
            And make her queene of his land.


25.    And he tooke leave of that ladye fayre,
            To goe to his owne countree,
        To fetche him dukes and lordes and knightes,
            That marryed the might bee.


26.    They had not ridden scant a myle,
          . A myle forthe of the towne,
        But in did come the Kyng of Spayne,
            With kempës many one.


27.    But in did come the Kyng of Spayne,
            With manye a bold barone,
        Tone day to marrye Kyng Adlands daughter,
            Tother daye to carrye her home.

28.  Shee sent one after Kyng Estmere
       In all the spede might bee,
     That he must either turne againe and fighte,
       Or goe home and loose his ladye.


29.  One whyle then the page he went,
       Another while he ranne ;
     Till he had oretaken King Estmere,
       I-wis he never blanne.


30.  ' Tydings, tydings, Kyng Estmere ! '
       ' What tydinges nowe, my boye ? '
     ' O tydinges I can tell to you,
       That will you sore annoye.


31.  ' You had not ridden scant a mile,
       A mile out of the towne,
     But in did come the Kyng of Spayne,
       With kempës many a one.


32.  ' But in did come the Kyng of Spayne,
       With manye a bold barone,
     Tone daye to marrye King Adlands daughter,
       Tother daye to carry her home.


33.  ' My ladye fayre she greetes you well,
       And ever-more well by mee :
     You must either turne againe and fighte,
       Or goe home and loose your ladye.'


34.  Saies, ' Reade me, reade me, deere brother,
       My reade shall ryse at thee,
     Whether it is better to turne and fighte,
       Or goe home and loose my ladye.'

35.   'Now hearken to me,' sayes Adler Yonge,
          'And your reade must rise at me ;
      I quicklye will devise a waye
          To sette thy ladye free.

36.   'My mother was.a westerne woman,
          And learned in gramarye,
      And when I learned at the schole,
          Something shee taught itt mee.

37.   'There growes an hearbe within this field,
          And iff it were but knowne,
      His color, which is whyte and redd,
          It will make blacke and browne.

38.   'His color, which is browne and blacke,
          Itt will make redd and whyte ;
      That sworde is not in all Englande
          Upon his coate will byte.

39.   'And you shal be a harper, brother,
          Out of the north countrye,
      And Ile be your boy, soe faine of fighte,
          And beare your harpe by your knee.

40.   'And you shal be the best harper
          That ever tooke harpe in hand,
      And I wil be the best singer
          That ever sung in this lande.

41.   'Itt shal be written in our forheads
          All and in grammarye,
      That we towe are the boldest men
          That are in all Christentye.'

42.   And thus they renisht them to ryde,
      Of tow good renisht steedes ;
  And when they came to King Adlands hall,
      Of redd gold shone their weedes.

43.   And whan the came to Kyng Adlands hall,
      Untill the fayre hall yate,
  There they found a proud porter
      Rearing himselfe thereatt.

44.   Sayes, 'Christ thee save, thou proud porter,'
      Sayes, 'Christ thee save and see :'
  'Nowe you be welcome,' sayd the porter,
      'Of what land soever ye bee.'

45.   'Wee beene harpers,' sayd Adler Younge,
      'Come out of the northe countrye ;
  Wee beene come hither untill this place
      This proud weddinge for to see.'

46.   Sayd, 'And your color were white and redd,
      As it is blacke and browne,
  I wold saye King Estmere and his brother
      Were comen untill this towne.'

47.   Then they pulled out a ryng of gold,
      Layd itt on the porters arme :
  'And ever we will thee, proud porter,
      Thou wilt saye us no harme.'

48.   Sore he looked on Kyng Estmere,
      And sore he handled the ryng,
  Then opened to them the fayre hall-yates,
      He lett for no kind of thyng.

49.  Kyng Estmere he stabled his steede
        Soe fayre att the hall-bord;
     The froth that came from his brydle bitte
        Light in Kyng Bremors beard.

50.  Saies, 'Stable thy steed, thou proud harper,'
        Saies, 'Stable him in the stalle;
     It doth not beseeme a proud harper
        To stable his steed in a kyngs halle.'

51.  'My ladde he is so lither,' he said,
        'He will doe nought that's meete;
     And is there any man in this hall
        Were able him to beate?'

52.  'Thou speakst proud words,' sayes the King of
           Spaine,
        'Thou harper, here to mee:
     There is a man within this halle,
        Will beate thy ladd and thee.'

53.  'O let that man come downe,' he said,
        'A sight of him wold I see;
     And when hee hath beaten well my ladd,
        Then he shall beate of mee.'

54.  Downe then came the kemperye man,
        And looked him in the eare;
     For all the gold that was under heaven,
        He durst not neigh him neare.

55.  'And how nowe, kempe,' said the Kyng of Spaine,
        'And how, what aileth thee?'
     He saies, 'It is writt in his forhead,
        All and in gramarye,
     That for all the gold that is under heaven,
        I dare not neigh him nye.'

56.　Then Kyng Estmere pulld forth his harpe,
　　　　　And plaid a pretty thinge :
　　　The lady upstart from the borde,
　　　　　And wold have gone from the king.

57.　' Stay thy harpe, thou proud harper,
　　　　　For Gods love I pray thee,
　　　For and thou playes as thou beginns,
　　　　　Thou 'lt till my bryde from mee.'

58.　He stroake upon his harpe againe,
　　　　　And playd a pretty thinge ;
　　　The lady lough a loud laughter,
　　　　　As shee sate by the king.

59.　Saies, ' Sell me thy harpe, thou proud harper,
　　　　　And thy stringes all,
　　　For as many gold nobles thou shalt have
　　　　　As heere bee ringes in the hall.'

60.　' What wold ye doe with my harpe,' he sayd,
　　　　　' If I did sell itt yee ? '
　　　' To playe my wiffe and me a fitt,
　　　　　When abed together wee bee.'

61.　' Now sell me,' quoth hee, ' thy bryde soe gay,
　　　　　As shee sitts by thy knee,
　　　And as many gold nobles I will give
　　　　　As leaves been on a tree.'

62.　' And what wold ye doe with my bryde soe gay,
　　　　　Iff I did sell her thee ?
　　　More seemelye it is for her fayre bodye
　　　　　To lye by me than thee.'

63.  Hee played agayne both loud and shrille
         And Adler he did syng,
      'O ladye, this is thy owne true love,
         Noe harper, but a kyng.

64.  'O ladye, this is thy owne true love,
         As playnlye thou mayest see,
      And Ile rid thee of that foule paynim
         Who partes thy love and thee.'

65.  The ladye looked, the ladye blushte,
         And blushte and lookt agayne,
      While Adler he hath drawne his brande
         And hath the sowdan slayne.

66.  Up then rose the kemperye men,
         And loud they gan to crye:
      'Ah! traytors, yee have slayne our kyng,
         And therefore yee shall dye.'

67.  Kyng Estmere threwe the harpe asyde
         And swith he drew his brand,
      And Estmere he and Adler Yonge
         Right stiffe in stour can stand.

68.  And aye their swordes soe sore can byte,
         Throughe help of gramarye,
      That soone they have slayne the kempery men,
         Or forst them forth to flee.

69.  Kyng Estmere tooke that fayre ladye,
         And marryed her to his wiffe,
      And brought her home to merry England
         With her to leade his life.

## KEMP OWYNE.

1.  Her mother died when she was young,
        Which gave her cause to make great moan;
    Her father married the warst woman
        That ever lived in Christendom.

2.  She served her with foot and hand,
        In every thing that she could dee,
    Till once, in an unlucky time,
        She threw her in ower Craigy's sea.

3.  Says, 'Lye you there, dove Isabel,
        And all my sorrows lye with thee;
    Till Kemp Owyne come ower the sea,
        And borrow you with kisses three:
    Let all the warld do what they will,
        Oh borrowed shall you never be.'

4.  Her breath grew strang, her hair grew lang,
        And twisted thrice about the tree,
    And all the people, far and near,
        Thought that a savage beast was she.

5.  These news did come to Kemp Owyne,
        Where he lived far beyond the sea;
    He hasted him to Craigy's sea,
        And on the savage beast lookt he.

6.  Her breath was strang, her hair was lang,
        And twisted was about the tree,
    And with a swing she came about:
        'Come to Craigy's sea, and kiss with me.

7.  'Here is a royal belt,' she cried,
        'That I have found in the green sea;
    And while your body it is on,
        Drawn shall your blood never be;
    But if you touch me, tail or fin,
        I vow my belt your death shall be.'


8.  He stepped in, gave her a kiss,
        The royal belt he brought him wi;
    Her breath was strang, her hair was lang,
        And twisted twice about the tree,
    And with a swing she came about:
        'Come to Craigy's sea, and kiss with me.


9.  'Here is a royal ring,' she said,
        'That I have found in the green sea;
    And while your finger it is on,
        Drawn shall your blood never be;
    But if you touch me, tail or fin,
        I swear my ring your death shall be.'


10. He stepped in, gave her a kiss,
        The royal ring he brought him wi;
    Her breath was strang, her hair was lang,
        And twisted ance about the tree,
    And with a swing she came about:
        'Come to Craigy's sea, and kiss with me.


11. 'Here is a royal brand,' she said,
        'That I have found in the green sea;
    And while your body it is on,
        Drawn shall your blood never be;
    But if you touch me, tail or fin,
        I swear my brand your death shall be.'

12.   He stepped in, gave her a kiss,
          The royal brand he brought him wi ;
      Her breath was sweet, her hair grew short,
          And twisted nane about the tree ;
      And smilingly she came about,
          As fair a woman as fair could be.

## TAM LIN.

1.   O I forbid you, maidens a',
    That wear gowd on your hair,
To come or gae by Carterhaugh,
    For young Tam Lin is there.

2.   Janet has kilted her green kirtle
    A little aboon her knee,
And she has broded her yellow hair
    A little aboon her bree,
And she 's awa to Carterhaugh,
    As fast as she can hie.

3.   When she came to Carterhaugh,
    Tam Lin was at the well,
And there she fand his steed standing,
    But away was himsel.

4.   She had na pu'd a double rose,
    A rose but only twa,
Till up then started young Tam Lin,
    Says, ' Lady, thou 's pu nae mae.

5.   ' Why pu's thou the rose, Janet,
    And why breaks thou the wand ?
Or why comes thou to Carterhaugh
    Withoutten my command ? '

6.   ' Carterhaugh, it is my ain,
    My daddie gave it me ;
I 'll come and gang by Carterhaugh,
    And ask nae leave at thee.'

\*    \*    \*    \*    \*    \*    \*

7.    Janet has kilted her green kirtle
          A little aboon her knee,
      And she has snooded her yellow hair
          A little aboon her bree,
      And she is to her father's ha,
          As fast as she can hie.


8.    Four and twenty ladies fair
          Were playing at the ba,
      And out there cam the fair Janet,
          Ance the flower amang them a'.


9.    Four and twenty ladies fair
          Were playing at the chess,
      And out then cam the fair Janet,
          As green as onie glass.


10.   Out then spak an auld grey knight,
          Lay oer the castle wa,
      And says, 'Alas, fair Janet, for thee
          But we'll be blamed a'.'


11.   'Haud your tongue, ye auld fac'd knight,
          Some ill death may ye die!
      Father my bairn on whom I will,
          I'll father nane on thee.'


12.   Out then spak her father dear,
          And he spak meek and mild;
      'And ever alas, sweet Janet,' he says,
          'I think thou gaes wi child.'


13.   'If that I gae wi child, father,
          Mysel maun bear the blame;
      There's neer a laird about your ha
          Shall get the bairn's name.

14.  'If my love were an earthly knight,
        As he's an elfin grey,
     I wad na gie my ain true-love
        For nae lord that ye hae.

15.  'The steed that my true-love rides on
        Is lighter than the wind ;
     Wi siller he is shod before,
        Wi burning gowd behind.'

16.  Janet has kilted her green kirtle
        A little aboon her knee,
     And she has snooded her yellow hair
        A little aboon her bree,
     And she's awa to Carterhaugh,
        As fast as she can hie.

17.  When she cam to Carterhaugh,
        Tam Lin was at the well,
     And there she fand his steed standing,
        But away was himsel.

18.  She had na pu'd a double rose,
        A rose but only twa,
     Till up then started young Tam Lin,
        Says, 'Lady, thou pu's nae mae.

19.  'Why pu's thou the rose, Janet,
        Amang the groves sae green,
     An a' to kill the bonie babe
        That we gat us between?'

20.  'O tell me, tell me, Tam Lin,' she says,
        'For's sake that died on tree,
     If eer ye was in holy chapel,
        Or Christendom did see?'

21.   ' Roxbrugh he was my grandfather,
      Took me with him to bide,
  And ance it fell upon a day
      That wae did me betide.

22.   ' And ance it fell upon a day,
      A cauld day and a snell,
  When we were frae the hunting come,
      That frae my horse I fell;
  The Queen o Fairies she caught me,
      In yon green hill to dwell.

23.   ' And pleasant is the fairy land,
      But, an eerie tale to tell,
  Ay at the end of seven years
      We pay a tiend to hell;
  I am sae fair and fu o flesh,
      I 'm feard it be mysel.

24.   ' But the night is Halloween, lady,
      The morn is Hallowday;
  Then win me, win me, an ye will,
      For weel I wat ye may.

25.   ' Just at the mirk and midnight hour
      The fairy folk will ride,
  And they that wad their true-love win,
      At Miles Cross they maun bide.'

26.   ' But how shall I thee ken, Tam Lin,
      Or how my true-love know,
  Amang sae mony unco knights
      The like I never saw?'

27.   'O first let pass the black, lady,
          And syne let pass the brown,
      But quickly run to the milk-white steed,
          Pu ye his rider down.

28.   'For I'll ride on the milk-white steed,
          And ay nearest the town ;
      Because I was an earthly knight
          They gie me that renown.

29.   'My right hand will be glovd, lady,
          My left hand will be bare,
      Cockt up shall my bonnet be
          And kaimd down shall my hair,
      And thae's the takens I gie thee,
          Nae doubt I will be there.

30.   'They'll turn me in your arms, lady,
          Into an esk and adder ;
      But hold me fast and fear me not,
          I am your bairn's father.

31.   'They'll turn me to a bear sae grim,
          And then a lion bold,
      But hold me fast and fear me not,
          As ye shall love your child.

32.   'Again they'll turn me in your arms
          To a red het gaud of airn ;
      But hold me fast and fear me not,
          I'll do to you nae harm.

33.   'And last they'll turn me in your arms
          Into the burning gleed ;
      Then throw me into well water,
          O throw me in wi speed.

34.  'And then I'll be your ain true-love,
      I'll turn a naked knight;
  Then cover me wi your green mantle,
      And cover me out o sight.'

35.  Gloomy, gloomy was the night,
      And eerie was the way,
  As fair Jenny in her green mantle
      To Miles Cross she did gae.

36.  About the middle o the night
      She heard the bridles ring;
  This lady was as glad at that
      As any earthly thing.

37.  First she let the black pass by,
      And syne she let the brown;
  But quickly she ran to the milk-white steed,
      And pu'd the rider down.

38.  Sae weel she minded whae he did say,
      And young Tam Lin did win;
  Syne coverd him wi her green mantle,
      As blyth's a bird in spring.

39.  Out then spak the Queen o Fairies,
      Out of a bush o broom:
  'Them that has gotten young Tam Lin
      Has gotten a stately groom.'

40.  Out then spak the Queen o Fairies,
      And an angry woman was she:
  'Shame betide her ill-far'd face,
      And an ill death may she die,
  For she's taen awa the boniest knight
      In a' my companie.

41. 'But had I kend, Tam Lin,' she says,
       'What now this night I see,
     I wad hae taen out thy twa grey een,
       And put in twa een o tree.'

## THOMAS RYMER.

*[the — handwritten insertion above "THOMAS"]*

*[familiar charact— handwritten note at right]*

1.   True Thomas lay oer yond grassy bank,
     And he beheld a ladie gay,
  A ladie that was brisk and bold,
     Come riding oer the fernie brae.

2.   Her skirt was of the grass-green silk,
     Her mantle of the velvet fine,
  At ilka tett of her horse's mane
     Hung fifty silver bells and nine.

3.   True Thomas he took off his hat
     And bowed him low down till his knee:
  'All hail, thou mighty Queen of Heaven!
     For your peer on earth I never did see.'

4.   'O no, O no, True Thomas,' she says,
     'That name does not belong to me;
  I am but the queen of fair Elfland,
     And I'm come here for to visit thee.

5.   'Harp and carp, Thomas,' she said,
     'Harp and carp along wi me;
  But if ye dare to kiss my lips,
     Sure of your bodie I will be.'

6.   'Betide me weal, betide me woe,
     That weird shall never daunton me;'—
  Syne he has kissed her rosy lips
     All underneath the Eildon Tree.

7. 'But ye maun go wi me now, Thomas,
   True Thomas, ye maun go wi me,
For ye maun serve me seven years,
   Thro weel or wae as may chance to be.'

8. She turned about her milk-white steed,
   And took True Thomas up behind,
And aye when eer her bridle rang,
   The steed flew swifter than the wind.

9. For forty days and forty nights
   He wade thro red blude to the knee,
And he saw neither sun nor moon,
   But heard the roaring of the sea.

10. O they rade on and further on,
    Until they came to a garden green;
'Light down, light down, ye ladie free,
    Some of that fruit let me pull to thee.'

11. 'O no, O no, True Thomas,' she says,
    'That fruit maun not be touched by thee,
For a' the plagues that are in hell
    Light on the fruit of this countrie.

12. 'But I have a loaf here in my lap,
    Likewise a bottle of claret wine,
And here ere we go farther on,
    We'll rest a while, and ye may dine.'

13. When he had eaten and drunk his fill,
    'Lay down your head upon my knee,'
The lady sayd, 'ere we climb yon hill,
    And I will show you ferlies three.

14.   'O see ye not yon narrow road,
          So thick beset wi thorns and briers?
      That is the path of righteousness,
          Tho after it but few enquires.


15.   'And see not ye that braid braid road,
          That lies across yon lillie leven?
      That is the path of wickedness,
          Tho some call it the road to heaven.


16.   'And see ye not that bonny road,
          Which winds about the fernie brae?
      That is the road to fair Elfland,
          Where you and I this night maun gae.


17.   'But Thomas, ye maun hold your tongue,
          Whatever ye may hear or see,
      For gin ae word you should chance to speak,
          You will neer get back to your ain countrie.'


18.   He has gotten a coat of the even cloth,
          And a pair of shoes of velvet green,
      And till seven years were past and gone
          True Thomas on earth was never seen.

## THE WEE WEE MAN.

1. As I was wa'king all alone,
      Between a water and a wa,
   And there I spy'd a wee wee man,
      And he was the least that ere I saw.

2. His legs were scarce a shathmont's length,
      And thick and thimber was his thigh;
   Between his brows there was a span,
      And between his shoulders there was three.

3. He took up a meikle stane,
      And he flang 't as far as I could see;
   Though I had been a Wallace wight,
      I couldna liften 't to my knee.

4. 'O wee wee man, but thou be strang!
      O tell me where thy dwelling be?'
   'My dwelling 's down at yon bonny bower;
      O will you go with me and see?'

5. On we lap, and awa we rade,
      Till we came to yon bonny green;
   We lighted down for to bait our horse,
      And out there came a lady fine.

6. Four and twenty at her back,
      And they were a' clad out in green;
   Though the King of Scotland had been there,
      The warst o' them might hae been his queen.

7.   On we lap, and awa we rade,
        Till we came to yon bonny ha,
     Whare the roof was o the beaten gould,
        And the floor was o the cristal a'.


8.   When we came to the stair-foot,
        Ladies were dancing, jimp and sma,
     But in the twinkling of an eye,
        My wee wee man was clean awa.

## ST. STEPHEN AND HEROD.

1. Seynt Stevene was a clerk in Kyng Herowdes halle,
   And servyd him of bred and cloth, as every kyng befalle.

2. Stevyn out of kechone cam, wyth boris hed on honde ;
   He saw a sterre was fayr and brygt over Bedlem stonde.

3. He kyst adoun the boris hed and went in to the halle :
   'I forsak the, Kyng Herowdes, and thi werkes alle.

4. 'I forsak the, Kyng Herowdes, and thi werkes alle ;
   Ther is a chyld in Bedlem born is beter than we alle.'

5. 'What eylyt the, Stevene ?   What is the befalle ?
   Lakkyt the eyther mete or drynk in Kyng Herowdes halle ? '

6. 'Lakit me neyther mete nor drynk in Kyng Herowdes halle ;
   Ther is a chyld in Bedlem born is beter than we alle.'

7. 'What eylyt the, Stevyn ?   Art thu wôd, or thu gynnyst to brede ?
   Lakkyt the eyther gold or fe, or ony ryche wede ? '

8.   'Lakyt me neyther gold ne fe, ne non ryche wede ;
     Ther is a chyld in Bedlem born sal helpyn us at our
         nede.'

9.   'That is al so soth, Stevyn, al so soth, iwys,
     As this capoun crowe sal that lyth here in myn
         dysh.'

10.  That word was not so sone seyd, that word in that
         halle,
     The capoun crew *Cristus natus est!* among the
         lordes alle.

11.  'Rysyt up, myn turmentowres, be to and al be on,
     And ledyt Stevyn out of this toun, and stonyt hym
         wyth ston !'

12.  Tokyn he Stevene, and stonyd hym in the way,
     And therfore is his evyn on Crystes owyn day.

# APPENDIX I.

———◦◇◦———

## THE BALLADS OF EUROPE.

Narrative songs were known to the ancient Germans and along
with choral hymns formed the chief part of their poetry: Tacitus,
*Germ.* 2; *Ann.* ii, 88; iv, 47; *Hist.* ii, 22; iv, 18; v, 15. Jordanes,
*de Origine Actibusque Getarum,* c. 4, says that the migration of the
Goths "in priscis eorum carminibus pene storico ritu in commune
recolitur"; and again, c. 5, "cantu majorum facta modulationibus
citharisque canebant." Many other passages could be quoted to
the same effect. In the seventh century, among the Franks, we
have an example of events passing directly into song: See *Vita S.
Faronis* in Mabillon, *Acta Sanctorum ord. S. Bened.,* Venetis, 1733,
II, 590, with introductory words quoted above, p. lxxix; after the song
(given in Latin), the historian says in apology: "hoc enim rustico
carmine placuit ostendere, quantum ab omnibus celeberrimus habe-
batur." Famous is Charlemagne's love of these songs: "barbara
et antiquissima carmina quibus veterum actus et bella canebantur
scripsit memoriaeque mandavit," *Vita Karoli,* c. 29; and much the
same is told later of English Alfred: "sed Saxonica poemata" —
ballads, one hopes — "saepissime audiens," and of his children:
"maxime Saxonica carmina studiose didicere," *Asser de Aelfredi
rebus gestis,* ed. 1603, Frankfort, pp. 5, 13. What these *carmina*
were is a parlous question; but perhaps we are not to think simply
of poems like the later "Maldon." Aldhelm was fond of ballads;
he made songs which were still known in Alfred's time, — a fragile
prop for the modern rationalist, — and better yet, he stood on that
famous bridge and sang the recalcitrant people, somewhat like him
of Hamelin, sheer into church, such was his *peritia canendi,* and such
the power of the ballad! See Mabillon, *Act. S. ord. S. Bened.,* III,
224. Here, however, one suspects artistry: these were hardly
*vulgaria carmina.* One must not omit Cnut's song: "Cantilenam
his verbis Anglice composuit," says the chronicle, *Historia Eliensis,*
II, 27, in Gale, *Hist. Script.,* I, 505; but after giving the well-known

verses, it adds: "et caetera quae sequuntur, quae usque hodie *in choris publice cantantur* et in proverbiis memorantur," so that Cnut probably had as much to do with his song as Alfred had with those proverbs which are stamped with the earlier royalty.  Hereward the Wake had ballads sung about him : " ejusque gesta fortia etiam Angliam ingressa canerentur ; " and again : "ingenta praelia et mille pericula . . . prout adhuc *in triviis canuntur*." See *Ingulph. Hist. Croyland.*, in Michel's *Chron. Norm.* II, v f.; though this particular document is a forgery, and belongs some two centuries after the events, the statement about ballads has a definite value. The chronicling ballads were used by early historians of England, even by the critical and careful William of Malmesbury.  Thus far, he says in his second book (*Gest. Reg. Angl.*, ed. Stubbs, I, 155), he has written upon trustworthy evidence : "sequentia magis cantilenis per successiones temporum detritis, quam libris ad instructiones posteriorum elucubratis, didicerim." — See also same edition, I, 165; and for the reports spread in ballads about the return of Arthur, II, 342.  There can be no doubt that poets like Layamon and the author of " King Horn " owed much to ballads : see Wülcker, *Ueb. d. Quellen Layamons*, Paul-Braune, *Beiträge*, III, 524 ff.; Wissmann, *Untersuchungen zu King Horn*, p. 58.  With the thirteenth century, ballads come even more into prominence as affecting the style of other poems : see ten Brink, *Gesch. d. engl. Lit.*, I, 381 f., 421, who thinks, moreover, that the refrain 'Blow, northerne wynd' is popular, and not the work of the poet in whose lyric it is preserved.

Such — and the list could be greatly enlarged — are some of the references which prove that ballads were made and sung from the earliest historical periods of the Germanic race down through the middle ages.  Unfortunately, we find nothing which enables us to say just what these ballads were.  The powers of the church were doing their best to suppress such poetry, mainly because of its heathen origins, but here and there for moral reasons.  Hence, too, it failed to be recorded.  From this time, however, — that is, for England from the thirteenth century, and earlier elsewhere, — we begin to meet actual specimens of the poem which we know as the narrative ballad.  The Germanic ballad, " which is not preserved in its original form or original extent " (see Grundtvig, Introduction to Rosa Warrens, *Dänische Volkslieder*, for this and immediately following quotations), can be traced in Denmark, Norway, Sweden, Iceland, the Färöe Islands, Scotland, England, Netherlands and

Germany. "Almost every Norwegian, Swedish or Icelandic ballad is found in a Danish version. Of Scandinavian ballads, moreover, a larger number can be found in English and Scottish versions than in German or Dutch versions." England and Scotland preserved none of the old heroic lays (*kœmpeviser*) which are so plentiful in Scandinavia, and which in Germany, though unknown to the ballad, have been worked into the national epic (Grundtvig, p. xxix). Again, while the British Isles have kept little of a mythic character, and Germany nothing at all, Scandinavia is very rich in this respect. So far as oral tradition goes, the Färöe islanders and the Norwegians have preserved the oldest and the most genuine versions of the Germanic ballad ; but Denmark has manuscripts of ballads three or four hundred years old. Grundtvig divides the subject-matter of Danish ballads (see his noble collection, *Danmarks Gamle Folkeviser*, 5 vols., incomplete, Copenhagen, 1853, ff.) into (1) Heroic Ballads, (2) Ballads of Myth and Enchantment, (3) Historic Ballads, (4) Ballads of Chivalry ; and he puts the probable date of composition for the first class in the twelfth and thirteenth centuries, for the mythological class as early as the eleventh century.

As regards England, Professor Child assigns the origin of the Robin Hood ballads to the thirteenth century, and with them probably belongs *Hugh of Lincoln*. The Battle of Otterburn, 1388, gives us a certain date, "from which time we have a succession of ballads founded on ascertained events down to the middle of the eighteenth century " (Child, in Johnson's *Cyclopœdia*). The most important sources of our ballads, besides such printed pieces as *The Gest of Robin Hood* (about 1489), are the Percy Manuscript, "written just before 1650," and "the oral tradition of Scotland " during "the last 130 years " (Child). This brings us to the earliest collections, especially Bishop Percy and his famous *Reliques*.

Percy was more collector than critic, and even his enthusiasm was dampened by the sneers of Dr. Johnson. Dr. Johnson, however, appears to have given Percy some help about the ballads. Boswell's *Johnson*, ed. Dr. G. B. Hill, III, 314, note, quotes Cradock's *Memoirs:* "Almost the last time I ever saw Johnson, he said to me: 'Notwithstanding all the pains Dr. Farmer and I took to serve Dr. Percy in regard to his *Ancient Ballads*, he has left town for Ireland without taking leave of either of us.'" Among his undoubted and enthusiastic helpers, Percy counted "the elegant Mr. Shenstone," Grainger, Garrick, Warton, and even Goldsmith. At one time, if we may believe report, six amanuenses were busy copying ballads for Percy from the Pepys collection at Cambridge; and he had correspondents "in Wales, in the wilds of Staffordshire and Derbyshire, in the West Indies, and in Ireland." Thus the famous folio was not sole basis of the *Reliques*. This book appeared in 1765; a fourth edition, "improved," in 1794. Good modern editions are H. B. Wheatley, 3 vols., London, 1876–77, and A. Schröer, Heilbronn, 1889, ff. The Folio, after long seclusion, was edited by Hales and Furnivall, 4 vols., 1867–68. The *Reliques* owed little to predecessors. Besides "Garlands" and random collections (see Brandl, in Paul's *Grundriss*, II, i, 844 ff.), we note Dryden printing "Chevy Chase," "Johnie Armstrong," and other ballads, in his *Miscellany Poems* (1684, and continued after Dryden's death till 1708). The first distinct collection of ballads printed in English appeared 1723, 1724, 1727, with an editor anonymous, but inspired by Addison's praise of "Chevy Chase," and timorous and bold by turns. The *Reliques*, however, really heads the list of ballad collections in England; it may be noted that Denmark and Spain had each made collections of ballads in the sixteenth century.

It was when "very young" that Percy found his folio; "sadly torn," it was "lying dirty on the floor" of Humphrey Pitt, Esq., whose maids had used it to light fires (see Hales and Furnivall, *Folio*, II, xx). Percy scribbled on this manuscript and tore out leaves for the printer, thus depriving us of all control over "King Estmere"; but his greatest sin was lack of fidelity to the text. Out of 39 lines of "The Childe of Elle" he made 200 lines in his book. Since the *Reliques*, many collections have appeared: see Professor Child in Johnson's *Cyclopædia*, and the Bibliography of his earlier edition (1860) of Ballads, I, xiii ff. The forthcoming tenth and final part of his new collection (*The English and Scottish Popular Ballads*, Boston, 8 Parts, 1882–1892), "will contain a full bibliography." In a way, this noble work makes all earlier collections superfluous; but we may mention Herd's *Ancient and Modern Scottish Songs*, 1769, 1776, distinguished for fidelity and accuracy in regard to sources; Ritson's *Ancient Songs*, 1790, but not brought out till 1792, *Robin Hood*, 1795, and other collections; Scott's *Minstrelsy of the Scottish Border*, 3 vols., 1802–3, with later editions, mainly traditional and containing much that was new; and Motherwell's *Minstrelsy, Ancient and Modern*, 1827. Some critical remarks by Lemcke on these collections will be found in the *Jahrbuch f. rom. u. engl. Lit.*, IV, 1 ff., 142 ff., 297 ff.

We can give but a hasty glance at the ballads of other nations. Ballads have been pointed out in the Bible: *Numbers*, xxi, 17, where

" Israel sang this song," for example.   The primitive Aryans must
have had ballads along with the other heavy responsibilities laid upon
them; but this is to consider too curiously : see Meyer, Haupt's
*Zts.*, XXIX, 235.   The battle over ballads and the Greek Epos is
still raging, and need not be approached ; but Modern Greek ballads
are deservedly famous.   Ballads may well have formed the basis of
early Roman history as we read it in Livy, but did not, as Niebuhr
thought, furnish the substance: Niebuhr, *Hist. Rome*, transl., London,
1855, I, 254 ff., and Macaulay, preface to the *Lays of Ancient Rome*.
Apparent references to Roman ballads are: Cicero, *Tusc.* iv, 2, 3,
*Brutus*, xviii, xix ; and Horace, *Carm.* iv, 15, 25. —— Spanish ballads rank high, and received early notice.   In modern times, it was
Herder who called attention to them : see F. Wolf's elaborate
article, *Wiener Jahrbücher*, CXIV, 1 ff., and CXVII, 82 ff.   First
printed in broadsides, they were collected about 1550 in a volume,
partly from the broadsides, partly from oral tradition.   Their origin
is referred to the eleventh and twelfth centuries, but they cannot be
traced earlier than the fifteenth. — For Italian ballads one may find a
good summary of facts in the introduction to Nigra's *Canti Popolari
del Piemonte.* — France was almost the last nation to take up the
study of ballads ; Villemarqué was a pioneer in the movement.
See Crane, Introduction to *Chansons Populaires de France*, New
York, 1891 ; Tiersot, *Histoire de la Chanson Populaire en France*,
Paris, 1889 ; and Jeanroy, *Les Origines de la Poesie Lyrique en France
au Moyen-âge*, same place and date.— The German revival has been
considered in detail above ; Uhland, *Alte Hoch- und Niederdeutsche
Volkslieder*, 2 vols., Stuttgart, 1844–45, along with the *Abhandlungen*,
published after the author's death, may be noted for older times, and
Böhme, *Altdeutsches Liederbuch*, Leipzig, 1877, for the new. — For
the ballads of the Netherlands much was done by the German Hoffmann von Fallersleben : see his *Niederländische Volkslieder*, 2nd. ed.,
Hannover, 1856. —— Slavonic popular poetry, such as that of the
Servians, who have little literature save their ballads, shows a marked
difference from Germanic poetry of the same order, and lacks the
romantic element of the latter.   J. Grimm was interested in Servian
ballads, and reviewed a collection of them with considerable praise.
— An account of the collecting of such poetry among the Russians
is given by Ralston, *Songs of the Russian People*, pp. 63–76. — But
no collecting was ever done so zealously as among the Finns and
Esthonians: see *La Tradition* (Paris, 1889), III, 237 f.   Between
1871 and 1880 the Society for Esthonian Folk Lore received 7300

"chansons"; one woman alone recited 700 songs. Later, in response
to another appeal, the peasants sent in this almost incredible harvest : "8532 vielles chansons, 1131 contes, 7963 proverbes, 8457
énigmes,"— evidence of a marvelous if not suspicious fertility.   A
collector in the grand style was " J. Hurt, traditionniste esthonien!"
The Finns had an old reputation for magic and incantations.   Random collections of their forms of exorcism, and the like, were made
as early as 1640 : see Krohn, *La Tradition*, IV, 45 ff.   In 1841 Cas-
trén brought out the *Kalevala*.   In 1854 the Society for Finnish
Literature began to look after popular melodies, and sent out three
musicians to collect them.   These investigated the original songs of
the *Kalevala*, and gathered a few more "chants épiques."

# APPENDIX II.

———◆———

## METRE, STYLE, AND FORM.

Two absolute conditions of English ballads, so far as form is concerned, are the stanza and rime. Instead of continuous epic verse,
one finds a stanza made up of two verses. This stanza may be a
couplet with verses of four accents each, — apparently the oldest
form (Steenstrup, *Vore Folkeviser*, p. 120), or else there are two long
verses of seven accents each, which are so divided, occasionally with
middle rime, that a four-line stanza is the result, with first and third
line of four accents, and second and fourth of three. Brandl, Paul's
*Grundriss*, II, i, 840, recognizes no English ballads which are not in
one of these two stanzas. Of course, occasional overflow occurs,
with resulting stanza of six lines : see *Otterburn, Cheviot, Johnie
Cock, Sir Hugh, Child Waters;* but the typical stanza, if not a
couplet, has four lines: This four-line stanza is itself the old *septenarius* couplet with a new division ; but we are not to discuss the
difficult question of metrical origin : see Schipper, *Englische Metrik*,
I, 89, 349, and in Paul's *Grundriss*, II, i, 1048 ; Brandl, *ibid.*, II, i,
658 : "das zersungene septenarpar der sächsischen epiker" ; and
compare that popular elegy, composed about 1200, the *Poema Morale.*
The prevailing view is that the metrical scheme came from the
Latin hymns of the church, and the irregularities of practice from
influence of older native verse (Brandl) ; but there are difficulties
even in this simple assumption. For example, the *septenarius* was
not used in England until the twelfth century, and it is absurd to
suppose that England had no ballads until that date. In what
metre were the earlier ballads ? Müllenhoff, *Sagen, Lieder, u. s. w.*,
p. xiii, says that in Germany the old alliterative verse died a natural
death, so that in the course of the tenth century popular poetry had
to take up rime. In England, however, alliterative poetry was not
at all dead when the ballad-metre began. There is a possibility that
these popular metres, like the refrain, which came out of the church
to the people, had previously gone out of the people into the church;
and we may thus think of a continuity in metre from older ballads :

see Luick in Paul's *Grundriss*, II, i, 997. The stanza certainly seems
a necessity in ballads, and hence we are not to look to the older
recited and continuous verse of Anglo-Saxon records. We have
seen that there is the same metrical gap in the case of Scandinavian
ballads and the older poetry: Steenstrup, *Vore Folkeviser*, p. 123 f.,
322, and Lundell in Paul's *Grundriss*, II, i, 728 f.

Secondly, all our ballads employ rime in its modern sense. Initial
rime, or alliteration, affected the verse; end-rime concerns the stanza:
see Schipper, *Engl. Metr.*, I, 83 f., 309 f. Indeed, rime marks nearly
all ballad-poetry known to us, Germanic, Celtic and Romance (Wolf,
*Lais*, p. 162); for the regular assonance in place of rime, found in
Spanish ballads, is not original, but was once a matter of chance, as
in English, becoming normal in the sixteenth century: Wolf,
*Romanzenpoesie d. Spanier*, *Wiener Jahrb.*, CXVII, 112 f., 121. In
our English ballads we note considerable assonance, but always as a
license. Such are: have-drawe, *Monk*, 9; taen-hame, *J. Cock*, 3;
came-belong, *Bart.*, 19; marke-heart, *ibid.*, 63; stane-in, *Sisters*, 8;
yard-there, *2 Bro.*, 5; grasse-Maurice, *Maur.*, 6; age-side, *Brand*, 2;
gate-it, *ibid.*, 28; fast-burst, *C. Waters*, 13; hand-Hunting, *Hunt.*, 11;
lefe-tethe, *Gest*, 225; sweet-sleep, *J. Cock*, 9, and very common; red-
bride, *Cruel Br.*, 2; deed-me, *Babylon*, 17; men-hame, *F. Annie*, 20;
lyne-meane, *Guy*, 2; thinge-behynde, *ibid.*, 9; stye-lynde, *Monk*, 76;
king-queen, *Cruel Br.*, 5; white-alike, *Armstr.*, 2; din-men, *Brackley*,
7; iwys-dysh, *Stephen*, 9; Hode-stout, *Gest*, 355; Hood-golde, *Guy*,
25 (good rime?); grone-slayne, *Otterb.*, 57; stone-man, *Maur.*, 7;
more-fall, *Bart.*, 55; home-toun, *Car*, 6; gone-burn, *Brack.*, 26;
gone-kind, *W. Lady*, 5; son-in, *2 Sist.*, 16; John-ring, *2 Bro.*, 9; on-
maidén, *Colven*, 4; bord-beard, *Estmere*, 49; bold-child, *Lin*, 32;
town-again, *Bewick*, 23; cup-about, *W. Lady*, 6; fly-play, *Brack.*, 10.
Often the assonance is only a matter of spelling: gun-in, *Brack.*, 14;
son-man, *Randal*, 1; and perhaps Hood-golde, *Guy*, 25. Feminine
assonance is rare, as are indeed feminine rimes: gallowe-arrowe,
*Guy*, 18; playin-dawin, *Brack.*, 1; lasses-rashes, *B. B. and M. G.*, 1;
middle-girdle, *2 Sist.*, 11; adder-father (?), *Lin*, 31. Utter lack of
rime occurs: see especially *Willie's Lady*, and also, face-night,
*Hunting*, 2; to-day-quite, *Car*, 29, may be remedied by adding
"away." "Perfect rime" is rare: get-forget, *Gest*, 175; he-he, *Bewick*,
43; alle-alle, *Stephen*, 4; wood-wood, *Maur.*, 18; well-well (with
different meanings, as in Chaucer), *Usher*, 7; him-him, *Sweet Wm.*,
11; Mahound-hound, *Estmere*, 13.

The rime falls usually on the second and fourth verses only: *a, b,
c, b;* but *a, b, a, b*, is fairly frequent. About half of *The Hunting of*

*the Cheviot* has the latter form, and it occurs elsewhere sporadically. Rime within the verse itself is less frequent: *Earl Brand*, 9; *Gest*, 354; *Otterburn*, 2, 40, 48; *J. Cock*, 3, 18; often in *Sir Andrew Barton;* and rarely in other ballads. On the whole, the ballads are not rich in variety of rime; see particularly *Bewick and Grahame*, where *he, me, be, thee, stand, land*, and the like, must do yeoman service.

Initial rime, or so-called alliteration, is always an adornment, and never a principle or stay of the metre; at least, it never takes the place of rime. It is much more frequent in the older than in the later ballads: see *Monk, Guy, Otterburn, Cheviot*, and parts of the *Gest;* for general examples, *Monk*, 1; *Otterburn*, 14; *Cheviot*, 6. Alliteration occasionally connects verses: *Guy*, 3 1-2; 16 3-4; *Monk*, 29 1-2; *Otterburn*, 50 3-4; *Cheviot*, 31 3-4; 32 1-2; 66 3-4; 68 1-2; *Cock*, 5 3-4; *Car*, 4 1-2; *Campbell*, 5 3-4; and elsewhere. *Bewick and Grahame* shows a tendency to this connection: 12, 13, 14, 34. —— Again, Alliterating Phrases are very common: bete and bynde, *Gest*, 12; buske and brome, *Monk*, 12; browght in bale, *ibid.*, 51; bear your bowe, *Death*, 6; a berne upon the bent, *Ott.*, 5; to batell make you boune, *ibid.*, 28; busk and boun, *Cock*, 2, and often; blyth as birds, *Armstr.*, 5; *Lin*, 39; bigget a bower, *B. B. M. G.*, 1; big wi bairn, *F. Mary*, 4; barn and byre, *Usher*, 12; banke to brim, *C. Waters*, 14; bed and board, *Janet*, 3; brisk and bold, *Rymer*, 1; blood and bone, *Cheviot*, 3; Kith nor kin, *Guy*, 36; of comfort that was not colde, *Ott.*, 5; cawte and kene, *ibid.*, 26; carpe of care, *Cheviot*, 58; caste [the] kevels, *Robyn*, 2; cups and cans, *F. Mary*, 20; kaims o care; *W. Lady*, 35; cheek and chin, *Janet*, 12; Dale and doune, *Guy*, 20; dye before his day, *ibid.*, 39; dawnynge of the day, *Ott.*, 20; to deth was dyght, *Cheviot*, 40; dule ye drie, *Edward*, 3; A fote would flee, *Ott.*, 61; fyght in a fylde, *Cheviot*, 23; fight or flee, *Car*, 24; fetters o his feet, *Y. Waters*, 10; fashes in the flood, *Usher*, 4; fame of fight, *Estmere*, 39; fat fadge by the fire, *Lord Thomas*, 8; Goune of greene, *Guy*, 44; gravell and . . . greete, *Death*, 26; glytteryde as did a gleed, *Cheviot*, 14; gets no gaine, *Barton*, 57; green as . . . glass, *Lin*, 10; greene as . . . grass, *Maur.*, 7; gowd and gear, *Fair A.*, 1; girdle of gold, *C. Waters*, 2; Hart nor hand, *Cheviot*, 11; harpe in hand, *Estmere*, 40; by halke and eke by hill, *Gest*, 366; houndes and horn, *ibid.*, 182; horse and harness, *Armstr.*, 2; Lothe or lefe, *Gest*, 225; leaves of lyne, *Guy*, 22; leaned under a lowe, *ibid.*, 46; light as lef on lynde, *Monk*, 76; lord of land, *Cheviot*, 19; lord nor loune, *Car*, 13; lyvar and longes, *Cheviot*, 37; laird nor lord, *Y. Waters*, 8; lie your lane, *Fair A.*, 1;

lands and livings, *Barton*, 78; large and long, *Armstr.*, 4; Mete and mele, *Gest*, 384; might and main, *Guy*, 14; mother and may, *ibid.*, 39; mornynge of May, *Monk*, 5; mas nor matyns, *ibid.*, 6; man of might, *Ott.*, 52; male and myneyple, *Cheviot*, 30; mickle of might, *Barton*, 5; misse my mark, *ibid.*, 13; maid o the mill, *Brack.*, 19; moss and moor, *Brand*, 6; make her moan, *C. Waters*, 33; meek and mild, *Lin*, 13; Nicked him [of] nay, *Estmere*, 12; Robbe and reve, *Gest*, 12; reken with . . . reves, *ibid.*, 254; redy on a rowe, *ibid.*, 448; reacheless on a root, *Guy*, 38; roke . . . in the rayne, *Ott.*, 51; rede full ryght, *ibid.*, 53; rynde and rent, *ibid.*, 42; Seker and sad, *Gest*, 215; sad and sar, *Cheviot*, 46; sayle the sea, *Barton*, 37; sail this ship, *Spens*, 1; save and see, *Maur.*, 10, and often; sark o silk, *Colven*, 5; slaine in a slade, *Guy*, 24; sichin and sobbin, *Brack.*, 19; sistar's son, *Cheviot*, 55; for soth as I yow sey, *Monk*, 27, and often; for soth and sertenly, *Ott.*, 59; stand you still, *Guy*, 8; stay and stand, *Barton*, 18; stiffly in stoure can stand, *Ott.*, 58; stiffly she stode, *Car*, 12; styffe and strong, *Gest*, 437; styll and stalworthlye, *Ott.*, 6; still as any stone, *Monk*, 31; stout and stalwart, *Usher*, 1; stockes and stone, *Guy*, 13; strete and stye, *Monk*, 76; strete and stalle, *ibid.*, 89; styrande many a stag, *Ott.*, 3; spendyd a spear, *Cheviot*, 40; at supper set, *Car*, 7; stable thy steed, *Estmere*, 50; sun was set, *Lord Thomas*, 1; sweavens are swift, *Guy*, 4; Thick and thimber, *Wee Man*, 2; the thistle and the thorn, *Lady Maisry*, 17; telle him tale, *Monk*, 51; top to toe, *Guy*, 44; trusty and trewe, *Gest*, 215; Wilful of my way, *Guy*, 24; went by the way, *Monk*, 13; wyrke him woo, *ibid.*, 28; welth in the worlde, *Ott.*, 6; welth at wyll, *ibid.*, 15; world to winne, *Death*, 10; waken with wynne, *Ott.*, 22; water from the well, *Usher*, 7; wed a wife, *Lord Thomas*, 2; woo'd a wife, *W. Lady*, 1; well I wat, *Lin*, 25; weppone welde, *Cheviot*, 23; woo and wouche, *ibid.*, 26; wounde full wyde, *ibid.*, 28; win[d] and weet, *Lady Maisry*, 20; woman's weede, *Maur.*, 32. Not to prolong the list with less striking cases, we may further note the form of phrase where adjective and noun, adverb and verb, are bound together by alliteration : baylefulle bronde, *Ott.*, 58; bryght bronde, *Gest*, 202; bonny boy, *Fair Mary*, 8; bosome braid, *ibid.*, 3; cherry cheeks, 2 *Sist.*, 14; deerly dight, *Barton*, 28; dungeon deep, *Y. Waters*, 10; gowden graithed, *ibid.*, 4; gowden girdle, *2 Sist.*, 11; groves sae green, *Lin*, 20; hanged hye, *Maur.*, 16; leeve London, *ibid.*, 5; limmer loon, *Bewick*, 15; lilly lee, *Fair A.*, 24; lilly leven, *Rymer*, 13; maidens mild, *Fair Mary*, 1; ribbon sae red, *Brand*, 14; siller shod, *Y. Waters*, 4; trusty tree, *Cheviot*, 44; weary wight, *W. Lady*, 11; wondrous wide, *Cock*, 7.

## VERSE.

Of the ballads in this collection, the so-called *ballad-measure*, — four verses, riming mostly *a, b, c, b*, with four measures or accents each for the first and third, and three each for the second and fourth, — claims all the *Robin Hood* ballads, *Otterburn, The Hunting of the Cheviot, Johnie Cock, Brown Robyn, Spens, Captain Car, Young Waters, Bessie Bell and Mary Gray, Sir Hugh, Twa Brothers, Maurice, Wife of Usher's Well, Fair Margaret and Sweet William, Young Hunting, Fair Janet, Lady Maisry, Lass of Roch Royal, Willie and Lady Maisry, Lord Thomas and Fair Annet, Fair Mary of Livingston, Child Waters, Fair Annie, Katharine Jaffray, Gay Goshawk, King Estmere,* and *Tam Lin.* In *The Hunting of the Cheviot,* the form: 4*a*, 4*b*, 4*ac*, 4*b*, prevails in stanzas 2, 40, 58, and others, where one cannot reduce the measure by such slurring as Schipper recommends (*Englische Metrik,* I, 351). Slurring, of course, will often keep the verse in limits, but in the fourth line of the stanza overflow is sometimes certain: *Gest,* 224; *R. H. Death,* 25³; *Otterburn,* 69⁴; *Cheviot,* 7⁴, 17⁴, 40⁴, 58⁴; and *Fair Annie,* 23⁴. Slurring is evident in *Fair Margaret and Sweet William,* 3²; *Earl Brand,* 1²; *Willie and Lady Maisry,* 9³, and elsewhere; but it is useless to catalogue minutely all such variations, and it must be remembered that great license in number and weight of syllables is one of the chief marks of ballad-metre. Moreover, we may right many a verse by leaving out a phrase like "quoth the sheriffe" in *Guy of Gisborne,* 20³, or "he says" in *Cheviot,* 16³. Another ballad in this measure, with interwoven refrain, is *Edward.*

A second group of ballads have the stanza in four-accent verse throughout. Here belong *Kinmont Willie, Johnie Armstrong, Sir Andrew Barton, Bewick and Grahame, Clerk Colven, Sweet William's Ghost, Young Beichan, Kemp Owyne, Thomas Rymer,* and *The Wee Wee Man.* A single ballad has the stanza in three-beat verse throughout, with a lilt due to the feminine ending of the odd lines and the triple measure in the following foot: *The Bonny Earl of Murray.*

All the other ballads, except one, are in the couplet of four beats to the verse, and often have a "tumbling" effect. They are *The Three Ravens, The Twa Sisters, The Cruel Brother, Babylon, Earl Brand, Willie's Lady, Hind Horn. Brackley* and *Lord Randal* show abounding triple measure; *Bonnie George Campbell* has a quite regular movement in the triple measure, with "dactylic" effect.

Peculiar is the metrical form of *St. Stephen and Herod,* where we come closer to such models as the *Poema Morale;* we note, however, the six-beat verses which once or twice combine with the regular *septenarius* in something like "Poulter's Measure." The verses of the last stanza have six measures each.

The general movement in all these metres is "iambic," though the verse very often begins with an accented syllable: *Gest,* 280:

> God, that syt in heven hye,
> Graunte us well to fare.

Unaccented syllables are frequently omitted: *Gest,* 20: These yémen áll thrée; 419: Nów práy I thée; 202: Ón my bríght brónde; *Three Ravens,* 3: Dówne in yónder gréene féeld; *Brand,* 8: Eárl Bránd, if yé love mé; *Gest,* 44: The knýght sháll begýnne; 256: The sóth múst we sée; 294: Évermóre wás the bést, For sóth, Róbyn Hóde; so also 351¹, 352¹, 373¹, 395², 400², etc.; *Monk,* 20: Oút át the dúrre he rán; *Cheviot,* 11¹; *Sir A. Barton,* 43³; *Captain Car,* 11: Fétch mé my péstilétt, and chárge mé my gónne. Three considerations are suggested for this matter of omitted light syllables. In the first place, ballads were sung, and it is easier thus to dispose of the metrical hiatus than in recitation. Secondly, many syllables may be resolved into two: *Gest,* 352⁴: myre; 337²: slayne; 378⁴: saynt; *Cheviot,* 39²: years; *Lady Maisry,* 19⁴: world; *Otterburn,* 37⁸: desyres; and, for inflectional reasons, *Guy,* 7²: had been many a *man's* bane; see *Lin,* 30⁴: I am your *bairn's* father. Thirdly, one must reckon with the final *ë.* It is not pretended that all such cases are marked in this collection, nor that those marked are invariably necessary. There is a subjective element always present in scanning these lines; but it may be suggested that even where a final *ë* is no longer sounded, it may affect the metre, precisely as the disappearance of terminal vowels in oldest Germanic, according to Scherer (*Gesch. d. d. Spr.²,* p. 625, note), and Möller (*Ahd. Alliterationspoesie,* p. 152), may account for omitted light syllables in that older verse.

There remains the matter of shifted accent, whether for the verse or for thé word. For the former one example will suffice: *Gest,* 246²: And the tróuthe téll thou mé. For the latter, "hovering accent" will account for most cases, though outright "wrenched accent" is not uncommon. For Germanic words, those in *-ing* are most affected: fastínge, *Gest,* 25³, 220⁴; lesýnge, 322²; spendýng, 383²; syngýnge: mornýnge, 445; tydýnge, 386⁴; lordýnge, 380⁴; endýng, *Cheviot,* 68⁴; wakín, *Brackley,* 3¹; compare further: dygh-

tánde, *Gest,* 388[4]; monánd, *C. Waters,* 33[4]. Other cases are Eng-
lánde, *Gest,* 361[4]; pený, 40[2] (but pény, 41[4]); burý, *Bewick,* 51[2];
trulýe, *Maurice,* 29[4]; ladíe, *Hamilton,* 9[4]; lemán, *Ravens,* 10[2]. For
hovering accent, not forced by rime : hàrpèr, *Estmere,* 40[1]; wìndòw,
*Hugh,* 2[3]; wèlcòme, *Bewick,* 28[2]; the whỳte lỳòn, *Otterburn,* 46[1];
ròse-wàtèr, *Lord T. and F. A.,* 24[1]. For words of foreign derivation
we may note : dynére, *Gest,* 16[4]; ryvére, 33[2]; arschére, 147[3]
chartér, 36[1]; mastér, *Spens,* 7[3]; velvét, *Cock,* 5[1]; forést, *Gest,* 297[4];
abbaý, 84[4]; servaúnt, 154[3]; sertaýn, *Otterburn,* 49[2]; portér, *Estmere,* 44[1]; castéll, *Car,* 3[1]; for a verb, enviéd, *Twa Sisters,* 4[2];
and often in proper names : Ellén, Robín, Watérs, Gregór, Margarét.


## GENERAL STYLE.

Simplicity is the key-note to the style of Germanic ballads. Iteration and parallelism are the constant factors; standing phrases,
recurring epithets — "comely king," "lovely London," "bluid-red
wine," "berry-brown steed," — are plentiful; metaphors are rare in
any artistic and intentional sort, — "byte" for "cut," *Otterburn,* 56[1],
is as old as our literature; similes are few and rarely sustained : see
*Guy,* 4; *Otterburn,* 51; *Cheviot,* 32; *Armstrong,* 5, and the like.
Antithesis is rare, except where iteration is concerned; while the
anacoluthon, sign of imperfect artistic control, is fairly abundant :
see *Gest,* 253[3,4], or *Spens,* 3[4] for a less important phrase. For other
qualities the reader is referred to the ballads themselves. While
they have no artifices to increase interest, and while they are not
uniform in movement, they know how to tell a story : see the end of
*Robin Hood and the Monk,* stanzas 61 ff. The poet Gray praises
this unconscious art : see his letter to Mason, *Works,* ed. Gosse, II,
316. "I have got the old Scotch ballad [a version of *Child Maurice*]
on which Douglas [Home's tragedy] was founded. It is divine . . .
Aristotle's best rules are observed in it in a manner which shews the
author never had heard of Aristotle. It begins in the fifth act of
the play. You may read it two-thirds through without guessing
what it is about; and yet, when you come to the end, it is impossible
not to understand the whole story."

# APPENDIX III.

———•◆•———

## MINSTRELS, AND THE AUTHORSHIP OF BALLADS.

There is no doubt in regard to the existence of professional singers among the early Germans; but the precise nature of their "profession" is not easy to define. For the facts we have simply to read the statements of Wídsíð, a typical Germanic singer: see ten Brink, *Gesch. d. engl. Lit.*, I, 29, and Möller, *Das altengl. Volksepos*, p. 31 f. Of such a singer it was said that he knew his business; so one must interpret "sé þe wel cúðe," *Béowulf*, 90 f., or even "sô hê uuola conda," used of Wodan in the Merseburg incantation, Müllenhoff-Scherer, *Denkmäler*[3], I, 16; II, 46: see also their reference to Otfrid's similar phrase, as well as the "þá þe wel cúðan" of Wídsíð, 106 f. Déor, too, was certainly a singer to the court. W. Grimm, *Heldensage*[2], p. 382 ff., has ample material to prove that trained singers were known among the Germans from earliest times; but he emphasizes the "free" singing of kings, heroes, and particularly the people at large (p. 385). Song, he concludes, was both "free" and professional. The "blind crowder" may be mentioned here: Demodokos, Homer, Ossian, and the blind singers of Servia, are all in point, not to speak of the Spanish *Romances de Ciegos;* and a well-known quotation from *Titurel:* "sô singent uns die blinden, daz Sîvrit hürnîn wære," tells of German custom: see W. Grimm, *Heldensage*[2], p. 384, and J. Grimm, *Kl. Schr.*, V, 169 f. In the eighth century there was a famous Frisian singer, blind Bernlef, "qui a vicinis suis valde diligebatur eo quod esset affabalis et antiquorum actus regumque certamina bene noverat psallendo [i. e., striking the harp as he sang] promere": *Vita Liudgeri*, Pertz, *Mon. Germ.*, *Scriptores*, II, 412. Scherer, leaning on Milton and J. Grimm, is fain to go farther and count blindness as a factor in the making of poets themselves: *Poetik*, p. 175 f. We must certainly follow Müllenhoff (*Sagen, Lieder, u. s. w.*, p. xviii f.) in sundering nobler minstrels from the mob of gleemen who ran in bands and sang farces or played tricks in attempts to evoke the coarser gaiety of nations; so, too, we must sunder the blind singer and recorder of the best ballads from the gleeman whose dog furnished an apt comparison to the poet of the Vision about Piers Plowman (ed. Skeat, B, v, 353).

Writers about the minstrel have fixed their attention too exclusively on one side of the picture. We have evidence of almost royal splendor, privileges of the knight and the noble; and we have evidence of utter squalor. It was on the latter spectacle that Ritson dwelt with such delight, hurling phrases parliamentary ("Beggars they are with one consent, And Rogues by act of Parliament") or scurrilous at these *protégés* of Percy; while the Bishop and Scott had a far nobler person in mind. There is no doubt about the degeneration of minstrels: W. Grimm, *Heldensage*[2], p. 285. Motherwell notes (*Minstrelsy*, Amer. ed., I, 50 f.) that they kept good character longer in Scotland than in England. It was the rabble of mountebanks, coarse singers and jugglers, who brought contempt upon an honest calling; and we have fallen upon evil tongues as well as evil times when we find gross immorality flung in the faces of the profession as their invariable failing: see Dunbar's *Poems*, ed. Schipper, I, 83, *The Devil's Inquest*, st. 14; and compare the "commone menstrallis," — town-pipers, says Schipper, — p. 86, st. 5. But a Bernlef, as well as a Homer, must be otherwise considered; and Scott and Motherwell would trace much of our ballad poetry to the composition of humbler but worthy singers: "minstrels . . . and fellow-poets, as opposed to mere reciters," says the latter, *Minstrelsy*, Amer. ed., I, 9; and Paul (*Grundriss*, I, 231) declares that in times of oral transmission, poet and minstrel are one and the same person.

We do not need the minstrels as a class, however, to account for the origin of ballads; they were probably agents in the preservation of popular song, and incidentally may have added to the stock. Who, for example, wrote *The Battle of Otterburn?* Not a community, — as the poem lies before us, at least. Certainly not a ballad-maker like the later Tom Deloney. Not, we may add, the professional though popular minstrel. Let us bear in mind ten Brink's account of the process; let us fancy much of this homogeneous social condition still existing along the border, even in 1388. After such a glorious fight, we may think, at merry-makings of the village, in the hall of the knight, and among the men-at-arms, not forgetting the dance and chorus, "*the carols of the maidens and minstrels of Scotland*," and even the laments for fallen heroes, stanzas in a traditional metre, with traditional tune, phrases, and style, would spring into being here, there, and everywhere. The strongest consideration in such a case is the acknowledged aptitude of the older peasant for improvisation and spontaneous narrative song. Special names, special deeds, special points of view; a traditional art; spontaneous singing. Out of all this, by a survival, we will hope, of the fittest, some singer of note would in time chant a ballad into unity; we do not exclude a certain amount of invention here, for the ballad as we have it, is not a mere improvisation for the dance, but a thing of some art, meant to entertain listeners, whose share in singing was limited to a refrain. So we may think of a traditional ballad founded on known events. When we are dealing with ballads from a tale, from some borrowed bit of history or sensation, we can still think of the *schnaderhüpfl*, the tendency to improvise stanzas on a given subject; but we must of course give more room to the art of a singer. In any case, what we do not admit, about any of these ballads, is the notion of a " self-taught bard " rapt into poetic mood by the deeds of battle or a tale of woe, and inventing *de longue haleine*, — our modern composition is out of the question, — some stirring ballad for the edification of a passive if enthusiastic audience. The question, then, is not of the minstrels of a people so much as of a people of minstrels. Hence, too, we are not necessarily to think of a single and definite original, the *urtext*, of a ballad. The versions are not necessarily variations of an original, which has been left to the chances of oral transmission; they may be, and often are, contemporary results of the original artistic process which tended to stamp form and unity upon material mainly due to communal and spontaneous singing.

From this point of view, it is of little importance to pursue the minstrel through all his haunts and adventures. Often he may have helped to hand down good ballads, and, in the sense defined above, even to make them. Often, on the other hand, he was a mere town-piper and musician. Now and then he was an artist, and, like Blind Harry, composed a sort of epic. If Sidney heard the *Cheviot* — or *Otterburn ?* — from a " blind crowder," Shakspere sends us for ballads to " the spinsters and the knitters in the sun." The ballad belonged to the people, and was exclusive property of minstrels as little in the making as in the singing. — For particulars about the minstrels of Europe, see Schultz, *Das höfische Leben zur Zeit d. Minnesinger*, I, 565; E. Freymond, *Jongleurs u. Menestrels*, Halle, 1883, mainly for Romance relations; Talvj, *Charakteristik*, p. 481 f; I. von Döllinger, *Beiträge zur Sektengeschichte des Mittelalters*, II, 621–4; Axel Olrik, *Middelalderens vandrende Spillemænd, Opuscula Philologica*, Copenh., 1887, p. 74 ff.

# NOTES.

*The figures refer to stanza and line.*

## A GEST OF ROBYN HODE.

See Child, *Ballads*, V, 39 ff.;[1] Ritson, *Robin Hood*, ed. 1832: 'Notes and Illustrations'; Hales, 'Introduction to the Robin Hood Ballads,' in the *Percy Folio*, I, 1 ff.; Fricke, *Die Robin-Hood Balladen* (Dissertation), Braunschweig, 1883; Brandl, in Paul's *Grundriss*, II, i, 657 f., 842 ff. The present text is mainly *a* (Child), the 'last piece in a volume in the Advocates' Library, Edinburgh.' The date is uncertain, but should be placed early in the sixteenth century. Another version, *b*, which supplies deficiencies in *a*, was printed by Wynkyn de Worde; a fragment, *c*, printed not earlier than 1489, and other editions or fragments, are used for occasional variation. The text of *a* would seem to be the oldest. 'The whole poem may have been put together as early as 1400, or before' (Child), and it is based on older ballads. Fyttes 1, 2 and 4 seem to have the closest relationship; 3 has a digression about Little John. It seems also as if different persons of independent ballads had been fused into one person of the *Gest*: *e.g.*, Syr Richarde at the Lee and the knight of the first fytte were perhaps different persons. Professor Child supposes at least four ballads as basis for this little epos : ' Robin Hood, the Knight, and the Monk ; Robin Hood, Little John, and the Sheriff; Robin Hood and the King ; Robin Hood's Death ' (p. 42), and no one of these 'is extant in a separate shape, and some portions of the story may have been of the compiler's own invention' (p. 49). The conclusion is 'a mere epilogue,' leaving three distinct stories : Robin's doings with the knight, with the sheriff, and with the king. The sheriff, of course, is no individual, but Robin's official enemy ; which accounts, says Fricke (p. 31), for the repeated deceptions practised on him. The other ballads which

---

[1] For convenience, all references to this work will be made by Parts.

belong to the same ancient date with the *Gest*, are *Robin Hood and the Monk*, and *Robin Hood and the Potter* (Child, V, 108 ff.). — For the topography, one must not demand any accuracy from the *Gest*. 'There was evidently at one time a Barnsdale cycle and a Sherwood cycle of Robin Hood ballads. The Sheriff of Nottingham would belong to the Sherwood cycle.' For special localities, see the notes. — To identify Robin Hood with Woden (Kuhn, in Haupt's *Zts.*, V, 472 ff.), or with a historical personage in England, is sheer conjecture, and utterly lacks foundation. Robin Hood is an idealized outlaw.— Ritson collected many references to Robin Hood, and others have added to the list. The oldest of which we know is in *Piers Plowman*, version B (1377), v, 401 f. Sloth knows 'rymes of Robyn Hood and Randolf, erle of Chester.' Ritson also collected a number of proverbs (*R. H.*, p. xcix ff.), one of which we still use daily: 'to go round Robin Hood's barn.'

2 1.    Similar favorites of ballads were Hereward, about whom we have no ballads preserved, and Gamelyn, whose story is told in the interpolated tale of the cook in the *Canterbury Tales;* see Skeat, *Gamelyn*, Oxford, 1884.

3 1.    *Bernesdale.* — Barnsdale, 'a woodland region in the West Riding of Yorkshire.' For discussion of the general topography see Child, *Ballads*, V, 50 f.

3 3.    *Litell Johnn.* — He is associated with Robin from earliest times. Wyntoun, *Chronicle of Scotland*, 1420:

> 'Lytill Ihon and Robyne Hude,
>   Waythmen ware commendyd gude.'

4 1.    *Scarlok.* — In *b*, and later in *a*, Scathelok.

4 4.    An inch of his body was worth an ordinary man.

7 1.    The line is lacking in all versions.

10.    For courtesy, says Professor Child, Robin is 'a popular Gawain,' that is, the Gawain of the old romances, not of Tennyson.

15 3.    Nottingham as a locality would naturally belong to the 'Sherwood cycle,' and Sherwood has nothing to do with the *Gest* (Child, V, 51, note); but these irregularities are of no moment.

16 3.    *fer dayes* = far on in the day, late. It was the custom of Arthur not to eat 'until he had heard of some adventure or strange news'; and Robin here imitates the blameless king. See note to *The Boy and the Mantle*, Child, II, 257.

18 1.    'The Sayles appears to be some place in the neighborhood of Barnsdale. . . .'— Ritson. 'A very small tenancy of the manor of Pontefract.'— Child.

18 2. *Watlinge Strete.* — 'The name generally used by the vulgar for Erming-street. The course of the real Watling Street was from Dover to Chester.'— Ritson. Here the Great North Road is meant.

20. See 220.

22 4. *That othere.* — That = def. article. Cf. 'the tother.'

25 1. *Grenë wode.*—Whether so pronounced, or read with omitted light syllable, is really of little moment for the metre.

29 3. It is common in these ballads (so *Gest*, 134 3, 268 4; *Monk*, 38 4, 62 4) to omit the personal pronoun as subject of a sentence or clause when it may be readily conjectured by reference to the preceding clause. Here it is probably Róbin (cf. 263) who kneels, though it may be the knight.

31 2. Note the alliterating formula, and cf. the specimens given above, p. 305 f.

32 1. There was rigid etiquette in those times in regard to this custom; see Furnivall, *Babees Book*, E. E. T. S., p. 322, for the duties of the *euwere* (Ewerer) before meat.

39 2. Like our 'So help you God.'

45 3. 'I think you must have been forced to accept knighthood.' Child refers to Stubbs, *Constitutional Hist.*, II, 281 f.

46 1. 'A bad manager.'

49 2. Wanting in *f* and *g*; while 50 2, 3, are transposed in all versions. Child, [1] V, 53, v. 194, and Allingham in his *Ballad Book*, read 'kende' for 'knowe,' restoring the rime, and leaving 50 2, 3, transposed.

54 4. *Mary*, genitive fem. Cf. modern 'lady-day,' and Chaucer's 'his lady grace,' *Prol., C. T.*, 88. —'St. Mary's Abbey was at York, and must have been a good twenty miles from Barnsdale.' — Child.

56 2. 'What shall become of thee?'

62–66. See Professor Child's comments, V, 51 f.

68 4. In *b, f, g,* 'eighteen score,' which is obviously wrong. — *Eight and twenty score* is 'twenty score and over,'— a generous count.

70 3. *lyveray* here = suit of clothes; but see note to 161 3.

73 1. *met* = measured.

81 3. Compare the knight's yeoman in the *Canterbury Tales, Prologue,* 101 ff.

83 4–118 3. Wanting in *a*, supplied from *b*.

87 1, 98 1. Wanting in all versions.

87 4. *Disherited* = dispossessed.

88 1. 'The prior, in an abbey, was the officer immediately under the abbot; in priories and conventual cathedrals he was the superior.' — Ritson.

**91** 2. Ritson mentions three St. Richards.

**92** 3. In other words, if the knight failed to pay this relatively trifling sum upon ' his day,' all his estates fell to the abbey,— a most iniquitous arrangement, for which the substitution of regular interest on borrowed money, of mortgage and the like, might well be reckoned an advance in civilization.

**93** 3, 4. That is, the Chief Justice was retained, or bribed (see 107), by the abbot. 'Abbot' is subject of 'did holde.'

**96** 3. In grievous or bad time; 'in an evil hour.' 'Sorrow' was early confused with 'sorry.'

**100** 3. *Coresed?* — The 'harnessed' or 'caparisoned' of the glossaries is a guess.

**104** 3. *shrewed* = 'cursed.'

**116** 1, 2. See description of the knight in *Canterbury Tales, Prologue*, v. 43 ff., where these foreign parts are mentioned in detail.

**117.** The justice foresees legal troubles if sheer confiscation be attempted, and advises a payment of money to the knight in return for a quittance or release by the latter. As it is, the knight pays back the money without any interest (cf. 121 3, 4); while to Robin Hood (cf. 270) he offers additional money, besides gifts.

**126** 4. 'Wierysdale is the name of a forest in Lancashire.' — Ritson. 'It is very likely, therefore, that the knight's castle, in the original ballad, was in Lancashire. However this may be, it is put in the *Gest*, 309 f., on the way between Nottingham and Robin Hood's retreat, which must be assumed to be Barnsdale.' Child, V, 50. We have here the confusion of two ballad-cycles, mentioned above.

**128** 3. 'Had it not been for his kindness.'

**132.** Chaucer's Yeoman bears 'a shef of pococke arwes'; there were usually twenty-four arrows in a 'sheaf.'

**133** 3–136 3. Wanting in *a*, supplied from *b*.

**135** 1. On the Went, the northern boundary of Barnsdale. The original reads: 'But as he went at a bridge.' Professor Child suggests the reading adopted in the text. Wentbridge is named in *Robin Hood and the Potter*, Child, V, 109.

**136** f. The value of the prizes indicates an extraordinary occasion.

**138** 3. 'Because he was a stranger.'

**145** ff. Ritson in his 'Notes and Illustrations,' *Robin Hood*, 1832, xliii, remarks that archery was cultivated assiduously until 'about the year 1540, when owing to the introduction of artillery and matchlock guns, it became neglected.' See his references.

148 4.  *Wonyng* (A.-S. *wunung*) and *wane* (A.-S. *gewuna*) mean the same thing, a dwelling.

149 2.  *Dame* = mother.

152 4.  A good and strong horse.

160 4.  *go* = walk.

161 3.  *Lyveray* was 'the quantity of provisions delivered at one time by the butler.' — Ritson.

163 3, 4.  For a heroic cook of even grander proportions, see Rumolt in the *Nibelungen*.

170 1.  'Many men talk of Robin Hood that never shot *in his bow*,' was a common proverb, quoted by Ritson, *R. H.*, p. xcix f.

170 3.  See Wright's note, *King Lear*, Clarendon Press Ed., ii, 2, 14, on 'three-suited.'  He thinks it probable 'that three suits of clothes a year were part of a servant's allowance.'

176 4.  'A forest highe and hore,' *Morte Arthur*, 314, quoted by Stratmann, *Dictionary*.  *Hoar* is a very common epithet for a wood: see Kölbing's note to *Beves of Hamtoun*, 95, E. E. T. S., p. 225.

177 2.  'Christ save and protect thee!'

182 3.  'Knew what courtesy demanded.'

184 2.  *can = gan =* 'did.'

185 2.  Allingham changes to 'full shene'; but of course Robin Hood is meant (see 188 4) with his coat of green.  Little John asks the sheriff to come see a marvellous sight.

186 1, 2.  Sixty tines, forks, of the antlers would be 'marvellous' indeed.

189 3.  *Wo the worthe* = 'Woe be to thee!'  *Worthe* = A.-S. *weorþe*, subj. pres. of *weorþan*, to become.

198 1.  'This is a harder discipline, a more severe order,' — as of friars or anchorites.

202 1, 2.  A common form of oath : see *Hamlet*, i, 5.  In 358 the princes of the Quadi drew their swords, 'which they worship as deities,' and swore to keep faith.  Ammianus Marcell., xvii, 12.

202 3.  'Thou wilt never lie in wait to harm me.'

204 4.  *Hepe* = hip.  As the hip has 'woolly seeds,' Allingham changed to 'haw.'

208 4–314 1.  Wanting in *a*, supplied from *b*.

210 3, 4.  To save the rime, these verses are inverted from the order of all the versions.

213 3.  Black monks = Benedictines.

215 2.  *Frese?* a crux.

221 3.  *Strong thefe* = a violent robber, a highwayman.

223 1. A bolt 'was an arrow . . . used chiefly for shooting at birds; having a round or blunt head.' — Ritson.

223 4. So that he fell to the ground. *Can* = did.

225 4. The common phrase 'maugre thy teeth' (a modern poem has : 'In spite of all her teeth ') is here confused with more vulgar exclamations.

229 4. Pricking (= spurring) seems here to mean 'hurrying.'

230 2. *Raye.* 'Cloth not coloured or dyed . . .' — Ritson. 'Striped cloth.' — Halliwell, who is probably right.

240 4. See 149 2.

242 3. 'Owe thee more thanks,' — am so much the more grateful.

246 4. 'No penny let me see,' *g.*

248 4. *Cast* = a throw, as in dice ; *f* and *g* have *cost.*

249 4. *me* = ethical dative.

253 2. The monk was going to institute legal proceedings against the knight, on whatever grounds. *Mote* = meeting, is constantly associated with law, and in view of the monk's cause we may well quote *Piers Plowman* (ed. Skeat, B, iv, 152) :

'For I seige [=saw] Mede in the moot-halle on men of lawe wynke.'

The whole *passus* is in point, and so is iii.

256 1. 'And what is on the other courser?' 'And what is in the other coffer?' are the readings of *f* and *g*. Professor Kittredge suggests *forcer* = coffer.

268 1. Professor Kittredge would read : *But take not a-grefe,* a-grief, in grief (*i.e.* as a grievance).

274 4. 'This trusty tree,' *f, g.*

282 4. *dyde crye* = 'caused to cry'; cf. 'I do you to wit.'

297 1. See note to *Monk*, 19 2.

307 4. 'Depart,' *f, g.*

310 2. *at the Lee* = the knight's surname, as if Atlee. Cf. names like 'Atwood,' or the German 'im Thurm.'

316 1. The 'bord' or table was commonly laid on trestles, which were folded up when the board was removed : the Usher

Awoydes [removes] þo borde into þo flore,
Tase away þo trestes þat ben so store [big, strong].

*Babees Book*, ed. Furnivall, p. 326.

318 2. This was probably the *posse comitatus*, or a sort of hue and cry.

322 2. A recurring formula, useful in patching out the stanza : cf. 353 2.

334 2.   See note 31 2.  *Free* here means 'noble, full of grace and favor.'

346 4.   'For thy boote,' reads *g*, to make better rime.

349 4   to the end, wanting in *a*, supplied from *b*.

357 1.   *Passe* = limits, bounds, extent ; *f*, *g*, read ' compass.'

363 3.   ' May ride or walk.'

364 2.   A jocose expression of old standing.

366 4.   *welt* = pret. (otherwise *walde*, *welde*, *wolde* in Middle-English : A.-S. *wéold*) of *welden* = to have power over, to govern or control.

367 4.   'You must follow my advice.'

385 1.   *targe* ? *f*, *g*, have *seale*.

388 4.   *dyghtande* = the original form of the present participle which afterwards, as in modern English, became confused with the verbal noun in *-ing*.  In A.-S., *-ende* was the normal ending, with *-ande* as a Northern form ; in M.-E. *-ende* becomes *-inde*, *-inge*, *ing*, while Scottish and Northern *-and* held its place with obstinacy.  See Koch, *Laut· u. Flexionslehre d. Engl. Spr.*,[2] p. 342 f.

403 2.   Notwithstanding his friend's experience.  *Fare* = ' doings.' See Chaucer, *Knight's Tale*, 951.

417 1.   ' Unless your service please me.'

418 1–422 1.   See Ritson, p. xlv f., who quotes Spenser, *Faerie Queene*, vi, 2, 5 :

> 'All in a woodman's jacket he was clad
>      Of Lincoln greene . . .'

and Drayton, *Polyolbion*, xxv, with note.  ' Lincoln anciently dyed the best green in England.'  Kendal green was also famous.  ' This colour was adopted by the foresters to prevent their being too readily discovered by the deer,'—a questionable though exquisite reason.

423 1.   As if they were outlaws.

424 3.   It is suggested to the editor that *plucke-buffet* is an adverbial phrase modifying *shote*, and consists of a verb *plucke* = ' take, pluck,' and its object ' buffet.'  However this may be, the sport is evidently much the same as that described above (st. 400), and *plucke-buffet* may be simply the name of the sport. — The exchanging of buffets or hard blows is a practice common enough in the romances ; but this is an affair of archery.

428 3.   ' If R. H. came to the town,' *etc*.  *Come* = subjunctive of condition ; *lefte* = ' would leave.'

434 2.   This liberal expenditure was the proper thing for knights and men of rank ; and the minstrel's point of view in the matter is well known from the days of *Widsíð* down.

442 3. Cf. *Piers Plowman*, ed. Skeat, B, xviii, 1:

> 'Wolleward and wete-shoed went I forth after';

to which Skeat remarks (*Notes*, E. E. T. S., No. 67, p. 395), quoting Palsgrave's 'without any lynnen nexte ones body. *Sans chemyse*,' that it clearly means 'with wool next to one's body.' It is a kind of penance, and is prescribed in Hampole's *Pricke of Conscience*, v. 3512 f.

451 3. See Ritson, p. lii. — 'Kirkleys, Kirklees, or Kirkleghes, formerly Kuthale, in the deaconry of Pontefract, and archdeaconry of the west riding of Yorkshire, was a Cistercian, or, as some say, a Benedictine nunnery, founded . . . in the reign of King Henry II.'

---

## ROBIN HOOD AND GUY OF GISBORNE.

Printed from *Percy Folio*, ed. Hales-Furnivall, II, 227 ff.; Child, *Ballads*, V, 89 ff.— A few verses are lost between 2 and 3.— For the probable tune of the ballad, see Chappell, *Pop. Mus. Old. Time*, II, 397.— Gisborne 'is a market town in the West Riding of the County of York, on the borders of Lancashire.' H.-F.— This ballad is rich in alliterative and proverbial phrases.

2. *Woodweele:* MS. *woodweete*. Glossary H.-F.: 'wodewale, bryd *idem quod* reynefowle or wodehake (or nothac. *Picus*) *et lucar.*' (*Promptorium*.) That is, = '*witwall*, the great spotted woodpecker.' But Chappell, II, 396, referring to *Rom. Rose*, (attributed to Chaucer), vv. 658, 914 [where Morris, Aldine ed., glosses 'witwall' or woodpecker], insists that this woodweele is a singing bird, say the woodlark. Possibly woodweete is right, after all; though cf. *Thomas of Erceldoune*, ed. Brandl, v. 31:

> I herde the jaye and the throstell,
>     The mawys menyde of hir songe,
> The wodewale beryde as a belle,
>     That alle the wode abowte me ronge.

2 2. *A lyne* = On lime, linden. 'I would read "so greene,"' says Percy.

3 1. *They* are the two wight yeomen who, Robin dreamed, beat and bound him. Sir Guy of Gisborne is one, — the name 'yeoman' need make no trouble ; and Professor Child points out (V, 89) that the other must be the sheriff of Nottingham. 'The dream simply foreshadows danger from two quarters.'

20 1. *downe* seems to rime with *John;* and Percy is probably right that 'quoth the sheriffe' was added by some 'explainer.'

27 4. 'Many men meet at unset steven,' at an unappointed time. See Chaucer, *C. T., Knight's Tale*, v. 666.

28 3. *In twinn* = apart. '330 yards must have been a long range. . . . *Prickes* seem to have been the long-range targets, *butts* the near.'— Furnivall. See also Ritson, *R. H.*, 1832, p. xli, and his references.

31 2. The *garlande* has been defined as 'the ring within which the prick was set'; and the *prick* seems to have been now a wand, now a white mark, 'bull's eye, or peg in the middle of the target,' with *prickewande* as a pole or stick. A 'rover' was any accidental mark, — tree or the like. The precise meaning of these terms, however, is open to dispute: see Furnivall, *Babees Book*, E. E. T. Soc., p. ci; also, *Percy Folio*, II, 232.

40 3. *Awkwarde* = unusual, unexpected, dangerous. This is the regular phrase for a decisive blow in ballad warfare. See *auk*, Stratmann's *Dict.*, p. 40: 'sinister, perversus.'— It may also mean a backward, backhanded stroke.

44. Professor Child points out that we are not told how Robin knew of the trouble among his men.

---

## ROBIN HOOD AND THE MONK.

Printed by various editors from the manuscript 'of about 1450' in the Cambridge University Library. Verses are lost at 30 2. From the beautiful opening of this old ballad to its close, it deserves the highest praise.

6. For Robin's great piety, see Professor Child's comments and illustrations, *Ballads*, V, 96.

7 2. Since I took the sacrament, — attended mass.

11 4. Gives him odds of three to one.

17 2. A formula, like *Gest*, 322 2: see note.

19 1. See *Gest*, 91 3.

19 2. 'Woe is me' and 'Woe am I' occur indifferently in older English.

22 3–4. It is your fault if he escapes.

23 1. *traytur:* genitive. See 24 3, *moder;* 38 3, *Moch;* and note to *Gest*, 54 4.

29 3. *But if* = unless.

**31.** The lost verses doubtless told how word of Robin's captivity came to his band in the forest. They are all overwhelmed by the news, except Little John.

**32** 1. *rule*, for which some editors read *dule*, might be a form of 'revel' : see *Century Dictionary*, s. v. *rule*.[2] But it is suggested to the editor that *rule* is here our common word, in the sense of 'conduct,'—the way one 'regulates' one's behavior. That is, John says: 'Let this behavior cease!'

**35** 3. John evidently knows that the monk is going to London with the news of Robin's capture.

**38** 3. 'And looked in at the house of Much's uncle, which lay near the highway.' Relative omitted.

**39** 2. *stage ?* Child, early edition (with ?), — 'story of a house.'

**41** 4. Notice the plural form *frende*.

**57** 4. *after the way* = upon the way.

**61 ff.** This account may be compared with that in 'Adam Bell,' 56 ff., Child, *Ballads*, V, 25.

**73** 4. Had the city bell rung, sounded an alarm.

**77** 4. A fragment (*b*), of same date with text, reads here : *Quit me*, which gives a better meaning.

**80** 4. 'I care to be no other.' No noder = none other.

**90** 3. Prayers were common at the end of a story ; cf. Chaucer, *Nonne Prestes Tale*, end, *Otterburn*, *Cheviot*, and other ballads, as well as the romances.

---

## ROBIN HOOD'S DEATH.

*Percy Folio*, ed. H.-F., I, 50 ff.; Child, *Ballads*, V, 102. The story agrees with the conclusion of the *Gest*, and opens much as *R. H. and Monk* opens. 'The yeoman in stanza 3,' says Professor Child, 'should be Red Roger; but a suspicion has more than once come over me that the beginning of this ballad has been affected by some version of *Guy of Gisborne*.'

**1** 3. *Churchlees.* See note, *Gest*, 451 3. H.-F. quote Drayton, *Polyolbion*, of the Calder :

> It chanced she in her course on Kirkley cast her eye,
> Where merry Robin Hood, that honest thief, doth lie.

For traditions, epitaphs, etc., see Child, *Ballads*, V, 103 f., 107, and H.-F., *Fol.*, I, 51 ff.

6 1.   *you'st* = you shall, you must.

7 2.   Shot by turns.

7 4.   *laid* = elliptical construction : 'and a plank was laid over it.'

9.   Half a page of the MS. is missing,— say nine stanzas,— which must have told why the old woman was cursing Robin, and must have mentioned other people who were blessing him or weeping for him.

14 2.   'In that same time.'— Furnivall.

18.   John calls from outside.   Another half-page is missing here. Professor Child supposes an altercation to take place between Robin and Red Roger, who is below; so that when Robin slips out of the window, Roger wounds him.   John is probably on the other side of the house.

23 1.   *Mood* hardly means 'help' or 'courage,' as Furnivall suggests.   It must have something to do with the 'houzle.'   Professor Child conjectured 'Give me my God!' (*Ballads*, V, 103, note), but without confidence.   He is now inclined, however, to think this the right reading, relying on an equivalent phrase in the *Romaunt of the Rose* (ed. Morris, v. 6436), '*yeve me my savyour*,' meaning (cf. v. 6440) the 'housele.'

27 4.   Again a half-page is missing.

---

## THE BATTLE OF OTTERBURN.

This fine ballad, based upon an incident of a Scottish invasion of England in 1388, tempts to notes and comment beyond our limits of space, and we must refer the reader to Professor Child's admirable summary, *Ballads*, VI, 289 ff., while we give the barest outline. There are several versions ; this (A) is incomparably the best, and is based upon two MSS. in the British Museum, the better text dating from about 1550.   An account of the battle, derived from men who fought in it, is given by Froissart (ed. Kervyn de Letten-hove, XIII, 214 ff.); see the translation of Lord Berners, Pynson, 1525, vol. II, ch. 42 ff., fo. clvii ff.   See also Harding's *Chronicle*, ch. 190, ed. 1812, p. 342, and Wyntoun's *Cronykil*, ed. Laing, III, 32 ff.   The date of the battle was August (probably the 19th : Child, VI, 292, and note), 1388.   Otterburn is thirty miles northwest from Newcastle, in the parish of Elsdon.   The field of the fight 'is still called Battle Riggs': see Percy's *Reliques*, ed. Wheatley, I, 42.

1 1.   *Lamasse* = loaf-mass, August 1.

1 3.   This refers to the Scottish detachment which ravaged about Newcastle, and at last fought the battle of Otterburn.   They were

commanded by James, Earl of Douglas, and others, and numbered two or three thousand.

2 1. The Earl of Fife, son of the Scottish king, with the main army, was harrying in the northwest of England, about Carlisle. He then passed over Solway Frith.

3. 'The several stations here mentioned are well-known places in Northumberland.'— Percy. — Hoppertope = Ottercap.

3 4. *Styrande* (= stirring), present participle; cf. *dyghtande, Gest*, 388 4. MS., 'Many a styrande,' which moved Motherwell unnecessarily to make *stage* = 'stallion.'

4 3. Shows the English origin (or adaptation : discussed by Child, VI, 293) of this version. See 35.

5 1. Phrases of this kind (*bent* = field) may be compared with the *wéox under wolcnum* of older epic (*Béowulf*, v. 8 = 'grew under welkin,' on earth).

6 1. Bamborowe. See note, *Cheviot*, 3 4.

7 2. See *Knight's Tale*, v. 117 ff.

8 1. *Syr Henry Perssye*. This is the famous Hotspur, killed at Shrewsbury fight, fifteen years after Otterburn. He is said 'to have been appointed Governor of Berwick and Warden of the Marches in 1385.'

8 2. A patch-verse: see 18 2, 40 2, and *Gest*, 322 2, with other cases noted above.

9 2. *On hyght* = aloud.

10 4. In a satirical sense.

12 4. *The tone* = the one.

13 4. 'The "hygh way" is the old Watling-street road.'— Percy.

15 1. *they* = either an interpolation, or 'the,' ethical dative.

24 4. A *b* reads 'gare me out to dyne.' Child (1860), VII, 323, explains : 'give one his fill of fighting.' *Out* = aught.

25 2. *lesse* = *leas* = lie, falsehood; cf. 'leasing' in the Bible.

26. See Child, VI, 293 f. Mentaye = Menteith.

27 1. Bowghan = Buchan.

29 4. 'I will keep my promise': *that* = what.

32–33. See *The Battle of Maldon*, v. 2 ff.; and Freeman, *Norman Conquest*, III, 472 : at the battle of Senlac, 'Omnes descendunt et equos post terga relinquunt,'— said of the Saxons.

37. The Earl of Northumberland, remaining at Alnwick, had sent his sons to Newcastle to look after Douglas and his detachment.

42 4. *with* = by.

44 2. Cross himself in the name of the Trinity.

45. 'The crowned harte, and Above stode starres thre,' says Percy, would be an exact description of the Douglas arms 'at this day.'

46. The Percy arms.

47 1. St. Andrew, of course, for Scotland.

47 3. 'Fixed their eyes on, took aim at.'—Child, *Ballads* (1860), VII, 326.

48. On 'our ladies knyght,' see Child, VI, 294, 520.

50. This is the English account; but Froissart and the Scots say Douglas was killed in the confusion of the night attack.

50 3. *whyll that the* = 'until they.'

50 3, 4. See note, *Cheviot*, 31 3, 4.

63 3. Fitz-Hugh.

67 3. See *As You Like It*, ii, 4 : '. . . said with weeping tears.'

69 4. Was exchanged for Percy.

---

## THE HUNTING OF THE CHEVIOT.

There are two versions of this ballad. The younger and more corrupted version (*Chevy Chace*) is the one which Addison criticised, with so much praise, in the *Spectator* (70, 74); it was common in broadsides, and enormously popular throughout England. The older and better version, which we print here, is from a MS. in the Bodleian Library : see Skeat, *Specimens of English Literature from the 'Ploughman's Crede' to the 'Shepheardes Calender,'* 1881, 67 ff., and Child, *Ballads*, VI, 303 ff. Both versions were printed by Percy in the *Reliques.* The name of Richard Sheale, who sang and wrote ballads early in Queen Elizabeth's reign, is written at the end of the MS. of the older version, but, of course, merely as the signature of the transcriber.—As regards the ballad itself, it has manifold points of contact with *Otterburn*, and is probably a later and confused account of the same fight, a hunt in Scotland being substituted for a raid in England. See, for this and other details, Child, VI, 304, and H.-F., *Percy Folio*, II, 4 ff. Sidney's famous praise of 'the olde song of Percy and Duglas' (see *Defense of Poesy*, ed. Cook, p. 29) is generally referred to this ballad, though, as Professor Child remarks, it would fit *Otterburn* as well in all respects save that of poetic merit, where *Cheviot* has some advantage.

1 2. *And avowe* may = 'an avowe' = a vow; or else, as is suggested, we may supply 'came' before 'out.' Cf. 'Stand fast, Titinius :

we must out and talk.'—Shakspere, *Jul. Caes.*, v, 1, 22. *Up* is similarly used without a verb, as, 'When this was don this Pandare up anoon. . . . and forth gan for to wende.'—Chaucer, *Troilus*, ii, 214.

3 3. *off blood and bone* is superfluous.

3 4. *Shyars thre*, 'meaning, probably, three districts in Northumberland, which still go by the name of *shires*, and are all in the neighborhood of *Cheviot*. These are *Islandshire . . . Noreham-shire . . .* and *Bamboroughshire*, the ward or hundred belonging to Bamborough-castle and town.'—Percy.

4 3, 4. See 51 3, 4.

7 3. *be that* = when.

8, 9, are connected by rime into one stanza; 'to this standard the whole poem may have been intended to conform,' says Skeat, *Spec.*, p. 394. See also 3, 4; 5, 6; 15–16; 18–19; 25–26; 27–28; 29–30; 31–32; 33–34; 36–37; 38–39; 40, 41; 42, 43; 44, 45; 48, 49; 50, 51; 52, 53; 54, 55, 56; 63–64. See also other connections by rime, as 13, 14; 65, 66.

8 2. They came up from all sides. *The* = they; *shear*, for *sere* = 'several.'

10 2. Observed near at hand.

12 4. *Tividale* = Teviotdale. So Chevy = Cheviot.

13 2. *boÿs* = bowys = bows.

13 3. *On* = of. See 45 4 and 46 2.

15 3. *Chays* = hunting-ground. 'Common in local names.'

19 4. *do* = 'let us do.' Let our men all stand aside while we fight.

21 4. *On* = one.

22 2. See Percy's note.

24 2. *fynde* may be a corruption of *fyne*, that is, 'end, finish,' with *d* inserted by copyist for the sake of the rime.

26 4. *wouche*, 'also spelt *wough* . . . A.-S. *woh*,' rimes correctly with *yenoughe*.

30 2. Many bold ones (*sterne*) they struck down.

31 3, 4. See *Otterburn*, 50 3, 4. Myllan = Milan steel; see 'Cologne' in *Otterburn*. *Tylle* (until) and *whyll* (while) are occasionally confused in meaning: see *Sir A. Barton*, 66 4.

36 2. *wane* = multitude, says Skeat, hence 'a single arrow out of a vast quantity'; but this goes ill with 'folke.' *Wane* might = *wone* (see 47 1) = one: 'a mighty one'; but this is unsatisfactory.

38. Addison compared Vergil, *Æn.*, x, 821 ff.

> At vero ut voltum vidit morientis et ora,
> Ora modis Anchisiades pallentia miris,
> Ingemuit miserans graviter, dextramque tetendit. . . .

39.   When Lessing heard of Winckelmann's death, he wrote to Nicolai : 'That is the second man of letters, within a short time, to whom I would gladly have given a few years of my own life.'

40 2.   Montgomery.

40 4.   Skeat reads 'a spear a [= of] trusti tre.'

44 2.   'Saw [that] slain was,' *etc.*

45 2.   *Stele.*   He pulled the arrow to its [steel] head.

49 1.   'They took' . . . Words are missing in the MS., and Skeat supplies 'the fight,' = they fought.   Child, early edition, suggested 'rest.'   Could it be 'they took them off,' took themselves off, retreated?   See 50.

53.   Loumle = Lumley ;  Raff = Ralph.

54 3, 4.   See parallels, Child VI, 306 ;  VIII, 502.

55 3.   Lwdale, in later version = Lambwell.

56 1.   Sir Charles of Murray.

57.   Compare *Otterburn*, 67.

59 2.   James I.

61 1.   Lovely London.   See Child, VI, 306.

62.   Addison pointed out the difference, not only in numbers slain, but in the replies of James and Henry, due to the patriotism of an English singer.

63 4.   There was a battle of Homildon, resulting in victory for the English, in 1402 ; though the Percy of *Otterburn* and *Cheviot* fought in it.

64 3.   Glendale is the district or ward in which Homildon is situated. — Percy.

65 2.   Skeat says this is a proverb : 'That tear, or pull, brought about this kick.'   But this is extremely doubtful : see Child, VI, 307, who suggests [Alas] 'that e'er began this spurn; or possibly *that tear* is for that there, meaning simply there.'— The MS. has *Expliceth* [= *explicit*], *quoth Rychard Sheale*.

---

## KINMONT WILLIE.

A traditional ballad of the border, based upon an occurrence in 1596, first printed by Scott in his *Minstrelsy*, and upon his own testimony rescued by more or less emendation from a 'mangled' state.   It is impossible to say just how much is tradition, and how much is due to Scott. For the historical and personal references, see Child, *Ballads*, VI, 469 ff. Kinmont Willie was William Armstrong, or 'Will of Kinmonth.' Lord Scroop was 'Warden of the West-Marches of England'; Salkeld was his deputy. The rescuer was Sir Walter Scott, of Branxholm, laird of Buccleugh. — In the actual affair, no lives were lost.

1 4. *Hairibee* is 'the place of execution at Carlisle.'

3 4. *rack* = 'A very shallow ford, of considerable breadth.' — Jamieson.

18, 19. Four squads of ten men each. 'Broken men' are outlaws.

31 4. A favorite Liddesdale tune. See Chambers, *Book of Days*, I, 200.

---

## JOHNIE COCK.

This admirable traditional ballad, as printed here, is made up of stanzas from the following versions (Child, V, 1 ff.): D: 1, 2; A: 2, 3; D: 5, 7; A: 7, 8, 9, 10, 11; D: 12; F: 12; A: 14, 15, 16, 17, 18, 19, 20, 21. The localities, now in Northumberland, now in Dumfriesshire, are confused; and indeed import little or nothing.

5 2. See above, note to *Gest*, 418, 422.

8 4. *bot* = 'but' = also, besides; *bot and* = 'as well as.'

15 3. It is easy to exaggerate the importance of these things; but the place of affection assigned here and there in the ballads to a *sister's son* certainly deserves attention : see *Cheviot*, 55 ; *Sir A. Barton*, 55, a capital instance; *King Arthur and King Cornwall*, I, Child, II, 283 ; and other places which the editor has failed to note. Tacitus, *Germania*, c. 20, says of the Germans that a sister's sons stand with the uncle as high as with the father; 'some even think this tie of blood to be holier and closer, and they have regard to it in the choice of hostages.' The commentators refer us to an 'Indo-Germanic law'; but Lippert's anthropological explanation seems more reasonable,— that by the old *Mutterrecht*, the principle of inheritance through the mother, a man 'would part more readily from his wife's child than from his sister's child; for in his eyes there was more blood-relationship with the latter.'— See the editor's *Germanic Origins*, p. 132.

17. Wolves were found in the north of England long after the south was clear of them.

20 1. The original has 'boy'—manifestly 'a corruption of "bird."' (Child.)

## JOHNIE ARMSTRONG.

Often printed, and in another version known as 'John Armstrong's Last Good Night.' The Armstrongs were a powerful border family, on the Scottish side, to be sure, but almost as troublesome to their own king as to the English. In 1530, James V. of Scotland undertook, with help of his nobles and an army, to put down the lawlessness and robbery of the border, in which our hero was chief offender; not, it would seem, without artifice, he was persuaded to appear with a few followers before the king, and was summarily hanged.— See Child, VI, 362 ff.

1 1. Westmoreland is, of course, impossible; but this is an English ballad. The Armstrongs were originally settled in Liddesdale.

1 3-4. His revenues were somewhat like those of Robin Hood.

11 3. The phrase is given in a historical account of this affair : see Child, VI, 365. It was probably a favorite : see *Mary Hamilton*.

16. See *Sir A. Barton*, 65. This stanza is taken from Child, B, 18.

---

## SIR ANDREW BARTON.

*Percy Folio*, ed. Hales and Furnivall, III, 399 ff.; Child, *Ballads*, VI, 334 ff. Percy printed this ballad in the *Reliques*, with additions from another version in broadside in the Pepys collection (Child's B, p. 343 ff.), and emendations of his own.— See H.-F., *Folio*, and Child's *Ballads* as above, for fuller historical references. Andrew Barton, one of three brothers, all 'men of note in the naval history of Scotland,' had been capturing and robbing Portuguese trading-ships, and now (1511) began to rob English vessels. Our ballad tells the rest, with some inaccuracies : see Child, p. 337.

3 2. Supplied by Percy. See Furnivall's note, *Fol.*, III, 404. Another version (Child, VIII, 503) has : 'The best salers in Christiantie.'

7 1. See *Armstrong*, 11.

8 1. Lord Charles Howard, a famous naval commander in his day, 'was not born till twenty-five years after the fight' described in our ballad. Barton was captured by Lord Thomas and Sir Edward Howard.

**12** 4. *thoust* = thou shalt.

**20** 2. In this ludicrous line, 'poor' has been suggested for 'pure,'— that is, 'a weary heart.' Another version (Child, VIII, 504, 21) has 'woeful hart and a sorrowefull minde.'

**23** 3. In the MS. *archborde.*—H.-F., *Folio*, III, 407, and in the Glossary, make *archborde* = 'ship, or side of a ship.' See, however, 36 1, 70 2; and in 29 2 *charke-bord* (MS.) may also be read *hachbord*, as *hall* may be *hull* (Child, VI, 334, note), so as to mean : 'if his beams hit your deck,'— that is, the timber of or about the hatches,—'or your hull.' Barton's body (70 2) is cast over the 'hatch-bord' into the sea ; and Professor Kittredge quotes *Batayle of Egyngecourte*, 109 f., Hazlitt, *Early Pop. Poetry*, III, 97 :

> With theyr takyls they launched many a longe bote,
> And over hache threw them into the streame.

**27** 2. *beames.*— Another nautical puzzle. The MS. has *beaues* or *beanes*. Percy changed to *beams*, and remarked the similarity of the old 'Dolphins made of lead or iron . . . which [the ancient Greeks] suspended from beams or yards fastened to the mast and which they precipitately let fall on the enemies' ships.' The top-castle is properly 'a stage at the very tip of the mast '; but might, of course, be lower. See Professor Child's note, p. 337. The point is that Lord Howard must at any risk keep Barton's men out of this top-castle, and so escape all havoc wrought by the beams.

**29** 2. See note on 23 3. In a version from a MS. of the sixteenth century, printed by Professor Child, *Ballads*, VIII, 502 ff., these lines read (st. 30):

> Were yowe twentie shippes, my lorde,
> As your Honor is but one,
> Ethere bye lerbord or by lowe
> That Scootte would overcome yowe, everye one.

Professor Child suggests that *lowe* may = hull.

**32** 4. *glasse*, perhaps a lantern ; but this is doubtful.

**35.** *peeces* = guns.

**36.** In the version referred to above (Child, VIII, 504), stanza 38 runs as follows :

> A larborde, wher Sir Andrew laye,
> They saide he tould his gold in the light ;
> 'Now by my faith,' saide my lord Charles Howarde,
> 'I se yonne Scootte, a worthë wight.'

As 'larborde' here = 'hache-bord' in our version, we have additional reason to make the change in 29 2.

43 4. Nine yards of chain. — At this point the ballad 'strikes its pace,' and the description of the fight is admirable and clear, provided one does not consider too curiously the working of the beams.

47 2. *Weate?* — See VIII, 505, 51 2: 'I like not of this geare, said he'; and 66 2: 'For howe soe ever this geare doth goe.'

53 1. *Swarved.* Perhaps *swarmd* (= climbed), as in VIII, 505, 56. — So, too, 56 1.

53 3. *Bearing arrow* = one meant for long range, one that carries well, like the 'broad' arrow below. See VIII, 505, 56: 'broode-headed arrow.'

55 2. See note, *Cock,* 15 3.

64 3, 4. *Jacke* is a leather coat. The direction of the arrow might be such as to reach the brain. In the other versions Sir Andrew is shot through the heart.

65. See *Armstrong,* 16.

66. *Till* = while; 'during the time that': Jamieson, citing Barbour.

71 3. Another version more sensibly brings them home July 20th: VIII, 506, 74 4.

## BROWN ROBYN'S CONFESSION.

First printed by Buchan, *Ballads of the North of Scotland.* See Child, III, 13 ff., and his remarks on the unique character of the ballad in English.

2 1. *kevels* = lots, originally blocks or staves of wood, properly marked; see a description of the process of divination, Tacitus, *Germania,* c. 10. In an Anglo-Saxon charm against poisons (Wülker-Grein, *Bibliothek,* I, 320 ff.), Woden takes nine 'Wonder-Twigs.'— See also the 'black bullet' which decided Bonnie Annie's fate as causing trouble on shipboard: *Bonnie Annie,* Child, I, 245.

3. In the omitted lines Brown Robyn confesses certain monstrous crimes.

## SIR PATRICK SPENS.

Often printed: see Child, III, 17 ff., for particulars. This is the version of the *Reliques,* and loses nothing by its brevity. The ballad may be founded on actual fact, but it points to no definite and unmistakable occurrence. Professor Child calls attention to the delicacy and beauty of stanzas 9, 10. Praise of the ballad itself is superfluous.

1 1. Dunfermline palace.

3 1. '*A braid letter, i.e.*, open or patent; in opposition to close rolls.'— Percy.

5. Percy calls attention to a law of James III. forbidding ships with certain cargoes to sail between October 28 and February 2.

7. It is the sight of the new moon '*late, late* yestreen,' which makes the bad omen: Child, p. 18.

8 4. 'Floated on the water.'

---

## CAPTAIN CAR, OR EDOM O GORDON.

We now enter upon the particular or domestic cycle of border-ballads. *Otterburn* and *Cheviot* were international. — Printed here from a MS. (late sixteenth century) in the British Museum, as given by Child, *Ballads*, VI, 430 f., with substitution of 19 4, 23 3, from B, the version of the *Percy Folio*, ed. H.-F., I, 79 ff., and of 20 from F, Child, VI, 435. — Adam Gordon, a deputy of the Scottish queen Mary, in November, 1571, sent one Captain Ker to the house of one of the Forbeses, a family attached to the protestant or regent's party. Captain Ker demanded surrender; the lady of the house refused; and thereupon he burned down the house, to the destruction of the inmates, whose numbers are variously given. — For the particulars, see Child, as above, p. 424 ff. — As Chambers pointed out, Gordon, being held responsible for the act of his subordinate, was in some ballads treated as the principal actor himself.— Chappell, I, 226, gives the tune of this ballad and refrain.

2 1. We are ready to go whither you please.

4 4. *towne*, in the old sense of an enclosed place.

8 4. That is, he will legally marry her: see D, 7.

22 1. Evidently a former retainer or servant who has shown Car how to come at the house.

24 3. *in close* = in a narrow place, in extremities.

25. Lord Hamilton is a blunder for one of the Forbeses.

28 4. Add *away?* *Quite* = free, clear, 'quit.'

## THE BARON OF BRACKLEY.

See Child, *Ballads*, VII, 84, printed from Laing's *Scarce Ancient Ballads*, 1822. — The ballad is based upon a Scottish feud and its culmination, September, 1666 : for particulars see Child, p. 80 ff. — Probably there were two ballads of this name, for a Baron of Brackley was killed in 1592, an old man, in his own house, while dispensing hospitality to his murderers. Professor Child leans to the assumption of two ballads (as above, p. 83); and we seem to have a confusion of them at the opening of this version. The editor has therefore omitted 5–10, which run as follows :

5.     Out spak the brave baronne, owre the castell-wa :
       'Are ye cum to spulyie and plunder mi ha?

6.     'But gin ye be gentlemen, licht and cum in :
       Gin ye drink o my wine, ye'll nae gar my bluid spin.

7.     'Gin ye be hir'd widifus, ye may gang by,
       Ye may gang to the lawlands and steal their fat ky.

8.     'Ther spulyie like reivers o wyld kettrin clan,
       Who plunder unspairing baith houses and lan.

9.     'Gin ye be gentlemen, licht and cum in,
       Ther's meat an drink i my ha for every man.

10.    'Gin ye be hir'd widifus, ye may gang by,
       Gang down to the lawlands, and steal horse and ky.'

These stanzas belong to a ballad of a good old man, with a false young wife; whereas the following seem to involve a brave but sluggard husband, and an energetic wife. Moreover, in our 5, the 'Get up, get up,' and the laconic foreboding reply, do not accord with the previous garrulity of the talk over the castle-wall. The Baron surely does not speak from his bed. See also versions C and D, Child, as above; and Mr. Macmath's note, VIII, 522.

3 2. See *Hen. V*, iv, 2, 10 : 'That their hot blood may spin.'

8 1. *Marys* = handmaids, like the later 'Abigail.' Cf. Queen's Maries in *Mary Hamilton*, note to 3, 17.

35. See *Armstrong*, 17.

## THE BONNY EARL OF MURRAY.

Printed in the *Reliques*, and often; Child, VI, 447 ff. James
Stewart, Earl of Murray, was killed by the Earl of Huntly's
followers, February, 1592.

2. This is said, of course, by the king.

3 2. Riding at the ring, or piercing with a lance a suspended ring
as one rode at full speed. See Strutt, *Sports and Pastimes*, Bk. iii,
12, and on the *quintain*, iii, 2 f. 'At the commencement of the
seventeenth century,' says Strutt, 'the pastime of running at the
ring was reduced to a science.' For the implied connection here
with the queen's love, cf. the well-known lines of another Scottish
noble (Palgrave's *Golden Treasury*, cxxxiii, p. 152):

> For you alone I ride the ring,
> For you I wear the blue,
> For you alone I strive to sing,—
> O tell me how to woo!

5 2. 'To claim a glove worn as a lady's favor, was a form of
challenge, — which is perhaps the reference here.' — Child, *Ballads*
(1860), VII, 324.

6 2. Murray's father was Sir James Stewart, of Doune. — The
murdered man was handsome, strong, and exceedingly popular.

---

## YOUNG WATERS.

*Reliques;* Child, IV, 342 f.

1 2. *Tables*, a sort of backgammon, was very popular even in the
13th century; and the round-tables, that is, an in-door recreation,
may have been something of the sort. See Strutt, *Sports and
Pastimes*, p. 419.

3 3. For *burning*, 'burned' = burnished, has been suggested.

---

## MARY HAMILTON.

For the numerous versions of this fine ballad see Child, VI,
379 ff., and VIII, 507 ff. — The occurrence on which it is based
seems to have taken place at the Russian court in the time of Peter

the Great (Child, VI, 382 ff.), while the names and the treatment are distinctly Scottish. The ballad, says Professor Child, must have arisen between 1719 and 1764.

1.  A common form : see *Lady Maisry*, version H, 2, Child, Part III, 122, where in a similar case, —

> Word's gane to her mother's kitchen,
> And to her father's ha. . . .

2.  Child-murder led to the death of Russian Mary Hamilton ; but the ballad is thinking of the old exposure or 'exposition' of infants.  In some other versions Mary kills the baby outright; but in Y (VIII, 512) 5 :

> I put it in a bottomless boat
> And bad it sail the sea.

See also U, 14 : VIII, 509.

3.  The 'auld' queen is Mary of Scotland, who has four Maries in waiting upon her : see the final stanza.  The king is presumably Darnley.

6 3.  In the Russian account, Mary dresses in white silk, 'hoping thereby to touch Peter's heart': Child, VI, 383.  See *Fair Mary*, E, 4, Child, IV, 315.

10.  So far we have followed Version A, but this stanza is E, 13. See also *Armstrong*, 11 ; and Scott, *Minstrelsy*, I, 20, note.

15 2.  *held up* = took up, recognized as his child by lifting her in his arms.  Saxo Grammaticus, speaking of a child whom a man had begotten, uses the phrase 'quem sustulerat.'  See the editor's *Germanic Origins*, p. 189.

17.  For *Maries*, see *Lass of Rochroyal*, B, 8, 9, Child, III, 218. As name for ladies' maids, see *Brackley*, 8, and *Willie and Lady Maisry*, B, 13, III, 169.

---

## BONNIE GEORGE CAMPBELL.

This is Motherwell's combination of several versions, *Minstrelsy*, Amer. ed. I, 194. — With questionable propriety Allingham has distorted the refrain 'for rhyme's sake,' reading 'gallant to see' for 'gallant rade he,' and 'wi boots to the knee' and 'careless and free' for the 'booted rade he' of 4 and 6.  See *The Ballad Book*, Amer. ed., pp. 236 f., 386.

### BESSY BELL AND MARY GRAY.

Founded on an actual event during the plague, near Perth, in 1645. See Professor Child's interesting account, VII, 75 f.

3 3.   The proper name is Dranoch Haugh.

3 4.   'To bake against (in the rays of) the sun.'

---

### SIR HUGH.

An old ballad, often printed, and based on an alleged murder which took place in 1255. See contemporary and other records, Child, V, 235 ff. A similar story is told in the *Prioresses Tale* of Chaucer.

1 3.   *him :* dative of subject with verbs of motion.

8.   See *Death of Robin Hood*, 17.

---

### THE THREE RAVENS.

Not as well known as the counterpart or perhaps parody of this ballad, *The Twa Corbies*, which is in many of the anthologies. See Child, I, 253 f. In Motherwell's *Minstrelsy*, Amer. ed., II, 270, there is a different refrain.

4 2.   *keepe* = guard.

6 1.   Cf. 10 2. — *Leman* (*lief-man,* dear one) has no offensive suggestion.

8 2.   *earthen lake* = 'shroud of earth.' *Lake* = winding sheet, shroud. Cf. *Sweet William's Ghost*, 15 :

> 'Cold meal (= mould) is my covering owre,
> But an my winding sheet.'

9 1.   *Prime* = about nine o'clock in the morning.

---

### LORD RANDAL.

This is Scott's familiar version in the *Minstrelsy*. Other versions add a dialogue, like that of *Edward* and *The Cruel Brother*, in which Lord Randal leaves to his mother his cattle, to his sister his gold and silver, to his brother his houses and lands, and to his true-love 'hell and fire.' The many and widely distributed versions of this ballad deserve attention ; and the student should read Professor Child's exhaustive study of them and the related ballads of Europe, *Ballads*, I, 151 ff.

The group of ballads involving a domestic tragedy through faithlessness or folly of true-love, as here, of mother (*Edward*), of brother, of sister, of father (*Bewick and Grahame*), and of husband (*Clerk Colven*), must be completed by the ballad of the false wife and the ballad of the false servant. *Little Musgrave and Lady Barnard* and *Glasgerion*, admirable both, were omitted for obvious reasons from the text, but are given here, with slight omissions and no change or addition, in order that the cycle may be complete. See Child, III, 244 ff., 138 ff. Several versions are used here.

---

## LITTLE MUSGRAVE AND LADY BARNARD.

1. As it fell one holy-day,
       Hay downe,
     As many be in the yeare,
   When young men and maids together did goe
       Their mattins and masse to heare,

2. Little Musgrave came to the church-dore;
       The preist was at private masse;
   But he had more minde of the faire women
       Than he had of our lady grace.

3. The one of them was clad in green,
       Another was clad in pall;
   And then came in my lord Barnard's wife,
       The fairest amongst them all.

4. She cast an eye on little Musgrave,
       As bright as the summer sun;
   And then bethought this Little Musgrave,
       ' This lady's heart have I woonn.'

5. Quoth she, ' I have loved thee, Little Musgrave,
       Full long and many a day ; '
   ' So have I loved you, fair lady,
       Yet never word durst I say.'

6. ' I have a bower at Buckelsfordbery,
       Full daintyly it is deight;
   If thou wilt wend thither, thou Little Musgrave,
       Thou's lig in mine armes all night.'

7.  Quoth he, ' I thank yee, fair lady,
        This kindnes thou showest to me ;
        But whether it be to my weal or woe,
        This night I will lig with thee.'

8.  With that he heard, a little tynë page,
        By his ladye's coach as he ran :
    ' All though I am my ladye's foot-page,
        Yet I am Lord Barnard's man.

9.  ' My lord Barnard shall knowe of this,
        Whether I sink or swim ; '
    And ever where the bridges were broake
        He laid him downe to swimme.

10.  ' A sleepe or wake, thou Lord Barnard,
        As thou art a man of life,
    For Little Musgrave is at Bucklesfordbery,
        A bed with thy own wedded wife.'

11.  ' If this be true, thou little tinny page,
        This thing thou tellest to me,
    Then all the land in Bucklesfordbery
        I freely will give to thee.

12.  ' But if it be a ly, thou little tinny page,
        This thing thou tellest to me,
    On the hyest tree in Bucklesfordbery
        Then hanged shalt thou be.'

13.  He called up his merry men all :
        ' Come saddle me my steed ;
    This night must I to Bucklesfordbery,
        For I never had greater need.'

14.  And some of them whistld, and some of them sung,
        And some these words did say,
    And ever when my lord Barnard's horn blew,
        ' Away, Musgrave, away ! '

15.  ' Methinks I hear the thresel-cock,
        Methinks I hear the jaye ;
    Methinks I hear my Lord Barnard,
        And I would I were away ! '

16.  ' Lye still, lye still, thou little Musgrave,
        And huggell me from the cold ;
    'Tis nothing but a shephard's boy
        A driving his sheep to the fold.

8.  ' But come you hither, master,' quoth hee,
    ' Lay your head downe on this stone ;
  For I will waken you, master deere,
    Afore it be time to gone.'

9.  But upp then rose that lither ladd,
    And did on hose and shoone ;
  A coller he cast upon his necke,
    Hee seemed a gentleman.

10.  And when he came to that ladie's chamber,
    He thrild upon a pinn ;
  The lady was true of her promise,
    Rose up and lett him in.

11.  He did not kisse that lady gay
    When he came nor when he youd ;
  And sore mistrusted that lady gay
    He was of some churlës blood.

12.  But home then came that lither ladd,
    And did of his hose and shoone,
  And cast that coller from about his necke ;
    He was but a churlës sonne :
  ' Awaken,' quoth hee, ' my master deere,
    I hold it time to be gone.

13.  ' For I have sadled your horsse, master,
    Well bridled I have your steed ;
  Have not I served a good breakfast,
    When time comes I have need.'

14.  But up then rose good Glasgerryon,
    And did on both hose and shoone,
  And cast a coller about his necke ;
    He was a kingës sonne.

15.  And when he came to that ladie's chamber,
    He thrild upon a pinn ;
  The Lady was more then true of promise,
    Rose up and let him in.

16.  Saies, ' Whether have you left with me
    Your braclett or your glove ?
  Or are you returned backe againe
    To know more of my love ? '

17.   Glasgerryon swore a full great othe
        By oake and ashe and thorne :
      ' Lady, I was never in your chamber
        Sith the time that I was borne.'

18.   ' O then it was your little foot-page
        Falsly hath beguiled me ; '
      And then shee pulld forth a little pen-kniffe
        That hanged by her knee,
      Says, ' There shall never noe churlës blood
        Spring within my body.'

19.   But home then went Glasgerryon,
        A woe man, good [Lord] was hee ;
      Sayes, ' Come hither, thou Jacke, my boy,
        Come thou hither to me.

20.   ' Ffor if I had killed a man to-night,
        Jacke, I wold tell it thee ;
      But if I have not killed a man to-night,
        Jacke, thou hast killed three ! '

21.   And he puld out his bright browne sword,
        And dryed it on his sleeve,
      And he smote off that lither ladd's head,
        And asked noe man noe leave.

22.   He sett the sword's poynt till his brest,
        The pumill till a stone ;
      Thorrow that falseness of that lither ladd
        These three lives werne all gone.

---

## EDWARD.

See Herder's praise of this ballad, *Works*, XXV, 19.— Printed in
the *Reliques*, and communicated to Percy by Sir David Dalrymple.
4 7.   In Motherwell's version, 'Son Davie' says :

            ' I'll set my foot in a bottomless ship
              And ye'll never see mair o me.'

Flosi in the *Niálssaga* (c. 160) thus takes a bad boat for his last
voyage, saying that he is old and 'fey.'

## THE TWA SISTERS.

This remarkable ballad exists in many versions, and in that melancholy proof of popularity, burlesque. The reader is referred to Professor Child's exhaustive account, *Ballads*, I, 118 ff. — We print B, omitting 5. The refrain made popular by Scott's version, — 'Binnorie, O Binnorie,'— occurs in I, K, M.

6 1. A regrettable confusion of ocean and mill-stream ; see 15 2.

25 ff. In A the 'violl,' made of the breast-bone, plays of itself :

> Then bespake the treble string,
> 'O yonder is my father the king.'
> Then bespake the second string,
> 'O yonder sits my mother the queen.'
> And then bespake the strings all three,
> 'O yonder is my sister that drowned me.'

## THE TWA BROTHERS.

Printed in Sharpe's *Ballad Book*, and Child, II, 435 ff., A. Professor Child prints seven other versions, one American.

2 3–4. Motherwell insists that this must be accidental, or the ballad is spoiled ; but Professor Child points out that 'the generosity of the dying man is plainly greater if his brother has killed him in an outburst of passion.'

10 3. *Kirk-land*, evidently for the kirk-yard of 5 and 6.

## BEWICK AND GRAHAME.

From a printed copy ; see Child, VII, 144 ff. The ballad, as Scott pointed out, 'is remarkable as containing probably the very latest allusion to the institution of brotherhood in arms.'— The tragic motive of a struggle between two duties, with decision fatal in either case, is used here with admirable if homely power. Hamlet, Rüdiger in the *Nibelungen*, Rodrigue in the *Cid*, and all the rest, are presented, of course, with far more art, but not with more fidelity to nature.    There are some weak verses, due to broadside influence ; but delicate touches (as stanza 16) are not wanting.

1 3.    Scott notes that this 'custom of going armed to festive meetings' often made serious trouble.

5 2.    *bully*, in the other versions *billy*, = comrade, brother in arms.

8 2.    See 48 2.

19.    By the old blood-brotherhood, and later forms of it, it was disgraceful for one of the pair to survive the other.

43.    This is the awkward stroke by which Robin Hood killed Guy of Gisborne, stanza 40.

---

## THE CRUEL BROTHER.

This is one of the ballads recited by Mrs. Brown of Falkland. She was born in 1747, and learned her ballads before she was twelve years old.    See Child, I, 142 ff., II, 455, note, who also quotes Prior in regard to the great importance 'in ballad times' of asking a brother's assent to his sister's marriage.    As printed here, the ballad is made up of A and B (Child, p. 145 f.) as follows:  A = 1, 9, 10, 11, 12, 13, 14, 15, 16, 19, 20, 21, 22, 23, 24, 25;  B = 2, 3, 4, 5, 6, 7, 8, 17, 18.

1.    For ball-playing, see *Introduction*, p. lxxxi.

11.    See Suckling, *Ballad upon a Wedding*, of the bride and groom :

> Till every woman wish'd her place,
> And every man wish'd his.

19.    For the testament, cf. *Edward*, p. 170.

---

## BABYLON, OR THE BONNIE BANKS O' FORDIE.

Printed in Motherwell's *Minstrelsy ;*  Child, I, 170 ff.

1 4.    Fordie is a stream 'about six miles to the east of Dunkeld' in Scotland.

2 1.    This peculiar form of trespass invariably summons the outlaw, enchanted person, or whatever power of the place.    See *Tam Lin*, 4.

17 2.    *o me* = by me.

18 2.    *twyned* = twinned = parted, divided.

## CHILD MAURICE.

H.-F., *Percy Folio*, II, 500 ff.; Child, IV, 263 ff.  A popular Scottish version is *Gill Morice ;* see Gray's letter, above, p. 309.

Upon this vivid and admirable ballad Home founded his tragedy of *Douglas.* — For the Silver Wood, see *Jellon Grame*, 1; Child, IV, 303.

1 3.  *that* is superfluous.

2.  In the MS. this is preceded by a defective stanza :

> . . . And he tooke his silver combe in his hand,
> To kembe his yellow lockes.

4–5.  The sense is that the page must greet the lady as many times as there are knots in nets for the hair, or merchant-men faring to London, or thoughts of the heart, or schoolmasters in all the school-houses ; in short :

> 'Grüss mir mein Liebchen zehntausend mal !'

4 3.  Sometimes 'lovely London.'  So 'fair Edinburgh' in *Armstrong*, and 'merry Lincoln' in *Sir Hugh.*

6–7.  He sends her tokens of his identity.

7 4.  *Let* (infinitive) = desist.

20 1.  *him :* dative of subject with verbs of motion.

25 1.  As in *Gest*, 305 1, and often in the ballads, swords are both 'brown' and 'bright,' and the former adjective probably means 'burnished,' or 'glistening.'  Cf. *brún* and *brúnecg* (*Béowulf*, vv. 2574, 1546) used in A.-S. of the sword, and evidently in the sense of 'bright,' not 'dark' or 'brown,' as Grein defined the words.  If the adjective has such venerable traditions, however, one is half inclined to follow it further back to those bronze swords, found so plentifully in Denmark, and elsewhere in reasonable abundance, and exquisite enough in their workmanship to have come from the hand of Wéland himself.

26 1.  *hee* = John Steward.

30–31.  See (above, p. 339) conclusion of *Little Musgrave and Lady Barnard.*

## THE WIFE OF USHER'S WELL.

This ballad, which introduces a small group dealing with the supernatural, was printed by Scott in the *Minstrelsy;* Child, III, 238 f. — Allingham patches with two stanzas, inserted after 11, from a version of *The Clerk's Twa Sons o' Owsenford* (printed by Child as B, with *The Wife of Usher's Well*), and actually adds another stanza (of his own?) 'to complete the sense.' See *The Ballad Book*, pp. 32 ff., 375. But we are more than content with the noble simplicity of A; and Allingham, gaining little or nothing by his borrowing, has lost pitiably by his inventing. A touch in version B is that the mother wraps her sons in the mantle; in A she wraps herself in it. Allingham thus 'completes the sense' by making the brother remark:

> Our mother has nae mair but us;
>   See where she leans asleep;
> The mantle that was on herself,
>   She has happ'd it round our feet.

It is not said in our ballad that the sons have come back to protest against their mother's excessive grief (see Child, III, 238); but this motive is so common in folk-lore that we add for comparison a ballad called *The Unquiet Grave*, printed by Child, III, 236:

> 1. ' The wind doth blow to-day, my love,
>       And a few small drops of rain;
>    I never had but one true-love,
>       In cold grave she was lain.
>
> 2. ' I'll do as much for my true-love
>       As any young man may;
>    I'll sit and mourn all at her grave
>       For a twelvemonth and a day.'
>
> 3. The twelvemonth and a day being up,
>       The dead began to speak:
>    ' O who sits weeping on my grave,
>       And will not let me sleep?'
>
> 4. ''Tis I, my love, sits on your grave,
>       And will not let you sleep;
>    For I crave one kiss of your clay-cold lips,
>       And that is all I seek.'

5. ' You crave one kiss of my clay-cold lips;
    But my breath smells earthy strong;
    If you have one kiss of my clay-cold lips,
    Your time will not be long.

6. ' 'Tis down in yonder garden green,
    Love, where we used to walk,
    The finest flower that ere was seen
    Is withered to a stalk.

7. ' The stalk is withered dry, my love,
    So will our hearts decay;
    So make yourself content, my love,
    Till God calls you away.'

See *Sweet William's Ghost* for st. 5 of the above.

4 2. *fashes*. MS. *fishes*. Lockhart suggested the reading *fashes* = troubles, disturbance, storms.

5 1. B puts the time as 'the hallow days of Yule.' — Martinmas = 11 November.

5 4. 'The notion that the souls of the blessed wear garlands, seems to be of Jewish origin.' — Scott.

9 1, 2. Cf. Child, *Ballads*, III, 229, st. 14. — Extravagant and erring spirits are usually supposed to be warned by any cockcrow which they may hear; but R. Köhler, *Germania*, XI, 85 ff., shows more elaborate distinctions in folk-lore. Three, sometimes (as in this ballad) two cocks, distinguished by color, — white, red and black, — announce to ghosts and demons the approach of day; and it is when the third (or second: in each case, the last) cock crows that the spirits vanish. Köhler notes that in our ballad the gray cock takes the place of the black. In Scandinavian myth, the dark-red cock crows in the under-world ; but every one knows how devil and demons have been substituted for perfectly harmless spirits. Here, at any rate, no evil is at work ; the sons simply obey the ghostly signal of recall.

12 3, 4. The beauty of reticence in this last farewell is as delicate as anything in literature.

---

## CLERK COLVEN.

Child, II, 371 ff. — See his full account of similar European ballads.

'Clerk' is what Allingham calls 'a learned young knight'; see *Clerk Saunders*, 10 4, Child, III, 159.

1 1.  This 'gay ladie' is his newly married wife; hence the ven-
geance of the forsaken mermaid, — not forsaken, however, as the
sequel shows, but sufficiently slighted.

1 3.  'About her slender waist.'

3 2.  'Be not so anxious about me.'

5 2.  *And ay's ye wash* = 'And it is ever that you wash,' 'You are
always washing your sark o' silk.'

6 2.  See *Tam Lin*, 7.  Scott remarks, in a note to the latter
ballad, that 'the ladies are always represented, in Dunbar's Poems,
with green mantles and yellow hair.'

-----

## FAIR MARGARET AND SWEET WILLIAM.

Printed in the *Reliques*, and an early favorite with the stalls;
Child, III, 199 ff.; and quoted, from whatever source, in Beaumont
and Fletcher's *Knight of the Burning Pestle*, ii, 8, and iii, 5.  The
final stanza is here omitted, — a mere tag.  For the tune, see
Chappell, I, 182 f.

1.  See *Lord Thomas and Fair Annet*.

17–19.  See note to 29, 30, of same ballad.

-----

## SWEET WILLIAM'S GHOST.

In Herd's MSS. this ballad is the continuation of *Clerk Saunders*,
and is so treated by Scott in the *Minstrelsy;* see Child, III, 226 ff. —
It would be too large a task to point out nearer or remote parallels
in literature; but a good measure of difference between poetry of
the schools and poetry of the people may be gained by comparing
this ballad with either Wordsworth's *Laodamia* or Goethe's *Braut
von Corinth*.

1 1.  *A wat* = 'I wot,' like 'in sooth.'

2.  'Are ye at present sleeping or waking?'

3.  She does not yet know that he is dead.

4.  See *The Unquiet Grave*, 5, above, p. 347.

5 1.  Professor Kittredge very plausibly suggests that this unintelligible *mid-larf* is really the corrupted name of some town.  Thus
*Usher's Well*, B, 4 (Child, III, 239), says of a similar situation:

> O the young cock crew i the merry Linkem,
> An the wild fowl chirp'd for day.

So here (*a* = 'in'); 'the cocks are crowing in merry ——.'

6 4. That die in childbirth.

9 2. In other cases — see the passage quoted by Professor Child, III, 227, from Scott's Advertisement to *The Pirate* — it is the surviving lover who desires to take back the troth-plight bestowed upon the dead. — As for the wand upon which Margaret 'strokes' her troth, it seems not unlikely that we are dealing with a confused survival of the common method by which savages and even European peasants get rid of a disease by rubbing the affected part upon a stick, a tree, or what not. See Tylor, *Primitive Culture* (1873), II, 146, 148 f.

11 1. With no dress save hose, shoes and gown.

13 3, 4. In some versions she is told that there is no room.

14 1. *Meal* = mould, earth.

---

## EARL BRAND.

This is the older and fuller version, printed by Bell in his *Ancient Poems*, of a ballad known best in the form to which Scott gave the name of *The Douglas Tragedy*. See Child, I, 88 ff. See also the fragment in the *Percy Folio*, ed. H.-F., I, 132 ff., out of which Percy made his *Child of Elle*. — The related ballads of Europe are very interesting : see Child, as above, and compare the ballad which follows in his collection, — *Erlinton*. In these two ballads there are distinct traces of the Germanic Hilde legends. The elopement and the fight with pursuers recall the story of Walter and Hildegund, as told in the A.-S. fragment *Waldere*, in the *Waltharius* of the German Ekkehard, and elsewhere. — This version of *Earl Brand* (see Child, p. 92 f.) has many points of contact with Scandinavian ballads on the same subject.

7 1. Carl Hood, as Scandinavian sagas give us plainly to understand, is here Odin himself, who, 'though not a thoroughly malignant divinity, had his dark side.' . . . (Child).

11 1. *lee-lang* = lief-long, corrupted into livelong (defined by some dictionaries = 'long as life'!); 'this dear long day.' Cf. German 'den lieben langen tag.'

13. 'Almost literally' the same in certain Danish ballads. — Child.

14 1.  *dead* = death.

24.  This is the last member of the attacking party, and, like the slayer of Johnie Armstrong (15 3), he comes behind Earl Brand's back to give the mortal wound.  But the oldest form of the ballad doubtless retained a feature found in most of the Scandinavian versions: all will go well if the maid remember the knight's command that she shall not name his name.  It is when she sees her youngest brother come to his fate that she calls upon her lover by name, and asks him to have mercy; thus she brings about the tragedy.  There is a touch of this in Scott's version, though father takes the place of youngest brother:

> She held his steed in her milk-white hand,
> And never shed one tear,
> Until that she saw her seven brethren fa',
> And her father hard fighting, who lov'd her so dear.

> 'O hold your hand, Lord William!' she said,
> 'For your strokes they are wondrous sair;
> True lovers I can get many a ane
> But a father I can never get mair.'

## YOUNG HUNTING.

See Child, III, 142 ff., printed from Herd's MSS., with the aid of which Scott made up his version, *Earl Richard*.  He added, for example, st. 28:

> The maiden touched the clay-cauld corpse,
> A drap it never bled;
> The ladye laid her hand on him,
> And soon the ground was red,

which is the well-known test of a murderer's presence, most familiar to us in Shakspere's *Richard III*, i, 2.  In our ballad the only test is the trial by fire.

3 1.  Has plied him with ale and beer; literally, 'has poured in (*i.e.* into the cup) for him,' *him* being the dative case.

5 1.  A commonplace of the ballads.

8 3, 4.  From G (Child, p. 151).  'You shall have a cage of gold instead of a cage of wood.'

12 1.  'The deep holes, scooped in the rock by the eddies of a river, are called pots; the motion of the water having there some resemblance to a boiling caldron.'—Scott.

14 2, 15 2. She swears by corn and by moon ; in another version by 'grass sae greene and by the corn ' ; again (K, 26) by the thorn. Glasgerion's oath (see above, p. 342) was 'by oak and ash and thorn,' — a 'full-great' oath, with distinctly heathen elements.

16 3. *duckers* = divers.

17 1. *the tae* = the one.

18 3, 4. From K. — For a bird revealing secrets, cf. the parrot in *Lady Isabel and the Elf Knight* (Child, I, 22 ff.), C, 13 ff. (p. 57); D, 22 ; E, 14 ff., where a cage is promised ; and especially *The Bonnie Birdy* (Child, III, 260 f.), a Scottish pendant to the English *Little Musgrave.* Here the bird tells the knight of his wife's sin because the latter has treated the bird ill. Birds carry messages ; cf. *Johnie Cock*, 20, and *Gay Goshawk*, with Professor Child's note, IV, 356 f.

20 3, 4. Scott thinks these are 'unquestionably' the corpse-lights 'which are sometimes seen to illuminate the spot where a dead body is concealed'; but Professor Child urges that the meaning 'is as likely to be that a candle, floated on the water, would burn brighter when it came to the spot where the body lay.'

23 6. Note the dative with substantive force.

25 6. *hokey-gren.* In Scott's version, *hollin green* = green holly.

---

## FAIR JANET.

Printed in Sharpe's *Ballad Book ;* Child, *Ballads*, III, 100 ff.

4 4. *He's* = he shall.

5 4. *jo* = sweetheart.

18 4. *the morn* = the morrow.

19. Cf. *Mary Hamilton*, 6.

20 3. White steeds have sacred associations (Tacitus, *Germania,* c. 10), are reserved for royalty, and are the best of three colors in times of need : see *Lady Maisry*, B (Child, III, 116), and *Fair Mary of Livingston*, 20–22. Tam Lin, too, rides not the black, nor the brown, but — he is a favorite of the queen — a milk-white steed : 27, 28. 'Saddle *white Surrey* for the field to-morrow,' commands the king, *Richard III*, v, 3. 'Dem Pabst ist gesetzt,' ran an old regulation, 'dass er reyte auf einem *blancken Pferde.*' For a deeper glimpse, see Hehn, *Kulturpflanzen u. Haustiere*, pp. 44 f., 478.

24. In came, etc.

24 4. *downa* = am not able ; 'occasionally denoting want of inclination, even reluctance or disgust.' Jamieson. — 'I cannot bear to look upon your face.'

26 2. *Many mae* = 'many more,' — 'many others.'

29 3, 4. Cf. *Twa Brothers*, 7 ff.

30. See note to *Fair Margaret and Sweet William*, 17 ff.

---

## LADY MAISRY.

Printed by Jamieson, *Popular Ballads:* see Child, III, 112 ff.

1 3. *Maisry* is for Margery, Marjory.

2 2. *a' kin kind* = all kinds of.

6 1. 'Kitchen-boy.'

11 1. Who is it that owns (*aught*); to whom belongs?

20 4. *sat* = salt.

22 2. He waited not to knock or call.

23 3. *lighter* = delivered.

---

## THE LASS OF ROCH ROYAL.

This is the version E of Child, *Ballads*, III, 221 f., from Mrs. Brown's recitation (1800), and in good part (see Child, p. 226, for changes) that printed by Scott in his *Minstrelsy* as *The Lass of Lochroyan*. Lochryan 'lies in Galloway,' says Scott ; and he notes that Burns has 'celebrated' the same story. See *Works of Burns*, Globe Edition, p. 181, *Love Gregory*, a slight and not very impressive song.

10. Said by the 'fause mother' who personates Love Gregor while he sleeps.

17 3. *him :* substantive dative, and not reflexive; cf. *raise* in 24 4.

18 2. *gars me greet* = makes me weep.

---

## WILLIE AND LADY MAISRY.

Printed by Motherwell in his *Minstrelsy ;* Child, III, 167 ff. — Compare *Clerk Saunders*, the ballad which precedes it in Professor Child's collection. — Maisry is here substituted for Margery.

5 2.   A 'whang' is a thong; he has thus a full 'sheaf.'

10 2.   Note the 'run-on' verse, a rare occurrence in ballad metre.

11 2.   *gare* often = a strip of cloth, a part of the dress : 'used vaguely in romances,' says Professor Child (*Ballads*, first collection, II, 397), 'for clothing.' Jamieson : 'A triangular piece of cloth inserted at the bottom of a shift or robe.' Cf. *gore*.

----

## LORD THOMAS AND FAIR ANNET.

Printed in the *Reliques* 'from a MS. copy transmitted from Scotland'; an English version was printed as broadside in the reign of Charles II. 'One of the most beautiful of our ballads, and indeed of all ballads,' says Professor Child, *Ballads*, III, 180.

4 3.   *nut-browne* is here the opposite of fair or beautiful, though we can hardly assume the same insinuation for that type of constancy and amiability, the Nut-brown Maid. In C (Child, p. 186) the fair one grows scurrilous, addressing Lord Thomas:

> 'Brown, brown is your steed,' she says,
>   'But browner is your bride;
> But gallant is that handkerchy,
>   That hideth her din hide.'

The brunette was certainly undesired in Germanic Europe : see *Twa Sisters*, 14, with the line of another version: 'ye was fair and I was din [= dun]'; and an army of similar expressions could be marshalled, including Shakspere's famous apologies for his 'dark lady.'

8 2.   'And her cattle in the stable.'

11 2.   *owt o hand* = immediately.

15 3.   The finest linen was made in Holland, and so named.

16 4.   See note to *Young Waters*, 3 3.

29–30.   This well-known substitute in tragic ballads for the 'lived happily ever after' of ordinary tales is fully treated by Professor Child, *Ballads*, I, 96–99. See also Talvj, *Charakteristik*, 139 f. The former notes that in English ballads the plants, separated at the roots, but twining their branches lovingly together, are 'either a brier and a rose, or a brier and a birk.' — See *Fair Margaret and Sweet William*, *Fair Janet*, and the familiar ballad of *Lord Lovel*.

## FAIR MARY OF LIVINGSTON.

The story is told better in *Fair Mary of Wallington* (Child, **IV**, 309 ff., version A), but the present version — to be consistent, the title should be *Fair Maisry* — from Herd, and printed by Professor Child as B, is better suited to the purposes of our collection. The editor has ventured to change the order of stanzas as follows: B, 5, 6 have been placed after 26, and 7, 27 have been omitted altogether, so that B, 5, 6 = 24, 25 of our copy, with distinct gain in clearness, and no loss by the trifling omissions. If stanza 7 (B) is retained (see Professor Child's note, p. 316), restoration of the right order is 'impracticable.'

2 2.   An lords? (Child).

5 2.   *shoon* may well be *sheen* as elsewhere, making a good rime.

9 4.   *Bird her lane* = 'a lonely maid,' or possibly nothing more than 'utterly alone.' Still, whatever the etymology of *bird, burd* (see Murray's *Dictionary,* s. v. *burd*), the ballads understand by *burd* a maiden, a young lady. Cf. *Fair Annie,* 1 2.

17.   This is the proper ballad behavior for any one surprised by a great piece of news.

20–22.   See note to *Fair Janet,* 20 3. — For this passage, see *Lady Maisry*, B, 14–16 (Child, III, 117):

> Fair fall the mare that foaled the foal
> Took him to Janet's lyke.

The rime — or assonance — requires *lyke* instead of *lear*, which = *lair*, resting-place, bed or tomb.

26.   Spoken by the mother.

28 4.   *rathes.* 'Raith, reath. The fourth part of a year.' Jamieson, *Dictionary.*

---

## CHILD WATERS.

*Percy Folio,* ed. H.-F., II, 269 ff. 'It was not necessary,' noted Percy, 'to correct this much for the press.' For other versions like *Burd Ellen*, see Child, III, 83 ff. — The great praise awarded to this ballad by Child and Grundtvig must not be thwarted in the mind of readers by the impression of irritating cruelty in the hero and irritating patience in the heroine. We must take the only point of view recognized in ballad times; this done, and allowances made for the roughness — not coarseness — of the details, we shall be ready to concede that no better ballad can be found in any tongue. An obvious comparison brings us to the same obstacles and the same triumph in judging Chaucer's *Clerke's Tale,* as well as to that admirable 'dramatic lyric,' *The Nut-brown Maid.* The editor has taken a surely pardonable liberty in omitting the one passage which jars hopelessly with our modern sentiment, — stanzas 27, 28, 29 as printed by Professor Child. Hence A, 30 is 27 of this copy.

3 3.   *strayght* = narrow.

28 1.   MS. 'This, and itt drove now afterward.' Professor Child inserts 'night,' but says it is an emendation 'made without confidence,' and assuming *and* to be superfluous, as in *Sir Cawline:* see notes, *Ballads,* III, 99, 57 (on *and*).

33 4.   *monand* = moaning.

34 3, 4.   To wish one's child born and one's self in the grave is common with forsaken sweethearts in popular lyric (cf. the song *Waly, Waly*); but this touch is final. Mr. Furnivall pours out his wrath on the Child's cursedness and brutality (*Folio,* II, 278); but he goes too far. Child Waters is abominably callous, but he has heart enough to respond to this last and unconscious appeal. Moreover, the response is no sentiment, but practical amends.

---

## FAIR ANNIE.

Printed by Scott in the *Minstrelsy;* Child, III, 63 ff. The same story is told by Marie de France in the *Lai del Freisne,* 'three hundred years older than any manuscript of the ballad,' though not the source of the latter. Scott was moved by the resemblance, or identity, of the stories to remark 'that the romantic ballads of later times are, for the most part, abridgments of the ancient metrical romances, narrated in a smoother stanza and more modern language.'

1 2.   *your lane* = alone. Cf. *Fair Mary,* 9 4.

4 4.   Married women wore their hair bound up, or under a cap; maidens 'wore it loose or in a braid.' See Child, III, 64, note.

22 2.   *lilly lee* = lilied or flowery meadow.

22 3.   *grew* means a greyhound.

## WILLIE'S LADY.

From Mrs. Brown of Falkland, and printed, with some alterations, in Scott's *Minstrelsy;* see Child, I, 81 ff., for interesting
illustrations and parallels.

3 2.  *lighter* = delivered of her child.

7 2.  'Let her be . . . and this goodlie gift . . .'

11 2.  Seems to be spoken by the husband; but it may be the
suffering wife, as in Professor Child's earlier collection, I, 164.

13 2.  *Leed.*  'Perhaps Lydia,' says Scott, — a bold suggestion.

15 2.  *chess* is for *jess*, 'the strap or cord attached to a hawk's leg
and to the leash.'

29 1.  *Billy Blin.*  See Child, I, 67, introduction to Gil Brenton.
This 'serviceable household demon' is one of the friendly spirits of
the home so common in folk-lore and familiar in another guise even
to Milton (*L'Allegro*, 'the drudging goblin'). The word *bil* 'seems
to point to a just and kindly-tempered being.' Scott, in a note,
pointed out the Billy Blind 'in the rustic game of Bogle,' a sort of
blindman's-buff.

31, 32.  Verses have apparently dropped out at this point; and
the rimes, as elsewhere, leave a great deal to be desired. Probably,
too, a stanza is omitted between 33 and 34.

34.  On the malignant effects of these knots, see Professor Child,
p. 85.

37 1.  *master* = big.

---

## YOUNG BEICHAN.

Version A, Child, II, 454 ff., with 4, 5, 6, 7, 8 from H (Kinloch's
*Ballads:* in H = 7, 8, 9, 10, 11), and the name Beichan instead of
Bicham as in A.  A favorite ballad, especially in such versions as
*The Loving Ballad of Lord Bateman*, which Cruikshank illustrated
(1839); as a story, it is related to the following ballad of *Hind
Horn*. For the connection of Beichan (or Bekie) with Gilbert Beket,
father of the Canterbury saint, see Child, p. 457 ff.

2.  In some versions this treatment is caused by Beichan's refusal
to bow a knee to 'onie of their stocks' in 'Grand Turkie.'

2 2.  *tree* = piece of wood: cf. our *axletree.*

11 2.  *white money* = silver.

14. In two other versions, as undoubtedly in the original forms of the ballad, it is the Billy Blin (see preceding ballad) who warns the heroine of Beichan's impending marriage.

15 4. We must, in all civility, concede this line to the minstrel.

22 1. In other versions, cups and cans fly, as Beichan very properly kicks over his table.

----

## HIND HORN.

See Child, I, 201, for this version from Motherwell's MS.; and I, 192 f., for the relations of the ballads to the famous *gest* of *King Horn* (13th century), the latter being in all probability founded on older ballads now lost beyond chance of recovery. As Professor Child remarks, this ballad gives only the catastrophe of the story. — *Hind* = young man, stripling.

4 2. *lavrocks* = larks.

6 2. Not literally 'gone', of course, for she remains always true to Horn, but rather 'in danger.'— For other warnings of trouble at home, see Child, p. 200 f. Somewhat similar sympathy with human emotions is felt by a stone in a certain Rathhaus (Kuhn-Schwarz, *Norddeutsche Sagen*, p. 249), which turns from red to blue when a maiden whispers to it her story of misfortune. Grimm (*Deutsche Sagen*, No. 41) tells of a sword belonging to Countess Rantzau : if it turned black, it meant the death of one of her family. — Other instances are given by Child, II, 268 f., under the head of tests for loyalty, virtue, and the like.

11 2. Prolonged, of course, by the bride, who hopes for her lover to the last.

----

## KATHARINE JAFFRAY.

This is the ballad which Scott imitated in his *Young Lochinvar*. As here printed it is Child's A (VII, 219) from Herd's MSS.— For the make-up of Scott's version in the *Minstrelsy* (*The Laird of Lamington ;* in later editions *Katharine Janfarie*), see Child, p. 230 f. — Other ballads of bride-stealing, — peace, however, to primitive Germans, modern peasants, and above all, the Sabines, — are *Bonny Baby Livingston*, *The Lady of Arngosk*, and *Eppie Morrie ;* the latter tells in vigorous fashion of an attempt of this sort which was frustrated by the heroine's affinity to Brunhild in the *Nibelungen*. A graphic description of Highland bride-stealing is given by Scott in his Introduction to *Rob Roy :* see the ballad of that name, Child, VII, 243 ff.

11 3. Evidently *she* is wrong. We must assume the bride to be faithful to her first love, and consenting to the abduction ; hence one version alters to ‘ It's a’ fair play.’ Perhaps it is the deserted bridegroom who gars the trumpets sound ‘foul play.’

13 1. ‘*To haik up and down, to haik about,* to drag from one place to another to little purpose, conveying the idea of fatigue caused to the person who is thus carried about.’— Jamieson, *Dictionary.*

13 3. Frogs, toads, snakes are served for fish, and act as a poison : see *Lord Randal,* and remarks, Child, I, 155, 157.

## THE GAY GOSHAWK.

Printed by Scott in the *Minstrelsy :* here from Version A, Child, IV, 357 f.

7. See 4.— Although the Jamieson-Brown MS. has *she* in 7 3, it seems evident that we should read *he,* the goshawk being meant : see also 1 2.

8 2. *Shot-windows :* see Glossary.

10 4. See note to *Young Hunting,* 18 3, 4. Professor Child notes that rationalism, working its way into ballads, is fain to substitute parrots for all these birds that speak and understand.

19. A ‘ drowsy syrup.’

26. For parallel cases, see Child, IV, 355 f.

28 2. *Sound your horn* is evidently a taunt ; cf. Chaucer's phrase ‘ blowe the bukkes horn ’ (*Miller's Tale,* v. 201), and the fate of a rejected lover (*Knight's Tale,* v. 980):

‘ He mot go pypen in an ivy-leef.’

See Morris's note to the latter, Clarendon Press Ed., p. 151.

## KING ESTMERE.

Percy tore from his MS. the leaves on which this ballad was written, and sent them to the press ; it is certain that he made both alterations and interpolations, only material, however, near the end. The edition of the *Reliques* published in 1794 professed to restore

the ballad to closer relations with the original; but critics agree
that 63–66 are Percy's own manufacture, and we have to reckon
with the usual editorial corrections in other parts of the text. — See
Child, III, 49 ff.

1 4. *borne* = dissyllable (*borën*).

4 4. *able* = of proper rank: cf. 'capable' in *Lear*, ii, 1: 'Loyal
and natural boy, I'll work the means To make thee capable,'—*i.e.*
'able to inherit, though illegitimate,'— said to Edmund.

6 4. 'Between me and the lady.'

11 3. 'Take her to wife.'

12 3. The usual phrase is 'nicked *with* nay.' See *Scotish Ffeilde*,
*Percy Folio*, I, 215, v. 53.

15 2. *in halle* = among the men. So, in the *Nibelungen*, it is a
great favor to Siegfried that Kriemhild is brought to court where
he may see her. The attendance, moreover, is much the same as
Kriemhild's : *N. L.*, st. 277 ff.

25 4. *the* = they.

36 2. *gramarye* = magic, which of course had its connection with
runes, with writing, and then with abstruse lore of every kind.

47 1. The gift of an arm-ring was the commonest form of reward
among the Germanic races. A king, from his habit of breaking off
rings from the long spiral on his arm, and giving these as rewards,
was called in A.-S. 'the ring-breaker.' It is with arm-rings that
Hildebrand makes a last appeal to his son: see *Hildebrandslied*,
v. 33 ff.

47 3. 'And ever we desire thee,' etc.

49. Cf. Chaucer, *Squire's Tale*, v. 69 ff.:

> Whil that the kyng sit thus . . .
> In atte halle dore al sodeynly
> Ther com a knight upon a steed of bras.

For other references for this custom, as well as for that of stabling
the steed in the hall, see Child, III, 51.

54 2. Looked at him narrowly, at close quarters.

## KEMP OWYNE.

Child, II, 306; printed in Motherwell's *Minstrelsy*. Another
version is *Kempion* in Scott's *Minstrelsy*. The central motive of
the ballad is found frequently in popular tradition: see Child, p. 307 f.
Owyne is in name identical with the Owain or Ywein of the romances,
though the latter say nothing of this adventure.

## TAM LIN.

This ballad, interesting in so many ways, is printed here in the version communicated by Burns to Johnson's *Museum* (Child, II, 340), and freely used by Scott in compounding *The Young Tamlane* for his *Minstrelsy*. It is impossible in this place to discuss such features of the ballad as the transformation, and the hints of faery, or the relations and parallels in other literature. Scott wrote an admirable essay ' On the Fairies of Popular Superstition' by way of introduction to the ballad.

1 3. 'Carterhaugh is a plain at the confluence of the Ettrick and Yarrow in Selkirkshire.'— Scott.

5–6. See *Babylon*, 2.

14 2. *elfin grey.* 'The usual dress of the Fairies,' says Scott in his Introduction, 'is green; though on the moors, they have been sometimes observed in heath-brown, or in weeds dyed with the stone-raw or lichen,'— and in a note : ' Hence the hero of the ballad is termed an *elfin grey*.'

20. 'Were you ever christened ? '

24. Hallowe'en is the eve of All Saints (1 November), which is easily merged in All Souls (2 November), a festival once purely heathen and celebrated as a part of the universal manes-cult or worship of the dead. A general feast was held at which the dead were thought to be present; and Widukind, describing such a feast which took place in 980, explicitly tells us of the move by which these rites got a slight change in character and a great change in name. Evidently this is the proper time for spirits to visit the earth. On the night of the second of November European peasants until lately set out food for the spirits, and even went so far as to offer them a bath.

28. See note to *Fair Janet*, 20 3.

33 3, 4. 'Immersion in a liquid, generally water, but sometimes milk, is a process requisite for passing from a non-human shape, produced by enchantment, back into the human. . . .'— Child, II, 338.

36 2. The proper sign of a fairy procession.

39 4. *groom* = man.

41 4. *tree* = wood. Tam can recognize fairy folk.

## THOMAS RYMER.

From Mrs. Brown's recitation; see Child, II, 317 ff.— This ballad retains the essential features of a story which has served the purposes of political prophecy, and is to some extent connected with historical personages. These essential features are the love of a fairy and a mortal, and the visit which the latter makes to fairyland. In fuller detail this story is told in the poem known as *Thomas of Erceldoune* (ed. Murray, E. E. T. Soc., and Brandl, Berlin, 1880), which is probably the source of the ballad. At the end of his visit, Thomas receives from the elf-queen the gift of prophecy, and at his request she tells him a number of things which concern the future of Scotland, — often surprisingly close to history, though clothed in mystical expressions, and made, of course, after the event. Thomas Rymour, 'True Thomas,' thus obtained a great reputation, and was potent to console or alarm the Scottish peasant 'down to the beginning of this century.' For an analysis of the prophecies, see Brandl, p. 29 ff.; for the historic foundation and the personality of the author, Child, p. 318. It is probable that in the original story True Thomas went back to fairyland, never, or, like Arthur, Barbarossa, and the rest, only at some far-off consummation of things or stress of fate, to return to earth : see Professor Child (p. 319 f.) on Ogier le Danois and Morgan the Fay. Two stanzas (5, 6) are inserted from Scott's version in the *Minstrelsy*.

3. This is a trait of the poem as well as of the related romances.

5 1. 'Harp and sing': see Introduction, above, p. lxxiii.

5 3, 4. To kiss a fairy or a spirit puts a mortal in the jurisdiction of the other world : see *Sweet William's Ghost*, 4 :

> And if I kiss thy comely mouth,
> Thy life-days will not be long.

The motive is artistically treated in Goethe's *Braut von Corinth*.

6 4. 'The Eildon Tree . . . now no longer exists; but the spot is marked by a large stone called Eildon Tree Stone.'— Scott.

9 4. In the poem this passage of the waters is better emphasized (ed. Brandl, xxviii f.):

> Scho [she] ledde hym in at Eldonehill
> Undirnethe a derne [secret] lee,
> Where it was dirke as mydnyght myrke
> And ever water till his knee.

> The montenans of dayes three
> He herd bot swoghyng of the flode. . . .

11 2.   A well-known precaution from Proserpine's day to this.

12.   As Professor Child remarks, this is 'honest bread and wine' which the fairy has considerately brought with her.

15 2.   *lillie leven* = a lawn covered with lilies and flowers, — 'the primrose path of dalliance,' or rather the route described by Macbeth's porter.

17.   Another well-known precaution: see Child, p. 322, note, who quotes Falstaff (*Merry Wives*, v, 5): 'They are fairies ; he that speaks to them shall die.' Of course, if a colloquy was unavoidable, Latin was the only refuge.

18 1.   *even cloth* = smooth, fine texture?

---

## THE WEE WEE MAN.

Printed by Herd in his *Ancient and Modern Scottish Songs ;* Child, II, 330. — For the older poem, and added prophecies, connected with the ballad but not the source of it, see Child, pp. 329 f., 333 f.

2 2.   Another version has:

> 'And sma' and limber was his thie.'

---

## ST. STEPHEN AND HEROD.

Often printed from a MS. said to be of the time of Henry VI. For the legend and related literature, see Professor Child's introduction, I, 233 ff.   The ballad 'was sung as a carol for St. Stephen's day,'— 26 December.

1 2.   *befalle*, subjunctive for indicative: 'as befits,'— 'as is customary with. . . .'

2 1.   The Christmas dish of old England, brought into hall with pomp of procession and a carol and Latin refrain :

> 'Caput apri defero,
>   Reddens laudes Domino . . .'

Two English carols for the occasion are printed by Ritson, *Ancient Songs* (1790), p. 125 ff.

4 2.   *Bedlem* = Bethlehem.

7 1.   *or thu gynnyst to brede* = 'beginnest to entertain capricious fancies, like a woman.'— Child.

12 2.   The eve of St. Stephen's is, of course, Christmas night.

# GLOSSARY.

———◆◆———

*A* (in *a wat, wot*), I : *Sweet William's Ghost*, 1²; *Beichan*, 23⁴.
*a, a'*, all.
*a*, on, of.
*abone, aboon*, above.
*ae*, one : see *tae, tone*.
*ain*, own.
*airn, airns*, iron.
*alther, alder, alre* (gen. pl.), of all.
*almus*, alms.
*ancients*, ensigns.
*and*, if.
*ane*, one.
*ankir*, anchorite.
*as* (with subjunctive), as if.
*aught*, owns (*Lady Maisry*, 11⁶).
*auld*, old.
*avowe*, vow.
*avowë*, founder or patron.
*awayte*, to lie in wait.
*awkwarde, ackward*, unexpected, evil (*auk*); or perhaps simply 'backward,' back-handed.
*ayre*, heir.

*Ba, ba'*, ball.
*baffled*, disgraced.
*bale, balys*, evil, harm, ruin.
*ban*, band.
*bande*, bond, agreement.
*bane, banis*, murderer.
*bar*, bore, carried.
*barne, berne*, a man.
*basnet, basnites, bassonnettes*, helmet.

*bauld*, bold.
*be*, p. p., been.
*be, by, bi*, near.
*beams* (MS. *beanes*), see note, *Barton*, 27².
*bearing-arrow*, an arrow that carries well (?).
*bedone*, wrought.
*beerys*, biers.
*begoud* (*Beichan*, 8³), began ; cf. *begouth*, Barbour, *Bruce*, ix, 183 (Murray).
*behote*, promise (*Gest*, 315¹); promised (*Gest*, 297³).
*belive, blive*, quickly.
*ben*, within (the house).
*benbow*, bent bow ; bow.
*bent*, open grassy place, field.
*ber* (*Cheviot*, 42⁴), thrust, pierced ; cf. Chaucer, *Knight's Tale*, v. 1398.
*berne* (see *barne*), a man.
*bestand* (*R. H. Death*, 23⁴), to bestead, avail.
*bested*, placed, circumstanced : see note, *Gest*, 138³.
*bestis*, beasts.
*bete*, to remedy, to mend.
*beth*, be, are.
*bi*, by; *bi west*, in the west.
*biek*, to bask.
*bigget*, builded.
*biggins*, buildings.
*bigly*, spacious, ample.
*billie, bully*, brother, comrade.

*bird, burd,* maiden, young woman.

*birk,* birch.

*birld,* poured out.

*blan, blane, blanne (blinne),* stopped, ceased.

*blawn (Lady Maisry,* 20³) = blawin', blowing : present participle in elliptical construction (?).

*blinne,* to stop, cease.

*blood-irons,* lancets.

*blowe,* to brag (*Gest,* 59⁴).

*blyve, belyve,* quickly.

*bode,* bidden, invited.

*bolte,* arrow with blunt head.

*bond,* bound.

*bone,* boon.

*boote,* remedy.

*bord, borde,* table.

*borowe,* surety.

*borrow, borowed,* to ransom.

*boteler,* butler.

*botery,* buttery, place for liquors.

*both,* be, are.

*bowne, bowynd,* to prepare.

*boun, bowyn,* prepared, made ready.

*boÿs (bowys),* bows.

*brae (Cock,* 17⁴), brow.

*brae,* hill, hill-side.

*braider,* broader.

*braw,* brave, handsome.

*bread,* breadth.

*brede,* see note, *St. Stephen,* 7¹.

*bree,* brow.

*brente,* burnt.

*brether,* brothers.

*briddis,* birds.

*briggs,* bridges.

*broad-arrow* (see *bearing-arrow*), an arrow with broad head, 'for cleaving.'

*broche,* tap : *a broche,* abroach, on tap.

*broded,* braided.

*broke, brook,* to enjoy, use.

*broken (men),* outlaws.

*brome,* broom.

*broo,* broth.

*brook,* see *broke.*

*brown, browne* (of swords), glittering, bright ; or simply, 'browned against rust?' See note, *Maurice,* 25¹.

*bryttlynge,* breaking or cutting up, quartering of slain animals.

*bully* (see *billie*), friend, comrade, brother-in-arms.

*burd,* see *bird.*

*burn,* a brook.

*burn-brae,* 'the acclivity at the bottom of which a rivulet runs.' — Jamieson.

*buske,* to dress, prepare, make ready to go.

*buske,* bush.

*buss,* bush.

*busshement,* ambush.

*but,* except, unless.

*byckarte,* skirmished.

*byddys,* abides, remains.

*bydene* ('for *bĩ êne?*' conjectures Stratmann ; but see Hempl, *Academy,* 25 April, 1891, p. 395: *bi þe ēne* > *biðe-ēne* > *bidēne*), together, at once.

*bylle,* bill, sword, battle-axe.

*byn,* be, are.

*byre,* cowhouse, stable.

*byst,* art.

*Ca,* to call.

*ca'd,* drove, hit.

*can,* for *gan,* often combined with an infinitive to express the past tense : *can I see (Gest,* 184²), I saw.

*can (Gest,* 210²), knows.

*canst,* knowest.

*capull-hyde,* horse's hide.

*care*, anxiety.

*care-bed*, sick-bed ; *care-bed taen*, fallen sick with anxiety.

*carefull*, full of care, sorrowful.

*carl*, man.

*carlin, carline*, old woman.

*carp, carpe*, sing, narrate.

*cast*, to intend.

*cast*, a throw, as in dice.

*cawte*, wary.

*channerin*, fretting.

*chap*, to knock.

*chays*, chase, hunting-park.

*chepe*, bargain.

*chere*, face (*Gest*, 28[2]); entertainment (*Gest*, 61[4]).

*chess* (for *jess*), strap : see note, *Willie's Lady*, 15[2].

*child, children* (*R. H. Death*, 7[1]), title of honor, knight, brave fellow.

*christendom* (*Tam Lin*, 20[4]), christening, baptism.

*clame*, climbed.

*cleading*, clothing.

*close, closs*, a narrow place; a courtyard.

*coffer* (*Sir Hugh*, 11[2]), though ridiculous enough in this place, must mean box, small trunk.

*cole*, cowl.

*collayne*, Cologne [steel].

*coped*, knocked, struck.

*corbie*, crow.

*coresed* (*Gest*, 100[3]) ? Professor Child suggests 'possibly *bodied*, in fine condition.'

*cors*, curse.

*corser*, see note, *Gest*, 256[1].

*corsiare*, courser.

*cote-a-pye*, upper garment, short coat : cf. *courtepy*.

*coud*, knew.

*coulters*, iron blade of a plough.

*couth* (*Gay Goshawk*, 2[3]), word, saying (*cwide*).

*covent*, convent.

*cowthe*, could.

*cracked* (*Bewick*, 4[4]), defied, bid boastful defiance to.

*craftely*, skillfully.

*craw*, to crow.

*cressawntes*, crescents.

*crye*, to announce by a crier.

*cun* (*can*), know; *cun . . . thanks*, feel gratitude, 'savoir gré.'

*curch*, kerchief, head-covering.

*Dame*, mother.

*daunton*, to frighten.

*daw*, to dawn.

*dawin*, dawning.

*de*, to die.

*dead, deed*, death.

*deal* (*Fair Marg. and Sweet W.*, 16[1]), give out as 'dole.'

*dee*, to do.

*dele*, part, bit ; *no dele*, not at all.

*demed*, judged.

*departed*, divided, parted.

*dere*, harm, injury.

*derne*, secret, dark.

*did, dyde*, caused.

*did* (*them*), betook themselves, went.

*dight, dyght*, prepared, done ; furnished (*Barton*, 28[4]).

*ding*, to beat, cast.

*disgrate*, fallen in fortune, innocently disgraced.

*disherited*, dispossessed.

*do*, to cause.

*doen* (*he's doen him*), betaken himself, gone.

*done*, down (*Cheviot*, 30[2]).

*donne*, dun.

*dool, doole, dule*, sorrow.

*dout*, dread, danger.

*downa* (*I*), I dislike to, cannot bear to.

*dowy*, *dowie*, sad, sadly.

*doys*, does.

*dre*, *dree*, *drie*, *drye*, to endure, suffer.

*duckers*, divers.

*dughty*, doughty, capable.

*dule*, see *dool*.

*dyghtande*, preparing, in preparation: see note, *Gest*, 388[4]. — See *dight*.

*dynte*, a blow.


*Eare*, heir.

*een*, eyes.

*eerie*, sad, melancholy.

*eftsoones*, again, afterwards.

*eke* (*Otterburn*, 57[1]), each.

*eldern*, elderly.

*eme*, uncle.

*emys*, gen. sing., uncle's.

*envye*, injury.

*ere*, previously.

*ere*, to inherit, possess.

*esk*, ask, lizard, newt (A.-S. *aðexe*).

*even*, precisely, exactly.

*even*, smooth.

*everilkon*, everyone.

*eylyt*, aileth.


*Fa*, to befall, betide.

*fache*, to fetch.

*fadge*, a thick cake (Jamieson), and figuratively a clumsy woman.

*faem*, foam.

*fall*, to happen, become, chance.

*fare*, doings.

*farley*, *ferley*, strange, wonderful.

*farleys*, *ferlies*, strange things.

*fashes* (MS. *fishes*), troubles, disturbances, storms.

*fause*, false.

*fawken*, falcon.

*fay*, faith.

*faylyd*, missed.

*fe*, *fee*, pay, money, property.

*feale*, fail.

*feders*, feathers.

*fer*, *ferre*, far.

*ferd* (*Monk*, 52[4]), fear.

*fere*, fellowship, company: *in fere* together.

*ferly*, see *farley*.

*ferlies*, see *farleys*.

*fet*, *fette*, fetched.

*fetteled*, made ready.

*firstin*, the first.

*fit*, *fytte*, division of a ballad.

*fitt*, strain of music (*Estmere*, 60[3]).

*fivesome*, five together: cf. A.-S. *sum* with genitives of the cardinal numbers (*eahta sum*), or in a phrase like *féara sum* (Béow., v. 1412), 'one of a few,' 'a few together.'

*flatters*, flutters, moves quickly about.

*flattering*, fluttering (*Young Hunting*, 7[2]).

*flee*, to fly.

*fleed*, flood.

*fleyd* (*Kinmont W.*, 36[2]), frightened, put to flight.

*fo'd*, foaled.

*fone*, foes.

*forbye*, beyond.

*force*, *fors*, matter, account: *do no fors*, 'lay no stress upon.'

*forehammers*, sledge-hammers.

*forenent*, in the face of.

*forgone*, to forego, lose.

*foriete*, forgotten.

*forlorn*, utterly lost, forfeited.

*fors*, see *force*.

*forsters*, foresters.

*fostere*, forester.

*fou,* full.

*fourthin,* the fourth.

*fowarde,* the van.

*frebore,* freeborn, gentle.

*free,* noble, open, excellent.

*freke, freyke,* man; pl., *freckys.*

*frembde, fremde,* strange.

*frere,* friar.

*frese?*

*fu,* full.

*fule,* fowl.

*furs,* furrows, ground.

*fynde,* perhaps for *fine,* to end, conclude, *Cheviot,* 24³.

*fynly,* fine, goodly.

*Ga, gae,* to go.

*gaed,* went.

*gan,* with infinitives; see *can: Gest,* 21⁴, and often.

*gang, gange,* to go.

*gar, garre, gard, garde,* to cause, make : and see note, *Otterburn,* 24⁴.

*gare,* a piece of cloth; a part of the dress : see note, *W. and Lady Maisry,* 11².

*garlande,* see note, *Guy,* 31².

*gate,* got.

*gate,* went.

*gates,* paths.

*gaud,* a bar.

*gear,* property (*Fair Annie,* 1⁵); dress (*Cruel Bro.,* 21³).

*geare,* (*Barton,* 47²), affair.

*gete,* got.

*gettyng,* booty.

*gied,* gave.

*gimp,* slender : see *jimp.*

*gin,* if.

*girds,* hoops.

*glave,* sword.

*gleat,* glitter.

*glede, gleed,* flame, fire, a live coal.

*goe, gone,* to walk.

*golett,* throat, part of hood covering the throat.

*goud, gowd,* gold.

*gound,* gown.

*gowden,* golden.

*gowden-graithed,* caparisoned with gold.

*gramarcy,* thanks.

*gramarye,* learning, magic.

*grat,* (see *greet*), wept.

*greahondes,* greyhounds.

*gree,* satisfaction.

*greet,* to weep, wail.

*greete,* gravel, grit.

*greffe,* grief.

*gresse,* grass.

*grevis,* groves.

*grew,* greyhound.

*grith,* peace, security.

*grome, groom,* a man.

*grounde,* sharpened.

*growende,* ground.

*grysely,* direfully.

*gryte,* (*Two Sisters,* 21²), great.

*Ha,* hall.

*hacheborde,* see note, *Barton,* 23³.

*hached,* (*Barton,* 36²), chased, marked, overlaid.

*had,* to hold.

*hae,* to have.

*haik,* to drag about : see note, *K. Jaffray,* 13¹.

*halden,* held.

*halfendell,* half.

*half-gate,* half-way.

*halke,* corner, recess, covert.

*haly,* holy.

*halyd, haled,* hauled, pulled.

*haud,* to hold.

*haugh,* flat ground on the border of a river.

*haylle,* hale, strong.

*haysell,* hazel.

*he,* high.

*heal*, hail.

*heiding-hill*, hill of beheading, execution.

*hem*, them.

*hendë*, courteous, gentle.

*heng*, to hang.

*hente*, seized.

*hepe*, hip, 'the fruit of the dog-rose.'

*her*, their.

*herry*, to harm, plunder, spoil.

*he's*, he shall, must.

*het*, hot.

*he[ve]de*, head, person.

*hight, hyght*, promise, promised.

*hight (on)*, on high.

*him*, reflexive pronoun, 'himself'; *Gest*, 24².

*him*, substantive dative.

*hind*, a young man.

*hinde (hende)*, gentle.

*hoky-gren (Young Hunting, 25⁶)?* — Jamieson, s. v. *hoakie*, 'a fire that has been covered up with cinders, when all the fuel has become red.' — *gren* = twig, bough.

*hol, hole*, whole.

*holde*, shelter (*Car*, 1⁴); possession, stronghold.

*holde*, to retain as counsel or advocate.

*holland*, a kind of linen.

*holtes*, woods.

*hom (= hem)*, them.

*hongut*, hanged.

*hooly*, slowly.

*hors*, horses.

*houzle*, housel, the Eucharist.

*hoved*, remained, waited, hovered about.

*hunds*, hounds, dogs.

*husbonde*, head of a family, farm-er, manager.

*hy*, high : *on hy*, upright.

*hye, (upon)*, aloud.

*hye*, haste (*Monk*, 50²).

*hyght (on)*, aloud.

*hyght* (see *hight*), promised.

*hypped*, hopped, limped.


*I*, see y-.

*ifedred*, feathered.

*ilka*, each one, each.

*ill-far'd*, ill-favored.

*in-fere*, together.

*inocked*, notched.

*intill, into*, in.

*ipyght*, pitched, set up.

*iquyt*, requited, rewarded.

*I'se*, I shall, I must.

*iwys, iwysse*, certainly.

*iyn*, eyes.


*Jacke*, a leather coat, or coat of mail.

*japis*, jokes.

*jaw*, wave (*Two Sisters*, 9²).

*jimp*, slender; tightly, closely (*Fair Annie*, 4³).

*jo*, sweetheart.

*just*, joust.


*Kaim, kems*, comb.

*keepe, kepe*, to guard ; to care for, to like, to esteem.

*kell*, head-dress or net worn by women.

*kembing*, combing.

*kempe, kempes*, warrior, champion; also may have meant 'giant': see Möller, *A. E. Volksepos*, p. 74, note.

*kemperye-man*, see *kempe*.

*kettrin*, cataran, band of High-land marauders.

*kevels*, lots.

*kilt*, to tuck up.

*kin*, kind (*a' kin kind* = all kinds of).

*kirtell*, short gown or tunic.
*kitchy-boy*, kitchen-boy.
*knave*, boy, servant.
*knet*, knitted, knotted.
*ky*, kine, cattle.
*kyst*, to cast, throw.
*kythe*, to become known.

*Laith*, loath.
*lake*, shroud.
*lakit, lakkyt*, lacketh.
*lane*, lone ; *your lane, her lane*, alone.
*lap, lappe, lapt*, to wrap.
*lap*, leapt.
*lasten*, last.
*lat*, cease, desist, let.
*late*, let.
*launsgay*, a kind of spear.
*lavrocks*, larks.
*lawing*, inn-reckoning, account.
*layde down*, spent.
*layn, layne*, sb. and verb, lying, deception ; to lie.
*lear*, lore, learning.
*lear*, lair, resting-place.
*lease*, leash.
*lede*, train, retinue (*Gest*, 368²).
*ledes-man*, leader, guide.
*ledyt*, imperative plur., lead (*Stephen*, 11²).
*lee* (*lee-lang*), lief, dear (see note, *Brand*, 11¹).
*leeve*, dear, lovely.
*leeve*, to believe.
*lefe*, lief, glad.
*leman*, sweetheart.
*lende*, to grant, lend.
*lende*, to dwell.
*lent*, leaned.
*lere* (*Gest*, 28⁴), cheek.
*lere*, to learn ; to teach.
*lese*, to lose.
*lesse* (*Otterburn*, 25², A.-S. *léas*), a lie.

*lesyng, leasyng*, lying.
*let*, to let ; to cause.
*let*, to hinder.
*let*, to desist, be hindered (*Child Maur.*, 7⁴).
*lette*, past tense of *let*, to desist.
*leugh*, laughed.
*leutye, lewte*, loyalty.
*leve*, to permit.
*leven*, lawn.
*lewte*, see *leutye*.
*lig*, to lie.
*light, lighte*, alighted.
*lighter*, delivered (of a child).
*lightly*, to undervalue, treat with contempt.
*lillie, lilly*, explained in note to *Thomas Rymer*, 15², as 'lilied, flowery'; but Professor Child refers to *Ballads*, VIII, 485, ' lilly Londeen,' which, he thinks, = ' leeve London,' of other passages ; so that *lilly* =lovely, fair (A.-S., *léoflíc*).
*limmer*, scoundrel, general term of reproach.
*lin*, to cease.
*lither*, bad.
*lock*, look.
*lodging-maill*, rent.
*loe*, to love.
*long* (*of*), owing to, dependent upon (*Monk*, 22³).
*looten, lotten*, let (past part.).
*lorne*, lost.
*loset*, loosed.
*loughe*, laughed.
*loup*, leap.
*louten*, bowed, bent.
*lowe*, a hillock.
*lowe*, fire, flame.
*lowe*, humbly (*Gest*, 43²).
*lowne, loun*, a servant, a worthless person.
*lucettes*, luces, pikes.

*luikt*, looked.

*lyed*, 'lay,' dwelt.

*lyed* (*Monk*, 14[1]), gave the lie to.

*lyked*, pleased.

*lynde*, *lyne*, linden; tree in general.

*lyng*, heather, long grass.

*lyste*, pleases; *me lyste*, I desire.

*lythe*, *lithe*, listen.

*lyveray*, allowance of clothes (*Gest*, 70[3]), of food (*Gest*, 161[3]).

*Made*, caused.

*mae*, more.

*magger*, maugre; *in the magger of*, in spite of.

*make*, to cause.

*make*, *makes*, *makys*, mate.

*male*, a large bag or portmanteau (*Gest*, 134[2]).

*male*, mail, armor.

*march-man*, warrior of the border.

*march-parti*, border side.

*marke* (*hym*), 'sign' himself, commit himself to the Trinity by making the sign of the cross (Child, 1860).

*marke*, *merke*, the value of about 13*s*. 4*d*., but not a coin.

*marys*, handmaids, ladies in waiting.

*masars*, cups, bowls.

*master* (*Willie's Lady*, 37[1]), big.

*mast*, mayst.

*masteryes*, trials of skill.

*maun*, must.

*may*, maid.

*meal*, mould, earth.

*mede*, reward.

*meen*, moan.

*meikle*, mickle, great.

*merked* (*one* = on: *Otterburn*, 47[3]), aimed at.

*messis*, masses.

*met*, *mete*, measured.

*mete*, meat; *to meat*, at meat, dinner.

*met-yard*, 'a measuring-rod, generally a tailor's.'

*meynë*, *menë*, *menye*, *meany*, company.

*mickle*, *mykkel*, great, mighty.

*mid-larf*, see note, *Sweet William's Ghost*, 5[1].

*molde*, mould, earth.

*monand*, moaning.

*mood*, error for *my God?* See note, *R. H. Death*, 23[1].

*morne*, morrow.

*mort*, death, — the blast blown by hunters when game has been killed.

*most*, greatest.

*mote*, moot, meeting, court.

*mote*, may; *mote I the*, 'may I prosper.'

*moudie-hill*, mole hillock (Jamieson).

*mountnance*, amount, durance.

*myllan*, Milan steel.

*mylner*, miller.

*myneple*, 'manople, a gauntlet covering hand and forearm,' Skeat, *Spec.*, p. 396 f.

*myster*, need.

*Nare*, nor.

*neigh*, to approach (*Estmere*, 55[6]).

*nere*, nearer.

*nextin*, the next.

*nicked*, shook the head.

*nie*, to neigh.

*noder*, other; *no noder*, none other.

*noumbles*, entrails, 'those parts which are usually baked in a pie.'

*nourice*, nurse.

*O*, of (= by, *Babylon*, 17²); on.
*of*, off.
*okerer*, usurer.
*on*, one.
*on*, of, in.
*ones*, once.
*or*, before.
*order*, *ordre*, rule or discipline of a monastic order.
*ought*, owned, had (*Car.* 31¹).
*overtolde*, counted too much.
*oware*, hour.
*owre*, or, before (*Spens*, 8³).
*owre*, over.
*owtlay*, outlaw.

*Palfray*, palfrey, saddle-horse.
*pall*, cloak.
*parti*, side; *uppone à parti*, on one side.
*passe*, limits, extent.
*pastes*, pasties, pies.
*pavyleon*, tent.
*pecis*, cups, vessels.
*peecis*, pieces, guns.
*pellettes*, bullets.
*perte*, part, side.
*pestilett*, pistol.
*pety*, pity.
*peyses*, pieces.
*pin*, 'the metal peg under a knocker,' Furnivall.
*pine*, pain, torture.
*pit*, *pitten*, put.
*plate-jack*, coat of mail.
*plucke-buffet*, see note, *Gest*, 424³.
*pot*, deep place in a river.
*prees*, stress of battle, attack.
*pricke*, target.
*pricke-wand*, see note, *Guy*, 31².
*prime*, about nine o'clock in the morning (originally a term applied to the first hour of the canonical day).
*prude*, proud.

*prycked*, spurred.
*pyght*, pitched.
*pyne*, suffering, torture.

*Quarter* (*Cock*, 8²), the fourth part of a yard.
*quyrry*, quarry, slaughtered game.
*quyt*, *quitt*, requited.
*quyte*, to requite, pay.

*Radly* (see *redly*), quickly.
*ranke*, turn, series.
*rashes*, rushes.
*rathes* (*raith*), periods of three months.
*rawe*, row.
*rawstye*, rusty.
*raye*, striped cloth.
*raysse*, raid, incursion.
*reacheles*, reckless, careless.
*reade*, counsel, advice.
*reade*, *rede*, to advise, interpret, guess.
*reane*, rain.
*reas*, to rouse.
*reave*, to rob.
*rede*, p. p., guessed.
*reden*, rode.
*redly*, *redely*, quickly.
*reiver*, robber.
*renisht*, prepared, arranged, caparisoned (?).
*reve*, to rob.
*reves*, stewards, bailiffs.
*rin*, to run.
*rise* (*at*), to spring from, come from.
*rivin'*, tearing.
*rocks*, distaffs.
*rode*, *rood*, cross.
*roke*, reek, steam.
*rome*, room.
*route*, to assemble in a band.
*rout*, *rowght*, attack, battle.
*row*, *rowd*, *rowed*, to roll, wrap.

*row-footed*, rough-footed.

*rule*, see note, *Monk*, **32¹**.

*rung*, staff.

*ryall*, royal.

*rynde*, flayed.

*rysyt*, imperative pl., **arise**.

*Sad*, earnest, serious, heavy.

*sae*, so.

*sair*, sore.

*sakeless*, guiltless, innocent.

*salued*, greeted.

*sark*, a shirt.

*sat*, salt.

*sawten*, assault.

*say*, to essay, try (*Child Waters*, 27⁴).

*sayne*, to say.

*scathe*, harm, injury.

*schoote*, shot, *i.e.* let go, sent off (*Otterburn*, 32³).

*scobs*, gags.

*se* (*Cheviot*, 40¹), saw.

*se*, *see*, to protect (in the phrase 'save and see').

*seke*, to search.

*seker*, secure, sure.

*selerer*, cellarer, the officer who furnished the convent with provisions (Ritson).

*semblyde*, assembled.

*sen*, since.

*sen*, sent.

*sent*, sendeth.

*sent* (*sent I me*), to assent.

*set* (*to fore : Gest*, 223³), hit, struck upon.

*sett*, to aim (*Barton*, 31²).

*sette*, leased, placed in pledge (in *sette to wedde*).

*settled*, aimed.

*shanna*, shall not.

*shathmont*, a span, a measure of about **six** inches; A.-S. *scæft-mund*.

*shawe*, wood, grove, thicket.

*shear* (*Cheviot*, 6², 8²), probably for *sér*, *sere* = several, particular.

*sheave*, slice.

*shee*, shoe.

*sheene*, *sheyne*, beautiful.

*shefe* (of arrows), 'sheaf,' twenty-four.

*shende*, to harm, rebuke, punish.

*shent*, hurt.

*shet*, shot.

*shete*, to shoot.

*sheugh*, *seugh*, furrow, ditch.

*shift*, change, resource.

*shope*, created.

*shot-window*, a projected window (?) ; a window opening outwards, on a hinge (not set in a sash), still, or till lately, in use in Scotland. — Jamieson.

*shradds*, coppices, openings in a wood.

*shrewed*, cursed.

*shroggs*, stunted shrubs.

*shryve*, sheriff.

*sich*, sigh.

*sichin*, sighing.

*sicke*, such.

*siller*, silver.

*sin*, sun.

*sindry*, sundry, 'all sorts of people.'

*sith*, since.

*skinkled*, sparkled.

*slack* (*Fair Mary of L.*, 20⁴), low ground, hollow, narrow pass between hills.

*slade*, greensward between two woods, valley.

*slan*, slain.

*slawe*, slain.

*slight* (*Kinmont W.*, 13³), raze, dismantle, level to the ground.

*slist*, sliced.

*slo*, *sloo*, *slon*, to slay.

*slogan*, the clan-cry.
*sloken*, to slake.
*sloughe*, slew.
*sma*, small.
*snell*, keen, sharp.
*snood*, a fillet for the hair.
*somers*, pack-horses.
*sowdan* (*Estmere*, 65⁴), sultan, any infidel king.
*spait*, flood, freshet.
*sparred*, barred.
*sparris*, barrest.
*spauld*, shoulder.
*spede* (p. p., *sped*), to prosper.
*speer*, to ask.
*spendyd*, spanned, placed in rest.
*splent*, armor.
*spole*, shoulder.
*sprente*, sprang out, spouted.
*spulyie*, to plunder.
*spurne* (see note, *Cheviot*, 65², 66¹), trouble, cause of disaster: ‘offendiculum.’— Stratmann. (?)
*spyrred*, asked.
*stage*, stag.
*stage* (*Monk*, 39²)?
*stalle*, place.
*stean*, stone.
*stear*, stir, fright.
*sterte*, bold ones.
*sterte*, started, hurried.
*steven*, voice (*Guy*, 52²); time (*Guy*, 27⁴).
*stonyt*, imperative pl., stone.
*stownde*, time.
*stour, stowre*, stress of battle, attack.
*straked*, stroked.
*strayght*, narrow.
*streen*, yestreen, yesterday evening.
*strocke*, struck.
*strong* (*Armstrong*, 10¹), violent, with a shade of ‘infamous.’
*stye*, path, road.

*styntyd*, stopped.
*styrande*, stirring, raising.
*suar*, sure.
*swapped, swapte*, struck, smote.
*swarved = swarmed*, climbed (?) (*Barton*, 56¹).
*sweavens*, dreams.
*syke*, ‘a marshy bottom with a small stream in it.’—Jamieson.
*syne*, since, afterwards.
*syt*, sitteth.

*Tae* (for *ae*), one; *the tae = that ae; that* being an old form of the definite article. Cf. *tone, tother*.
*take*, to give.
*takles*, arrows.
*talents* (*Estmere*, 17¹), abundance, great weight.
*taryed*, p.p., delayed.
*tene*, trouble.
*tet, tett*, lock or knot of hair.
*the*, they.
*the*, to prosper, thrive.
*theekit*, thatched.
*thimber*, gross, thick.
*thinketh*, with dative, seems.
*thirdin*, the third.
*thought*, with dative, seemed.
*thrast*, thrust, pressed.
*threw*, twisted, entwined.
*thrild* (*tirled*), shook, rattled (at the latch).
*throly*, vehemently.
*throwe*, space of time.
*tiend*, a tithe, a tax or tribute.
*tift*, puff.
*till, tyll*, to; while (*Barton*, 66⁴)
*till*, to entice.
*tine, tyne*, to lose.
*tither* (*tother*), other (*that other*).
*tobroke*, broken in pieces.
*toke*, gave.
*told*, counted.

*tone*, one; *the tone* = that one.
  Cf. *tae.*
*toom*, empty.
*topcastle*, 'ledgings surrounding
  the mast-head.'
*tother*, other.   Cf. *tae, tone.*
*to-towe*, too-too, excessively.
*toune, towne*, often means simply
  an enclosed or fortified place.
*tow*, two.
*tray*, grief.
*tre, tree*, wood, staff, piece of wood.
*trew*, to trust.
*trystell-tree*, trysting-tree, meeting-
  place.
*tul*, till.
*twa*, two.
*twal*, twelve.
*twin, twind, twyned*, v. t. and v. i.,
  to part, separate.
*twine*, (*Cock*, 5³), a woven fabric,
  cloth.
*twinn* (*in*), apart, in twain.
*tyll*, see *till.*
*tyndes*, tines, antlers.
*tyne*, see *tine.*

*Unco*, strange, 'uncouth.'
*unkouth, unkuth*, unknown,
  strange.
*unneth*, scarcely.
*unsett*, not previously appointed.
*untyll*, unto ; while.
*up-chance*, by chance, perhaps.
  Cf. 'up peril of . . .'

*Veiwe-bow* (*Guy*, 15¹), yew-
  bow (?).
*verament*, truly.
*vew-bow* (*R. H. Death*, 27³), yew-
  bow (?).
*vylaynesly*, churlishly, rudely.

*Wache*, watch, sentinel.
*wad*, would.

*wae*, woe.
*Wallace wight* (*Wee Wee Man*, 3³),
  strong (*wicht*) as Wallace.
*wame*, womb.
*wan* (pret. of *win*), came.
*wand*, stick, wood ; *cage o' wand*,
  wooden cage.
*wane* (*wone, wune*), habitation.
*wane* (*Cheviot*, 36²) ? — See note.
*war, waur*, worse.
*waran*, protection, surety.
*warison*, reward.
*warlock*, wizard, demon.
*warsle*, wrestle.
*wat*, know ; *a wat*, I wot, for-
  sooth.
*wayte*, to watch ; *wayte after*, to
  lie in wait for.
*waythmen*, hunters.
*weal* (*Cheviot*, 60¹), clench, so as
  to leave 'wales': Skeat (with ?),
  who also suggests altering
  the phrase to 'wringe and
  wayle.'
*weate* (*Barton*, 47²)?
*wedde*, pledge.
*weede, wedes*, clothes.
*weet, weit*, wet.
*well-fared*, well-favored, handsome : cf. *ill-far'd face, Tam
  Lin*, 40³.
*well-wight* (*Cock*, 16¹), right
  hardy.
*welt* (past tense of *welden*), commanded, disposed of.
*wete*, to know.
*wether*, whither.
*whae*, who, what.
*whang*, thong.
*whatten*, what kind of.
*whereas*, where.
*whether*, whither.
*whun*, whin, furze.
*whyll, while*, until (*Otterburn*,
  50³).

*widifus* (sing. *widifu*), rascals, thieves, those who deserve to be hanged in a 'widdy,' to fill a withy, *i.e.* a rope of willow-twigs, here equivalent to 'gallows.' Cf. Dunbar, *The Fengeit Freir of Tungland*, v. 47 f.: 'He had purgatioun to mak a theif To dee without a widdy.'

*wife*, woman.

*wight*, person, being, thing.

*wight*, *wyght*, *wighty*, strong, brave, hardy.

*wile*, vile, wicked.

*wilfull* (*Guy*, 24¹), mistaken : *wilful of my way*, having lost my way.

*win*, to go.

*winna*, will not.

*wit*, knowledge.

*with* (*Otterburn*, 42⁴), by.

*wôd*, *wode*, *wood*, mad.

*wolwarde*, see note, *Gest*, 442³.

*won* (*Armstrong*, 3³, 7¹), one.

*wonder*, wonderfully.

*wone* (*Monk*, 25²), abundance, quantity.

*wonnest*, dwellest.

*wonyng*, dwelling.

*wood-wroth*, mad with rage.

*woodweele*, see note, *Guy*, 2¹.

*worthe*, see note, *Gest*, 189³.

*wouche*, wrong, damage.

*wrocken*, revenged.

*wyld*, game, animals.

*wynne*, joy.

*wynnes*, pl., get in, gather.

*wynne* (*win*), to go.

*wystly*, intently.

*wyte*, blame.

*wyte* (*wete*), to know.

*Y-* prefixed to a word usually indicates the past participle of the verb ; also spelled *i-*. It is the older *ge-*.

*yae*, every.

*yare*, ready.

*yates*, gates.

*ychon*, each one, everybody.

*yebent*, bent.

*yede*, *yode*, went.

*yee* (*Otterburn*, 39⁴), eye.

*yefeth*, in faith.

*yerdes*, sticks, rods.

*yerlle*, earl.

*yerly*, early.

*yett*, gate.

*ylke*, *ilke*, same.

*yole*, yule, Christmas.

*yont*, beyond, further off.

*youd*, *yode*, went.

*yth*, i' th', in the.

### Addendum.

*he* (*Stephen*, 12¹), they.

# INDEX

TO

## INTRODUCTION, NOTES, AND APPENDIXES.

———◆◇◆———

Seek never grace from a graceless face,
For that you'll never see

2 types of ballad meter

ballad with refrain, ~~stanza~~

nearly always a couplet.

[8 syllable couplet or 4 measured]

occasional exception

Ballad of Domestic Relations

Adventure Ballad

1. Border Ballad

2. Outlaw

Characters in Domestic Relations

are individuals —

In Border Ballads — characters

represent classes

Adventure

C B E 5
C□

Hayes Int. Soc. Ch. I

L -3 Lindsey

R 6 - Thom,

N 8 Prather

I 11 Haller

eupeptic
auxillary